Polish Cities of Migration

Polish Cities of Migration

The migration transition in Kalisz, Piła and Płock

Anne White

First published in 2024 by
UCL Press
University College London
Gower Street
London WC1E 6BT

Available to download free: www.uclpress.co.uk

Text © Author, 2024
Images © Copyright holders named in captions, 2024

The author has asserted her rights under the Copyright, Designs and Patents Act 1988 to be identified as the author of this work.

A CIP catalogue record for this book is available from The British Library.

Any third-party material in this book is not covered by the book's Creative Commons licence. Details of the copyright ownership and permitted use of third-party material is given in the image (or extract) credit lines. If you would like to reuse any third-party material not covered by the book's Creative Commons licence, you will need to obtain permission directly from the copyright owner.

This book is published under a Creative Commons Attribution-Non-Commercial 4.0 International licence (CC BY-NC 4.0), https://creativecommons.org/licenses/by-nc/4.0/. This licence allows you to share and adapt the work for non-commercial use providing attribution is made to the author and publisher (but not in any way that suggests that they endorse you or your use of the work) and any changes are indicated. Attribution should include the following information:

White, A. 2024. *Polish Cities of Migration: The migration transition in Kalisz, Piła and Płock*. London: UCL Press. https://doi.org/10.14324/111.9781800087354

Further details about Creative Commons licences are available at https://creativecommons.org/licenses/

ISBN: 978-1-80008-731-6 (Hbk.)
ISBN: 978-1-80008-733-0 (Pbk.)
ISBN: 978-1-80008-735-4 (PDF)
ISBN: 978-1-80008-736-1 (epub)
DOI: https://doi.org/10.14324/111.9781800087354

Contents

List of figures vii
List of tables ix
Acknowledgements xi

1 Introduction 1
2 Kalisz, Płock and Piła and the research 23
3 Motives to live in smaller cities: jobs versus quality of life 43
4 Polish migration patterns, motivations and experiences 65
5 Polish return mobilities 95
6 Polish reflections on migration to Poland 109
7 Motives for leaving Ukraine 133
8 Migration to Poland: agencies, families and friends 165
9 Ukrainian jobs and integration 189
10 Ukrainian place attachment in Kalisz, Piła and Płock and likelihood of moving on 211
11 Ukrainian–Polish networks and relations 233
12 Minority minorities 265
13 Conclusions 295

References 303
Index 319

List of figures

6.1 Polish attitudes towards Ukrainians, 2001–23 (CBOS)   112
7.1 Ukrainian interviewees' arrival dates   145
7.2 Ukrainians' ages when interviewed   145

List of tables

2.1	Selected indicators, Płock and Kalisz cities and Piła urban commune	28
2.2	Interviewees	35
4.1	Registered unemployment (percentages)	67
4.2	Polish interviewees by date and type of migration	70

Acknowledgements

I am very grateful to my 124 interviewees and 40 key informants for sharing their information and thoughts. I would also like to thank everyone who helped me find interviewees, including: Iwona Erturan, Barbara Janta, Andrzej Kansy, Katarzyna Kobuszewska, Krystyna Kalota Kornatowska, Kalina Michocka, Agata Mikolajewska, Michał Nowosielski, Marek Przybył, Bogumiła Przygoda, Dorota Pszczółkowska and Iwona Towgin. Izabela Main and Michał Buchowski generously hosted me for the first six months of 2022 at Poznań's Adam Mickiewicz University Centre for Migration Studies and Institute of Anthropology. It was an honour to be associated with the University and its anthropologists. The visit was funded by a Ulam Scholarship from the Polish Agency for Academic Exchange (NAWA). I also thank my colleagues at the UCL School of Slavonic and East European Studies for covering for my absence during a year's sabbatical leave 2021–2.

The Covid-19 pandemic led to a two-year gap in my fieldwork. However, one advantage of this was that I had more time to test out my ideas and initial findings at conferences and in conversations with Polish friends and colleagues. In particular, I received invaluable feedback from Katarzyna Andrejuk, Izabela Grabowska and researchers from the Warsaw Centre of Migration Research. Finally, I thank my family and friends, particularly my husband Howard, for their support throughout the research project.

1
Introduction

'For me it's no different whether I live in Nottingham or Płock. I spend most of my time in the recording studio.'
(Jan, Polish return migrant, interviewed by Anne White)

'At last, after waiting so long, I've been able to buy a house ... I want my grandchildren to be born here ... There's a lake and a forest. I want to take my grandsons fishing.'
(Sergei, Ukrainian interviewed by Anne White in Piła, mid-February 2022)

Introduction

Polish Cities of Migration analyses how Poland, with its strong and continuing 'country of emigration' identity, is transitioning to a new identity as a 'country of immigration'. In the past few years, millions[1] of migrants have been arriving to work, study and join family members in Poland. The book explores two interconnected puzzles. The first is whether the nature of Poland's migration transition is influenced by the fact that it is simultaneously a country of emigration. In Poland, immigrants encounter Polish circular and return migrants, as well as Polish neighbours and workmates who have not migrated, but have family and friends living abroad. The book discusses how these mobile and transnationally connected Poles respond to the newcomers in their midst. What parallels do they perceive, and do they behave in a more welcoming way because of their shared experiences? The second puzzle concerns the decision-making of the non-Polish migrants. Why are they beginning to spread out beyond the metropolises, often settling with their families in smaller cities, such as Kalisz, Piła and Płock, with limited economic opportunities? I argue that their feeling of comfort in such locations links to lifestyle considerations, and is partly connected to their impression that local Poles have a pragmatic and accepting attitude towards migration. The early twenty-first century context is significant for Poland's migration transition. *Polish Cities* aims to shed light on some typical aspects of twenty-first century mobility, and it compares the experiences of Polish and other migrants. Drawing on my in-depth interviews with 70 Ukrainians, 37 Poles and 17 people from different countries around the globe, I illustrate some actual – not just perceived – parallels between (ex)migrants, irrespective of their nationality. These include, for example, how parents quite soon after their arrival abroad decide to bring over their partners and children. Parallels between Ukrainian and Polish migration are often particularly striking, as also found, for example, by Brzozowska (2018). The book investigates why.

This chapter begins by introducing the main themes and arguments of the book. It outlines the story of the Polish migration transition and the particular role played by Ukrainians. It also looks at the phenomenon from the Ukrainian perspective. For Ukrainians, this is not a migration transition, but a story of mobility and emigration connected directly and indirectly to Putin's 2014 invasion. The chapter then discusses central concepts of the book: migration transitions and migration (or mobility) cultures. It relates these to the Polish experience and explains how the concepts shed light on local-level experiences of becoming a country of immigration.[2] Because of space limitations, the chapter does not discuss other concepts used in *Polish Cities*, such as livelihood strategies, place attachment, intersectionality, integration, anchoring, contact hypothesis, ethnic hierarchies and social networks. These are introduced in later chapters.

Countries are often considered to be either 'countries of immigration' or 'countries of emigration'. For example, Australia is seen as a 'country of immigration', unlike Ireland, which until the 1990s was a 'country of emigration'. These reputations are not just linked to statistics about net migration flows, but are also based in culture and historical tradition. Moreover, 'emigration' and 'immigration' in English (although not in other languages, such as Polish) imply migration for settlement, suggesting significant, sustained losses or gains of population. Given these connotations of migration for settlement, the phrase 'country of immigration' captures the idea of a country which is acquiring a more permanent identity as a place where foreigners come to settle. The book argues that becoming a new receiving country on a major scale is not just a matter of statistics but also implies acquiring a 'country of immigration' self-identity. In this connection, one could study the top-down process of adopting legislation, institutions and policies. My focus instead is on grassroots self-identification, the bottom-up process of ordinary people adjusting to the new identity as a receiving society. However, as discussed later, migrants have to become somewhat visible within local society for the majority population to acknowledge that this change has occurred. The book shows that on the eve of the 2022 refugee influx, Ukrainians, whom I label the 'majority minority', were already more visible and acknowledged to be part of composition of the local population in the fieldwork cities than were the 'minority minorities'. These other migrants were individuals or tiny groups, not communities of co-nationals. They hailed from countries across the globe, from Uruguay to Nigeria and Taiwan.

Chapter 2 discusses the book's intersectional approach. However, it seems important here in Chapter 1 to highlight that 'migrants' is a category as diverse as 'humankind'. Any person could become a migrant. One type of differentiation which is particularly salient for this book is that different migrants have different expectations about whether their migration may result in settlement. Sergei and Jan, quoted at the head of the chapter, were Ukrainian and Polish respectively, but their ages and overall outlooks on life were at least as important as nationality in explaining their different degrees of place attachment and attitudes towards mobility. Sergei, having transplanted himself and his family to Piła, and achieved his life's ambition of buying a house, dreamed on the eve of war of being settled in idyllic surroundings for the rest of his life. He was one of a group of interviewees for whom migration appeared to represent a 'happy ending'. Jan, a younger person and a musician, was highly mobile and transnational, and typified another group: people of different nationalities whose occupations meant they could have lived almost anywhere, but nonetheless chose to be based – sometimes part-time and temporarily – in the smaller city or its environs.

Poland's migration transition

Okólski (2021: 152, 159–62), after outlining 'the enduring perception' of 'Poland as a country of sustained emigration', collates statistical evidence and concludes that Poland statistically became an immigration country around 2018. However, as he shows, net immigration derived less from declining out-migration than from increased migration to Poland. Labour migration was encouraged by Polish governments, starting in 2006–7 with the simplification of procedures for labour migrants from former Soviet countries such as Ukraine (Duszczyk and Matuszczyk 2018: 57–8;

Górny et al 2018: 4).[3] This had the effect that Poland became 'the most important recipient of a seasonal workforce worldwide, well ahead of the United States' (Górny and Kaczmarczyk 2021: 88). The policy was matched by a post-2015 approach of rejecting most asylum claims, and generally attempting to keep out refugees (Klaus 2020). Although the Civic Platform government, in power until 2015, had been developing a comprehensive immigration policy, this was abandoned by the Law and Justice party when it won the 2015 elections, and never replaced (Bukowski and Duszczyk 2022: 18; Ślęzak and Bielewska 2022: 177). The Polish government was consequently caught unprepared when millions of refugees from Ukraine arrived in Poland in 2022, and Poland's migration transition took an unexpected turn. The suddenness of the transition – happening while Poland was still a sending country – distinguishes it from countries of Southern Europe, where the process was more gradual and the two identities did not overlap.[4] According to Arango (2012: 3), in Spain, Greece and Italy 'out-migration prevailed until the mid-1970s, then return migration was prominent, and only since the 1980s could they be perceived as primarily receiving countries'.[5] By contrast, Poland is an example of a society which has been experiencing overlap, with both out-migration and immigration relevant to people living through the migration transition. This begs the question – discussed later in this chapter – of whether countries which still maintain a strong 'emigration' identity experience the transition differently to those which have lost that identity.

Like many of its neighbours in Central and Eastern Europe (CEE), Poland is also used by transit migrants. Transit can take the form of a single journey, for instance from Belarus via Poland to Sweden. It can also consist of migration to live in Poland for months or even years, before the migrant departs for a third country, because of a change of heart or circumstances, or in line with their original hopes and plans. Only time will tell whether Poland from 2014–22 had really been becoming a country of 'immigration', in the sense of settlement, or whether much of this migration turned out to be prolonged transit migration – with many Ukrainians in particular using Poland as a stepping stone to Western Europe. The book does not make predictions. However, through qualitative research it illustrates how migrants are making decisions about how long to stay, and when to move on.

The book has a special focus on Ukrainians. Even before 2022, they constituted by far the largest population of foreigners in Poland, including 70–95 per cent of all economic migrants (Górny and Kaczmarczyk 2023: 2). Moreover, their share of the foreign population was increasing. For example, Ukrainians constituted 55 per cent of foreigners paying social security contributions in Poland in 2015, and 72 per cent in 2021 (ZUS 2022: 9). An estimated 1.3 million Ukrainians were located in Poland on the eve of the 2022 full-scale war (Bukowski and Duszczyk 2022: 11). Without Ukrainians, Poland would still have net emigration. Most Ukrainians had come to Poland to work, although there was also a fast-growing student population (Gońda 2020; Hoły-Łuczaj 2022; Kruk 2020). Some Ukrainian workers and students were technically 'repatriates', since they held identity documents known as Polish Cards on the basis of Polish family origins (Gońda and Lesińska 2022).

Few Ukrainians before February 2022 claimed or were awarded refugee status (Jóźwiak and Piechowska 2017: 13; UdSC 2022).[6] Nonetheless, arrivals after 2014 included people displaced as a result of Putin's 2014 invasion. Many others lost or abandoned their livelihoods as circular migrants to Russia because of the war (Blum and Malynovska 2023: 20; Górny and Jaźwińska 2019; Grzymała-Kazłowska and Brzozowska 2017: 105; Libanova 2019: 316–17). This redirecting of the migration flow, away from Russia and towards Poland – as well as Czechia, Lithuania and other points west – does much to explain how Poland suddenly achieved net immigration. The overall volume of migration from Ukraine also grew, since all regions suffered from the economic consequences of the ongoing war, adding to the economic stimulus for migration (Chugaievska and Rusak 2022). Finally, in accordance with migration network theory, the more people migrated from Ukraine, the more other migrants were encouraged to follow in their footsteps. The Covid-19 pandemic created short-term setbacks, but the overall number of Ukrainians holding resident permits in Poland continued to rise in 2020 and 2021 (Churski et al 2021; UdSC 2023). Hence Ukrainians in Poland before 2022 constituted a definite migration 'wave'. This book argues that it shared many similarities with the wave of Poles arriving in the UK and Ireland in the years around and after 2004.

In the last years before 2022, Ukrainian labour migration was also evolving, and becoming more long-term (Górny et al 2019: 2; Musiyezdov 2019; UdSC 2021). Qualitative studies, for example Andrejuk (2017a), backed up statistics showing that Ukrainians were increasingly interested in settlement. When a new population of migrants settles in a receiving country, this usually entails family reunification (Castles et al 2014: 34). More Ukrainians were coming to Poland officially for 'family reasons' (UdSC 2023: 5–6) and more Ukrainian children were studying in Polish schools in the years before the 2022 invasion (Nowosielski et al 2021). More Poles and Ukrainians were getting married (Brzozowska

2015; Szukalski 2020). Increasingly dense co-ethnic networks helped 'anchor' the Ukrainian population in Poland (Grzymała-Kazłowska and Brzozowska 2017), while also revealing fissures and stratification within Ukrainian diasporic society, which to some extent is a microcosm of Ukrainian society in Ukraine, akin to 'Polish society abroad' in countries like the UK (White 2018c). Another sign of leaving behind their temporary migrant identities was that Ukrainians were increasingly unwilling to let themselves be exploited and to do the worst-quality work (Górny et al 2018: 109).

With Putin's launching of full-scale war, Poland's migration identity changed almost overnight: it became a country of refugees. Within weeks, refugees outnumbered Ukrainians already living in Poland. By May, mobile phone data suggested that there were nearly 3.5 million Ukrainians in Poland (Pędziwiatr et al 2022: 5). Meanwhile, by 2023 an estimated 100,000–400,000 male labour migrants had returned to fight in Ukraine (Pacewicz 2023). Since Ukrainian men of fighting age were forbidden to leave Ukraine, most refugees were women and children, leading to a change in the gender and age composition of the Ukrainian population in Poland. For many, Poland was a temporary resting point on the way to countries such as Germany, but others decided to stay, often because their friends or family were already in Poland (Długosz et al 2022: 2; Jarosz and Klaus 2023: 19).

Despite the significance of Ukrainian migration, Poland's migration transition is also the story of migrants from around the globe (Górny and Kindler 2018). This has led to the beginnings of a 'new ethnic diversity' (Grzymała-Kazłowska 2021) in a country which, following the Holocaust and post-World War II border changes and deportations, had been ethnically almost homogeneous. The number of non-EU or Ukrainian foreigners paying social security contributions almost quadrupled between 2015 and 2021, reaching 209,454; this compared with 36,608 EU citizens (ZUS 2022: 9). Before 2014, foreigners in Poland had included economic migrants from former Soviet countries, Vietnam and China; spouses of Polish nationals; a handful of refugees, mostly from Chechnya; employees of international companies; Western lifestyle migrants, especially in Kraków and Warsaw; and some foreign students. Subsequently, all these groups increased in number, but also – as for example happened during Italy's migration transition (King et al 1997: 2) – the range of sending countries suddenly became highly diverse. Thus, for example, in 2021 in Wielkopolska region, where Kalisz and Piła are located, work permits were issued in the largest numbers to Ukrainians, followed by Filipinos, Belarusians, Indians, Nepalese people,

Moldovans and Uzbeks (USwP 2022: 2). Workers from outside Europe were particularly liable to exploitation (Górny et al 2018: 109; Józefiak and Wójcik 2022; Roszkowska 2018). Entrepreneurs are also well-represented among certain nationalities, although types of entreneurship vary (as discussed for example by Andrejuk (2017b) regarding differences between EU-15 and EU-12 migrants). There is a trend towards internal diversification among new migrant populations (Andrejuk 2019a, Kardaszewicz 2018).

The book uses the concept of 'minority minorities' to understand the experiences of these non-Ukrainian foreigners. They did not visibly arrive in 'waves', with the partial exception of Belarusians, who, after the political repressions of 2020, came to big cities in Poland in increasing numbers. Up to 150,000 Belarusians were living in Poland by spring 2023 (Homel et al 2023). Relatively well-established migration flows existed from Vietnam, dating back to student migration in the communist period (Szymańska-Matusiewicz 2017) and, since the 1990s, from China (Kardaszewicz 2018). As Bielewska (2021: 620–1) shows with reference to Wrocław, even in the largest cities, other nationalities were often present only in very small groups. They did not have the critical mass to constitute local 'communities'. As I discovered, the minority minorities were even more isolated in smaller cities. On the other hand, as this book frequently illustrates, migrants inhabit a social media world beyond the local streets and squares. For example, a Bangladeshi informant told me that there were only five other Bangladeshis in Piła, but then showed me on his mobile phone that there was a Facebook community of 25,000 Bangladeshis in Poland – thanks to whom he had changed his job and place of residence. A to-date barely explored research topic is that of inter-ethnic networks and relations, between Ukrainians and minority minorities, or between the different minority minorities. Chapter 12 discusses whether and when they associate and see parallels between their own experiences, or instead engage in the same kind of ethnic hierarchising which typifies receiving societies. This is important to the story of the migration transition, since it has a bearing on how migrants are forming place attachments and settling, or not.

Another significant aspect of Poland's migration transition is that it can only be understood by taking into account the fact that 'Poland' is not a uniform space. The transition is happening at different speeds in different locations. The largest cities are the main magnets for immigrants (Górny and Kaczmarczyk 2021: 89). By 2022, Warsaw, Kraków, Wrocław, the Tri-City of Gdańsk-Gdynia-Sopot and Poznań seemed to have lost their 'city of emigration' status and become migrant destinations. The big cities, especially the 12 members of the Union of Polish Metropolises, had been starting to develop integration policies, collaborating with local NGOs, and emphasising their respect for diversity and openness to migrants from abroad. In doing so, they were bypassing the national government and positioning themselves in opposition to its nationalist narrative (Jarosz and Klaus 2023; Main 2020; Matusz and Pawłak 2020; Ślęzak and Bielewska 2022). Nonetheless, since 2014, and perhaps rather puzzlingly, Ukrainians and other foreigners have increasingly been moving to other cities, beyond these metropolises (Górny and Śleszyński 2019; Kałuża-Kopias 2023), as well as to almost all Polish regions (Bukowski and Duszczyk 2022: 18; ZUS 2022: 21–3). As suggested at the beginning of this chapter, this is a puzzle which *Polish Cities* seeks to address.

The book also considers the opposite side of the coin – migration by Poles. If cities like Warsaw have become cities with net immigration, this is partly because out-migration has declined. The situation had looked very different in the years immediately after 2004. In the 1990s, most Polish international migrants came from small towns and rural areas, located in peripheral regions (Anacka et al 2011). However, with EU accession, Poles began to migrate from everywhere in the country. Between 2004 and 2007, 'nearly one in ten people in their late twenties left Poland' (Anacka and Okólski 2010: 155); they included many residents of the biggest cities, including students and recent graduates. This middle-class exodus slowed after 2007. By 2022, attractive and prospering cities with over 500,000 inhabitants had shed their role as emigration locations, both statistically and in terms of their self-identity. With a few exceptions,[7] it is the 500+ metropolises which both keep their residents and serve as magnets for internal migrants – particularly university graduates – from elsewhere in Poland. Moreover, young people can confidently return to these cities from study abroad to find suitable jobs.

Individual Polish migrants also return to smaller cities, towns and villages, but in such cases they are motivated more often by personal reasons, such as coming home after completing a specific earning project abroad, and/or missing family and friends, rather than because they have found a job (Rokitowska-Malcher 2021: 126).[8] Compared with the biggest cities, there usually exist fewer opportunities on the labour market which could attract a wave of economic return migration. Indeed, local Poles, particularly those without a university degree, continue to migrate abroad to find better work, engaging in the kind of circular migration which was typical before EU accession (Garapich et al 2023). *Polish Cities* argues that some Poles in Kalisz, Płock and Piła still possess a strong sense that these are cities of out-migration, whereas for others migration is more of a historical memory associated with the years after 2004. Either they themselves had been part of the middle-class post-2004 wave, or their friends and family had migrated then, settled and were still living in countries like the UK and Ireland. Interestingly, individuals who knew people who were still migrating abroad, or who were likely to adopt international migration as their own livelihood strategy, were often also the people who had most contact with foreign labour migrants, for example because they worked in factories.

As one of the impacts of Polish migration on Poland, several scholars, including Gawlewicz (2015) and Nowicka (2018), have studied how Poles abroad pick up and remit back to Poland racist or open-to-difference ideas. Slightly modifying Levitt's (1998) definition, Izabela Grabowska and I (White and Grabowska 2019: 34) have defined social remittances as 'ideas, practices, attitudes, values, norms, beliefs and identities which migrants bring from one society to another, as well as the non-economic capital of various kinds – knowledge, qualifications, social skills and useful contacts – which they acquire thanks to migration'. Social remitting in this sense is relevant to *Polish Cities,* since it partly explains how Poles in Poland regard immigration, and, more specifically, why polls indicate that they have become more welcoming towards labour migration in recent decades. As I show in White (2018a), individuals who become more accepting of diversity directly as a result of working abroad have a particular significance as social remitters. Even if they often find it hard to spread their views (Garapich 2016a; Grabowska et al 2017) they add to the stock of people in Polish society – including those living in smaller cities and towns – who possess a more cosmopolitan outlook. Opinion polls routinely show that the 500,000+ cities are the most liberal locations, but this is largely because Polish big city–dwellers are on average wealthier, highly educated and younger. If they espouse liberal views, these are often connected to these other identities, and often have other origins, rather than being picked up by working abroad.

Finally, as for example indicated by Gołębiowska (2014), the correlation between 'smaller in population size' and 'less open' is not always clear-cut. CBOS surveys about attitudes towards Ukrainians in 2012–15 showed that Ukrainians were most favourably regarded in locations with populations between 20,000 and 500,000, especially those of 100,000–500,000 (Boguszewski 2015: 5). This book attempts to dispel stereotypes that all Poles who live outside the largest cities are xenophobic. However, it is not trying to prove that smaller cities according to some objective criteria are friendlier than the metropolises. For immigrants to settle, and take the Polish migration transition to its next stage, it is sufficient that the new residents of those smaller cities personally have the impression of local friendliness and openness. Migrants with worse experiences might move on to the metropolises, where they would not be available for interview in a project on smaller cities.

Migration transitions: theory and practice

Launching the hypothesis of the 'mobility' transition, Zelinsky (1971) outlined different stages of modernisation as it interconnected with economic development; the demographic transition towards smaller family sizes; and migration patterns, including internal and return migration. Nowadays, 'migration' transition, as it is more commonly known, tends to refer to the final stage in this process, when a country reaches a level of economic development which enables it to shed its 'sending country' status. King and Gëdeshi (2022: 132) define migration transition as 'passage from a country of net emigration to one of net immigration'. Often migration transition is discussed with a view to supporting countries in the Global South to improve their levels of education and economic well-being, to the extent that, instead of seeking work in the Global North, their own nationals would return from abroad (Johnson 2020). Meanwhile, as labour markets in developing economies become more complex and segmented, certain sections are no longer attractive to local people, only to immigrants (Fassmann and Reeger 2012: 69–70).

Although migration transition scholars are usually demographers and economists, some researchers have noticed its sociological dimension. Arango suggests (2012: 46):

> No doubt, strictly speaking, it can be said that all countries are sending, receiving and transit countries at the same time … The decisive criterion for defining a country as immigration-receiving is not so much net migration in a given year in a receiving country – it can be occasionally negative – but rather the societal impact of receiving or hosting significant numbers of immigrants … a receiving country is one in which the most socially significant phenomenon in terms of international mobility is immigration.

Fassmann and Reeger (2012: 65–6) note there can be a discrepancy between the statistical situation and how ordinary people recognise and define themselves. Immigration may not actually be 'socially significant' if they do not feel like a migrant-receiving society, even when figures show net immigration. The USA, Canada and Australia are classic countries of immigration, but other countries have been more reluctant to adopt the identity, notably Germany and Austria (Stevenson 2006). Therefore populations 'learn' to become receiving societies. They achieve a 'self-image as an immigration society', to quote Berriane et al (2015: 516) on Morocco.

Within his framework of analysis, Arango (2012) includes Dassetto's (1990) concept of the 'migration cycle', a phenomenon referred to by Castles et al (2014: 34) as the 'migration process'. They observe that immigration typically proceeds in stages. The pioneers are single, often temporary migrants. In the second stage, migrants bring over their families and begin to settle. The third stage consists of long-term, multi-generational integration within the receiving society. This pattern can be seen to take place within particular flows from specific sending countries. Arango (2012) observes that, while migrant populations undergo these different stages, receiving societies go through a parallel process. At first, they adopt a neutral or instrumental attitude towards immigration. As immigrants arrive in greater numbers and begin to settle, the receiving society becomes more anxious and hostile. Eventually, however, they become reconciled to the presence of ethnic minorities. In line with Fausmann and Reeger's (2012) insight that societies 'learn' to become receiving ones, Arango (2012: 54) refers to a process of 'socialisation' into receiving country identity. On a sub-national level, Alexander (2003) describes how 'new immigration cities' of western Europe and Israel learned to adapt to their new identities. These (bigger) cities, such as Amsterdam, Birmingham and Rome, typically began by treating migrants as strangers and guestworkers, progressed through an 'assimilationist' phase, but then arrived at a policy of 'pluralism', i.e. multiculturalism. As mentioned above, the biggest Polish cities have already begun developing multicultural policies which include migrant integration as well as historical memory projects, but other cities still lack any integration policy, with the very recent exception of support for Ukrainian refugees.

The idea of 'learning' to be a receiving society is fundamental to the analysis in this book. 'Socialisation' is less apt, since it is a process typically undergone by children, whereas in Poland migration knowledge is also based on the recent, personal experience of many adults. 'Learning' to be a new receiving society is therefore superimposed onto existing migration cultures (discussed later in this chapter). Migration cultures are typically studied at sub-national level, making this a particularly suitable concept for understanding sub-national aspects of migration transitions.

As the migration transition proceeds, migrants spread to ever new locations (Janská et al 2014). Drbohlav (2003), for example, noted that by the turn of the twenty-first century Ukrainians in the Czech Republic were increasingly settling in destinations other than Prague. The process of spreading to new destinations is not uniform and immediate. Individual locations in well-established countries of immigration can remain almost untouched by migration, before suddenly becoming 'new immigrant destinations' (McAreavey and Argent 2018). This phenomenon of late immigration to new localities was strikingly illustrated by the case of CEE migration to the UK after 2004 (Bauere et al 2007; Jivraj et al 2012). According to Bauere et al (2007: 8):

> Traditionally, immigrants to the UK [since the 1940s] have tended to go predominantly to London and the South-East, the conurbations and a relatively small number of large towns and cities [but]... the A8 population has spread widely across the UK, no part of the country being untouched.

This phenomenon turned out to be significant, not just in the biographies of individual migrants – including some of the Polish returnees interviewed for this book. It also shaped UK politics, given that towns which had recently acquired particularly large EU migrant populations (in the context of the Global Economic Crisis and subsequent austerity measures, together with campaigns by populist politicians) voted solidly to leave the EU in the 2016 referendum.

The UK case illustrates why the migration transitions framework can fruitfully be combined with insights from scholarship on social cohesion. Particularly relevant is research which focuses on why some locations are more successful than others at incorporating migrants, for example: Fonseca and McGarrigle (2012); Glick Schiller and Çağlar (2009); Phillips and Robinson (2015); Robinson (2010). Platts-Fowler and Robinson (2015: 485), comparing ethnically diverse refugee flows from unfamiliar origin countries to the medium-sized cities of Sheffield and Hull, found that these new migrants considered Sheffield the more welcoming city, thanks to its 'more cosmopolitan neighbourhoods, which have a long history of accommodating diversity and difference'. 'Superdiverse' locations, such as areas of London where most people have migrant backgrounds and white British people are the minority, can be the most accommodating of all (Wessendorf 2015).

Countries which acquire EU membership are likely to become countries of immigration (Okólski 2012), although this cannot be taken for granted (Incaltaurau and Simionov 2017). However, the exact historical period at which countries acquire immigration status also helps shape the nature of their transition (Arango 2012: 47). Arango suggested that CEE countries would therefore experience their migration transitions differently from countries in north-western or southern Europe, which made that transition in the twentieth century. This book demonstrates the importance of the historical context, and more specifically, the twenty-first century 'mobility turn' (Sheller and Urry 2006) in shaping migration transitions today. 'Mobility' is viewed here as a subset of migration, not its antithesis. It is a term to be used when stressing individual migrants' frequency of motion and – in some cases – their capacity to be mobile. EU status in particular encourages citizens to experiment with mobility, although numerous authors have cautioned against overstating this mobility (Bygnes and Erdal 2017; Franceschelli 2022). However, despite not having EU status, and despite restrictions on their employment, Ukrainian labour migrants manifest a similar proclivity towards intense mobility. This helps explain how they have been rapidly spreading across CEE and beyond. Mobility is encouraged not just by improved transport, such as cheap and plentiful bus routes, but even more importantly by the efficient functioning of social networks based on easy and rapid transnational communication with family, friends and acquaintances. Potential migrants can be better-informed about what to expect in advance, and migration becomes overall less risky (White 2017). Paradoxically, the process of settlement (the end of mobility) is speeded up by these mobility options, because short-term experimental migration by some family members can quite quickly be followed by family reunification abroad.[9]

Migration (mobility) cultures in sending countries

Migration culture is a concept used in this book to analyse how people living in smaller cities conceptualise migrants and migration. It is generally studied with reference to sending locations, although qualitative researchers agree that migration culture cannot be understood outside its transnational context. A 'local' migration culture exists not just in that particular sending location, but also in a web of ties between people living there and their contacts abroad. All migration culture researchers acknowledge the significance of social networks and social capital, since information and opinions about migration are transmitted via networks, often in connection with invitations or offers of help from migrants already abroad. It is the density or absence of those networks which mean that some locales seem to have migration cultures and others not.[10] Generally, smaller sending communities are the focus of migration culture researchers.[11] When I looked for traces of migration culture in the biggest Polish cities, such as Warsaw and Wrocław, it was impossible to find any at city level. The bigger the city, the less likely that potential migrants will know one another. Within a city, however, there exist 'migration hotspots' – social and institutional settings which are more touched by migration than others (White 2016c). Warzywoda-Kruszyńska and Jankowski (2013) discovered a similar situation in 'poverty enclaves' in Łódź. This alerted me to look for 'migration hotspots' in Kalisz, Płock and Piła. Certain factories proved to be particular hotspots.

In its narrower sense, as used for example by Kandel and Massey (2002), a 'culture of migration' denotes a local acceptance that migration is a sensible livelihood strategy. Quantitative research considers a culture of migration to be one of the non-economic factors driving migration. For example, Van Mol et al (2018: 2) concluded on the basis of survey evidence that 'in some locations [in Ukraine], migration seems to be a "normal thing to do"'. Massey et al (1993) showed that people from some Mexican localities migrated to the USA partly because there existed a local 'culture of migration' in the sense of a tradition of out-migration. They also observed that migration has its own internal dynamics. The more migration, the stronger the 'culture of migration' (Kandel and Massey 2002). In this case, ever greater numbers of migrants were inviting their families and friends to join them in the USA, a process which Massey and his team labelled 'cumulative causation'.

Broader definitions, such as the 'cultural framing of migration' (Cohen and Sirkeci 2011: 16), view the community's acceptance that migration is normal and even desirable as just one of a set of migration-related beliefs and understandings. Examples of qualitative research on migration cultures include Connell 2008 (on the Pacific island of Niue); Horváth 2008 (on Romania); and, on Poland, Elrick (2008); and White (2017). This qualitative literature helps explain why people migrate from certain locations in large numbers, but also how they think and talk about migration, and the role of migration practices within the broader cultural environment. They can include, for example, views about how, when and where to migrate, as well as certain taboos about who should not migrate, such as mothers of young children (White 2017).

In this book, migration culture refers to how people understand and talk about migration, and how migrants act out those understandings and transmit them to others. My definition is similar to Morawska's (2001) idea of a 'socio-cultural tool kit' consisting of knowhow and social capital. However, the metaphor of the toolkit perhaps makes migration culture sound exclusively instrumental. People also have imaginings, dreams and emotions about migration which help shape their behaviour – for example, a kind of collective sadness about the absence of close family members, in locations where solo parental migration is the norm (White 2017: Chapter 7). Garapich (2019: 14) writes of 'an attitude towards migration (*wyjazdów*), its ethical valuation and meaning'. As my various research projects have indicated, aspects of migration culture include sharing information, impressions, myths and scare stories based on other people's migration experiences. This includes swapping stereotypes. For example, Ukrainians assert that in Poland Ukrainians work harder than Poles, and Poles assert that in the UK Poles work harder than British people. Understandings about how much local people should help each other migrate help shape perceptions about how to use social capital located in migrant networks. In some sending communities, there are also strong expectations of the 'Good Migrant'. Migrants are under the gaze of the sending locality. This may heighten the pressure to remit money to their families and to collective causes. Furthermore, the Good Migrant must not return empty-handed. It is preferable to stay on longer in the receiving country, in order to avoid a 'return of failure' (Cerase 1974). Migrants' return visits are also part of the culture in some locations. Their rituals, such as partying and present-giving, help to maintain the migrant's networks and social capital in the origin location.

Qualitative researchers acknowledge that migration cultures change over time (Morawska 2001). This happened, for example, in response to enhanced mobility opportunities in the twenty-first century (Garapich 2013). EU accession brought the right to free movement within the EU, but a mobility culture (believing, and persuading friends and family, that migration was 'easy' and worth 'giving a go') helped turn that mobility opportunity into mobility in practice (White 2017). As already mentioned, ideas today travel rapidly along transnational networks, hence people in sending communities can be inspired or persuaded by people abroad to migrate to new destinations. In 2006–9, when researching a book about why so many Polish parents had stopped migrating alone and were bringing their children to live in the UK and Ireland, I discovered – largely from talking to mothers in small Polish towns – that the migration culture seemed to be changing. Previously, solo-parent temporary migration had been the norm, despite the sadness it created. Now, families were emboldened by the experience of other migrants to take their own children abroad. This was confirmed in my opinion poll in small towns and villages of south-east Poland, which indicated widespread agreement, especially among younger respondents, that it was better for families to stick together, even if it meant them all quitting Poland (White 2017). *Polish Cities of Migration* therefore explores whether a similar cultural change had been occurring among Ukrainian migrants, leading to the increase in settlement and family reunification in Poland on the eve of the 2022 full-scale invasion of Ukraine.

Migration cultures in receiving countries

Polish Cities follows Garapich (2013; 2019) in extending the concept of migration culture to include beliefs, etc., about migration which circulate among migrants while they are still abroad. Literature on sending locations shows that potential migrants pick up information not just from local people but also from current migrants back on visits, or communicating via phone or online from abroad. Since sending and receiving countries constitute a single transnational space, it seems odd that most researchers fail to notice signs of migration culture in the lives of migrants abroad. The explanation is probably that, particularly over the last decade, scholars researching how ideas circulate in transnational social space have been using, and developing, the concept of social remittances, rather than migration culture. Migration culture, in its transnational manifestations, can be viewed as a sub-set of social remitting. Social remittance scholars focus on ideas migrants pick up from the receiving society, but in practice migrants' social networks in receiving countries often consist largely of other migrants. Therefore, they are likely to pick up and transmit ideas from fellow-migrants, including about migrants and migration (White 2024).

Can migration culture exist in the receiving society, among members of the majority population who have never migrated? One might suppose not, since migration culture is about how 'we' do migration. In cases where a majority population is largely mono-ethnic and static, migrants are 'they', hence the prevalence of stereotypes about migration, and its stigmatisation (Anderson 2013). Anderson's book is titled *Us and Them*. 'They' are the migrants, 'we' are the stayers. Typical receiving country stereotypes include, for example, the ideas that all migrants are 'low-skilled', or that 'culturally different' migrants will find it hard to assimilate. Instead of migration culture, such widely-accepted ideas about migration circulating in the receiving society are more likely to be classed as 'conventional wisdom' (Castles et al 2014: 25) or 'common sense'. They constitute a kind of mental short-cut. When Jaskulowski (2019) interviewed Poles about their views on refugees who might potentially come to Poland, he found that people drew on a menu of pre-existing stereotypes.

However, as already discussed in the section on migration transitions, where receiving societies are more diverse, many inhabitants identify themselves as being migrants or of migrant background. Hence, they know how migration is done and are familiar with the idea that migration is an everyday social phenomenon. Given that the smaller Polish cities currently combine both sending and receiving identities, local people, now becoming part of a receiving society, might be expected to feel that migrants were not only 'them' but also in some senses 'us'. Migration wisdom, accumulated from Poles' own direct experience, could coexist with migrant stereotyping. Overall, my fieldwork in this and earlier projects left me with the strong impression that for many Polish people labour migration is simply 'normal' – both a regular socio-historical phenomenon, and an obvious livelihood strategy for people in certain situations. In other words, their own migration culture guides them to see parallels between themselves and migrants from other countries, and backs up the social learning involved in becoming a new receiving society. I also looked for evidence of intersecting migration cultures, in the sense of migration toolkits: Polish former migrants providing tools for immigrants from other countries. This could include teaching foreigners what to expect from migration, how to do it and where to go, as well as sharing networks. The book presents a small amount of evidence showing that, particularly in migration hotspots such as factories and hostels, Ukrainians may indeed be picking up some local migration culture from Poles.

Labour migrants and refugees

The welcome Poles extended to Ukrainian refugees in 2022 – in striking contrast to the ongoing pushbacks of Kurds, Afghans, Syrians and other refugees on the Belarusian border – has been attributed to factors such as awareness of the common Russian enemy, shared whiteness and a sense of fellow Slav identity (Jarosz and Klaus 2023: 9; Kyliushyk and Jastrzębowska 2023: 2). However, compassion displayed in 2022 and to a large extent maintained into 2023 (Scovil 2023) also links back to pre-existing attitudes towards Ukrainians. They were the 'familiar Significant Others' as opposed to 'distant' non-white refugees (Buchowski 2020). It seems important to consider how attitudes towards Ukrainian labour migrants could help explain the positive response towards refugees in 2022. As Ociepa-Kicińska and Gorzałczyńska-Koczkodaj (2022: 3) point out, 'Thanks to this [influx of labour migrants], Poles had the opportunity to meet the citizens of Ukraine, accept their presence in their country, and establish relations, friendships and relationships with them.' Baszczak et al (2022: 49) show that Poles who already knew Ukrainians living in Poland were more likely to be engaged in refugee support. As mentioned above, Poles often display a matter-of-fact, accepting attitude towards labour migrants. In 2019, a nationwide CBOS survey showed that 62 per cent of respondents believed foreigners should have unrestricted access to the Polish labour market (Bożewicz and Głowacki 2020: 5). However, this pragmatism is not necessarily equivalent to extending migrants a warm welcome, or feeling empathy with their plight. This section therefore briefly considers the topic of empathy. 'Empathy', imagining oneself in someone else's situation, can happen in some cases purely as the result of an effort to see things from another person's perspective, in which case it shades into sympathy and even pity. In other situations, however, the empathiser is drawing parallels with their own previous experience.

A small literature on empathy exists with regard to countries undergoing – sometimes extended – migration transition. Glynn (2011) shows that when Ireland and Italy became countries of immigration, more parallels were drawn publicly between Irish migrants and new arrivals, whereas Italian media exhibited a more patronising approach. He suggests that, as a result, Irish people were more empathetic to newcomers than Italians. On the other hand, Sorge (2021), writing about Sicily, shows how local activists tried to create empathy and solidarity with migrants crossing the Mediterranean, at the same time as opposing the exclusionary policies of the Italian government. For example, Sorge (2021: 269) mentions that:

> One prominent moment was a protest in Agrigento in July 2019 against Matteo Salvini's port blockades, which included the participation of a range of civil society organisations, including activist collectives, youth groups, labour unions, as well as social cooperatives and resident refugees and asylum seekers ... Organisers of the protest made direct appeals to an awareness of Sicily's own history of emigration, crafting the chant, La storia siciliana ce l'ha insegnato: Emigrare non è reato! ('The history of Sicily has taught us: emigration is not a crime!')

In turn, Feischmidt and Zakariás (2020) show how different generations of Hungarians were differently motivated to welcome refugees crossing Hungary during the so-called migration crisis of 2015. Those who had been refugees in Germany after the 1956 Hungarian Revolution displayed more empathy, while younger generations of migrants were more interested in showing solidarity in face of Orbán's xenophobic regime.

In Poland, the authors of *Hospitable Poland* assert that 'the desire to support those fleeing the war in Ukraine also triggered large amounts of empathy' and 'the huge grassroots aid spurt of Poles indicates a high empathy and sense of solidarity with Ukrainians' (Bukowski and Duszczyk 2022: 87, 111). Similarly, in his (2019) study of attitudes towards putative refugee arrivals, Jaskułowski uses the term 'empathy' to characterise those Poles wanting to help refugees. As in the Sicilian case, 'empathy' here is being used for an emotion which is more akin to 'sympathy'; in both Sicily and Poland, empathy also combines with 'solidarity', in the sense of a wish to extend support and make common cause with someone else. With regard to the other type of empathy – the 'that was me' moment – Bielecka-Prus (2020)'s findings from her survey of Polish media help explain the warm reception for Ukrainian women refugees in 2022. She argues that the predominant image of a Ukrainian labour migrant, before 2022, was of a well-educated woman working below her qualifications in Poland. Such an image was almost guaranteed to generate empathy, considering how many Poles had found themselves in the same situation.

This book provides a few instances – stories related by both Polish and Ukrainian interviewees – of empathy displayed by Poles towards Ukrainian labour migrants. However, the more important point concerns the pragmatic migration culture in Kalisz, Płock and Piła, with its normalisation of migration, both in general, and with regard to Ukrainian economic migration to Poland. A contribution of this book is to suggest that the 2022 welcome can be partly linked to how Poles often already saw Ukrainians primarily as people on the move, not in national(ist), ethnic and racialised terms – something which could not have been taken for granted, given the history of difficult and sometimes violent Polish–Ukrainian relations.

Conclusions

Chapter 1 opened with the research questions underpinning *Polish Cities*. The first puzzle concerns how Poland's experience of becoming a 'country of immigration' is shaped by the fact that, in most locations, it is still a 'country of emigration'. The book answers this question 'from below', by investigating views and experiences of ordinary Poles and foreigners in 2019–22. The second research question is why migrants are spreading out beyond the largest cities and settling in locations with problematic labour markets, from which Poles continue to migrate abroad. This question is answered with emphasis on why Kalisz, Piła and Płock were attractive specifically for settlement, rather than temporary migration.

The chapter sketched out Poland's migration transition and considered its component parts: the post-2014 exodus of labour migrants from Ukraine without which Poland would still have net immigration; the growing range of other nationalities; and trends in the patterns of Poles' own migration abroad. It discussed migration transition theory and how migration transitions can be approached sociologically, as learning processes for migrants and receiving societies. It suggested combining migration transition theory with studies of social cohesion which shed light on why cities with more migration experience are often more welcoming to migrants. In the Polish case, however, this migration experience is the receiving population's own. The chapter then turned to the concept of 'migration cultures', used in a broad sense to refer to how people understand and talk about migration, and how migrants act out those understandings and transmit them to others. Here, the book's original contribution is to suggest that migration cultures brought from sending communities also exist among migrants in receiving societies, where they can intertwine with local cultures, when for example Polish factory workers instruct Ukrainians on how to 'do' migration. Finally, Chapter 1 explored links between attitudes to labour migrants and refugees, considering the concept of empathy in receiving populations. It concluded that the Polish welcome for Ukrainian refugees in 2022 can be partly explained by the fact that many Poles did not view Ukrainians already living in Poland in national terms, which would involve the recollection of historical enmities, but rather as 'normal people' – economic migrants with whom they shared experiences in common.

The book is structured as follows. Chapter 2 introduces Kalisz, Płock and Piła and describes the research project on which *Polish Cities* is based. Chapter 3 explores some particular characteristics of smaller cities vis-à-vis metropolises and presents interview evidence about why participants of all nationalities chose to remain specifically in KPP. Chapters 4 to 6 analyse the motivations and experiences of the Polish interviewees, as well as their reflections on recent immigration to their home cities. Chapters 7–11 present the project's findings about the largest group, the 70 Ukrainian participants. The chapters consider in turn: their diverse range of motivations for leaving Ukraine; why they chose KPP, focusing primarily on family and friendship networks, but also on recruitment agencies; Ukrainian jobs and integration; aspects of place attachment to KPP, as well as why some might move on to other destinations; Ukrainian–Polish networks and reflections on Polish attitudes towards Ukrainians. Chapter 12, 'Minority minorities', introduces the 17 non-Ukrainian migrants. It covers the same territory as the chapters on Ukrainians, highlighting where their experiences were different from those of Ukrainians, not just because of nationality and race but also because they lacked the critical mass of the local Ukrainian population. The final section considers the topic of relations between different nationalities living in KPP.

Notes

1. Statistics about immigration to Poland are always inexact, particularly because of the scale of temporary migration. Figures about temporary migration are based mostly on the number of documents issued, rather than identifying and counting migrants who arrived in Poland (Górny and Kindler 2018: 222–5).
2. Like most contemporary migration scholars, I use 'migration' and 'mobility' as shorthand for international migration and mobility, while recognising that internal (domestic) and international migration share many features (King and Skeldon 2010). The book also refers to 'countries of origin' interchangeably with 'sending countries', and 'destination countries' interchangeably with 'receiving countries'. It does not use the terms 'home country', since migrants often have homes in two or more countries, or 'host countries', since receiving societies are often unwelcoming.
3. Labour migrants could now be given visas to Poland on the basis of an employer's declaration of intent (*oświadczenie*) to the regional authorities to hire a certain number of foreign workers. These were then normally recruited by recruitment agencies. A smaller number of foreigners were still recruited on the basis of a work permit (*zezwolenie na pracę*) for a particular individual, and (from 2018) seasonal work permits.
4. Abella and Ducanes (2014: 249) identify Malaysia as another example of particularly rapid transition. Of course, even in slowly transitioning countries, there is an 'equilibrium point', where immigration and emigration statistics match, before immigration begins to transcend emigration.
5. They lost this status after the 2008 Global Economic Crisis, while nonetheless remaining at an overall level of development which meant that they could easily regain net immigration.
6. In 2021, 260 Ukrainians had claimed asylum, none successfully.
7. Łódź until recently was 'in the shadow of Warsaw' (Śleszyński 2018: 51) and is less clearly a member of this club (Gońda 2021). On the other hand, the smaller city of Rzeszów has been developing fast and attracting internal migrants (Hajduga and Rogowska 2020: 23).
8. Of the respondents, 21.5 per cent returning to the Wrocław Metropolitan Area (but only 12.9 per cent returning to other parts of Lower Silesia) said they did so because they found work.
9. The average time in my small sample of 25 Polish couples reunifying in the UK between 2004 and 2009 was about 11 months (White 2017: 106).
10. For some examples, see Jaźwińska and Grabowska (2017: 143).
11. Perhaps unexpectedly, the terms 'migration culture' and 'culture of migration' are not used by researchers to describe the ethno-cultural identities and practices of migrants living abroad.

range of motivations for leaving Ukraine; why they chose KPP, focusing primarily on family and friendship networks, but also on recruitment agencies; Ukrainian jobs and integration; aspects of place attachment to KPP, as well as why some might move on to other destinations; Ukrainian–Polish networks and reflections on Polish attitudes towards Ukrainians. Chapter 12, 'Minority minorities', introduces the 17 non-Ukrainian migrants. It covers the same territory as the chapters on Ukrainians, highlighting where their experiences were different from those of Ukrainians, not just because of nationality and race but also because they lacked the critical mass of the local Ukrainian population. The final section considers the topic of relations between different nationalities living in KPP.

Notes

1. Statistics about immigration to Poland are always inexact, particularly because of the scale of temporary migration. Figures about temporary migration are based mostly on the number of documents issued, rather than identifying and counting migrants who arrived in Poland (Górny and Kindler 2018: 222–5).
2. Like most contemporary migration scholars, I use 'migration' and 'mobility' as shorthand for international migration and mobility, while recognising that internal (domestic) and international migration share many features (King and Skeldon 2010). The book also refers to 'countries of origin' interchangeably with 'sending countries', and 'destination countries' interchangeably with 'receiving countries'. It does not use the terms 'home country', since migrants often have homes in two or more countries, or 'host countries', since receiving societies are often unwelcoming.
3. Labour migrants could now be given visas to Poland on the basis of an employer's declaration of intent (*oświadczenie*) to the regional authorities to hire a certain number of foreign workers. These were then normally recruited by recruitment agencies. A smaller number of foreigners were still recruited on the basis of a work permit (*zezwolenie na pracę*) for a particular individual, and (from 2018) seasonal work permits.
4. Abella and Ducanes (2014: 249) identify Malaysia as another example of particularly rapid transition. Of course, even in slowly transitioning countries, there is an 'equilibrium point', where immigration and emigration statistics match, before immigration begins to transcend emigration.
5. They lost this status after the 2008 Global Economic Crisis, while nonetheless remaining at an overall level of development which meant that they could easily regain net immigration.
6. In 2021, 260 Ukrainians had claimed asylum, none successfully.
7. Łódź until recently was 'in the shadow of Warsaw' (Śleszyński 2018: 51) and is less clearly a member of this club (Gońda 2021). On the other hand, the smaller city of Rzeszów has been developing fast and attracting internal migrants (Hajduga and Rogowska 2020: 23).
8. Of the respondents, 21.5 per cent returning to the Wrocław Metropolitan Area (but only 12.9 per cent returning to other parts of Lower Silesia) said they did so because they found work.
9. The average time in my small sample of 25 Polish couples reunifying in the UK between 2004 and 2009 was about 11 months (White 2017: 106).
10. For some examples, see Jaźwińska and Grabowska (2017: 143).
11. Perhaps unexpectedly, the terms 'migration culture' and 'culture of migration' are not used by researchers to describe the ethno-cultural identities and practices of migrants living abroad.

2
Kalisz, Płock and Piła and the research

Introduction

Chapter 2 presents information about the three cities where I conducted the fieldwork for this book. It highlights some similarities and differences between Kalisz, Płock and Piła. The cities were not chosen on the basis of any supposed typicality; there is no such thing as a 'typical' Polish city. However, by analysing several locations one can form some idea of the factors at play in determining how migration transition 'from below' might be occurring. Kalisz, Płock and Piła (KPP)[1] are located far from Ukraine, in central and north-west Poland. They lie within two of Poland's wealthiest regions, where there is plenty of factory work, and agencies recruiting foreign workers have been active. Nonetheless, all three cities suffer from a shortage of graduate-level jobs, and from Polish internal migration to nearby regional capitals and Warsaw. Originally, I had intended to make a more systematic comparison of the three cities, based on secondary data as well as my fieldwork. However, because of the Covid-19 pandemic and travel restrictions and the 2022 Ukrainian refugee exodus, my fieldwork took place in three very different historical periods: the last era of 'normality' (Płock, 2019); the final months of pandemic restrictions (Kalisz, September 2021–January 2022); and just before and after the full-scale invasion of Ukraine (Piła, February–June 2022). This made it difficult to compare the fieldwork material gathered in the three different cities. The second part of the chapter discusses the project on which *Polish Cities of Migration* is based. It explains my methods: observation, including online; 40 conversations with key informants such as recruitment agents, employment centre staff, teachers and NGO activists; and 124 in-depth interviews with migrants and former migrants. I explain how I recruited participants and present some information about the sample. The section details my livelihood strategies approach and use of the integration concept in preparing the topic guide and analysing the interview material.

Płock, Kalisz and Piła

Each city and town in Poland is unique. Their histories, locations and labour markets, as well as the size of the local population, its educational levels and age structure, are just some of the differentiating factors.[2] However, there exists a widespread perception that all smaller cities share similar disadvantages and challenges. For example, an analysis of Kalisz (Fazlagić et al 2021: 7) claimed that 'a significant share of the city's problems and challenges are typical of those faced by many other cities in Poland'. Regional economic inequality, measured by GDP, has been growing since 2000 (OECD 2020: 4). Furthermore, regional capitals are commonly viewed as benefiting at the expense of smaller cities, including through internal migration and 'brain drain' (Szczech-Pietkiewicz 2017). The cities in this study were chosen partly because they did share some common problems and features, while differing in other respects. For instance, the cities were situated in different partitions, with Płock and Kalisz in the Russian partition from 1815 to 1918 and Piła (Schneidemühl) in Prussia/Germany until 1945.

The populations of the three cities in December 2021 were: Płock 113,660; Kalisz 95,021; and Piła 71,846 (GUS 2022: 93, 98). Płock was the second largest city of the Mazowieckie region, after Warsaw, while Kalisz and Piła were second and third in Wielkopolska, after Poznań.[3] In 2021, they ranked 32nd, 38th and 48th among Polish cities according to population size.[4] Although for statistical purposes Płock is often characterised as 'big' (*duże*), many Poles would consider Płock as well as Kalisz and Piła to be 'middling' (*średnie*). The Polish word *miasto*, as in the phrases *duże miasto* and *średnie miasto*, covers all urban settlements, and is the equivalent of both 'city' and 'town' in English. KPP are middling *miasta* because they are neither big cities nor small towns.[5] Since English distinguishes between cities and towns, it seems more helpful not to use the words middling or medium-sized but instead to label KPP 'smaller cities'. They are too big to count as 'towns', but small by city standards. This use of the term city to describe KPP also accords with parameters set by Eurostat, which defines cities as having populations of over 50,000.[6]

Piła perhaps deserves the city label less than the other two. It is the smallest of the trio. It lacks a cathedral, so would not traditionally be considered in a city in the UK, unlike Kalisz and Płock. With regard to Polish markers: Kalisz and Płock are 'counties' (*powiaty*) in their own right, while the city of Piła is part of wider Piła county. Piła city has the status only of an 'urban commune' (*gmina miejska*) and this means, among other things, that fewer city-level statistics are available. For planning purposes the concept of the 'functional urban area' is often preferred to *miasto*. For example, Kalisz with its slightly smaller neighbour Ostrów Wielkopolski form the hub of a functional urban area of over 400,000 population. Płock and Kalisz–plus–Ostrów Wielkopolski are accorded regional significance in Poland's 2011–30 development plan (Żuber 2012: 26), whereas Piła, ringed by much smaller towns, has subregional status (Gwosdz et al 2019: 6).

Piła also lacks its own supplement to *Gazeta Wyborcza*, Poland's leading newspaper. Hence it does not feature as one of the 'Polish cities' ranged along the head of the *GW* homepage. When *Wyborcza Kalisz* was launched in 2021, the opening article proclaimed:

> *Wyborcza Kalisz* is the latest local edition to be launched in recent months. Outside the big cities, our newspaper now exists in Elbląg, Rybnik, Koszalin, Zakopane and Wałbrzych. With each new edition, we are impressed by how the Polish hundred-thousanders constitute a mine of fascinating stories – interesting to readers across Poland (Skalnicka-Kirpsza 2021).

Skalnicka-Kirpsza invokes a category of *stutysięcznik*, cities of 100,000, as if such places have some kind of collective and perhaps exotically provincial identity.

Kwaśny (2020: 7) asserts that 'in today's Poland only a few of the very largest urban centres are considered sufficiently attractive so that in-migration can cancel out, or nearly cancel out, unfavourable change in the areas of natural population loss and suburbanisation'. KPP are typical of all but the most flourishing Polish towns and cities in that they are losing population year on year. Ironically, in view of Skalnicka-Kirpsza's (2021) comment about 'hundred-thousanders', in 2020 Kalisz's population dropped below the psychologically important 100,000 mark (GUS 2021: 98). Urban population loss across Poland is largely connected to low birthrates, though also to suburbanisation – where richer people move beyond the city boundaries, and/or poorer people cannot afford rents in the city. Suburbanisation has been noted as a particular problem in Kalisz: it exacerbates inequalities both for residents of the poorer inner city area and for people who live in villages but do not own cars (Syska 2019). All three cities worry about the scale of out-migration by young people. Fazlagić et al (2021: 53) suggest that 'migration is responsible for about one half of Kalisz's drop in population'. However, migration statistics based on official de-registration from place of residence in the city underestimate the scale of both international and internal migration (Jakóbczyk-Gryszkiewicz 2018: 291–2). My fieldwork suggested that school-leavers who 'temporarily' go abroad are quite an important category here. However, this group is not much discussed, and the focus tends to be on highly-skilled migration, and the fact that young graduates prefer to stay in the big regional centres after graduating from university. My interviewees confirmed that internal migration to Warsaw, Poznań and (from Kalisz) Wrocław is intense. For example, Tomasz, a former student, reminisced, 'When I lived in Wrocław it was hard to meet anyone from Wrocław. We socialised with our friends from Kalisz, there are heaps of people from Kalisz.'

In 2019–21, local media mentioned the topic of immigration quite rarely. For instance, my searches for 'Ukrain' before 24 February 2022[7] revealed mostly cultural and sporting items, plus a few traffic accidents. Very occasionally, Ukrainians were mentioned in connection with the local economy. For instance, one story featured an orchard owner near Piła currently employing Ukrainian women to pick fruit because Poles would not do it, but expressing his concern that the Ukrainians would head for Germany as soon as it opened its labour market (MN 2018). Migrants of other nationalities were also mentioned sporadically. For instance, in December 2021, a special mass was held for refugees in Kalisz cathedral. The priest commented: 'Just as in a very tough period of Polish history, in the 1980s and early 1990s, our compatriots emigrated to Germany, France, England or Ireland … so now we can see the reverse process, with migrants arriving from Ukraine, Belarus and even far-away Asia, including Vietnam and Thailand' (Kotowska-Rasiak 2021). In 2021 Kalisz was in the national news when a local family was convicted of smuggling Vietnamese people across Poland (Józefiak 2021).

KPP are all 'post-regional' cities, places which from 1975–98 were regional capitals. In 1999 the number of regions was reduced to 16 and ex-capitals lost the administrative posts and office jobs attendant on regional capital functions (Fazlagić et al 2021: 20). The stereotypes and negative connotations associated with these demoted cities, and the actual diversity of the category, are discussed further in Chapter 3. In fact, according to Gwosdz et al (2019), all three cities should be included in the top ten in Poland for their investment potential. Of course, being attractive to investors does not necessarily mean that KPP seem appealing to residents or migrants. Among their various disadvantages is that they are somewhat 'out of the way'; the biggest cities, with their range of employment, are rather distant. By road KPP are 100–120 km from the nearest metropolitan centres, Poznań and Warsaw (Gwosdz et al 2019: 6). The railway line from Piła to Poznań is partly single track, while to reach Kalisz from Poznań or Płock from Warsaw one usually has to change trains. On the other hand, buses travel from all three cities to a string of destinations in Ukraine.[8] The cities are not visibly polluted, since factories are situated on the outskirts and there is little traffic in the city centre. However, in common with most cities in central and southern Poland, Płock and Kalisz both have 'poor' air quality. They were ranked 304 and 360 out of 375 in Europe in 2023 for fine particulates.[9]

The cities each possess a handful of higher educational institutions: branches of Poznań's Adam Mickiewicz University in Kalisz and Piła, and Warsaw Polytechnic in Płock, together with the Akademia Kaliska, Akademia Mazowiecka w Płocku and Paweł Włodkowic University College in Płock. However, the opportunities to study for a university degree in KPP are insufficient to stem educational migration to the bigger cities, particularly because the range of degree programmes is limited. Płock is also home to Poland's oldest scholarly society, the Towarzystwo Naukowe Płockie, founded in 1820, and Kalisz has its own Kaliskie Towarzystwo Przyjaciół Nauk. Their headquarters and libraries are located in the city centres.[10] Of special importance to migrants are the adult education colleges (*szkoły policealne*) which offer courses in Polish and vocational subjects and can provide a diploma which dispenses applicants for permanent residence from taking a language examination. I was told by a college administrator that, for example, one college in Piła had 80 Ukrainians on the books as well as two Russians, two Belarusians and a Moroccan.

Voters in KPP tended to support more liberal candidates, though not on the scale of the largest cities. For example, in the second round of the 2020 presidential elections, Rafał Trzaskowski scored higher than Andrzej Duda in all three cities, though the vote was more evenly divided in Płock.[11] In 2023, the Civic Platform party would defeat Law and Justice comfortably in Piła and Kalisz, with Law and Justice narrowly victorious in Płock.[12] None of the three cities declared itself an 'LGBT-free zone'.[13] The cities also house a number of (liberal) civil society initiatives, especially Kalisz. These included, in 2021, a series of informal get-togethers for local migrants and Poles organised by students and advertised on Facebook

Table 2.1 Selected indicators, Płock and Kalisz cities and Piła urban commune

	Płock	Kalisz	Piła
'Quality of life' according to Wałachowski & Król (2019)	1st	21st	97th
Functional urban area, population 2021[1]	231,088	408,671	136,621
Natural population growth, 2021	-7.47 [6.52]	-7.92 [6.52]	N/A
Spending from city budget per citizen, 2021 (zł.)	9,891 [8,314]	8,259 [8,314]	5,490
Average monthly wage, 2022 (zł.)[2]	7,898	5,781	6,004
Registered unemployment, 2021 (%)	6.1[3] [4.9] Mazowieckie 4.7	3.2 [4.9] Wielkopolska 3.2	3.0
Wooded areas (%)	5.0	5.8	50.1
% with higher education among economically active population, 2011[4]	16.2	16.3	15.1
Number of university students, 2019/20[5]	4,994	4,074	N/A

Source: https://svs.stat.gov.pl/ unless indicated in endnotes. Figures in square brackets refer to the average for Polish cities with powiat status, Płock and Kalisz's natural comparators.

---

1 Wałachowski and Król (2019: 19–20, 22)
2 https://www.polskawliczbach.pl/miasta_z_najwiekszym_wynagrodzeniem_w_polsce, last accessed 15.8.23
3 In 2019, the year I did the fieldwork, unemployment in Płock had also been 6.1.
4 Gwozds et al (2019: 52). Figures for powiats including surrounding rural ones.
5 USwP 2020; USwW 2020.

(*Rozmówki kaliskie*) (Anon 2021b). Civil society activists, at least in Kalisz and Piła, supported refugees on the Belarus–Poland border (Miklas 2021; Pieczyńska-Chamczyk 2022). However, before February 2022, none of the cities hosted any NGOs concerned primarily with migrants. This changed after the full-scale invasion, as in many other locations across Poland.

Płock

Płock[14] is often billed as a 'former capital of Poland' since it was the seat of several medieval rulers, including Bolesław III Wrymouth. It acquired city status in 1237, shortly before Kraków. The city is strikingly located on the high bank of the Vistula, with a ruined castle, cathedral and several streets of historic buildings around a picturesque market square. Tourist attractions include the Muzeum Mazowieckie and a Jewish museum with a lively cultural programme. The Orthodox cathedral, like its equivalent in Kalisz, was dismantled during the de-Russification of the 1920s (Fundacja Nobiscum 2021) but two modest Orthodox chapels and a cemetery remain. The city hosts many different events and festivals, is a magnet for pilgrims from around the world and aspires to become European capital of culture in 2029.

During the period of communist industrialisation, Płock was chosen as the site of an oil refinery, attracting workers from across Poland. The population grew by 273 per cent in the years 1950–1990 (Szmytkowska 2017: 93). Today, PKN Orlen, which owns the refinery, is by far the biggest company in Poland.[15] Wages at Orlen contribute to high average wages in the city and therefore to Płock's impressive standing in league tables, especially for 'quality of life'. Orlen invests substantially in sport and culture. However, as shown in Table 2.1, unemployment is higher than in the other cities. Wages outside Orlen are only average, and local opinion is divided about the benefits of the refinery and whether or not it is still a serious polluter. Although other factories coexist alongside Orlen, Zaborowski (2019: 59) claims that the city's 'economic power is based only on the one big factory'.

When I conducted the fieldwork in 2019, my interviewees and key informants did not perceive Orlen to be a large-scale employer of foreign labour. This changed dramatically in 2023 when it emerged that the company had built a 6000-person container-module 'workers' town' on the outskirts of Płock, by the site of its new Orfin III production complex (Szkwarek 2023a, 2023b). The town, the only one of its kind in Poland,[16] was designed for workers, engineers and managers from South Korea, Spain, India, Malaysia, Pakistan, Türkiye, the Philippines and Turkmenistan. In the few months before it opened in June, around 1000 foreign workers had already arrived and were quartered in rented accommodation and hotels in Płock and the surrounding area (Burzyńska and Adamkowski 2023). Given the close links between Orlen and the Law and Justice party, allowing Orlen to employ thousands of foreigners, including from Muslim countries, seemed a blatant example of government hypocrisy. It also dramatically increased the non-white population of Płock. Although people living in the hamlet where the new town was located became concerned about the future of their agrotourism businesses, the city's residents seemed to take it in their stride. Płock's 'emigration' identity was visible in some comments reported by the press. For instance, one woman stated: 'I worked for several years in Germany and I'm not afraid of newcomers' (Szkwarek 2023a). At the Corpus Christi celebrations in June 2023, Bishop Szymon Stułkowski 'reminded the people of Płock that, for years, many of them had gone abroad to work, like the foreigners working today at Olefin III ... and he asked them to pray for the foreign workers who had come from the ends of the world to earn money to support their families' (Burzyńska and Adamkowski 2023).

The city's relative proximity to Warsaw helps draw away talent, and net internal migration was −402 in 2019 (USwW 2020: 1). The scale of international migration by well-known people associated with Płock is indicated by Łakomski's (2010) hefty album *Płock na emigracji*. Płock featured in Filip Springer's 2016 book of *reportage* about Polish former regional capitals. Springer describes it as a hive of entrepreneurship, but also spotlights the scale of internal migration. One interviewee was said to dislike Christmas and Easter because he would bump into old friends visiting their parents, who asked him how long he was staying in Płock. When he said he lived there 'they [would] shake their heads sympathetically. As if something must have gone horribly wrong in my life, for me to be stuck here' (Springer 2016: 226).

Kalisz

Kalisz[17] claims the distinction of being the oldest recorded city in Poland, often pared down to 'Poland's oldest city'.[18] The second-century Alexandrian geographer Ptolemy mentioned a 'Calisia', located on the Amber route which crossed Europe from north to south. Kalisz acquired city status around 1257. It was home to one of Poland's earliest Jewish communities and in 1264 Duke Bolesław the Pious issued the Statute of Kalisz, setting out the rights and freedoms of Jews in Wielkopolska, later extended to the whole of Poland. The old town was practically destroyed by the German army in 1914. However, in the 1920s the centre was rebuilt, not as a copy (unlike Warsaw and Wrocław following World War II) but according to the medieval streetplan, with an impressive Renaissance-style white town hall. The city centre is encircled by the narrow River Prosna, the city park and a shady green strip, the Planty – a miniature version of its Kraków namesake. Some streets in the centre are run-down, and Fazlagić et al (2021: 56, 90) complain that resulting social problems include crime and difficulties in families where one parent is working abroad. Just outside the medieval city, some monumental nineteenth-century buildings remain from the periods of Prussian and Russian rule (Tabaka and Błachowicz 2010). An open-air museum presents Kalisz as it might have looked in the early medieval period.

The new 2021 Kalisz supplement to *Gazeta Wyborcza* addressed topics popularly associated with the city: its status as a former capital and whether this could be reinstated (Cylka 2021); the closure of its signature Calisia piano factory (Lehmann 2021); debates about whether it really was the oldest city in Poland (Walczak 2021b); and rivalries with neighbouring Ostrów Wielkopolski 'dating back to the Partitions' (Walczak 2021a) when Ostrów was in Prussia, a fact which means it supposedly functions more efficiently today. (This view was also espoused by several of my Kalisz informants, both Polish and Ukrainian. They claimed, for example, that Ostrów had better shops and nightclubs.) The headline referred to nicknames given to local inhabitants and also used for sports teams: Onion-eaters for people from Kalisz, and Pheasants for their rivals. Zaborowski (2019: 61) claims that Ostrów 'is growing to be an equal partner with the slightly bigger but worse-situated Kalisz'. Residents of Ostrów Wielkopolski work and shop in Kalisz and vice versa. In addition to Kalisz's old industrial base such as (Nestlé) Winiary and the Goplana chocolate factory, a number of large new factories have been established, such as several supplying furniture to IKEA. However, as in Płock, there is an insufficient supply of white-collar jobs attractive to young graduates (Fazlagić et al 2021: 24, 56).

Like Płock, Kalisz claims a multicultural history (Walczak and Andrysiak 2006). A large nineteenth-century Jewish cemetery with a small museum is situated in the suburbs. In the 1930s Jews still constituted about one third of the population (Przygodzki n.d.; Woźniak n.d.) and about 800 Jews are estimated to have been murdered in Kalisz during the war (Woźniak 2006). A plaque marks the spot from which over 20,000 people were deported to death camps and a statue in the shape of a book commemorates the destruction of local Jewish–Polish and ethnic Polish libraries by the Nazis. In the 1920s and 30s, Kalisz was home to a several thousand-strong Ukrainian exile community consisting of veterans from the army of the Ukrainian People's Republic and their families. The Ukrainian cemetery lies on the outskirts of the city (Kolańczuk 2006; Kurzajczyk 2021; Sribniak 2019). In 2021, it was not well-signposted, and none of my Ukrainian interviewees mentioned its existence.

Piła

Piła,[19] like Kalisz and Płock, was awarded city rights in the Middle Ages. It was the birthplace of the educationalist Stanisław Staszic, a leading light of the Polish Enlightenment. Staszic's museum-house is one of the few tourist attractions in the city, which also possesses a small local history museum. During the First Partition of Poland in 1772, Piła was incorporated into Prussia, and was part of Germany until 1945. Most of the city was destroyed in the Second World War; some of the bricks and other materials were used to rebuild Warsaw.[20] After the war, Piła was turned into a Soviet-style city as part of the de-Germanisation of the newly annexed territories, and in keeping with the communist party's hope that new settlers would become model socialist citizens (Kolasa-Nowak and Bucholc 2023: 12). Little Germanic architecture remains. In 2022, the maps prominently displayed in the city centre still showed Heroes of Stalingrad Street and other communist-era names. Springer (2016: 44), in his book on pre-1999 regional capitals, comments that 'Today Piła is like America. If something dates from the 19th century, it is very old.' There is no up-to-date guidebook, or even a recent printed city map.[21] A few small tourist brochures concentrate mostly on Piła's surrounding lakes and forests. The city is a centre for outdoor leisure activities and the local branch of Poznań's Adam Mickiewicz University specialises in water management.

Despite the forced resettlement of Ukrainians in the former German territories in the 1940s, as a result of extensive emigration only a few thousand Ukrainians remained in Piła county by the late communist period. It is impossible to estimate how many lived in Piła itself (Słabig 2013: 63, 70–78). Ukrainian identity was stronger across the nearby border with Pomerania. In Walcz, just across this border, an Orthodox church was established in 1947 and an informal Greek Catholic parish emerged in 1959 (Słabig 2013: 64–70). In 2021–22, the Orthodox Church in Walcz advertised services on the Russian-language (but chiefly Ukrainian) Facebook Group *Nashi w Pile*. Germans not expelled after the Second World War were stigmatised and persecuted under communism and had mostly emigrated by 1989 (Prawdzic 2021). Prawdzic (2021: 10) mentions one older woman who spoke German only to her cat and dog. Piła county was also home to an autochthonous population consisting of people who lived on the territory of Poland before it was settled by Poles or Germans, or Poles who became Germanised under the Prussian/German partition. Although they were courted as Poles by the communists they were recognised as German by West Germany and consequently also emigrated (Słabig 2013). Piła houses the only German society in Wielkopolska, the Niemieckie Towarzystwo Społeczno-Kulturalne, founded in 1992. In 2021, the Society had over 250 members, both from Piła and from neighbouring Złotów commune. It organised language classes, whose students included would-be migrants, and social events (Anon 2021a; Anon 2021c; Niskiewicz 2017).[22] Piła lies about 175 miles from today's German border. However, my interviews suggested that if Piła residents migrated to Germany they tended not to choose locations in the former German Democratic Republic (GDR), with the important exception of Berlin. One interviewee, Sylwia, claimed that in the late 1990s 'everyone in Berlin was from Piła'.

Piła's economic transition is said to have been more successful than that of many medium-sized towns and smaller cities because its state light bulb factory was sold to the international company Philips as early as 1991. This helped the factory to flourish and provide employment for about 5,000 Polish workers by 2007 (Jałowiecki 2007: 91). In 2016, over 10 per cent of the local workforce was employed by Philips Signify (Gwosdz et al 2019: 37). However, by 2021–2 the factory experienced a demand for Ukrainian labour, judging by the many job advertisements and the testimonies of my interviewees.

The research project

The original material which forms the basis of this book was gathered during fieldwork in Płock in February–April and September 2019; Kalisz in September and November–December 2021 and January 2022; and Piła from February–June 2022. During the first six months of 2022 I held a NAWA Ulam Scholarship at the Centre for Migration Studies and

Institute of Anthropology of Adam Mickiewicz University in Poznań. One of the many advantages of being based in Poznań was the comparisons it offered between the big city and the smaller city migration experiences.

The fieldwork obtained ethical approval from University College London Research Ethics Committee. It raised some common ethical dilemmas, such as how to strike the right balance between providing sufficient detail to illustrate particular points while protecting the confidentiality of interviewees. My solutions to these problems included using 'KPP' instead of the names of individual cities, unless the city's identity was relevant to the analysis, and omitting even a pseudonym for my interviewees in cases where I was reporting sensitive information or opinions. In general, my approach was to present only the information about each interviewee which was most relevant to the given context. Hence, for example, unlike some authors I did not record an interviewee's age next to their pseudonym every time they were mentioned. The full-scale invasion presented new challenges. I stopped interviewing Ukrainians, although I continued to read posts on the Ukrainian Facebook pages for the three cities. I also decided to omit some of the more negative comments interviewees had made about Ukraine, since I suspected that in retrospect they might regret these. It was also clear from Facebook that some interviewees radically revised their opinions about Russia after the full-scale invasion.

The research methods included participant observation as a volunteer English teacher at the Migrant Information Point in Poznań and many casual conversations about migration with people I happened to meet around Kalisz, Piła and Płock. Although I did not formally set out to count the foreign population of each city, I did keep a note of foreigners who were mentioned both in these casual conversations with strangers and by my formal interviewees. I also paid attention to opinions local residents expressed about the cities themselves. It was striking, for example, how seldom anyone mentioned the loss of regional capital status, although this is the lens through which all three cities are often seen by geographers or in the media. In addition, I looked out for street-level evidence of local foreigners. For instance, I photographed signs in Ukrainian in post offices, a bank and employment agencies. However, as also found by Levchuk (2021) Ukrainian was rarely present in public space before 2022.

I joined the Facebook groups 'Ukrainians in Poland Płock', 'Ukrainians in Kalisz', 'Our people (*nashi*) in Piła' and 'Poznan Expats'; Facebook groups intended for the Polish residents of each city; and 'Bigger and smaller returns from the UK and other places to Poland'. I also joined groups set up in 2022 to coordinate Polish support for Ukrainians: 'Piła residents for Ukraine' and 'Kalisz for Ukraine'. Before February 2022, it was rare to find Poles active on the Ukrainian sites or *vice versa*. However, the groups founded in February 2022 were used by both nationalities, sometimes in dialogue. The groups 'Our people in Piła' and 'Ukrainians in Kalisz/Płock' had in 2019–21 been mostly conducted in Russian, and were sometimes used by Georgians and Belarusians. They became predominantly but not exclusively Ukrainian-language after February 2022.

I was fortunate to be able to discuss KPP with 40 key informants, experts in particular fields. Usually I contacted them directly through their organisations and institutions. Eight of these experts worked in NGOs, six in job centres and five in centres for integration of foreigners, institutions set up in a number of Wielkopolska smaller cities in 2022 and originally intended to target all foreigners. Since they opened just after the invasion they concentrated on supporting Ukrainians. Four of my key informants were employers or managers of recruitment agencies, four were teachers and headteachers, and four were priests of various Christian denominations. Two managed migrant hostels, two worked in houses of culture and two were university lecturers (one African). The key informants also included: a Polish factory worker who worked alongside Ukrainians; a local official who managed the city's tourism department; and Eskan Darwich, a Syrian city councillor and businessman in Kalisz who did not want to be anonymous.

My main source was my 124 loosely-structured interviews with migrants and former migrants living in KPP. Their nationalities and gender are listed in Table 2.2. Fuller details about the sample are provided in Chapters 4, 7 and 12.

The Polish sample included two women who visited their children living abroad. I initially planned to include more stayers alongside migrants in my Polish sample, but then decided this would over-complicate the analysis.

Table 2.2 Interviewees

	Płock 2019 (n=48)	Kalisz 2021–2 (n=45)	Piła 2022 (n=31)	Total
F:M	27:21	25:20	19:12	71:53
Polish	16	10	11	37
Ukrainian	26	28	16	70
Others	6	7	4	17

I paid for interviews, which encouraged more participants to volunteer and seemed particularly important given that many interviewees were working long hours. In Płock, I found most interviewees through Polish friends and acquaintances and, in the case of Ukrainians, with the help of the warden of one of the two main migrant hostels. In Kalisz, I also had help from Polish acquaintances for locating Poles, but relied primarily on Facebook for the rest. In Piła, I used Facebook almost exclusively. In addition, I walked into some workplaces such as cafés and recruited participants directly. Quite often, interviewees recommended me to their friends, but not usually more than two, so these 'snowballs' were not large. The Piła sample was smaller than I intended largely because I stopped interviewing Ukrainians after the full-scale Russian invasion. However, although it had been easy to recruit Ukrainians in Piła, it proved harder to find other nationalities and there seemed to be fewer of them than in Kalisz and Płock. My Ukrainian interviewees in Piła did not work alongside other foreigners in local factories; there seem to be no language schools employing native speakers and there were fewer Asian eateries and kebab bars than in the other two cities.

I interviewed in Russian, Polish and English, asking interviewees to choose whichever language suited them best. A handful preferred to speak Ukrainian (which I understand quite well) but let me ask them questions in Polish or Russian. At the time I conducted the fieldwork, the participants did not seem to mind speaking Russian, in keeping with Maksimovtsova's observation (2022: 244) that Russian functioned as a normal language of communication in Ukraine despite the political tensions in the period before the full-scale invasion. I have transliterated all Ukrainian placenames as if the conversation had been in Ukrainian (for example Kyiv, even when my interlocutor used the Russian form Kiev). When allocating pseudonyms, I gave Ukrainian names to self-identified Ukrainian speakers and Russian speakers with Ukrainian names, and Russian names to Russian speakers with Russian names.

My own identity as a British researcher perhaps influenced some of the Polish return migrants from the UK to engage in nostalgic reminiscences of their time abroad; I tried to encourage them to be critical too. A similar situation occasionally arose with several Ukrainians who, enthusing about Poland, seemingly forgot that I was British and addressed me as a Pole.

The interviews were conversational in style and based on a topic guide which I had memorised. We discussed how and why the informants had chosen to migrate, as well as their choice of destination, their experiences of life abroad, their transnational practices and networks and their impressions of migration to and from KPP, as well as other aspects of local change. The concepts of migration transition and migration cultures are central to my interpretation of the overall situation in Poland, which is why they are discussed in depth in Chapter 1. However, to construct the topic guides and organise the initial analysis of the interview material I employed some other concepts, chiefly livelihood strategies and integration, but also place attachment.

I used a livelihood strategy approach in my interviews to understand how potential migrants choose between different livelihood options, how they think about different available economic resources and how these thoughts are influenced by non-economic factors. Why, for example, did so many interviewees reject internal migration in favour of migrating abroad? How did migrants decide between their obligations to different family members? Who influenced their decision-making? Non-economic factors include migration culture: norms and assumptions prevailing, but also evolving, in the locations and social worlds migrants inhabit both in the sending and receiving societies. Hence I asked about not just the interviewee's own story, but also their impressions about and reflections on local migration practices. I was interested in stories about local people and relatives who had migrated. Although I did not ask directly about divergent interests and opinions within households, I made a note of these when they were mentioned. Livelihood strategy approaches are often based on an assumption of household unity, but as demonstrated for example in my book on Polish families (White 2017) or by Hondagleu-Sotelo (1994) with reference to Mexican–US migration, family harmony cannot be taken for granted. Attention needs to be focused on 'the politics of gender in families and social networks' (Hondagleu-Sotelo 1994: 53). As everywhere in migration scholarship, it is vital to apply an intersectional analysis. In other words, one has to try to understand how migrant identities resulting from livelihood strategies intersect with other identities such as gender and age. I refer to this as a 'critical livelihood strategy approach'.

Migrants are incorporated into receiving societies in different ways and to differing extents. When asking the interviewees about their experiences abroad, I used a mental checklist drawn from Ager and Strang's (2008) indicators of integration. Since this was a qualitative study, I understood integration as a process, rather than a completed state. Integration is often a controversial topic, with nationalists and liberals holding opposing views. Unlike Ager and Strang, nationalists adopt a narrowly cultural approach to integration, ignoring the rights of migrants to decent housing, jobs, etc. They assume that the onus to integrate is on the migrant and they suspect that if migrants resist assimilation they are disloyal and potentially a security risk. By contrast, Ager and Strang's is a liberal approach. They take for granted that the receiving society needs to evolve to incorporate migrants and that it is not just the task of the migrants to integrate themselves. Moreover, Ager and Strang refer to 'sufficient' integration in different domains, rather than insisting on full assimilation. I asked about interviewees' integration in various of the domains identified by Ager and Strang. These were: their friendships with co-nationals, members of the receiving society and other migrants; their language use and learning and impressions about local cultures; and experiences of work, housing, health services and, if relevant, education. I also questioned migrants in Poland, and Poles who had returned from the UK after Brexit, about their residence status. In addition, the Ager and Strang framework was useful for analysing the interview material, particularly for considering how experiences in the different domains interlinked. Like Bell (2016: 83), I find that interviewees rarely refer to 'integration' themselves, and I avoid using the word in interviews, both because it is not part of most informants' everyday vocabulary and because it is ambiguous when used colloquially.

The rationale for using the integration concept only applies to certain types of analysis. It helps chart the progress of migrants towards becoming members of the receiving society. However, when the researcher is more interested in a migrant's own views about how they are settling in a particular place, it can be better to apply other concepts. Mulholland and Ryan (2022) and Grzymała-Kazłowska and Ryan (2022) propose the analytical framework of 'embedding' to understand this process. The term embedding can be more helpful than 'settling', since it emphasises the role of social networks, which are an important part of many migrants' experiences abroad. Grzymała-Kazłowska's (2016) concept of anchoring (which I had used as a metaphor in White (2011)) is also helpful to identify those particular aspects of migrants' lives which help them to stop 'drifting' and keep them moored, at least temporarily, in places they live abroad (Grzymała-Kazłowska and Brzozowska 2017). Settling is colloquially equated with 'putting down roots', but Polish migrants, with their often experimental attitude towards migration, were not necessarily interested in putting down 'roots'. Place attachment, discussed in more detail in Chapters 4 and 11, is a close cousin of integration, embedding and anchoring, but emphasises the emotional dimension of the process. The most important point to highlight is that, when this book uses the terms 'integration', 'embedding', 'anchoring' or 'place attachment', it always seeks to portray the interviewees' experiences over time. These transitions in a multitude of individual lives combined together to make up Poland's migration transition 'from below'.

As King et al (1997: 3) observed, 'there is no such creature as a net migrant'. The book uses an intersectional lens to reveal differences between the interviewees, including between people of the same nationality. The age, life stage, gender, educational level, skin colour and other features of individual research participants help explain their varied experiences as migrants: their mobility; transnational identities and practices; and integration journeys (White 2022a). Sergei and Jan, quoted at the beginning of Chapter 1, were Ukrainian and Polish respectively, but age rather than nationality is the most significant – though not the only – clue to understanding their different outlooks on settlement vis-à-vis ongoing mobility. The chapters consider in turn the views of Poles, Ukrainians, and other nationalities. This nationality-based grouping was a convenient way to organise the research material. However, 'groupism' (Brubaker 2004) can obscure salient facts about identities not used as the organising principle for creating the groups. In particular, when migrants are seen primarily in terms of their nationality the result is often excessive 'culturalisation' (Horolets et al 2020: 744). Intersectional approaches help avoid falling into this trap. Without introducing this level of nuance, considering the significance of the remainder of each interviewee's bundle of identities, it would have been impossible to build a composite picture of the internally differentiated Polish and Ukrainian groups within my sample. The jigsaw would have remained incomplete.

By highlighting other social identities it also became possible to compare across chapters and consider side-by-side the experiences of people of different nationalities: for example, comparing attitudes towards migration of young Ukrainians and young Poles. To some extent they shared a sense of experimentation and migrating for fun – an approach to life which might be linked to the overall twenty-first-century mobility context. Besides identifying sub-groups (McCall 2005), a further function of the intersectional approach is to sensitise the researcher to 'the interconnectedness of different identities' (Anthias 2012: 102), 'bringing existing concepts, such as gender, class and race, into the same analytical framework to try to understand how they relate to one another' (Bastia 2014: 245). Hence, for example, researchers commonly discover that male migrants of a particular nationality and status are more privileged than women. Several such situations are described in *Polish Cities*. For instance, Chapter 7 considers a sub-group of Ukrainian interviewees:

women with unusable university degrees married to highly-valued skilled manual workers such as welders. These families were likely to stay in KPP, adding to the cities' migration transitions. However, the reason was not that the whole family wanted to stay. The husbands were satisfied, but the wives would have preferred to move to bigger cities.

Rigorous comparisons are not feasible on the basis of qualitative research. I had originally intended to adopt a 'light touch' comparative approach between the three cities. I had to abandon the idea because, as mentioned in the Introduction, I ended up conducting the fieldwork in three discrete periods. Travel restrictions and my university's embargo on overseas research meant that I had to wait two years before resuming fieldwork in Kalisz – by which time, my interviewees' lives and migration experiences had of course also been affected by the pandemic. When Putin invaded Ukraine on 24 February 2022, I was in the middle of fieldwork in Piła. The war inevitably influenced interviewees' perceptions, making them unlike their counterparts in the first two cities. For example, it seemed ridiculous to ask whether they were aware of Ukrainians in the city in the midst of the influx of refugees. I also encountered some Polish and Belarusian negativity towards Ukrainians, which had not featured in the earlier interviews.

Before Putin's full-scale invasion of Ukraine, I had assumed that my task was to analyse the present (second) stage of Polish migration transition, particularly the everyday lives and plans of Ukrainians working in Poland. That stage of the transition ended abruptly on 24 February 2022. At first it seemed that all I could do with three years' of accumulated interview material was to present the lost world of Ukrainian labour migrants as a piece of history. I had to finish this project, and could not begin a separate one which analysed the new (third) stage of the refugee influx, although I was living in Poland in Spring 2022 and collecting information about the refugees and their reception. However, with time, and as refugees from Ukraine to Poland began to move on to other countries or return (sometimes temporarily) to Ukraine, I began to see more clearly the continuing relevance of trends which I had identified before the full-scale invasion. The Ukrainians I interviewed in KPP probably felt that their lives and country had changed irrevocably, but entering the third stage of Poland's migration transition provided me as a researcher with opportunity for exercising hindsight which helped my analysis of the overall trends. I summarise these trends in Chapter 13, the book's conclusion.

Notes

1. I use KPP as shorthand to refer to the three cities in preference to phrases such as 'smaller cities' where I want to avoid implying that they are typical of all smaller cities, and/or to conceal the identity of individual cities to protect the anonymity of interviewees.
2. See for example Gwosdz et al (2019: 10–11) for a more complete list.
3. https://svs.stat.gov.pl/ (last accessed 27 October 2023). This website, Statystyczny Vademecum Samorządowca, provides the information about individual cities and counties published in previous years as pdfs.
4. https://www.polskawliczbach.pl/ (last accessed 27 October 2023).
5. A *miasto* in Poland is normally defined as middling if it has a population of 20,000–100,000; larger cities are 'big'. According to this criterion, Płock should be considered a 'big city', as was Kalisz until 2019. However, according to the Polish Government's Strategy for Responsible Development for the period up to 2020, a middling *miasto* is a town/city which has a population of over 20,000 and is not a regional capital. See https://www.gov.pl/web/fundusze-regiony/informacje-o-strategii-na-rzecz-odpowiedzialnego-rozwoju. Runge (2012: 90) observes that often the term middling is not applied strictly.
6. https://ec.europa.eu/eurostat/web/cities/spatial-units
7. The newspapers were the Płock and Kalisz versions of *Gazeta Wyborcza*; portalplock.pl; faktykaliskie.info; kalisz.naszemiasto.pl; zycie.pila.pl; pila.naszemiasto.pl.
8. As the 2022 refugee influx revealed, there were already some quite large populations of Ukrainians in north-west Poland, at least in Świnoujście, a resort town with an 'absorbent labour market' (Jarosz and Klaus 2023: 11, 38).
9. https://www.eea.europa.eu/themes/air/urban-air-quality/european-city-air-quality-viewer. Piła was not included, but cities in north-west Poland generally scored 'moderate' for air quality.
10. A Towarzystwo Miłośników Miasta Piły has an internet presence but its premises were boarded up and it was impossible to contact.
11. https://prezydent20200628.pkw.gov.pl/prezydent20200628/pl/wyniki/pl (last accessed 14 August 2023).
12. https://www.wybory.gov.pl/sejmsenat2023/pl/sejm/wynik/pow/ (last accessed 22 October 2023).
13. https://atlasnienawisci.pl/
14. https://nowy.plock.eu/
15. See Rzeczpospolita's list of top Polish companies: https://rankingi.rp.pl/lista500/2022 ('Lista 500') (last accessed 26 June 2023). It is #283 on Forbes list of global top companies: https://www.forbes.com/companies/pkn-orlen/?sh=36f982d92429
16. https://www.propertynews.pl/hotele/jedyne-takie-miasteczko-w-polsce-to-gigantyczny-hotel-pracowniczy,133013.html (last accessed 12 October 2023).
17. www.kalisz.pl
18. This is still claimed at the top of the English-language version of the city's homepage, www.kalisz.pl/en (last accessed 27 October 2023). Its motto is now a more careful 'Kalisz: add your [his]story', but the previous motto, 'The oldest city in Poland, young in spirit', is still in use. For example, 'Kalisz młode duchem, najstarsze miasto w Polsce', a promotional video featuring Grzegorz Kulawinek, vice-president of Kalisz (MTV: 3/8/22) at https://www.youtube.com/watch?v=HgsegQFAr8o
19. www.pila.pl
20. https://um.warszawa.pl/-/pila-dla-warszawy. 'Piła dla Warszawy' 30.8.11. Exhibition in Sejm about the destruction of the two cities and Warsaw's reconstruction.
21. Information from independent bookshop owner.
22. Backed up by information from key informants at the Society.

3
Motives to live in smaller cities: jobs versus quality of life

Introduction

This chapter discusses the factors which made smaller cities like Kalisz, Piła and Płock attractive destinations for migrants, thereby addressing the research question of why Poland has progressed to the stage of migration transition when migrants begin to settle in smaller locations, beyond the biggest cities. It is often assumed that metropolises like Warsaw or Kraków are more likely to attract migrants. Borkowski et al (2021: 169) suggest for example that Kraków offers

> a dynamic business environment, progressing economic development, a sizable labour market and a vibrant social and cultural life. The city was also known as an important hub of immigrants. As such, migrants' decisions on their prospective destinations were also influenced by the existing networks other than family-related and possibility of harvesting benefits of being a member of the existing diaspora.

KPP lacked all these attractions, nor, before February 2022, did they possess Polish-run NGOs whose primary role was supporting migrants. Moreover, as mentioned in Chapter 1, before the Ukrainian refugee influx only the biggest Polish cities had policies for supporting and integrating migrants. If migrants were rational actors, it would in many cases make sense for them to go to a larger city.

This chapter shows that some people's choice of initial location is guided by identity factors: their sense of not being a 'big-city person'. However, the chapter is not particularly concerned with why migrants came to these cities in the first place. As discussed in Chapters 8 and 12, characteristics of individual cities were usually unimportant. Interviewees either came to a particular workplace or university, or to be with family members. One Ukrainian did not even know where she was until she arrived. Similarly, Polish interviewees did not choose to grow up in KPP. Since the book is about people settling in smaller cities, it is their decision to stay in or return to live in the smaller city which needs to be understood. Factors specific to individual cities became more important when labour migrants were considering destinations for a second trip to Poland, or when Poles chose to return to their home cities. Of course, other factors such as social networks and jobs remained very important; nonetheless, certain aspects of the cities themselves began to seem more relevant. These could include, for example, that they were known to have clean air, affordable rents, good schools or easy access to bigger cities or regular coach routes to Ukraine.

The story of migration transition from below is one which is above all about place attachment. According to Bierwiaczonek (2016: 103–4), identification with one's city of residence takes place on different levels – those you cannot change (you are stuck with certain attributes of the place, you may have nowhere else to go) and those you can choose to be important in your life. It depends on the criteria you decide are most important. The interview evidence presented in this chapter illustrates which criteria the interviewees selected to justify their choice of city, including retrospective justifications. Loosely following Scannell and Gifford's (2010) distinction between place, people and process[1] in place attachment, Chapter 3 focuses on physical aspects of the place, while Chapters 10–12 pay more attention to social aspects of place and to the bundles of intersecting identities, networks and practices which made each migrant's process of place attachment unique. Chapter 3 seeks to explain the precise attraction of the three case study cities as places to live, while also investigating the broader question of how a 'smaller city' is conceptualised and why smaller cities as a category are preferred. The chapter begins by discussing some aspects of differently-sized cities in Poland, before asking 'is bigger better?' with reference to Polish city rankings. It then analyses evidence about the fate of the particular category of smaller cities to which Kalisz, Płock and Piła belong: former regional capitals. Finally, the main part of the chapter considers interviewees' opinions about what made a good city, mostly with reference to city size. I argue that lifestyle considerations, networks and sociabilities are often more important than economics in both the Polish and other interviewees' choice of migration livelihood strategies. Overall, it seems that one fifth of Poles would prefer to live in a 'medium-sized *miasto*' – a phrase probably understood by respondents to include all larger towns and under-500,000-population cities (Omyła-Rudzka 2022: 5).[2] Clearly, therefore, smaller cities have their devotees.

Metropolises and lesser places

Official statistics in Poland distinguish between small, medium-sized and big towns/cities. Population sizes of 20,000 and 100,000 mark the boundaries between small, medium-sized and big. However, in practice other dividing lines are often used to indicate differences in status and growth trajectory. The context is low birthrates in Poland and overall population decline, which enhances rivalry between cities and makes city size a particular emblem of success. The elite among Polish cities – those cities which are most clearly growing and prospering – are sometimes[3] labelled the 'Big Five': Warsaw, the Tri-City of Gdańsk-Sopot-Gdynia, Poznań, Wrocław and Kraków. These largest cities are referrred to as 'metropolises', and they are regarded as the beneficiaries of the 'metropolitanisation' which has accompanied globalisation and tended to concentrate resources in the biggest cities (Gwosdz et al 2019: 10). Wałachowski and Król (2019) titled their report on Polish cities *Runaway Metropolises: 100 Polish Cities Ranked (Uciekające metropolie: Ranking 100 polskich miast)*. In their introduction to Śleszyński's (2018) *Middling-City Poland: Principles and Conception of Deglomeration*, Kędzierski and Musiałek (2018: 10) write that 'Poland's development is concentrated … mostly in the big metropolises, where the standard of living is very like that in the metropolises of highly-developed countries. However, when it comes to development in the provinces, Poland is different'.

A minimum population of 500,000 is often used to mark the boundary between the biggest and the rest, although population size on its own is not quite sufficient. Poland's third city, Łódź, is not one of the Big Five. Half a million is also used as a dividing line by CBOS, Poland's main polling agency, whose research is widely reported in the national media. Their analyses of Polish society indicate that in many respects the 500,000+ cities are different: wealthier, younger and more highly educated, and, linked to this, more liberal, secular and cosmopolitan (White et al 2018: 14–15). Just below the 500,000 line there is a group of second-order cities which includes most other regional capitals, as well as cities in the Katowice conurbation. They have populations of between 250,000 and 500,000. Sometimes these smaller regional capitals are also regarded as metropolitan. Poland's 2011 official development strategy in fact takes 300,000 as the dividing line between metropolises and the rest. The Union of Polish Metropolises, the self-styled '12 main cities of Poland', includes three-quarters of the regional capitals, including Rzeszów, which has a population of just under 200,000.[4]

The antithesis of the runaway metropolis is the 'lesser' city/town. In journalism and *reportage*, the term *mniejsze* ('smaller' or 'lesser') *miasto* frequently implies a provincial backwater. Springer's (2016) *reportage* of his journeys to the 31 towns and cities which lost regional capital status in 1999 is titled *City/town Archipelago: Poland of smaller/lesser cities/towns* (*Miasto Archipelag: Polska mniejszych miast*).[5] These ex-capitals have populations varying from 43,000 to 230,000; 'lesser' therefore refers to status as much as size. Szymaniak's (2021) *Collapse: Reportage from lesser cities* presents an even bleaker portrait of social problems in technically medium-sized towns and cities of under 100,000 population. Before launching his book, Szymaniak toured 10 cities, ex-capitals including Kalisz and Płock, to discuss their problems. These cities of *circa* 100,000 were apparently conflated with the collapsing medium-sized towns. A film of the wide-ranging Kalisz discussion was uploaded onto YouTube.[6] The unequal relationship with nearby metropolises was a recurring theme. For example, a local activist complained, 'We are between Poznań, Wrocław and Łódź but we don't feel any benefits from those cities.' The chair reported that transport was the biggest topic in all 10 cities. Many local residents would like to live in their smaller city and work in a metropolis, but poor communications made this barely feasible. Poor bus services with the smaller city's own hinterlands were also said to be holding back Kalisz in particular.[7] Furthermore, Kalisz was said to suffer from an identity problem. According to local councillor Barbara Oliwiecka, 'We have never quite found a vision for the city since 1999.' On the other hand, participants also identified positive characteristics, for example: 'Everything is close by, the services aren't the worst, we have good schools and cultural opportunities' (Syska 2019).

City size is politicised in Poland, particularly by those who frame Poland as a country polarised between winners and losers. Although Poland was the first post-communist country to recover overall from the economic depression accompanying market reforms in 1990, this achievement was thanks to the dynamism of growth in the metropolises, especially Warsaw. The biggest cities are often still seen as having benefited disproportionately from the system transformation of the 1990s. Law and Justice, the ruling party 2005–7 and 2015–23, staked its legitimacy on the narrative that liberal elites, represented by the Civic Platform party, 'stole' the transformation, and that only they represented ordinary Poles – people who live in the provinces. The biggest cities are accused of having been privileged by Civic Platform's 2011 'Poland 2030' development policy, which assumed that growth would spread out from big cities to smaller locations. In fact, statistics point to the evidence of continuing regional inequalities. Hence, proponents of 'deglomeration' advocate an opposite approach, of special treatment for 'middling cities'.

The correlation between city size and wealth is borne out both by Śleszyński (2018), and by Wałachowski and Król (2019) in their volume *Runaway Metropolises: 100 Polish Cities Ranked*.[8] Wałachowski and Król found correlations between population size of functional economic areas and indicators such as wages, investments, and local authority budgets, as well as 'networks'/infrastructure. This included access to airports and major roads; tourist infrastructure; participation in cultural life; and sporting excellence. Gwosdz et al (2019: 12) argue on the basis of their literature review that the labour market is the main hindrance to development in smaller towns and cities, because it is so unattractive to people with 'high levels of human capital'.

Nonetheless, when it comes to non-economic factors, the advantage of the biggest cities is not so clear-cut. According to Gwosdz et al (2019: 12):

> Szmytkowska (2017: 76–81) concludes on the basis of a wide-ranging literature review that the possible advantages of middling towns over the metropolises are primarily 'soft', qualitative and non-material development factors. These include the lower cost of living, especially when it comes to the ratio between housing and wages, a slower pace of life, more closely located services (middling towns are more compact) and more green areas within the town boundaries, as well as a good balance between anonymity and inter-personal relations.

This list encapsulates the reasons my own interviewees gave for preferring to live in KPP. The three cities, but especially Kalisz and Płock, appear quite high up in various rankings. Most notably, Wałachowski and Król (2019) placed Płock top of their ranking for 'quality of life'. They measured availability of housing, house prices compared with local average wages, air pollution, green areas, hospital places, number of doctors, length of bike paths per head of population and number of road accidents. Wałachowski and Król show that population size and life quality do not always go hand in hand. Similarly, Hajduga and Rogowska (2020) compared the 16 regional capitals for 13 indicators of life quality and found they were not in order of size. According to 2018 statistics, Rzeszów came first, with Opole, another small capital, in fourth place (Hajduga and Rogowska 2020: 25). Łachowski and Łęczek (2020: 79) cite the European Commission (2018) to the effect that progressive urban planners aim for cities which are both 'compact' and 'liveable'. Their article is about cities of over 100,000. Among these cities, Kalisz is singled out for meeting the criterion of 'compactness' (Łachowski and Łęczek 2020: 87). Zaborowski (2019: 54) identifies Kalisz as one of the smaller cities where one could buy a square metre of housing for under 3,000 zloties, but also points out that prices in Piła were comparatively high, at 3,400.

In general, opinion polls[9] tend to come up with different indicators and priorities from the rankings based on official statistics (Denis et al 2021:3). Local-level studies show that that even towns and cities which do not seem to have many inherent assets can be appreciated for their good amenities. One example is Belchatów, best known in Poland for its gigantic coal-fired power station, which came out top in Wojnarowska's (2017) study of six medium-sized towns in Łódź region. Another advantage of polls is that they can indicate how different social groups have different attitudes towards their cities. This was noted for example by Bierwiaczonek (2016), contrasting the emotional attachments of middle-aged residents with the instrumentalism of younger people in Gdańsk, Gliwice and Wrocław. Unfortunately, these polls do not capture the views of local migrants.

Ex-capitals: second-class cities?

In 1975, the number of Polish regions (*województwa*) increased from 22 to 49. Lewis (1989) argues that the communist party leadership under Gierek made the change to dilute the power of regional party secretaries *vis-à-vis* Warsaw. Nonetheless, the reform had positive consequences for the smaller cities which acquired the status of regional capital, partly because communist party regional bosses were able to direct investment towards their capital cities (Kurniewicz et al 2023: 26–8).[10] This period, particularly the 1970s, is remembered by some as a golden age for cities like Piła, Kalisz and Płock, and helps explain nostalgia for the communist regime. The local economy was often centred on one large industrial plant (Runge 2012), as in the case of Płock's oil refinery. My interviewee Dagmara, who had grown up in another ex-capital, commented: 'Piła and Tarnobrzeg are very similar. Because they are both former regional cities.

Once upon a time. So they have similar labour markets. In Tarnobrzeg it was sulphur and here it's lightbulbs. Lightbulbs and the railway.' Once they were regional capitals the cities could diversify their labour markets by offering a range of administrative jobs, partly at the expense of the liquidated county administrations (Kisiała 2017). Their populations grew by tens of thousands over their 24 years of capital status (Springer 2016: 4).

However, in 1999 the number of regions was reduced to 16.[11] The 31 cities which lost their administrative functions also then became deprived of investment, which went primarily to the new regional capitals (Śleszyński 2018; Wałachowski and Król 2019: 8). Kwaśny (2020) adds that the regional capitals were better able to tap into EU funding. Kurniewicz et al (2023: 27) cite qualitative studies showing that local people and administrators believed the cities lost out in numerous respects, not just economic, but also political clout and status. In media accounts, the word 'former' in 'former regional capitals' (*byłe miasta wojewódzkie* or even *miasta postwojewódzkie*) sometimes has a sad ring, akin to Former Soviet Union or Former Yugoslavia – identifying a place by what it used to be. These are cities with status problems.

Nonetheless, Kurniewicz et al (2023: 23–4) suggest that, while the cities undoubtedly flourished during 1975–98 because they were regional capitals, their twenty-first century fates are not so clear-cut. Quantitative studies particularly illustrate the wide range of outcomes. These suggest that their fates were not determined primarily by their loss of status (Kurniewicz et al 2023: 27–8). Kisiała (2017: 24) compared all 49 cities across a range of indicators over the years 1999–2015 and – plotting their positions according to their absolute standing in 2015 and their progress since 1999 – found that most of the current regional capitals were in the top right-hand quadrant and most of the ex-capitals were in the opposite corner. The ex-capitals were neither doing well in absolute terms, nor making progress. However, there were several exceptions. Bielsko-Biała scored higher than half the current capitals and Płock, in absolute terms, was also better than several. Springer's 2016 book of *reportage* about the ex-capitals, mentioned above, is titled *Archipelago* to indicate the impossibility of gathering together and characterising the cities according to common criteria.

I was curious about whether residents today cared about the 1999 demotion. Early in my very first conversation in Płock – with some friends of a friend, who were trying to explain to me what the city was like – one of them mentioned the loss of status: indicating that it might be a prism through which my analysis could be conducted. However, this proved not to be the case. My interviewees provided plenty of examples of why current regional capitals were advantaged vis-à-vis KPP. However, apart from Dagmara, who had just completed an economics degree, the interviewees never brought up directly the topic of the 1999 reform. When Kalisz gained a *Gazeta Wyborcza* supplement in 2021 (see Chapter 2), one of the first articles reported on a local movement, established back in 2002, campaigning for Kalisz to become the capital of a new 'Central Poland' region. However, this article provoked only a few comments from readers, none of them supporting the idea. For example: 'With all due respect – it's one thousand years since Kalisz could be compared with Poznań or Wrocław' (Cylka 2021). In the 2019 public debate about Kalisz, referenced above, a local historian was asked whether people still felt disadvantaged by having lost the 'prestige' of being a regional capital. He said he did not know the answer to this. However, he thought people did have a sense that Kalisz ought to be a bigger city, given its historical significance, and not a poor relation, compared for example to Wrocław (Syska 2019).

One of my own interviewees, Jolanta, clearly had been disadvantaged by the 1999 change. Her story was probably typical of the experiences of many middle-aged women. She lost her administrative job when her office was abolished in 1998 and Płock became part of Mazowieckie region, run from Warsaw. Jolanta's office was absorbed into its Warsaw equivalent and she was offered a job in Warsaw but had to decline because of her caring responsibilities in Płock. She never found another satisfactory job in Płock, probably partly because white-collar jobs across Poland have become increasingly reserved for university graduates. When I met her, Jolanta was selling tickets, had recently done some manual work in the Netherlands, and was looking for more work abroad. However, she did not mention the reform as the cause of her woes. Kurniewicz et al (2023: 32–3) suggest that cities of over 300,000 were rewarded in 1999 by keeping regional capital status because they had already been developing fast in the 1990s, while the under 300,000 cities had hard times after 1998 because of the Poland-wide economic crisis in the years preceding EU accession. They show that cities of 100–300,000 performed similarly for GDP 1998–2013 irrespective of whether they had regional capital status. However, they do not dispute that the administrative reform might have had bigger impact on the smaller ex-capitals, contributing to their downward spiral (Kurniewicz et al 2023: 38).

Interviewees' comparisons between KPP and larger cities

> I never wanted to go to city even to study. I could have gone to Toruń and Gdańsk, my favourite cities, but I don't like chasing after money, fame, a career. I have more mundane wishes: my garden, a child. More ambitious people wll choose a big city with more opportunities. I'm more emotional. (Jagoda, Płock)

The interviewees frequently made comparisons between KPP and other cities in Poland. A handful of Ukrainians had been able to travel to various places before definitively deciding to live in KPP. Inna, for instance, who with her husband was hoping to set up a restaurant, reported that 'We went to Łódź, Warsaw, Poznań, Wrocław … We had a look, travelled around, and came to the conclusion that all the same we'd stay in Kalisz'. Others had travelled about visiting Ukrainian friends, and could therefore make comparisons and choices. Kvitka (aged 21) described how she had been visiting but also job prospecting:

> I've visited other cities in Poland, my husband and I have travelled around, looking for better work. We did want some better jobs. But I realised that I like it here. It's peaceful. I have lots of friends, lots of Polish friends who could help me out in any situation, that's a big plus. And it's not so noisy. It's good for living.

Among the labour migrants from different countries interviewed for this book, KPP was sometimes the second or third place they had worked in Poland. Brzozowska (2023: 2379) refers to 'frequent job changes among circulants arriving on a visa basis, even if it required moving to another city or region'. In her sample of 32 Ukrainians, these moves resulted from the desire to find a steady job. The migrants I interviewed more often mentioned poor living and/or working conditions in their previous work. For example, Raisa reported that when she first went to Poland from Ukraine, through an agency: 'I came to a different city and worked two months in a different city but I didn't like the work conditions, and I didn't like the accommodation, so I changed it. My friend worked here [in Piła] and suggested I could come.' Raisa's account incorporates both push and pull factors: she was pushed to change location by work and living conditions, but pulled to Piła by her friend.

Ukrainian networking is discussed separately in later chapters. This chapter focuses more on opinions about attributes of individual cities.

However, it is important to remember that these opinions are formed in the context of processes of checking out places with friends, and inviting or being invited to move to a new city. To quote Raisa again: 'We exchange information. Experience. Who's been where, seen what, knows something'. It seems that such advice from other migrants can include being warned off big city destinations. For example, Hlib told the story of some Ukrainians who had experimented with moving from Kalisz to Łódź, but then returned to Kalisz. 'Łódź was too big ... They went to Łódź because they thought it would be better. But it turned out not to be. It's a very dirty city.' Networks are also important for emotional comfort, and sometimes it seems that these trump all other considerations. Anita, a Polish return migrant, said for example, 'All my friends are in Kalisz, so that's why I'm here.'

The rest of this chapter considers some reasons why interviewees chose to live in KPP. It is important to point out that this did not always constitute a ringing endorsement of the cities. When migrants try to decide on their best livelihood strategy, they weigh up different factors. Smallness can be a problem, but it can be outweighed by other advantages. This is implied in Tamara's comment that 'There are Ukrainians here who have come to stay [in Poland] for ever. Some of them are still trying to decide, will it be Kalisz or not. It's true it's a small town. But most of my friends have decided on Kalisz.' Tomasz, a Pole, explained that 'I didn't plan to return to Kalisz, because I prefer big cities, but I got the chance of a flat here'. Similarly, distance from Ukraine is a factor which can be disregarded if necessary. Lizaveta, for instance, reported that 'everyone [in Mikolayiv] says, "Where on earth have you ended up?" When we go home it takes six to seven hours to the border and then 1000 km more to drive. And they say, "Everybody else is at the beginning of Poland, and you've landed at the very end." Well, we like it here ... It's a good, peaceful little city.'

The next section considers some of the ways the interviewees justified their choices by explaining their subjective assessments of the cities, but also magnifying features which made them feel at home and helped them bond with their new place of residence. This was a type of place attachment involving 'reconstruction of places (bringing elements of a place people love to their current location)' (Smith 2017: 6). The transnational dimension is significant here and illustrates the significance of this bifocal lens for some migrants' migrant identities. Migrants and former migrants are always making comparisons between places – they have points of comparison because they are migrants. However, it is also worth noting that the comparisons can just relate to the interview setting.

The interviewees were trying to help me understand what KPP were like by contrasting them with other places. I also had the sense that some were motivated by honesty. They felt they had to mention the downsides of KPP vis-à-vis other destinations in our conversation, for the sake of balance, but they usually then downplayed the importance of these negative factors.

Positivity: size and location 'just right', infrastructure improving

Lewicka (2011: 211) observes that individuals can be divided into urbanophiles and urbanophobes, city persons and country persons. However, the situation is more nuanced, since, in my experience, there are also people who prefer either big cities (like Tomasz, quoted above) or smaller ones. Individuals in the latter category apply the Goldilocks test: not too big, not too small, but just right. However, unlike geographers, interviewees did not use the term 'middling' to indicate something between a small town and a metropolis; just right was defined as 'smaller', vis-à-vis 'too big'. In his interviews with Swedes about place attachment in Spain, Gustafson (2001: 13) concluded that 'distinction is not only about establishing the uniqueness of the place, but also about categorization, about telling what kind of place it is'. Among KPP interviewees, the 'kind of place' is the 'not-too-big' city vis-à-vis the 'too big and bustling city'. They tended to define the places they liked by invoking comparisons between locations in the origin and destination country – a trait which highlights their often 'translocal' rather than 'transnational' way of looking at the world.

Considerations of size help shape choices of migration destination (White 2011). Nina, a Ukrainian, explained why she chose Kalisz over Gdańsk. 'I've already been offered work [in a beauty salon] in Gdańsk … But somehow I can't. I don't know, I like Kalisz. I don't like such big cities.' I asked a Polish interviewee, Anita, whether she would like to move from Kalisz to a bigger city and she replied, 'But that was why I left Manchester.' Generally, if interviewees justified their dislike, they complained about bustle and noise. For instance, Barbara, a Polish return migrant to Płock, said that she stayed in the city because 'I don't like Warsaw. Too many people. Too much bustle.' Similarly, Alla, a Ukrainian, asserted, 'It's my character, I don't like big noisy cities. They make me stressed and tired. So Kalisz suits me. I'm not considering moving somewhere else [in Poland].' Crime was mentioned in a few interviews. Belinda, from Montivideo, said that 'KPP is especially safe. It's not the capital like Warsaw'. Melaniya mentioned 'Piła is a small little city with a low crime level, because nothing much happens here ... By comparison with Kyiv'. More often, it was the compact and convenient quality of KPP which was prized by migrants: everything was nearby, on foot, by bike or bus. Anzhela, for instance, commented: 'There are practically never any traffic jams in Piła. The bus service is excellent. You can go almost everywhere by bus.' Both Poles and Ukrainians with experience of working in big Polish cities observed that if you lived in a big city you would probably waste a lot of time commuting to work and not have time to take advantage of the city centre's cultural opportunities. Polish interviewees had also, to some extent, taken size into account when they went abroad. For instance, Kinga explained that her dislike of big cities was a reason to prefer Yeovil, which is roughly the size of Piła, 'a town where you can easily get where you need to go and there are no traffic jams'.

However, sometimes interviewees' geography was more elastic, illustrating the phenomenon described by Smith (2017: 6) 'as bringing elements of a place people love to their current location'. They asserted that much bigger cities were the same size as KPP. Jagoda for instance claimed that 'I'm not a big city person [*wielkomiastowa*] ... That's why when we went to Wales we decided on a smaller city' (Swansea, pop. 300,000). Aneta said, 'I had been to London several times and liked it very much but I wouldn't like to live there. It's too big a city for my taste. I prefer a smaller little town [*mniejsze miasteczko*] where you can get where you want to go on foot.' In this instance she was rationalising her choice of Dublin, which has a population of over one million, by placing it in the same category as Płock. Some Ukrainians and Poles claimed explicitly that another city or town was the same size as KPP, when this was not the case. For instance, Solomiya asserted: 'We don't want to move to another city. We don't like such big cities. Because in Ukraine we live in a small town, just like Kalisz' (which is actually five times bigger).[12]

Identifying as a not big-city person has essentialist overtones. It often seems that the interviewees are claiming it as a core part of their identity, something which cannot change. Logically, therefore, some interviewees invoked small-town origins when explaining why they preferred not to live in bigger places. Hlib, for instance, stated, 'I don't like big cities. When I came to Kalisz that was already a big city by my standards. Because I grew up in a very small town.' Sergei claimed:

> If you lived in a big city in your country of origin you'll like living in a big city [in Poland], especially if you're young, what with discos and all that. When you lived in a small town or village, then you

feel comfortable in Piła. You feel at home (*v svoei tarelke*) ... I lived near Dnepropetrovsk [Dnipro] ... in a small little town (*malen'kii gorodok*). So, I lived in a small little town and Piła is also a small town (*malen'kii gorod*). Although it's a bit bigger.

Varvara, born in a city three times the size of Piła, similarly asserted:

> I like Piła because it's small. I don't like big cities. For example near Piła you have Poznań and Bydgoszcz. Poznań is a big city, a beautiful city. But I don't like it. There are too many people there. I prefer Bydgoszcz. Polish people say 'How can you like Bydgoszcz? Poznań is much better!' I say I don't like such big cities ... In Ukraine I lived in a small little town, I was born in a small town and moved to Kryvyi Rih. And now I've come to Piła it really reminds me of the little town where I was born. I feel normal here.

Ukrainian interviewees also drew architectural parallels, particularly between their home cities and Kalisz, which was taken at face value as an ancient city, despite the fact that the 'old' town was rebuilt in the 1920s, not as an exact copy of its pre-1914 self. Olesya explained why she was fond of Kalisz: '[From the start] I liked Kalisz. Do you know why? Because it's similar to Lviv. In the centre, yes? The town hall, I liked it at once.' Milena also stated: 'It's like Lviv, even that city centre, the town hall, so I have the feeling I'm at home.' Alla, who enjoyed living in a quiet part of Kalisz city centre by the park, said:

> I like Kalisz a lot because it so reminds me of my home city, Chernihiv. The only difference is that my city is slightly bigger, we have a population of about 300,000. And Kalisz has 100,000. But the atmosphere is the same. Kalisz is one of the oldest towns, not one, but the oldest city in Poland. Yes. And my city in Ukraine is one of the oldest. We have lots of ancient Christian churches, there is an 11th century church, and I live near the historic centre. I've got used to being in that atmosphere of antiquity. So Kalisz reminds me of it a lot ... Of course Kalisz still needs a bit of restoration. But all the same.

Melaniya Ukrainianised Communist-style Piła and presented it therefore as familiar:

> When I came to Piła I was struck by the old Soviet-style buildings. That Hotel Gromada is a totally Soviet design … That's how they build in Ukraine as well, and those Soviet-era cities are full of the same buildings. It's like there hasn't been any major change.

In previous research projects I had noticed that Polish interviewees also used the terms 'near' and 'far' elastically, so that places abroad could be classified as 'near', whereas big cities in one's country of origin were 'too far'.[13] Places are close because people close to you live there. This could be applied to KPP, even though they are not located close to the Ukrainian-Polish border. Zinaida said:

> Poland is considered not far from home [Mariupol] … While I'm in Płock, any time I want to see my parents or [adult] children I can ask them to come to Lviv, get on a bus. We meet up, I bring them some little presents, and then we say goodbye. It's considered next door (*ryadyshkom*). After all it's not really very far.

Similarly, even if some Polish residents of KPP complained about being too far away from the big cities which were their main reference points, migrants can construe them as 'close', especially by Ukrainian standards. This view was expressed exclusively by car owners. Tamara mentioned for example: 'Everything is close by. Wrocław is just an hour and a half by car; an hour and a half in the other direction and you're in Poznań. It's all close. Not like the distances in Ukraine, where you can drive for hours and hours.' Ruslana mentioned that she and her husband went on trips to Warsaw and Poznań, and had visited Kraków, but still preferred to live in Kalisz. 'If we want to visit a bigger city we can just get in the car.' Some Polish interviewees answered my question about why they did not move to the big city in similar terms. For example, Zenon said that Poznań was 'near enough for his purposes'. One Pole did however mention that the Covid-19 pandemic had decreased the frequency of their visits to Poznań for leisure activities.

Some interviewees referred to children to make judgements about the balance of advantage. The smaller city was a good place to grow up, and the parents were sacrificing their own interests for the children's benefit. This was particularly emphasised by parents of both nationalities in Piła. For example:

> It's peaceful. I like the fact that it's good for families. You can let your [teenage] child go out for the evening and you don't have to

> worry that something might happen to her. A big city has more opportunities for study, work, self-development. But on the other hand it's more dangerous and stressful … Sometimes you'd like more choice, like I said, more options for work. It is a bit, well, if you want to change your job there are hardly any options. But the quality of life is very good. (Anzhela, Ukrainian)

> Probably I wouldn't live here if I didn't have a child … There are lots of activities for children in Piła, they have everything. Perhaps not on the scale of a big city, but truly, I don't know, football, martial arts, English, and all those activities are really close. We live five minutes from school, ten minutes from other activities. So life is convenient. Perhaps we don't have so much money, but we have more time. (Karolina, Polish)

Some Ukrainian interviewees mentioned that their children had vetoed a move.

> I don't like the health service here … You have to go other cities … Bydgoszcz or Poznań … and there's no suitable work for me [in finance]. I looked for work and couldn't find it. Piła is a bit too small for me. The children like it, they've got used to it … I was thinking about moving three years ago but the children said 'No, we have friends here and we love school.' It would be too stressful for them to move. (Irina)

Last, but definitely not least: some interviewees were convinced that people were friendlier in the smaller city. Sue, for example, remarked that 'My impression of Warsaw people, after I've been living in Płock, I like the quietness and the slow pace of life. And Warsaw people have a sense of superiority. And they are not so patient. They think that they are more superior than other people in Poland. It felt like in Taipei.'

For Poles, the reference point was often the past. The question I asked was usually 'How is KPP changing?' or 'Is it changing?'. Not surprisingly, considering changes in Poland overall, many interviewees could see a positive trajectory of improving infrastructure. Jerzy, for example, said, 'Plock always had bad luck with its authorities. But the mayor now is very good. He does a lot for the city. It's much prettier. It used to be a hole. Things are repaired, there are lots of roads.' Wojciech made the same point: 'Płock used to be a hole. But now you can see everything has been regenerated, with new lighting, repairs, roads, bypass ... although there is only one street with bars.' Poles also noted recent infrastructural improvements in Kalisz and Piła. For instance, Edyta said: 'Piła is actually aspiring to look like a city, to look more beautiful ... We have a lovely new children's playground in the Park on the Island, children can play in the fountain, it's super.' Dagmara commented that under new leadership 'they've repaired the streets, got rid of potholes, begun to renovate the blocks of flats ... made little green parks between the houses'.

Negative assessments: depopulated, small and remote

On the other hand, it was also common for Polish interviewees to lament that, overall, the cities had been better in the past. Feliks, whose sentiments were echoed almost exactly by two other middle-aged Kalisz interviewees, complained:

> Definitely it has got a bit prettier since Poland joined the EU, there's less unemployment, so you can somehow survive. But on the other hand it has emptied of people, lots of people have left. There are no clubs for young people, no student club. We have the University, we have the Kalisz Academy, but there's no student club. Perhaps things are just beginning to revive slowly. At one time, when I was a teenager, there were several clubs, concerts, things like that. And then it simply ended. Everything shut down and that was the end. Mostly because so many people had left. But I don't know. I suppose that's the main reason. Kalisz used to have 100,000 inhabitants and now it has 98,000.

Similarly, Karolina commented on Piła:

> It could be better culturally ... Somehow we lack events, concerts, that's a bit missing. Good films. They don't come often. It used to be better here. There were more of things like that, I used to go to them. Some places have shut down. I don't know why. That was before many people I knew had left, then some went abroad, some to bigger cities. Lots to Poznań and Wrocław. When I was still at school, before EU accession, Piła buzzed with life. There was lots happening. I had heaps of friends and there were constant concerts and things going on.

Feliks and Karolina were nostalgic for their youth, but also making objective observations on a vicious circle of out-migration and urban decline. It was unsurprising if Poles were often more negative than migrants to KPP. Unlike the newcomers, they did not need to domesticate their surroundings and make them their own.

Leo, married to a Pole, gave his outsider's perspective on Kalisz (in English):

> For someone who has travelled around the world, I'd expect there to be more support, something to show why this city is the oldest. You know, even the road network systems, there is nothing here. If you want to go for example to the autobahn you have to drive at least 50 minutes before you can get there ... Everywhere you go it's a minimum of two hours. So it's frustrating when you think about it, like, if it is one of the oldest cities, if you want to promote it's one of the oldest cities. You should do something about it ... A friend of mine ... asked me, 'What attractions do you have in Kalisz to show me?' I go, 'Nothing, really.'

As in many other smaller towns and cities, the world of KPP is perceived by some non-Ukrainian residents in terms of lack of anonymity, nepotism and an inward-looking approach. These interviewees referred to KPP as 'small towns', deliberately shrinking the population. Most of these comments concerned Płock. For instance, Jagoda, who worked in a shop, complained that although Płock's infrastructure was improving, the labour market seemed to be worse. 'As it's a small town it hangs together by networks and it's hard for the average person [without contacts] to make a career.' Barbara (also Polish) described Orlen as an 'enclave' and thought you would need to have connections or pay a bribe to secure a job. A long-term Russian migrant married to a Pole similarly complained: 'Płock is a little town (*malen'kii gorod*). Mostly you can only find a job through contacts.' Another foreigner, whose husband was a return migrant, said that 'he always advises me: "It's a very small town, whatever you say, you never know who is behind the wall"'. Two Polish interviewees, in Płock and Piła, asserted that local employers conspired among themselves to keep down wages. Some of the more negative interviewees were Poles from other cities who had moved to KPP for family reasons. Dagmara complained: 'Wielkopolska is supposed to be a rich region, but Piła is such a backwater, such a hole, it's hard to find well-paid work.'

Pollution: mixed impressions

Smaller cities are sometimes assumed to be cleaner and greener. Piła, which is the greenest and has the cleanest air by objective markers, was often mentioned as being attractive for these reasons. In fact, together with being compact and having a slow pace of life, this was often presented as its chief advantage. Among the Poles, Karolina, quoted above on why the city was good for bringing up a child, added, 'And it's green. We live near the river. We can be by the river in three minutes, and by the forest in ten. That's why I live here. You can't measure everything in money.' Similarly, Ewa said, 'Perhaps Piła is not a beautiful city [architecturally], but there's lots of greenery. Outside Piła it's really lovely, lots of forests and lakes'. Lech contrasted the Netherlands, where he had worked for many years, with Piła. 'I don't care how much money I have in my pocket. I can go fishing and mushrooming. I phone my son and say "let's go for a bike ride."' Ukrainians made similar observations. Sergei was quoted at the start of Chapter 1 on how he had bought a house outside Piła near a lake and dreamed of going fishing with his future grandsons. Raisa said, 'It's a green city. There's a nice park in the centre, and there's forest around the city, you can go for walks in the forest, in the fresh air, there are places to go and relax.' Ostap, definitely planning to settle, mentioned, 'The forests and lakes ... I like to go for walks in the forest. We go fishing.' Comparisons were also made with polluted cities in Ukraine, discussed in more detail in Chapter 7. Veronika, for instance, enthused: 'The air, in comparison with Kryvyi Rih ... That's very polluted. And when we came here, well, it was wonderful. So green and nice.'

Kalisz and Płock, despite their worse air quality indicators, were also construed by some migrants as 'green and nice'. For instance, Solomiya saw Kalisz, apart from parts of the city centre, as 'all beautiful and neat. Well, there are some messy bits, but basically, if you take the overall picture, it's clean here'. However, opinions in Płock were sharply divided. On the one hand, Ukrainians without many Polish friends mostly seemed to accept that the city was clean. On the other hand, Poles were suspicious about the Orlen oil refinery. For example, Jagoda said:

> No doubt half the population considers it does a lot for Płock, and that thanks to Orlen Płock is developing. But that doesn't mean much to me. It's true it provides lots of jobs. Many people's livelihoods depend on it. But in recent times I think everyone who wants a healthy life and cares for nature thinks it's dangerous. They try to convince us that nothing is happening, that only steam is coming from the chimney.

'Like so many people' Beata's father had worked at Orlen and died of cancer, so that their family – despite liking the city in other respects – sometimes considered moving to 'the opposite part of Poland where the air would be fresh'. Barbara said, 'All Orlen does is poison us … Płock is my hometown and I love Płock, but lots of people in Płock have cancer, asthma, thyroid problems. I have thyroid problems myself.' As a result, she and her family were considering moving to a seaside town in Poland. Mateusz described Orlen as a mixed blessing. On the one hand, he read in the media that it invested a lot of money in Płock. On the other, they might be poisoning the inhabitants. It was not as bad as in the 1970s and 1980s when people had been sick on the street. However, there were still days when there was a strange smell. Migrants who had close contacts with Poles were also wary about Orlen. One non-Ukrainian married to a Pole invited me to sniff the air outside her flat so I could recognise the typical Orlen smell, while another blamed the refinery for her small son's frequent illnesses.

Conclusions

The chapter addressed the book's second research question, about why migrants spread geographically beyond the largest cities during the second stage of migration transition. It discussed the 'former regional capitals' such as KPP, as well as other smaller cities declining in population and often characterised as 'lagging behind' or even 'collapsing', compared with the 500,000+ 'runaway metropolises'. It considered the question of whether 'bigger is better' by examining Polish city rankings. These suggest that, while bigger cities score best on economic indicators, smaller cities, even former regional capitals, sometimes have the edge when it comes to quality of life. According to one report, Płock tops the Polish city rankings. If migrants were bent on economic objectives, it would make sense for them to go to larger cities. However, lifestyle factors and networks often seem to trump economic motives. This can be particularly true for families with children, indicating the significance of life stage in migration decision-making.

My interviewees rarely chose KPP: the Poles had mostly been born and brought up in the cities, while the non-Poles had come to a particular workplace, or via networks. The important point is that interviewees had chosen to remain in or return for a second time to these particular cities, in preference to big-city destinations. Some interviewees invoked identity factors: self-identification as 'not big-city people'. Many others simply expressed their preference for smaller cities as places to live. In keeping with Bierwiaczonek's (2016) observation that residents choose certain aspects of their cities to be particularly relevant to them, the Ukrainian interviewees singled out friendly locals; safety and peace and quiet; green spaces; compactness; clean air (especially in Piła); and affordable rents (in Kalisz). These compensated for restricted job opportunities, particularly in the eyes of parents, who saw the cities as appropriate places to bring up children. The second stage of migration transition, as already observed, is characterised both by migration to smaller cities and family settlement; in these parents' choices one can see how the two processes intertwined. The migration transition is also, to a more limited extent, the story of returning Polish migrants. I interviewed both Polish returnees and foreigners married to Polish return migrants. They had made the same compromise between jobs and quality of life, although they were typically more critical of aspects of small-city life such as nepotism or pollution which were perhaps not so noticeable to the Ukrainian economic migrants.

Chapter 3, together with 10–12, illustrate that place attachment does much to explain migration transition from below. Migrants go through a process of familiarising themselves with a new place, finding out the attributes which become meaningful to them. The objective qualities of cities like KPP are important here, but subjective assessments are also relevant. One intriguing aspect of place attachment involves 'bringing elements of a place people love to their current location' (Smith 2017: 6). Among my research participants, this resulted in some creative comparisons and elastic geography. Interviewees asserted that KPP was 'the same size' as their home city, even if it was not, or was 'near' Mariupol, or that 'Kalisz looked like Lviv'. The chapter therefore illustrates that migrants, including Polish returnees, think transnationally in their mental city rankings. This chapter began by comparing Polish smaller cities and metropolises, but migrants do not necessarily make exactly those comparisons. Although they would answer my questions such as why they did not move to Warsaw or Poznań, their narratives spontaneously compared KPP not with these cities but with Skegness, Adelaide or Kryvyi Rih.

Notes

1. As psychologists, they use the term 'process' to refer to psychological processes, whereas I am using it more broadly.
2. It was the most popular answer not only among people living in locations of 20,000–99,999 but also among residents of cities sized 100,000–499,999 which are officially 'big' rather than 'medium'.
3. For example, by Śleszyński (2018), but also by journalists.
4. https://metropolie.pl/o-nas/miasta
5. Springer's website translates the main title into English as *Archipelag City*, but does not attempt to translate the subtitle. See http://filipspringer.com/?page_id=668&lang=en (accessed 7 July 2023).
6. 'Polska średnich miast' (Kalisz, 26.06.2019) https://www.youtube.com/watch?v=WYkJ016htqI [video no longer available].
7. Members of the audience claimed that the problem was particularly acute for students who need to travel in to Kalisz to study and one remarked that she could see Kalisz from her windows but without a car had no way of getting there.
8. Both books were published by the Jagiellonian Club, a right-of-centre think tank.
9. An early example of a published league table is Wallis's 'Hierarchia miast', published in *Studia Socjologiczne* in 1965.
10. They also state (2023: 27) that according to some authors these advantages persisted to some extent into the post-1989 period. Government in the 1990s remained quite centralised.
11. Including two paired capitals, Toruń-Bydgoszcz and Zielona Góra-Gorzów Wielkopolski. Hence 18 cities overall kept regional capital status.
12. Additionally, sometimes interviewees asserted similarities in size without expressing any preference one way or the other. For instance, Andrei said of Mykolayiv (470,000) that 'I don't know the size. It's like Kalisz. A medium-sized city. It's not Warsaw'. Yevhen commented that 'Płock is small, pretty much like Kherson [twice the size]. They have the same population'.
13. On similar ways of thinking in Bulgaria and Romania, see Koleva (2013) and Kulcsár and Brădăţan (2014).

4
Polish migration patterns, motivations and experiences

Introduction

Chapter 4 analyses KPP's evolving identities as cities of out-migration, by looking at the stories and opinions of some of their Polish residents. It considers both the motivations of Polish migrants, and their experiences abroad. By 2019–22, smaller cities shared one feature of big cities – diminished international out-migration by university graduates – but another feature of smaller towns and villages – continuing international migration by non-graduates. Most Polish migration literature refers to so-called 'post-accession' migration. The term is sometimes applied to all migration occurring since Poland joined the EU, implying it possesses common characteristics. However, it is analytically helpful to distinguish between two phenomena. Around 2004, many young people left Poland, including those who could be labelled 'middle-class'. They often came from the biggest cities and their lifestyle motives are highlighted by scholars. Nonetheless, interest in this group should not overshadow the existence of an ongoing stream of often temporary labour migrants, typically not university graduates, migrating away from Poland from the 1990s until today. For them, livelihoods are clearly more important migration motivations than lifestyles. EU accession was a significant moment for this type of labour migration, since it encouraged a greater range of people to migrate, from every corner of Poland, to a wide range of destination countries, and also facilitated family reunification and settlement. However, the sources of this post-2004 long-term outflow pre-dated EU accession. Hence these twenty-first century labour migrants, mostly originating from smaller locations, share similarities with economic migrants of the 1990s. The persistence of geographical labour-market inequalities in Poland underpins continuing mobility.

In KPP, as in big cities where I previously conducted research, the post-accession wave was remembered by many as a historical event. The common opinion was that most people who left Poland around 2004–7 stayed abroad and were well-settled. In Piła, Sylwia even labelled her nephew and his family 'English people' to indicate the extent of their 'embedding' (to use Mulholland and Ryan's (2022) terminology). In cities like Wrocław and Warsaw one sometimes encounters proud denials that anyone would want to migrate from those cities. This was almost never the case in KPP.[1] Nonetheless, a handful of interviewees and key informants, typically teachers and administrators, struggled to think of anyone they knew who had migrated abroad recently. 'Emigration' for them was associated with the 2004 wave. It often seemed that, by 2021–2, the 500,000+ Polish metropolises were considered to possess all the attractions formerly offered only by western countries. Justyna for example asserted that 'I don't think they migrate abroad any more – they go to big cities'. Janusz said, 'I don't have any close friends who would go abroad nowadays.' I asked, 'How about poorer people? Do they migrate?' and he replied, 'Some people go as carers to Germany. You hear that they go. But I don't actually know any of those poorer people.'

By contrast, many of my interviewees, especially non-graduates and poorer and/or younger informants, moved in circles where international labour migration was still a commonplace livelihood strategy in 2019–22. For instance, Tomasz, not a graduate, from a working-class background, suggested, 'There's less and less now … But an old friend who lives with his parents and doesn't have a car or anything, I found out that he's gone off to Germany, he's saving for a mortgage. And it's a well-known fact that even today it does give you a great headstart.' Jolanta, a temporary ticket-seller and would-be circular migrant, asserted that 'In Płock, to be honest, in every third or fourth family someone is working abroad'. She voiced the opinions of other interviewees from this part of the local population. 'I don't have anything against people here coming [to Poland] to earn money, but I'd also like to go somewhere myself!' Hence, it seems that insofar as there exists a local 'culture of migration' in the sense of a tradition of out-migration (Kandel and Massey 2002) this is socially located within poorer and less well-educated sections of society.

Nevertheless, as Chapter 4 illustrates, there is no sharp divide between adventure-seeking youth of 2004 and the rest. Migration networks were important to almost everyone: they went to certain destinations because they knew other Polish people who were already there.[2] Often they had been invited by those people to join them abroad, a common practice among Polish migrants (White 2024a). As mentioned in Chapter 1, migration has its own internal dynamics. The more migration, the stronger the 'culture of migration'. Moreover, all interviewees shared the same motivations: they went to earn money, and they had been curious about the places they lived abroad. Economic and lifestyle motives simply mixed in different proportions for different individuals. Linked to this, the balance varied between a sense of agency and choice, on the one hand, and of being economically 'forced' to migrate, on the other. Unemployment was also a phenomenon which touched people of different social backgrounds. The Polish economic crisis at the start of the twenty-first century, with high levels of graduate unemployment, had helped create the 'perfect migration storm' (Okólski and Salt 2014: 33). Subsequently, the Polish economy grew dynamically, and on a national level unemployment fell. However, as discussed in Chapter 2 and illustrated in Table 4.1, labour markets in KPP, particularly Płock, remained unsatisfactory for many years after 2004. Moreover, as has also been mentioned, overall employment figures can conceal a shortage of graduate-entry and conventionally 'women's' jobs.

A common feature of all migration from KPP was the historical context of the mobility turn – a wider phenomenon than EU freedom of movement. 'Easy' is a word often mentioned in my interviews with Polish migrants over the years. Easy transport and communication shaped their actions and experiences, promoting intensely transnational lifestyles, with constant contact between Poles in Poland and their close friends and family who had recently moved to countries such as the UK. This helps explain why the 2004–7 EU wave was succeeded in following years

Table 4.1 Registered unemployment[1] (percentages)

	April 2004	April 2009	April 2014
Poland	19.9	10.9	13
Warsaw	6.6	2.3	4.7
Poznań	7.4	2.5	4
Kalisz city	16.7	7.6	7.7
Piła county	19.9	9.8	12.4
Płock city	21	11.1	13

---

1 Data taken from https://stat.gov.pl/. Access to 2014 data: https://stat.gov.pl/obszary-tematyczne/rynek-pracy/bezrobocie-rejestrowane/bezrobotni-oraz-stopa-bezrobocia-wg-wojewodztw-podregionow-i-powiatow-stan-na-koniec-kwietnia-2014-r-,2,20.html.

by a kind of swell, as siblings, cousins and friends came to join people already living abroad. This group does not seem to have been analysed by previous researchers, but there were six or seven examples among my informants and the chapter considers how their experiences compared with those of the EU wave.

Chapter 4 presents Poles' accounts of their personal migration stories. Since one premise of the book is that Polish migrants might be able to see similarities between themselves and others, it collects their views on their own strategies and experiences. I look first at the motives of the 'middle-class' EU generation, not to privilege their case above other migrants, but because they can serve as a reference point against which to compare other types of migration. Despite being intensively researched, they are still not fully understood, partly because the fuzzy demarcation line between them and other, more economically-driven migrants still needs more exploration. The chapter continues by considering the special features of the EU swell. It then turns to the diverse population of migrants who focus predominantly on particular earning goals, whom I have labelled 'target earners'. This first part of the chapter also incorporates the interviewees' own impressions about the different migration patterns from KPP, a theme to which I return in Chapter 6, about migration by foreigners to KPP. The main argument is that, among my interviewees, migration was regarded as a normal and understandable phenomenon. Moreover, even those who might be considered to regard migration as an episode of their youth, around 2004, were now recommending migration to their own children.

The second part of the chapter considers the interviewees' comments on their lives abroad. Given the copious existing literature on Polish migrants, this might seem unnecessary, and the section is comparatively short. Nonetheless, as a minimum it seemed important in Chapter 4 to consider their attachment to the places they lived abroad; experiences of friendliness or hostility on the part of the receiving society; communication and language barriers; rewarding work *vis-à-vis* deskilling and exploitation; and relations with co-nationals. As detailed in Chapter 2, Ager and Strang's (2008) model of 10 domains of integration, widely adopted by researchers, was useful for analysing the interview material. Ager and Strang (2008) and Grzymała-Kazłowska and Ryan (2022) point out that migrants are often differently integrated or embedded in different spheres. They are also differently mobile and transnational (White 2022a). The chapter highlights these differences and shows how they linked to the interviewees' various identities, not just their wave, swell or target earner identity, but also particularly their life stage, educational background and linguistic competence. This second part of the chapter also reveals the commonalities between different types of migrant from KPP, and where possible pinpoints features which can be ascribed to their shared smaller-city origins, particularly their self-identities as part of a wave of migrants.

Motivations to migrate from KPP

To aid analysis, I have taken into account the different streams of migration outlined above, and used these to categorise the 35 migrant interviewees and two interviewees' migrant daughters.[3] Several disclaimers are in order. As with many typologies, there is overlap and movement between types. For example, Jolanta, who, as already mentioned, was scraping together an income from temporary jobs in KPP and might be considered a 'typical' potential economic migrant, stated, 'I'm the sort of person who likes to travel, not just stay in one spot, sit here with my blinkers on.' Furthermore, I am not claiming that the share of migrants of each type in Table 4.2 is representative of return migrants to the cities or to Poland as a whole. It was not my purpose to create a representative sample, even had that been possible.

The EU wave

Research on Polish migrants to the UK and Ireland around the time of EU accession highlights their youth and the high share of students and university graduates (Fihel and Kaczmarczyk 2009; Grabowska-Lusińska and Okólski 2009; Krings et al 2013; Okólski and Salt 2014). Unsurprisingly, in view of their life stage, they often did not know how long they would stay abroad, and waited to see what opportunities came their way. To use Garapich's memorable phrase, many seemed to pursue a strategy of 'intentional unpredictability' (Eade et al 2007). My own previous interviews with return migrants from Polish big cities (White et al 2018: 18–9) and small towns (White 2017) suggested that whatever their locations of origin, and to some extent irrespective of age, participants in this wave shared the same migration culture: a culture of experimentation. They often voiced a conviction that it was 'worth giving it a go' (*warto spróbować*). This sense of agency was founded partly on structural factors: their possession of EU citizenship and free movement rights, as well as the booming UK and Irish economies, offering a wide choice of employment. Also important was consciousness of their own cultural capital, notably English-language knowledge, and social capital

Table 4.2 Polish interviewees by date and type of migration

	Approximate age at first migration	Higher education (including incomplete)	female/male	Destinations
PRL, professional: 1	32	yes	f	GDR
Pre-EU, educational: 3	3x19	-	2f, 1m	Germany, UK (London)
EU wave (2001–8): 10	all in 20s	all	5f, 5m	Ireland and UK
EU swell (2009–14): 6	2 x 19 3 x 20s 1 x 30s	all	4f, 2m	UK
Target earners: 20 (including 3 who originally belonged to other types)	5 x 19-20 5 x mid-20s 2 x 30s 7 x 40s 1x 60s	4	11f, 9m	Austria, Belgium, Finland, France, Germany, Ireland, Netherlands, Portugal, Sweden, Switzerland, UK

founded on the mass nature of the migration wave. Networks of friends, siblings and cousins played a large role in determining migration destinations, including for almost all the interviewees in KPP. Konrad, a big-city return migrant whom I had interviewed in Poznań (in English) in 2011, presented an extreme example of this type of young migrant with copious agency.

> [In 2005] I was finishing my studies, and lots of people were going to Ireland, to Great Britain, and I thought I could try as well. Specially that quite a lot of my friends were in Dublin. That's why Dublin was the place to go … They were like, 'Yeah, it's quite fun, it's nice, you will see and learn lots of new things, so why not?' I wasn't pushed by anything or anybody in my life, to change everything, so it was like, OK, let's go, we'll see what happens.

As Konrad's example illustrates, not all migration is part of a livelihood strategy.

The KPP sample seemed to have shared the same migration culture to varying extents. Janusz went to Ireland in the vacation just for a working holiday. He did not save money on his first trip and did not need funds, because he was a day student in KPP living with his parents. The other interviewees were somewhat more 'pushed' than Janusz to earn money abroad, but they shared the sense that going to the UK or Ireland would be fun and was worth the experiment. Mateusz, for example, mentioned that though he had an internship at Orlen when he was a student, he could not find a job there when he graduated, so he went to England. 'I didn't have any precise time period in mind. I wanted to see what it was like.' The word 'easy' came up in numerous interviews. Justyna, for example, mentioned that 'When Poland joined the EU it was easier to migrate, that was when I went to London.' Easy transport offered by new budget airlines made even distant places seem near. Daniel commented that Cork, on the west coast of Ireland, 'was superconnected to Poznań. It was really close. It was cheaper to visit my mother then than it is to travel 30 km to see her today.'

Members of this group often had fond memories of their youthful time abroad, which in retrospect could seem like an extended holiday. Karol, for example, said that 'I have nice memories. It was a carefree time. My first time away from home'. Ewa reminisced, 'It was a great time, because there were lots of young [Polish] people and we had a wonderful social and cultural life … When I'm asked whether I didn't regret working abroad in my youth I say "I worked, but I lived as well."'

Several mentioned passing on their enthusiasm to the next generation: Irena's daughter had already worked in Germany, Aneta had taken her daughter to see her friends and favourite places in Ireland and Mateusz said he would recommend to his sons to go and work abroad for a while. Hence, despite the claims I heard in 2019–22 that the post-2004 wave had come to an end, it was not quite true that this phase was a closed episode, even if the former migrants themselves are now well-settled back in Poland.

Many participants in the EU wave displayed a sense of belonging to an exodus. Szewczyk (2015) refers to a 'European generation of migration'; Burrell (2011) discusses how this cohort underwent a 'double transition', since their transition to adulthood was shaped by their experiences as the first post-communist generation; and Krzaklewska (2019) refers to the 'boom/Martial Law' generation. The term refers to the baby boom of the early 1980s, a demographic feature which was partly responsible for the shortage of graduate-entry jobs around 2004. Interviewees were conscious of the existence of a wave from Poland overall, and they could estimate the scale from their experiences abroad. However, some also made comments about a wave from KPP. For instance, Feliks remembered: 'There were a great many. Everyone [in Kalisz] knew at least a few people who had gone abroad. To the UK, or the Netherlands, or Norway.'

Karolina reminisced:

> It was that time in Poland when it was hard to find work, particularly because I trained as a teacher ... I kept hearing 'So-and-so have gone' and 'These other people have gone' and I thought 'If they can go and find work, why don't I try too?' ... [If it didn't work out], I could always come back ... There were Poles everywhere, everywhere I worked there were Poles. In the cafes, on the building sites ... It was great that I made friends with other Poles in the UK, there were lots and lots of Poles. That was when lots of people went abroad. It happened several times I met people by chance, in huge London, or in Ireland. I was living in Cork and I met a girl from Piła in a shop. And in London, I was at a big party, and someone tapped my arm and said 'Hi! You're from Piła?' It's a small world.

The sense of community and common destiny was enhanced by the fact that this generation rapidly began to bring over their families and/or bear children in the destination countries. This enhanced their tendency to settle, returning to Poland only for short visits, or experimentally, before deciding definitively to live abroad – a phenomenon I have termed 'double return' (White 2014a and 2014b). To quote Karolina again: 'When we joined the EU there was an exodus of people who never came back. Well, fewer returned than stayed abroad … Some people did come back to live in Poland just for a short time, I have friends like that, but then they returned abroad.' As discussed in Chapter 5, having children abroad could serve as a reality check, forcing the end of 'intentional unpredictability' and imposing the need to choose between settling either abroad or back in Poland.

One feature of this migration wave was the number of young couples who went to the UK and Ireland together. Several interviewees were influenced by their partners. For instance, Aneta had a good job in logistics in KPP, but her engineer boyfriend could not find a suitable engineering job after graduation, and persuaded her to go with him to Ireland. However, in most cases, the economic stimulus to migrate was not unemployment, but earning money, to support themselves at university, buy a car or save up for a flat. They were to some extent target earners, so it would be wrong to draw a sharp line between them and the target-earner group among my interviewees. Moreover, some changed their strategies over time: their stay abroad began as a light-hearted working holiday, but changed into serious hard work and saving money.

The EU swell

This group of six or seven interviewees – all university graduates and students – had gone to the UK after the peak year for Polish migration of 2007, but before the 2016 Brexit referendum. For instance, Jagoda, who accompanied her boyfriend after his father invited them to join him in the UK, claimed late membership of the EU wave. She pointed out that the post-2004 exodus had been her own cohort at university: 'most people' had gone abroad, but she had stayed, found a teaching job, then become unemployed – a further example of unemployment in Płock. She said, 'Because I was part of that cohort where lots of people sought their fortune abroad, I wanted to try it out. So as not to be regretful in later life.' Her plans were characterised by intentional unpredictability, said to be a hallmark of the EU wave (Eade et al 2007). 'We had no concrete plans about how long to stay. We just decided that we would go and see what it would be like and how it would turn out. We thought perhaps we might stay for ever, or perhaps in three months we'd return. We had no responsibilities.' Feliks similarly waited to go to the UK until after he graduated, unlike his friends who interrupted their university studies. His plans were equally open-ended: 'I didn't really see any prospects here.

So I decided to try my luck in Scotland.' His main motive was to play music with members of his band who had migrated with the wave and were already living in Scotland. This was a period when it still seemed easy for groups of friends and extended families to join together in the UK.

However, despite links to their predecessors in the wave group, the EU swell's experiences were sometimes different, and to some extent less carefree. The job market was less buoyant and it was harder to find work one liked. Another change was in the UK's ethnic composition. Iwona's first job in London was working in a Romanian shop, an experience she enjoyed; Kinga, Beata and Anita had more mixed feelings about the Romanian influx. For instance, Anita complained about Romanians and Bulgarians 'taking jobs' in Manchester. Poland had changed as well. As indicated in Table 4.1, unemployment had fallen considerably in KPP. Hence, for example, Kinga and her husband did not leave Poland because they could not find the jobs they wanted. They had both been employed in professional, albeit not well-paid jobs. Their 2014 decision to spend time working in the rural area of the UK where her sister-in-law was already living was sparked by the recognition that they would never earn enough in Piła to save for the house they dreamed of buying. Since, by 2014, mortgages in Poland were more available than they had been 10 years before, this was also a personal decision based on their fear of taking on debt. Kinga explained, 'I couldn't sleep if I had any debts – who knows what could happen.'

Target earners

In the 1990s, 'incomplete migration' (Okólski 2001) had constituted a common livelihood. This was predominantly working-class circular migration from small towns and villages in peripheral regions such as Podkarpacie and Podlasie. When these migrants were parents, they migrated alone, leaving their spouses and children in Poland, hence the label 'incomplete'. Typical destinations included Germany, Belgium and (for women) Italy. Dagmara, an interviewee from Podkarpacie who subsequently moved to Piła, was a typical example: a live-in domestic worker in Rome. Since KPP are located in the central regions of Mazowieckie and Wielkopolska, they were less touched by such migration, and there were only two pre-2004 migrants born in KPP among the 20 'target earners'. They had worked in destinations already popular before 2004: Belgium and Berlin. Piła's proximity to the border seems to have been a factor here. As mentioned in Chapter 2, Sylwia claimed that in 2002 'everyone in Berlin was from Piła'.

This type of migration persisted after 2004. As I found in Polish small towns in eastern Poland (White 2017) a sense of being 'forced' was often acute, because local livelihoods were perceived to be inadequate. Small-town migrants used the phrase 'forced by the situation', referring to debts, or their inability to find any job to support a family in a Polish location where they could afford to rent accommodation, thus ruling out the biggest cities. A steady stream of economic international migration continued after 2004 (Garapich et al 2023), although the range of destination countries increased as EU member-states opened up their labour markets to Poles. There was also more settlement, including family reunification, since this was now more feasible, and culturally acceptable (White 2017). However, temporary migration persisted and took various forms: regular circularity; irregular, but repeated trips; and one-off stays abroad.

As indicated in Table 4.2, the EU wave and swell shared certain features, chiefly their youth and university education, but the 20 target earners were more diverse. They included people who were middle-aged at the time they first migrated, indicating that some shock to their established livelihoods had made them seek a living abroad. Sylwia, aged 67, referred to the threatening 'situation which forced one to migrate', both in relation to a friend and about herself. In 2002, aged about 47, she was divorced, with only a secondary education, an expensive medical condition and a daughter at school. 'Unfortunately, the situation simply forced me … I was on disability benefit, and then they took it away, and I had no income. That's why I started migrating … I worked part-time in a shop belonging to friends of my parents but it wasn't enough.' Jerzy was an IT specialist and his wife was a teacher, but their combined wages did not seem enough to match their expenses, hence he felt compelled to work abroad.

> It was a year after Poland joined the EU and my son was starting university. And suddenly it was necessary to find money to support him. But Poland at that time, well, it wasn't in a good place. So I thought to myself, I know English, because I did it at school, I can drive, so I could be a driver. I don't want to go to do heavy manual work in a factory. So it was England for me.

Jerzy's livelihood strategy was typical in a society where it was often accepted that parents should migrate to subsidise their children's higher education (White 2022b). Zenon, who migrated to the UK in 2013, was similarly motivated by the need to support his daughter through university, although she also came to England to work with him in the vacations. By contrast, Edyta's parents did not offer to migrate on her behalf, and since they could not afford to support her on their Polish wages she herself felt forced to migrate, going to the Netherlands and then Germany in 2012, originally to finance the university degree she hoped to do in Poland. Business failure and debts were additional motives for 'forced' migration, mentioned by two interviewees, who had left Poland in 2005 and 2012. Unemployment motivated Dariusz. He could not find a job in 2017, aged 25, with only a vocational qualification. He commented, 'Recently Płock has begun to develop but with regard to development possibilities for young people there isn't much.' Four mothers and one father had begun to migrate to provide for their children after divorce or widowhood.

Alicja's case illustrates the overlaps between this type of migration and the others. She several times stated firmly that they had gone abroad only to earn money and return; she was not a student or graduate; and (in 2010) she went to Belgium, a traditional destination for incomplete migrants. However, in many ways her story resembles that of the EU swell. Alicja's boyfriend had been persuaded to migrate to a small town in Belgium by a cousin, as soon as he finished school; when Alicja herself left school the boyfriend persuaded her to join him so they could earn money for their wedding and to give them a start in life in KPP. They worked long hours to save up as quickly as possible. However, opportunity rather than a sense of being 'forced' to migrate was uppermost in Alicja's account. Moreover, the couple manifested the adventurous spirit said to typify the EU wave, since they spent their weekends taking trips around Belgium with their Polish friends.

Like the other twenty-first century KPP migrants, target-earner interviewees were conscious of being part of a mass exodus of Poles. Dariusz asserted, 'Poles are everywhere.' Similarly, Edyta commented, 'There were huge numbers of Poles in Bremen. Mostly working for temp agencies ... There were three Polish shops, lots of Poles, only Poles living there. And two Polish restaurants.' Hence they shared a sense of 'wave' identity. Like the EU wave, they often enjoyed the Polish social life in the locations where they lived abroad. Indeed, this was one of the main reasons why Edyta stayed in Bremen after abandoning her plan to study in Poland.

The scale of target-earner migration suggests the existence of a migration culture in the narrow sense as used by Kandel and Massey (2002): a widespread acceptance that international migration is a sensible livelihood strategy, particularly among people who are not university graduates. In Piła, for instance, Dawid, who was 24 at time of interview in 2022, had gone abroad from Piła immediately after secondary school, without passing his exams. He said that many of his friends had done the same, typically going as circular migrants to the Netherlands or to work in factories and Amazon warehouses in Germany. They could have found factory jobs in Piła, 'but young people don't want to work there because the pay is too low'. His schoolfriends helped him find building work in a range of West European countries. Damian (26), a roofer, asserted that 'half' his friends from Piła were living in London or Holland. Edyta (29), a salesperson in Piła, commented:

> I know lots of people who go abroad. You can earn very nice money in Germany, Holland or Belgium. Much more than here. That's probably always going to be the case. So lots go abroad, really a lot. My friends who worked in construction in Poland for example earned a lot here but, in Germany, well!

It was not only young people who shared this opinion. Sylwia (67), who was currently a circular migrant caring for a dementia patient in Germany, claimed she knew several local people who worked abroad as carers, of different ages. She thought students primarily went to the Netherlands to work in horticulture in their vacations. This impression was backed up by the owner of a recruitment agency in Piła who told me that she always had a rush of customers as soon the school-leaving and college summer exams were over.

The fact that so many Poles from KPP work abroad provided social capital for the would-be target earners, as for the EU wave and swell. It was socially acceptable to ask for an invitation, or to invite or even pressurise a friend or relative to come abroad. In such circumstances, as in small towns I had researched for previous projects, some people felt they could not say no. For instance, Lech recounted how 'I was working in an OK job in Piła, just working away [in a factory] and suddenly my friend suggested I go and work abroad. Those were the days [2007] when the only possible reaction was "Wow, anyone would want to do that!"' Dariusz 'had a friend who'd been working there for a few months and he said it would be good, "you could earn some money," and I was in a transition period with work, I couldn't find a job, and he persuaded me … and I said, "I'll give it a go."' Sylwia, who had been cleaning in Berlin for many years, but injured herself, was back in Piła when 'my friend said, "Let's try what it's like to be carers." So I said, "Fine! We'll give it a go!."' Damian had always asserted that he would not work abroad. He had plenty of work as a roofer in Piła. But 'my friend suggested I could work on roofs [in Austria]. I know something about that. I'm a bit of an expert. So I said, "Why not? The Alps – great!"'

Clearly, there is no definite line between forced and opportunistic migration. In fact, some migrants find themselves in situations where they feel compelled to take up opportunities. Similarly, it is hard sometimes to distinguish between 'target earning' and 'intentional unpredictability', which is closely related to opportunism. Alicja, for example, as mentioned above, seemed to overlap between the EU swell and target earner categories. She said, 'We just had the idea to go, earn some money to give us a start in life, because we wanted to get married. But we never planned to stay.' However, they were open-minded as to the duration of their stay abroad.

The research provided insight into different types of circular migration. Many interviewees took advantage of work abroad opportunities as they came up, but did not view regular migration as their livelihood strategy. However, there were a handful of truly circular migrants. Wojciech, who was a fitter, highly in demand on oil rigs, said that he preferred to work three months abroad – in a range of countries – and then rest at home with his family. He said, 'Either you work in Płock for some rubbish amount, or you don't work in Płock and go abroad from time to time. If you don't work abroad you can't afford to buy things. You go abroad and work hard and long, but your work is paid properly.' Circular migrants varied in their degree of agency. Like Wojciech, Krystyna was an occasional migrant by choice. She lived on her retirement pension, but it was insufficient for major household repairs. By working through an agency as a carer in Germany she had been able to pay for a new kitchen and bathroom. Jan, as a musician, performed equally in the UK and Poland, so he was also a type of circular migrant. On the other hand, there were cases where repeated migration seemed to be forced by circumstances, although the migrants themselves enjoyed being abroad. Karolina, originally one of the EU wave, had returned from Ireland during the Global Economic Crisis and had a child, but found it impossible to make an adequate living in KPP. She and her husband began working abroad again, on short trips.

> If you go abroad a bit to earn some extra money, it's hard to accept wages here in Poland. So we used to constantly go and come back. We still haven't quite found our place here. I can't settle here. We were always thinking we might move, so we weren't sure [we wanted to buy property in KPP]. And now those house prices have hit the roof, particularly as a result of Covid.

At the extreme end of lack of agency, Sylwia also mentioned inflation and the cost of living in spring 2022. 'I said I wouldn't go to work in Germany again, but given the inflation today, I probably will.'

Target earners were more likely than the other types to use recruitment agencies. When I asked Edyta why she had initially gone abroad, in 2012, she said she had been bombarded with Facebook advertisements from recruiters based in the Netherlands. 'That was how it worked. And the general opinion was that it was OK, that's why I went. I was 19 and didn't have the same attitude to life as I do now. I read that I could earn eight euros an hour and for me that was amazing!' In recent years, employment agencies have become even more prolific, particularly for seasonal work in the Netherlands and care work in Germany; they have also become more regulated and reliable (Leiber et al 2019). They represented another type of migration livelihood opportunity. However, only a small handful of my interviewees had used Polish recruitment agencies. In my previous fieldwork locations in eastern Poland I had found that mistrust of agencies, particularly Polish agencies, was strongly present in local migration cultures: the mantra was that 'you have to go to be with someone you know'. This mistrust was not so evident in KPP, although it was sometimes expressed. For instance, Wojciech, a frequent migrant target earner in different countries, asserted that 'It's always risky if you don't know anyone. Especially since you invest money in the trip – you want it to work out'.

Poles from KPP mixed with Poles from other regions of Poland when they were abroad, so they picked up scare stories about agencies.

> It's better to go to be with someone you know than through a stranger. Because not all Poles abroad are good people. You don't know who you'll end up with. You have to watch out for that. Because there were lots of stories where someone went and paid 1000 zloties for a job and there turned out to be no work, for example. And they were left waiting at the bus stop. There are lots of stories like that which people tell. (Daniel, EU wave)

As can be seen in Daniel's comments, caution about using Polish recruitment agencies linked to a wider caution about the ill intentions of Polish strangers abroad – stories of the 'Polish conman' (Garapich 2013, 2016b) which circulate widely and can be considered part of the migration culture (White 2018b: 148–50). A couple of the EU wave who migrated individually – possibly before being exposed to this type of caution from other migrants – had in fact used agencies, admitting that they took a risk. Karol, for example, said it did cross his mind to worry: 'as I set off at midnight from the station, with all my bags, I thought "Hell, where am I going, what will it be like?."' Karolina, however, as an experienced target migrant, mentioned how she had become reconciled to using agencies:

> I used to be too afraid to use agencies ... but when we started to use them, about five years ago, it turned out that they were OK ... I have a good experience with agencies and I think they have improved a bit. They need their clients. But I have heard bad tales as well. I met some people who went to Germany and paid [in advance] for their accommodation, but there was no job. I thought that didn't happen, but it turns out it still does.

Experiences abroad

As amply illustrated, for example, in Cekiera et al's (2022) *Emigration as Experience*, Polish return migrant interviewees often reflect on their lives in migration as a time rich in new experiences, a 'school of life'. Because of space limitations, the next section touches on just a few, most salient aspects of those experiences.

Place attachment

Representatives of all three types, EU wave, swell and target earners, mentioned that they had been curious about the places they lived abroad, and many of them said they had become attached. With a couple of exceptions – mostly because they were socially isolated – they had not returned to Poland because they disliked where they were living. On the contrary, most were very positive. Chapter 3 has already discussed their preferences for locations of a particular size, and for the advantages to some of smaller and more peaceful settings. Although place attachment theory tends to stress that people become more attached over time (Lewicka 2011), in fact the interviewees seem to have become quickly attached to where they lived abroad. Similarly, Trąbka (2019) found that the 'place discovery' element of place attachment can be speedy for Polish migrants in Norway, even if deeper forms of attachment do need more time to develop. Polish women I interviewed in KPP sometimes mentioned how they 'fell in love' with foreign cities and how they missed them. Dagmara, for instance, said: 'Rome was lovely, and so was the Italian language. I've always felt drawn to Italy. And I am still in love with it. If only my life had taken a different turn there, I would have liked to live there my whole life.' Trąbka (2019: 71) also mentions the significance of life stage for place attachment. 'Migrating in early adulthood makes it more likely to gain life-shaping experiences in the destination country and thus facilitates deeper bonds with this place.' As illustrated in the first part of this chapter, many interviewees were very young when they first went abroad. Dagmara, for instance, had been 19.

Some people mentioned specific favourite places, which could be seen as 'anchoring' them to where they lived abroad. For instance, Sylwia, back in Piła, missed her outings from Berlin to Potsdam, where she used to drive her visiting Polish friends – a sharing and hosting activity which must have consolidated her personal sense of identification with this favourite place.[4] Although one might suppose that migrants who worked temporarily in a range of countries did not put down many anchors, or feel a sense of place attachment, some of these interviewees were also very enthusiastic about specific destinations. For instance, Damian, who had never been to the Tatras – claiming that from Piła people went on holiday to the Baltic seaside – fell in love with the Alps. He complained about the gentle landscape of north-west Poland ('round Piła people see some lake or other and say "Wow"') before launching into an extended description of places he had lived in Austria and Switzerland.

> We lived in an amazing little house, by a stream which became a whole river when it rained hard for a couple of days. Goats were running about, cows high up in those mountains ... When I went into Austria there was a moment when suddenly the snowy mountain peaks appeared ... I would love to travel the whole length of the Alps, to where they end in France.

Bonding with nature is often mentioned as an aspect of place attachment (Lewicka 2011; Lynnebakke 2021). As Horolets shows in her article about Polish post-2004 migrants in the English West Midlands, exploring locally leads to 'establishing a more personal relation with place'. Horolets found that younger single migrants or childless couples were more prone to this type of 'wandering around' (Horolets 2014: 5, 13). Among the KPP interviewees, the EU wave and swell in particular seem to have done plenty of exploring, but to some extent so did the target migrants. Youth and not having dependents as well as car ownership were the main facilitators. They travelled with their partners or with groups of friends, often Polish. These weekends and short holidays often had a fond place in their memories. Since foreign holidays were less common for Poles around 2004 than they have since become, in many cases this was the interviewees' first experience of foreign tourism. Even interviewees who had negative experiences in their workplaces, such as Jagoda or Feliks, spoke fondly about their local travels. Jagoda and her friends explored the Welsh seaside and mountains. Feliks enthused that 'Glasgow was super. And later, when we bought a car, we could be at the seaside in half an hour, in the mountains, anywhere.' In some accounts, as in Damian's quoted above, the place and the people were intertwined. Daniel said, 'We had a car and toured all of Ireland. It's really one of the loveliest countries … It was great, great, I have very nice memories. We met lots of people, Irish people, Poles who had come there to work. And we were all very glad to be there.'

For some interviewees, in line with Horolets' findings, travels were associated with their more carefree early years, before they had children and life abroad became more complicated and expensive. Ewa, for example, reminisced:

> We had more anonymity and a more relaxed life. In Ireland, it was like a life without stress, a bit different from here in Poland. There were places in Ireland I often visited. Because I've seen the sights in Ireland, and I know it very well. I have my favourite places which I'd like to go back and see again … We used to set off at weekends to see Ireland, for what we jokingly labelled 'cultural weekends'. We'd go to some city, to the museums, we'd eat supper in pubs – things our Polish earnings would never have let us do.

Being able to afford foreign holidays helped consolidate attachment to the country where they lived abroad. It was fondly remembered partly because it was a gateway to the wider world. Ewa, for instance, also mentioned, 'We could afford to go for weekends to London [where her brother was living] or Amsterdam or somewhere. And later, bigger trips, to the Peruvian Andes.' On the other hand, a few interviewees took every opportunity to go back to Poland. As a result, they did less exploring in the destination country. Justyna, a member of the EU wave, although she seemed well-embedded in London, said with a slightly embarrassed laugh, 'Generally, if we had any time off we would come back to Poland. So, unfortunately, we didn't see much of England. We used to come back to Poland about twice a year.'

Social ties and receiving society attitudes

Migration scholars writing about place attachment have highlighted the significance of social ties – even weak ties such as 'nodding relationships' and casual conversations with people around the neighbourhood. Kohlbacher et al (2015) found from their study of people of migrant background in Austria that these urban sociabilities (Glick Schiller and Çağlar 2016) were particularly appreciated by migrants, even if they did not seem so important to the receiving population. In addition, having real friends helps consolidate place attachment. In line with Allport's (1954) contact hypothesis, sustained contact with others, on an equal basis, helps break down barriers and promotes openness and understanding. Finally, Ager and Strang (2004: 5) write that migrants should be 'socially connected with members of a (national, ethnic, cultural, religious or other) community with which they identify'. Relations with co-ethnics often seemed to play an important role in helping the interviewees feel at home, or not. Those interviewees living in places like Cork, Dublin, London or Glasgow were able to enjoy being part of loose-knit Polish communities.

As other research has shown, post-2004 migrants were impressed by courtesy they encountered from local people in Ireland and the UK, and, particularly in Ireland, by friendliness towards strangers (Grabowska et al 2017: 122; White 2018b: 145–7). Ewa, for example, enthused:

> It's a completely other mentality. That Irish mentality, that culture, everyone was different. They'd constantly be saying 'Hi' and talking about the weather and making contact with other people. I came back to Poland and was in the bus and I tried to strike up a conversation with another passenger and she stared at me as if I was mad.

Interviewees who lived in the UK and Ireland as part of the EU wave and swell tended to highlight the extensiveness of their Polish friendship circles, but some also mentioned British or Irish friends. Whether they had local friends depended on their workplace. As also discovered by other researchers, such as Grzymała-Kazłowska and Ryan (2022), it was possible for Poles to work alongside other Poles for many years and hardly be embedded in British social networks. However, many KPP interviewees had made friends at work; the labour market was not totally segmented. Several interviewees also mentioned making friends of neighbours, particularly if they lived in small towns and villages. Kinga, for example, had kept in touch with her neighbour and invited her to come and visit them in KPP. Jerzy attributed his good experiences in England to the fact that he lived in a small town: 'There were no problems around the fact that I was a foreigner ... although my friends who lived in cities had different sorts of experiences.' Mateusz, who before the 2008 Global Economic Crisis and subsequent austerity policies worked in a small town in Lincolnshire, an area which in 2016 recorded one of the highest votes to leave the EU, found local people 'very open and ready to joke'.

However, a couple of interviewees also mentioned that attitudes changed over time, both in England and Ireland. Beata lived in a small town with a strong 'leave' vote in the 2016 referendum. She said that in the run-up to 2016 local people had begun to say that Poles were stealing their jobs. Aneta, based in Ireland, was not sure how far her impressions that Irish people became less friendly after 2008 linked to moving from Dublin to a small town, or whether it was the same in Dublin. Rather than blaming the economic crisis, she said the situation had worsened because more Polish labour migrants had come to Ireland, and they were less welcome than the original university-educated lifestyle migrants like herself. On the other hand, Jan, whose work at the time of interview still connected him with England, felt that attitudes were improving. He had noticed that the somewhat condescending attitudes towards Poles he encountered a few years previously were eroding.

The target earners, who had lived in various non-English speaking countries, mentioned hostility from locals more often than did the EU wave or swell. This might be connected not to those countries as such but rather to the work the migrants did, as well as language barriers. Some interviewees in fact were positive: for instance, Alicja, who lived in a small town in Belgium, highlighted the good neighbourliness of local people. Others complained about being treated without respect and in some cases exploited. In two instances they decided to stop working in the country where they had been made to feel unwelcome (Germany) and began working elsewhere. In other cases, their bad experiences in one country marked the end of their whole migration career. Tomasz was one of these. He complained, 'If a Swede finds out you're from Poland he'll be fine about it, because Swedes are, let's say, in colloquial language, they are laid back people. But they're not that nice and when they know [you're Polish] they immediately start treating you differently.' However, this impression of unfriendliness was not his only reason to return to Poland. By contrast, Lech stated that 'the main reason [to come back to Poland] was that we are made to feel so unwelcome. We are only welcome as slave labour. Just for work ... Even though I speak Dutch, I would go into shops and be treated as if I was dirt. They are racists.'

Migrants are well placed to compare different countries and the KPP interviewees organised their impressions by creating hierarchies and engaging in generalisations. Karolina, for example, asserted that 'In Switzerland and Austria you feel more you are being kept at a distance... not like in Ireland or London where you could go for a walk and start talking to strangers, sit on a bus and strike up a conversation.' They also reflected on their experiences of non-Polish migrants. Wojciech had worked in England with Czechs ('smart alecs'); in Finland with Russians ('easy-going'); and in the Netherlands with Germans ('worse than the Gestapo' for keeping an eye on you). In a few cases, generalisations seemed to reflect underlying racist views. For example, one person said that in Birmingham and Coventry he felt 'as if he were in Kabul'.

However, more often the interviewees seemed to find ethnic diversity attractive.[5] Unlike Wojciech, other construction workers mentioned that they had formed friendships with workmates from Bulgaria, Nigeria and other countries. Several interviewees mentioned making friends from Central and East European countries. For example, Dagmara socialised with other women working as carers in Rome. 'From our part of the world there were lots of Ukrainians, Russians, Czechs, Slovaks, lots of them ... and we used to be friends.' Two interviewees mentioned having Muslim friends. Jan had a British-Pakistani friend whom he met because they were both curious about the music in a local Baptist church, where Jan was the only white person and his friend the only Muslim in the congregation. They became close friends and started going to college together to study music. Jan became much more confident at speaking English as the result of talking to his friend every day. Jan had been in the UK at a time of 'continuous news coverage about terrorist attacks' but 'never encountered anything like that in everyday life ... So I wondered to myself how much it's true and how much a media creation'. Tomasz also made Muslim friends abroad. He said:

> It was a small town, just 10,000 people, and half were immigrants, Muslims, immigrants from different countries, like Somalia and Ethiopia ... Refugees. In our block of flats, we were the only white people. As a Kalisz resident, well we don't have that many black people in Kalisz. Of course, I'm in no way a racist, but at first I was a bit concerned: a whole town, my whole block of flats! But they turned out to be really good people, it was great.

Both Jan's and Tomasz's examples demonstrate a process of learning as the result of sustained encounters with people of other nationalities. They stressed friendship, rather than – like Wojciech – making generalisations about the national character of their new friends and acquaintances. In Tomasz's case, these friendships made his stay in the small town more tolerable. In Jan's, it helped consolidate his place attachment and integration in Nottingham, especially as it led to his studying at a local college. On the other hand, Wojciech's categorisation of different nationalities betokens a certain essentialism and incomplete learning, even if it was founded on his personal impressions and first-hand knowledge.[6]

Ethnic hierarchisation is a common phenomenon globally. However, theorists of ethnic hierarchies such as Ford (2011) argue that the subject's own nationality is always placed at the top of the hierarchy. Among Polish migrants, this often seems not to be the case. As found by many other researchers of Polish migration, such as Garapich (2016b: 451–61), Gill (2010) and Ryan (2010), Poles can be highly critical of other Poles. Expectations that Polish strangers might want to cheat you were mentioned in the section on recruitment agencies earlier in this chapter. A corollary of this is the conviction that, compared with other nationalities, Poles do not display ethnic solidarity when they are abroad and are particularly unfriendly towards one another. Wojciech, for example, despite his criticism of other nationalities, was equally scathing about Poles.

> Poles are an unpleasant nation, and Poles behave worst of all when they are abroad … instead of sticking together in a group, supporting one another and helping each other out … I worked with Russians and Lithuanians. They stick together … If one Russian has a problem all the others rally round. And a Pole? A Pole would drown you.[7] I've seen it a couple of times. Of course, I don't say that all Poles are like that.

A few interviewees had personally had bad experiences with fellow Poles. Jagoda found that her Polish co-workers in Swansea – after the Global Economic Crisis – were fiercely possessive of their factory jobs and hostile to newcomers. In other cases, when interviewees distanced themselves from their fellow Poles it was because they drank or took drugs. Usually these were men doing hard manual labour. Lech complained that on his Dutch farm 'payday is on Thursday and they receive their 300–400 euros and just go and get drunk. No money for bread even by Sunday. They don't really have the energy to work, but they just hang on from Thursday to Thursday … Every third person has a criminal record in Poland'.

Netherrtheless, instead of recounting their personal bad experiences with Poles abroad, the interviewees were more likely to report on migration lore about Poles – scare stories circulating among other migrants which were part of the migration culture. Tomasz, for example, explained how he found out about Poles' poor reputation.

> Probably you've heard this before, from other people you interviewed, but I didn't know it until I went abroad ... When you talk to other Poles [abroad] they say how other nations stick together when they're in a foreign country, but unfortunately we Poles don't do that. We want our friend to earn less than us, not to earn a lot when he's abroad. Poles abroad are quite envious of each other.

Agata, apparently basing her assertions on Polish migration lore, similarly claimed:

> When I lived in London, I was forever hearing that 'A Jew will always help a Jew, an Arab will always help an Arab, but a Pole will never help a Pole'. I kept on hearing that and I think it's partly true ... Perhaps it sounds silly, but I think Poles are a nation of conmen.

Feliks was more reflective:

> On the whole, I'd say that Poles are quite suspicious when they are abroad ... both towards native residents and Poles. It's different there. Even in Scotland they [Polish migrants] said that, if a Pole hadn't harmed you, he'd done you a favour. There were simply bad people there who would promise something, for example to pay for something, and then disappear. I heard those sorts of stories. I didn't have any such experiences, but [that was how it was].

When I asked Karol for his opinion about such tales, he said that there was probably something in it – every nation had its black sheep. This seems to be the most convincing explanation. There are so many Poles living abroad, that interviewees are bound to have heard about, and in some cases, encountered behaviour they consider to be 'bad'. It stands out abroad, because they are more sensitive to how Poles appear in the eyes of other nations, but it simply connects to the fact that in countries such as the UK every type of Polish person is to be found among Polish migrants – this is Polish society abroad (White 2018c). Sometimes, in fact, it seems that social stratification rather than immorality or criminality is the 'problem', when interviewees who are conscious of their higher socio-economic status are embarrassed by encounters with people from other walks of life.

Such negative emotions were counterbalanced by the advantages of being part of a wave – finding oneself in a situation where there were so many other Poles that one could choose friends who were similar in outlook and tastes to oneself. Eade et al (2007: 15), Ryan et al (2008) and others underline that discursive hostility towards Polish strangers goes hand in hand with strong reliance on bonding ties with friends and family. However, it is also worth pointing out that migrants do not just rely on the ties they bring from their place of origin. Extending the Polish friendship ties can be an important part of a migrant's experience abroad and of their place attachment. Erstwhile co-ethnic strangers become friends. From the KPP interviewees' accounts it often seemed that this was above all what had made their stays in the UK and Ireland enjoyable. Ewa, for instance, said that when she went for holidays to Poland, she would miss Ireland because 'that was my life. That was where my friends were. I told my mother, "I'm packing my bags and going home." "Oh, so that's home now?" They were friends from Poland, different parts of Poland, and from my hometown, people I'd met in Ireland ... I have warm memories.'

Language skills and occupational mobility

Andrzej probably expressed the views of many migrants when he said: 'The main problem for anyone going abroad is language. If you can at least communicate, you won't have problems.' It is often claimed that the EU wave were able to be so confident in the UK and Ireland because English had replaced Russian as the main foreign language taught in Polish schools. For the braver and more sociable migrants this school education was enough to see them through the experience. Andrzej for instance said that 'I had only four years [of English] at school, but I'm one of those people who always asks questions. I'll find my way anywhere'. Damian said:

> My boss would talk to me in his Swiss German or not-German and I could say a bit in English. But it wasn't a problem ... Actually, most people know some Polish words because so many Poles have found their way there ... But I used to speak English, or sign language. He showed me, I showed him, he said OK.

On the other hand, for other migrants even having a degree in English seemed insufficient. Jagoda, for instance, reminisced:

> Wales is a difficult place if it comes to English. I had a bit of a shock at first, because I thought I knew English to a good level, I had a teaching degree with English, so I had a big headstart. But that Welsh dialect! … I remember I went into a shop and didn't even understand when the woman asked if I needed a carrier bag.

Additionally, back in 2004 not quite all young Poles had learnt English at school, and if they went straight to work in Ireland or the UK, and socialised mostly with Poles, it could be difficult to achieve a good standard. Even after ten years, Daniel never felt confident: 'I didn't know English before we went … So the fact that there was still that language barrier was a reason for me [to return] … If I'd known it perfectly, I think I would have stayed, and opened my own business.' On the other hand, Daniel's wife had devoted her early days in Ireland to attending a language course. Presumably this was part of a family strategy, also mentioned by some other informants in this and my previous projects (White 2017: 152). Only one interviewee, one of the youngest and most recent, confessed to not bothering to learn the language, just relying on a Polish friend and on his phone – an option not available to migrants *circa* 2004. He said he did not need to learn because he was not planning to be abroad forever.

Almost all informants stressed the effort they put into learning languages over an extended period. They included those with least formal education, and/or middle-aged people who are sometimes supposed not to be successful language learners. Jerzy, for example, explained his English-learning journey:

> I learned English at school when I was 15 and I went to England 25 years later. So when I arrived I could just hear noise around me. I couldn't understand anything and it was really hard – I had to rely on sign language. So I went to college to work on my language … And since I was working as a driver I had to rely on myself, I had to go to new places, unload my van. I had to know what to say, there was no choice.

Linguistic progress was closely connected with the nature of the interviewee's work abroad. As it happened, with the exception of one person doing voluntary work, none of the KPP interviewees, even the university graduates, was doing a graduate-level job. This did not mean that they necessarily felt deskilled and disadvantaged. The EU defines high-skilled migrants as those with university degrees (European Commission 2022: 80). However, manual work can also require high levels of skill. Some interviewees were proud that they did skilled manual work abroad, and there was a virtuous circle whereby experiences gained abroad and in Poland were complementary. Damian, who was a roofer, seemed to have established a comfortable pattern of working mostly in KPP with summer breaks in different Alpine locations. He displayed a strong sense that his skills were valued wherever he worked. Wojciech stated:

> We're professionals, we go abroad to work as professionals, so we must know how to do our jobs. I didn't work abroad as a 'cleaner' [said in English], I worked as a fitter [on oil rigs]. It's an elite in England, and they have excellent wages. It's not comparable to being a cleaner. It's the elite.

A few other interviewees had not worked using their qualifications and past occupational expertise but found employment which used other skills. Karolina, for instance, worked on archaeological digs for part of her career abroad, saying, 'I didn't want to do manual labour.' Zenon chose to work at a hotel which was 'better than going to a factory to work'. Jerzy, an IT technician, used his driving skills, then bought a Polish shop for his wife, a teacher, so that she would not 'have to work in a factory' when she joined him abroad. Justyna, who interrupted her university studies in Poland to sell beauty products in London, emphasised how much she enjoyed and was skilled at this job. One of its chief advantages was the ample opportunities for training. Iwona had always dreamed of being a florist but could not find a floristry course in Poland. In the UK, she was able to work in florists' shops and gain the skills to which she aspired. Kinga began working as a vet's assistant on a farm with calves, including quite heavy physical work. This was a big change from her work in KPP, but she said, 'I enjoyed it. I like animals … It was work in the open air. It was relaxing.'

Moreover, some informants were proud of their work, even if the job was not very demanding, because their employers demonstrated how much they were valued. Janusz, for example, a student who made multiple trips to work in Dublin, always worked in the same café. He said, 'They knew I was a good worker and always wanted to re-employ me, so I that's where I always returned.' Zenon, who had been furloughed from his hotel in England when I interviewed him, was hesitating about whether or not to return. One factor encouraging him to return was that his employer was phoning and trying to persuade him back. As Kinga mentioned about her cows, it could also feel relaxing to do manual work. Andrzej said, 'You just get your job done, come home and relax – no homework to mark!'

The key point was that it was properly paid. As Andrzej's comment shows, work–life balance could be an important criterion. This emerged from numerous accounts, for instance with reference to the leisure activities and tourism mentioned earlier in this section. The social side of work was also important. Even if your work was boring and heavy, if you were collectively deskilled, working alongside dozens of other young Polish graduates and students from the same migration wave, the situation was much more tolerable. Moreover, part of the migration culture included acceptance that, if you went abroad, you probably would need to do manual work. As Feliks mentioned, 'Of course, we did miserable work, as you do when you're a migrant'.

With regard to deskilling, like many of their contemporaries, some of the EU wave and swell were students or between school and university, and some of the target earners had only a general secondary education, so there was no qualification to not use abroad. In addition, among those who gained a specific vocational qualification in Poland, many had not been using it in their Polish job before they left. Dariusz, who had a technical qualification in Poland but was working as a cook, found factory work in the UK acceptable. Even Wojciech, so proudly professional, had originally trained as a plumber. Lech, aged 50, provided a slightly different example. He had trained as metal worker and worked in a communist-era factory in KPP which has since been shut down. He described his trade as 'obsolete'.

Parutis (2014) shows how young Poles and Lithuanians living in London after 2004 expected to progress from 'any job' to a 'better job' and eventually, with luck, to their 'dream job'. Some of her interviewees were already in the middle of this journey. A few KPP interviewees also progressed to better jobs. However, it was mostly the case that they remained in the same or similar unchallenging jobs throughout their time abroad, perhaps indicating why they found it not too stressful to leave those jobs and return to Poland. In retrospect, some of them felt they could have aspired to more. Feliks, for example, became stuck in one job because it came with a National Health Service contract which offered good conditions. However, he said that 'if I had stayed, I would definitely have tried to switch my job for something more ambitious'. Karol reflected, 'When you're older you think in different categories ... When I went to England a couple of years ago to see my friend, I thought about returning [to work] in England. But I wouldn't like to do the work I did then. I would regret my university studies. Of course, if I could do qualified work, I could perhaps go for six months.' Mateusz said, 'If I went back I would have done it a bit differently and gone to university to achieve something.'

The conservative Polish press laments that Poles work in menial jobs abroad. As the above accounts suggest, hardly any KPP interviewees gave the impression that they felt humiliated by such work, and certainly this was not the reason they returned to Poland. However, Lech's account of his 15 years in the Netherlands provided a sharp contrast. Lech differed from the other interviewees in completely lacking agency. He had accumulated large debts, and the belief that he could only pay them off by continuing his work abroad delayed his return to Poland by several years. He had returned two weeks before I interviewed him.

> I'm 50 now and it's time to get an easy job at Philips making lightbulbs. [In the Netherlands] we'd get a text message saying 'chickens today, start at 8' and work until 10 in the evening. There were 200 people in the company and not a single Dutchman worked there … We'd be sent into France, Germany, the Netherlands, we used to travel around. I'd be away from base for up to 17 hours. For the same money the whole time I was there, 80 euros a day … They rent a flat for workers who don't have their own housing, bed crowded up against bed like in a prison. And it's just non-stop work. No opportunity to go fishing or mushrooming … A wall, your laptop, and there you sit … Some people are there with their children. They got social housing, but they live on the breadline. They just about make ends meet, the same as if they lived in Poland. That's the reality of life abroad today.

Conclusions

In Kalisz, Piła and Płock, as in big cities where I previously conducted research, the post-accession wave was remembered by middle-class informants as a historical event. Other sections of society knew that migration continued apace. In their eyes, KPP were still 'cities of emigration' and there still existed a strong migration culture, in the sense of widespread acceptance that international migration was a suitable and in some situations even necessary livelihood strategy. The interviewees had left and returned to KPP over the period from just before EU accession to 2022, and the chapter examined KPP's identities as cities of out-migration over this time. It demonstrated that medium-sized locations like KPP combine features of big cities (the experience of a 'wave' of youthful migration around 2004–7, followed by a 'swell' of friends and relations) and small towns (a steady stream of labour migrants of different ages focused mostly on earning money).

However, one should not draw too sharp a distinction between adventure-seeking youth and the rest. They shared motivations, experiences and, in some respects, a common migration culture. The interviewees all highlighted their experimental approach to migration: it was such a normal local livelihood strategy at the time they migrated that it seemed relatively risk-free. Livelihood and lifestyle motives mixed for everyone, albeit in different proportions. Curiosity and enthusiasm about travelling abroad were expressed even by those interviewees who had been in greatest financial need, for example because they were unemployed or wanted to subsidise their children's higher education. Interviewees' narratives were also often similar in that they underlined how it felt to be part of a large population of migrants. This was not always comfortable, particularly when Poles abroad warned each other not to trust Polish strangers and repeated stories about 'Polish conmen'. Nonetheless, interviewees more often mentioned making friends with other Polish people, and place attachment. The latter was based partly on embeddedness in Polish networks, although also on socialising with people of other nationalities, and on exploring and bonding with nature. The informants did possess various different integration trajectories, and they were differently integrated into local labour markets and differently competent at speaking foreign languages. However, almost without exception these particular interviewees did not return to Poland because they disliked the place where they lived abroad. Nor did they disapprove of migration, which they considered a normal social phenomenon. In some cases they were actively encouraging their children to follow in their footsteps. Of course, they may have been willing to be interviewed precisely because they had positive memories of their migration experiences.

Notes

1. The Kalisz priest quoted by Kotowska-Rasiak (2021) and mentioned in Chapter 2 is perhaps an exception. He equated immigration to Poland with Polish labour migration of the 1980s and 90s, neglecting to mention that Poles also migrate in the twenty-first century.
2. Pszczółkowska (2024) argues that Polish highly-skilled migrants are less dependent on networks to help them migrate, but the university graduates among my interviewees did not possess much cultural capital. They were generally fresh from university at time of migration or else they were invited by friends and family to migrate.
3. As mentioned in Chapter 2, two Polish interviewees were 'stayers': grandmothers with daughters and grandchildren whom they often visited abroad.
4. The two mothers I interviewed, who visited their daughters living abroad, had also been extensively shown around and adopted their children's enthusiasms for Ireland and Norway. Presumably this helped consolidate the daughters' sense of belonging in their new homes.

5 Similarly, a 2005 survey found that more than half the respondents had positive views towards diversity (Garapich 2016b: 254). However, as Garapich's (2016b: 252–66) discussion based on ethnographic data reveals, the situation is more complicated than simply 'positive' compared with 'negative' attitudes. For fuller analysis see also White (2018a).
6 I discuss similar examples in White (2018b).
7 The full expression, which I have heard several times and which is also recorded by other researchers, is that a Pole would drown you for one euro, or a Pole would drown you in a glass of water.

5
Polish return mobilities

Introduction

The first part of this chapter discusses why the Polish interviewees returned to KPP. Polish return migration seems to be small scale in KPP, adding to the impression that out-migration identity remains more important, and that in-migration is mostly by Ukrainians, not Poles. Structural factors, like economic crisis abroad, growth in KPP or Brexit could in theory trigger a wave of return. However, it seems that returns happen usually because migrants finish their project for earning abroad, and go back to the places they never stopped calling home, or because some personal factors intervene and trigger a return (Iglicka 2010: 80–85; Rokitowska-Malcher 2021: 117–43). In KPP, no one, including in my casual conversations around the cities, claimed that there had been any waves of return. Instead, there was a trickle of returns as individuals came back because of specific personal events. Sometimes these were unpredictable, such as inheriting housing, pregnancy and health problems. Life-stage, particularly parenthood, played a significant role in determining the timing. The second part of the chapter looks at re-integration, particularly into the job market. As mentioned in Chapter 3, interviewees were fairly positive about their cities as places to live, noting recent infrastructural improvements. They often chose KPP in preference to bigger cities. Some of them sacrificed options for more highly-paid and challenging work in larger cities for lifestyle benefits and social (especially family) networks in KPP. Others seemed to have no sense of sacrifice and were content with their work in KPP, if not the pay. When they returned to KPP, it had been easier for some to find work, for instance because of language skills gained abroad. Others, especially women, had struggled to find anything suitable.

'Return' is popularly understood to imply 'permanent return' unless it is qualified by an adjective such as 'temporary', or a specified purpose or time limit, such as a return visit, or return for three months. However, returns, particularly in the world of EU free movers, are often temporary, or at least open-ended and experimental: the return migrants continue to live in Poland, but do not exclude further trips abroad in the future (White 2014a and 2014b). Some unskilled returnees, like Lech, whose aspiration to work in the lightbulb factory was quoted in the previous chapter, were more likely to seek work in KPP in migration hotspots with strong migration cultures, from which they might be tempted to re-migrate abroad. Judging from the accounts of Ukrainian interviewees working in these factories, it was quite common for Poles to come and go. Hence 'return mobilities' could be a more useful concept than 'return migration'.

Scholars have constructed various typologies of return migrants (Cerase 1974; Dzięglewski 2020; Kuschminder 2022). This chapter does not introduce any new typologies. It continues to refer to the types created for Chapter 4, since one of the arguments is that there is often a link between the original migration motivation and the motivation for return. As before, the analysis is intersectional. By thinking intersectionally we can achieve a clearer understanding of individual motives, including emotions. Gender, life-stage and educational level seem to be particularly relevant factors explaining return. The significance of gender in Lower Silesia is illustrated, for example, by Rokitowska-Malcher (2021: 119, 128). She shows that women were even more likely than men to return for non-economic reasons. With regard to life stage: migration journeys and life courses each have their own milestones and turning points, which interconnect (Dzięglewski 2020; Dziekońska 2023; White 2014a and 2014b; Winogrodzka and Grabowska 2022). In particular, some people migrate in early youth to escape from their home location, but return a few years later to settle down. Rokitowska-Malcher (2021: 119) includes 'starting a family' among her return motives. However, life is often not that straightforward. For example, even if a potential returnee wants to go back to Poland, their partner may not agree with the plan, or return may not be sustainable for economic reasons. Pregnancies are not always planned. People may return to their parents but then find it hard to live with them. More highly-educated people can feel more confident to return to Poland's biggest cities, where they know that there are plenty of graduate-entry jobs. Gender and educational level have an impact not just on the decision to return but also on whether return is sustainable within the context of smaller-city labour markets in Poland, given their limitations. Karolak (2020) distinguishes between 'effortless return' and the more problematic transitions into the Polish labour market experienced by most of his interviewees. He concludes (2020: 117) that 'the migration episode should be perceived as a catalyst or inhibitor of certain biographical trajectories deriving from the intersection of migrants' origins, gender, age, class, education as well as structural settings and politics of (dis)integration'.

Return is often less strategic than the original migration. Migration is usually part of a livelihood strategy, but return is often more haphazard. This might help explain why some interviewees seemed puzzled by their own return, or attributed different weight to different motivating factors at different points in the interview. Comments included Feliks's 'Somehow I didn't feel like it any more' and Alicja's 'We simply decided that we'd had enough'. As mentioned in Chapter 2, social scientists often use the term 'strategy' loosely, to underline that people have agency and are not just at the mercy of structural forces. Dzięglewski's (2020) book about Polish returnees is subtitled 'Strategies of returning migrants'. Many decisions need to be made and the pros and cons of different potential livelihood strategies researched and weighed up in advance. This is vividly illustrated in the lively debates among returning and return migrants within Facebook groups such as Bigger and Smaller Returns to Poland.[1] Return migration scholars since at least Cerase (1974) have pointed out that some people return as part of a plan and others because they do not succeed abroad – so-called 'return of failure'. Cassarino (2004) argues that it is the degree of preparedness which does much to determine whether return migrants succeed after they return. Nonetheless, Polish return migration research up to today – including recent examples such as Rokitowska-Malcher (2021) and Trąbka et al (2022) – consistently illustrates the truth of King's (2000) observation about return in general: it is more often for emotional and family-connected reasons than for economic ones. This is why it is less likely to be 'strategic'.

Motives to return

Although haphazardness of one sort or another emerged as important in most accounts, an element of planning was more evident among accounts by the EU wave. Although this was the group whose migration was commonly supposed to be characterised by a strategy of intentional unpredictability, they enjoyed more agency and therefore capacity to plan. They possessed more cultural capital than less well-educated migrants, and they acquired economic capital by being abroad. Given that the period living abroad was also an extended transition to adulthood (Krzaklewska 2019; Szewczyk 2015; White 2014b) it is not surprising that over time migrants became more interested in predictability and stability. Being abroad concentrated their minds, and as illustrated in the previous chapter it could help them shape their ideas about what they really wanted to do in life. At a minimum, this often meant that they were determined to find white-collar jobs in Poland, even if they did not aspire to very high-status work.[2]

Mateusz presented an extreme case of strategic return. He had gone abroad as a recent university graduate because he could not find a suitable job in Płock in 2006, but while he was abroad the Polish economy had begun to recover. He said:

> All the time, I followed what was happening in Poland … I was checking what was happening on the labour market, I was in contact with people I knew, and looked at the internet … Only here in Płock. And I noticed that things were beginning to move, and I decided to return. If it still seemed to be weak, I could return [to the UK]. But within six weeks I found the job where I've been working ever since.

Justyna, who left Poland before taking her degree, but acquired excellent language skills, was also in a position to choose for herself. She had a job she enjoyed in London, but found it an expensive place to live. On the other hand, she could return to Poland to live in her own flat, which she had bought from her London savings. She said 'When I weighed up the pros and cons, the pros were more for Kalisz.' Although at first she took a succession of low-paid jobs in Kalisz, while she tried to find something better, she strategically kept her options open. 'I didn't shut the door on London. I kept my bank account going, and I knew that if I didn't manage to get a job in Kalisz I could go back. I knew my manager would find me some work.' Other examples of strategic return among the EU wave and swell included Aneta and her husband. He, as an English-speaking engineer, had interviews in different places in Poland, and could choose his destination; she then followed him.

Agata's case demonstrates the multi-stranded qualities of some strategies. She had migrated as part of the EU wave, lived in London for 20 years, and expected to stay, partly because she thought her child had a brighter future in the UK. She said she came back unexpectedly, because her son persuaded her, and because, in the UK, the Covid pandemic increased her sense of isolation from her extended family in

Poland. However, she planned their return carefully. They waited until the son completed primary school in London. At the same time, Agata developed her business in Poland. Over recent years she had built up a transnational livelihood practising Chinese medicine both in the UK and in KPP when she came back for holidays. Hence she returned to Poland to an established client base. Her son, a UK citizen, could go to university in the UK, so the way back was open for him later if he chose that option. Agata's secure transnational livelihood as well as her general confidence and sense of her own adaptability enabled her to feel that she was in control of her destiny.

Karolak (2016: 27) refers to return 'as a test', whereby some returnees try out return, to see how they succeed, but are open to further migration. The EU wave migrants who 'kept the door open' in case their return failed were treating return 'as a test'. Among the KPP interviewees, there was also one target earner who fell into this category. Aged 24, Dawid had been working abroad since leaving school, but then decided to come back to Poland. He experimentally set up as a self-employed builder and decorator, taking advantage of tax breaks for young people. However, this livelihood strategy did not derive from any perception of new opportunities in KPP, since he moved to Poznań.

As already mentioned, some migrants' return is linked to the original migration motive in that they return because they achieve the targets they set for their stay abroad. Among this particular sample Kinga was the only clear-cut case of someone who met their target – buying housing – and returned to settle in Poland. Justyna, cited above, treated her recently-purchased flat in KPP as a 'pull factor', but it was not the main reason to return to Poland, nor was she sure that she would settle back for good. In several other cases, the target of acquiring property was achieved, but not by the interviewee: they inherited a flat, or an older relative moved out, and this seemed a good moment to come back to Poland. Return can also happen partly for the opposite reason: because the migrant recognises that they are unlikely ever to achieve their aspirations abroad. The case of Daniel was mentioned in Chapter 4. He had decided that his English would never be good enough to enable him to set up his own business in Ireland. Nonetheless, his return was part of a family livelihood strategy, and connected to inheriting a flat in Poland. Hence it cannot be viewed as a simple return of failure. In another case, someone went primarily to be with his band, but then this did not work out, apparently for musical reasons. Again, this should not be viewed as a simple failure, since there were many other factors at play.

Several families found themselves unable to continue abroad, even though they had liked being there originally. Here, lifestage was the important identity. They said that had they remained childless they might have stayed. However, it was expensive to support children abroad, and they usually lacked childcare – since their extended families were in Poland – so they gave up and came back. It should be noted that they made the choice to return as a whole family, not to revert to the old model of incomplete migration. They did not seem to regard this as a 'return of failure', emphasising that they appreciated the benefits of family life in the smaller city. Anita confessed that one reason to migrate to the UK, as a very young woman, had been to escape from living with her mother. However, she later returned to KPP because she missed her mother and needed her mother's help to care for her own child, who was born abroad. To describe the state of 'absence making the heart beat fonder', interviewees talked of attaching increasing value to their 'family orientation'. In other words, priorities changed with age. A particular type of unexpected return occurred when other family members made the decision for the interviewee. Agata's son persuaded Agata, as described previously. In addition, two interviewees reluctantly returned because their wives, whom they had persuaded to join them abroad, did not like it enough to stay. Other interviewees returned to Poland, or decided to stop circulating, when they were expecting a child – as also found by Kijonka and Żak (2020: 130). Return could also happen when, on visits back to KPP, the migrant had met a new partner, who wanted to continue living in KPP. Perhaps as result of Covid making the topic of mental health less taboo, several interviewees mentioned that their mental health had been a reason to return to Poland – to quote one of them, 'mental health is more important than money'. Other types of illness and health conditions, their own or their family members', also prompted return, either unexpectedly or supplementing other reasons.

With regard to structural factors, in three cases involuntary return linked to crisis in the construction industry in Ireland and Spain. This was only temporary in two cases, and in the third it coincided with having a small child and needing extended family support. Beata mentioned the lead-up to Brexit in the sense that attitudes towards Poles in the UK were souring (circa 2013); she lived in a small town which had recorded a number of hate incidents and which voted 'leave' in the referendum. No one else attributed their returns to Brexit, and one person, who had also been living in a rural area, flatly denied it. In Agata's and Zenon's cases Covid played a role. Zenon was furloughed, came back to KPP and then extended his stay for health reasons. When interviewed, he was toying with the idea of permanently returning to Poland. The rest from his job in England gave him mental space to sort out his priorities.

A handful of interviewees returned to Płock or Piła but at the time of interview were working or studying, usually part-time, in Warsaw or Poznań. For most, the reasons to return to KPP were also reasons not to 'return' to a bigger Polish city. Chapter 3 already mentioned the cases of individuals who defined themselves as 'not big-city people' or in various ways denied the advantages of bigger cities. The cost of living was also a big disincentive. As Dariusz put it, 'You wouldn't go there just to earn 2000 zl. like you might in Płock'. Several interviewees followed this line of reasoning, explaining that you would need to find a really special job to justify moving to a big city. A couple of interviewees expressed scepticism about the labour market all over Poland, including the large cities. Zenon described Poland as lacklustre (*szara*) and Wojciech stated, 'I don't believe in Poland. I've worked in different places in Poland, as a posted worker, and that was quite enough.' One interviewee tried living in Wrocław after returning from abroad, since her husband had found a job there, but decided they would prefer to live in KPP, partly for childcare reasons. For very many interviewees, in fact, the prime reason not to move to a big city seemed to be their family ties in KPP. Nonetheless, they could be more ambitious for their children. Jerzy, for example, was glad that his son had become a property developer in Warsaw, which he described as 'another class of city'.

Re-acculturation

The interviewees had returned over the period 2008–22. They could be positioned along a continuum of 'settledness'. There were some who seemed definitely settled, mostly members of the EU wave and swell. In other cases, return appeared somewhat provisional, though there were different degrees of likelihood of going abroad again. These ranged through 'I would if I could [but family considerations definitely prevent that]' to 'We might temporarily if the opportunity comes up' to 'I probably will, though temporarily' and, the least settled category, 'I will definitely go back abroad, but probably temporarily'. One person said they would go if they got divorced. Predictably, the poorer interviewees often seemed the most unsettled, like their small-town equivalents (White 2016b). As King (2000) points out, re-integration has both emic and etic aspects – it depends on the returnee, but also on the environment in which they find themselves, which has often changed in their absence. The re-integration process is partly a process of re-acculturation, which can involve culture shock.

Lech exemplified the positivity of the very recent returnee. He enthused:

> This is my home, and I feel free here, normal. I'd rather eat bread and lard here than bread and ham abroad ... I have a 2002 model car, it still goes ... I'll come back from work and it will be peaceful, no alcoholics ... I can return home, be on my own, get my fishing rod and go fishing ... Piła is the place for me, this is my home and my roots. Perhaps the outskirts, I like the countryside. If I could get to Piła by bike or car. No Poznań or Warsaw for me ... I like it here, that's how I am. There are forests everywhere. Piła is big, but not too big ... I feel I am master here in my own home (*czuję się panem u siebie*).

Lech's sense of local belonging, based on a (hunter-gatherer) bonding with nature, eased this early stage of re-integration. Often, however, it seems that after the initial euphoria the returnee begins to be assailed by doubt, and sometimes feels anxious and depressed. At this point, some ex-migrants return abroad. Several interviewees mentioned having been dismayed in the early days. Kinga, for example, with family and a good job in KPP, was pleased they returned. However, even she 'found it hard to adapt to the Polish mentality and unfriendliness and bad driving'. She commented that 'you get used to it'. Daniel, also returning to family and property in Poland, said that 'the return wasn't easy because we had good wages in Ireland, and here the salaries were so low, well, we had to laugh, it was so little. But we had to begin somewhere.' He also commented on their mental resilience acquired as a result of living abroad: 'People who have never left Poland are grim and pessimistic. But if you come back from abroad there is a residue of that positivity. They can take low wages in their stride. Although it does depend on the individual.' These stories are reminiscent of those reported by social remittances researchers such as Grabowska et al (2017: 117–22), showing how difficult it can be initially to get used to common patterns of behaviour in Poland which are viewed as different from behaviour encountered abroad.

It seems to happen quite commonly that migrants ease themselves back into the new environment by giving themselves time off after they return, to relax and look for new opportunities at their own pace. Since this appears to be socially acceptable behaviour, it could in fact be considered part of the migration culture. Feliks, for instance, said, 'I partied for six months and then looked for a job.' Alicja reported: 'When we came back to Poland we had the opportunity not to go straight to work but just to spend a bit of time at home. It didn't last too long, about a month, and then we found jobs. We regenerated ourselves and went to work.' Sometimes re-acculturation is eased by the fact that interviewees feel they are better people than before they migrated. Tomasz explained how he had taken heed of the bad example of other Polish migrants to turn over a new leaf:

> I've stopped drinking alcohol … And the fact that I'd lived abroad perhaps had some influence on that … They [middle-aged Polish foresters] only think about drinking, because what else can they do? They work, then just sit all evening, they're mostly blokes, they buy a bottle and sit and drink, they drink a lot with their friends, and say stupid stuff, and drink alcohol. So that definitely had some influence on me.

Grzymała-Kazłowska's (2016) concept of anchoring is helpful in understanding the case of Ewa, who seems to have had one of the most protracted re-acculturation experiences, partly because KPP was her husband's home city, not her own. Ewa was initially a stay-at-home mother, and in frail health. She was also dismayed by the cost of rented accommodation in Piła, which seemed comparable to prices in Poznań. However, when Ewa eventually found a job this constituted an anchor.

> I didn't know anyone or have any [extended] family. I just stayed at home with the children and if I simply had to go to some office to organise something I didn't know where to go. I even had a problem that I couldn't understand Polish money. I'd go into a shop and calculate the prices in euros. It lasted about a year, before I got used to life here, and I used to miss Ireland a lot … It was very tough, that first year. I would wonder whether it was a good idea that I came back instead of staying in Ireland. But what probably really helped me was that I managed to find work using my qualifications, and I'm very happy about that.

Not surprisingly, interviewees whose instincts told them to stay abroad, but who came back to please their partners, could have problems with re-integration. This illustrates how a household livelihood strategy – in this case a return migration strategy – can seem to be agreed by different members of the household, but is not really accepted by some. Edyta was a case in point. Her partner, a skilled manual worker, was based in KPP, and she returned from Germany after she met him because he wanted to stay in Poland. They also had a child soon after her return – her second. Hence Edyta's process of re-integration in Poland was strongly marked by her comparisons between the experiences of bringing up a small child in Germany and receiving plenty of state support, as a lone parent, with her parallel experiences of motherhood in Poland. She said, 'It was much better for me than it is here … To be honest, I'd be very glad to return to Germany … I really regret it. I left Germany for love … And my partner doesn't want to go [abroad]. No, no, no. He likes it here.'

Labour market re-integration

While recognising that infrastructure had improved in KPP (see Chapter 3), people who returned between 2008 and 2015, mostly from the EU wave, tended to be negative about the current labour market situation. This was despite the fact that Kalisz and Piła, as mentioned in Chapter 2, have little registered unemployment – below the Polish average. Interviewees were aware there was plenty of manual work. Justyna commented that:

> shopping centres have opened, they didn't exist before, but it's definitely not the best work, because the hours are very long. But there are definitely more workplaces. Big factories have opened or are being built so there will be more workplaces. Lots of people work in Ostrów, there is migration between Ostrów and Kalisz, and people in Ostrów also work in Kalisz, and there are big factories in the direction of Ostrów.

The problem was with white-collar work, both in terms of availability and perceived low wages. Mateusz, for example, stated that 'I think there is a particular problem with work for women in Płock. There isn't anywhere particularly for them to work. There is a shortage of office jobs.' Other Płock interviewees complained that the best jobs, at Orlen, were accessible only through contacts or even paying a bribe. The EU wave interviewees themselves had found jobs which were good by local standards, working mostly for local companies. Given that they did not want to move to a bigger city, they were prepared to moderate their ambitions. Unlike Karolak's (2020: 110) return migrant interviewees, some of whom lived in Wrocław and Warsaw, they did not seem much fixed on 'professional advancement'. Karol, for example, who had returned to Poland to do his university degree, did try living in Warsaw after graduation 'but somehow it didn't work out. And later I felt a bit too lazy, I rested on my laurels, so to speak ... I feel annoyed because there aren't many prospects in Płock. I could get a job with more responsibility, that would be easy, but it's hard to get a higher-paid job.'

Karolak (2020: 111) refers to an 'experience path'. A non-graduate job abroad, unconnected with a person's previous qualifications, turns into a passion developed back in Poland. Alicja's experiences fell into this category. As mentioned in Chapter 4, she was a target earner (with an unused technical qualification) who had migrated to Belgium at the same time as the EU swell were going to the UK and Ireland. On return to KPP she was prepared to work 'wherever there was a job and a wage' but eventually acquired a congenial job as a car salesperson. Her father was a lorry driver who had inspired her with an interest in cars, and Alicja had driven a delivery van in Belgium, so this could be seen as a continuation of her rather unusual career.

The remainder of this section considers examples of interviewees, target earners and EU swell, who had returned quite recently to KPP, since 2015. It considers the cases of people who had quite secure jobs, meaning that they were probably settled in KPP, before discussing those whose situation was more precarious. Two women, both with teaching degrees, were happily working as social workers, one of them having retrained after she returned from abroad. Several interviewees in different cities had found jobs in logistics companies. They were differently satisfied with these, partly because they offered different amounts of contact with English. Among the most satisfied was Anita, not a university graduate.

> When I returned [in 2016] I had no problems getting work [in a logistics company] ... It [the labour market] is much better than it was. But it depends what you do. If you have some qualification or talent. For instance, I have my English language, and that helps me earn a better salary ... If someone wants to work, they can get a job. Before, even those [manual] jobs weren't available. It's much better, but on the other hand you have to have some extra competences to earn more than the minimum wage ... If I hadn't gone abroad and got my English to such a high level I wouldn't be where I am today. I'd probably be earning the minimum wage and living from payday to payday. So my standard of living has definitely improved compared to before I went abroad.

Feliks, a graduate, also working in logistics, was more moderate in his appraisal. He was on his second job since returning, since the first company had folded.

> It's not exactly stunning, but it's OK ... I'd rather earn a bit less, but have work I enjoy. The atmosphere at work is really good and so are the boss and the whole team. That's important to me. After all, you spend a third of your life at work. So at the moment I'm not looking for another job.

Tomasz, also in logistics, had abandoned his dream of owning his own business, but was reconciled to his new job. His attitude had been that he needed 'to give it a go' (i.e. the same phrase I often heard about the migration motive). The salary could be higher, and he did not really like office jobs, but it was 'OK'. He had fun communicating with foreigners. The main thing was that he could spend time with his family. Life was not all about work. Daniel was an example of someone who had set up his own business upon return. He said he had returned with the attitude that 'I could become whatever I wanted'. His confidence was largely on the basis that with building skills he could always find work. He took a job in a local building supplies firm on the minimum wage, to get to know the building market and various companies currently operating in KPP, but he was rapidly promoted and although the firm later folded he was able to find another job as a sales advisor, and at the same time set up his own business in green energy.

At the 'less settled' end of the spectrum were women who had not managed to find satisfactory work in KPP and who were either strongly tempted or else actively planning to migrate again. Edyta, not a graduate, was an example of a woman who had taken on work in a shopping centre. This was better than her initial, very low-paid job in a bar. She liked her workmates and felt she had developed professionally. However, she complained of 'never seeing' her children, since she had to work until 6 pm every day, and she had had to give up being manager of the shop because she could not combine it with her domestic responsibilities. She was trying to find a job for a big company which was not located in a shopping centre. Jagoda, also manager of a shop in a shopping centre, complained, 'It's hard to find a job that you 100 per cent want to do. I've been working in trade for 10 years and there are moments when you feel really wrecked, you get tired of it. I looked twice for something calmer, more stable, perhaps an office job, but I couldn't find anything.' Karolina had tried but failed to use her teaching degree after returning to KPP in

2008. In her later career as a stay-at-home mother she also tried various business endeavours, but without success. Hence, she started doing seasonal work abroad every year. Her circular lifestyle was also enforced by her problems on the KPP labour market. She complained, 'It's not easy with work in KPP. There are jobs, but only for the minimum wage. There's more for men of course than women. And even if you can get an office job it pays barely above the minimum wage.' The case of Jolanta the ticket-seller has also been described.

It is sometimes possible to scale down transnational practices gradually, as I discovered in previous research and as seems to be common with migrants of other nationalities (Carling and Erdal 2014). Hence one livelihood strategy for mitigating low-paid work after the initial return to Poland is to keep connections with the employer abroad and make use of this gateway to migrate again on short working trips. Janusz and even Tomasz, who so hated Sweden, had done precisely this. Zenon, who had been furloughed from his job in England and thought he might stay in Poland for good, was beginning to waver and reconsider at least a temporary return to the UK. It was so hard to find a job in KPP with what he considered to be a normal wage. Even Lech, despite his enthusiasm about returning to Piła, was toying with the idea. Out of all the interviewees, Lech was the only one prepared to take a factory job. He was quoted in Chapter 4 as hankering after a quiet job making lightbulbs rather than dealing with pigs and chickens abroad. When interviewed, despite being 50 years old, he was holding offers from four factories in Piła, and trying to decide between them. However, for all his brave talk about eating bread and lard in Poland rather than bread and ham in Holland, he already seemed anxious about working for the minimum Polish wage. He was wondering whether it might be possible to combine working in a factory in Poland with short trips abroad to earn extra money.

Conclusions

From the interviewees' accounts as well as conversations with other local people, it seemed that Polish return migration to KPP was unpredictable, based on individual personal motivations, and could not be depended upon to constitute a significant component of Poland's migration transition. Even if big cities were beginning to attract more return migration because of structural factors – improvements on the local labour market – this was not (yet) true of KPP. Interviewees tended to work in small private companies or in the state sector, for instance as teachers and social workers. They mostly seemed quite satisfied with their jobs, while sometimes recognising that they could have been more ambitious if they had moved to a bigger city. Other interviewees, especially women, complained about the difficulty of finding suitable work and about low wages, particularly in shopping centres.

The chapter also illustrated that 'return' should not be assumed to be permanent. Returnees to KPP who found themselves in precarious employment or self-employment often seemed tempted to migrate again, an act which would enhance KPP's reputations as 'cities of emigration'. The interviewees could be placed along a continuum according to how settled they seemed to be in KPP. Factors influencing their positioning on this continuum included, for example, whether they had returned of their own volition or whether the decision had belonged to another family member. They were differently anchored in KPP according to their family status. Those whose children were minors were particularly likely to mention their expectation of staying in KPP, because of smaller-city lifestyle attractions for families. On the other hand, single people and parents of adult children sometimes envisaged or definitely planned to continue their mobile livelihoods.

Notes

1 *Wielkie i małe powroty z UK i innych zakątków do PL*. In October 2023 the group had 61,000 members.
2 Only two interviewees returned because they had been offered work contracts in Poland.

6
Polish reflections on migration to Poland

Introduction

Chapter 6 discusses how the interviewees in Kalisz, Piła and Płock talked about recent migration to those cities. The first part considers the visibility of foreigners in KPP, and interviewees' comments on when and where they encountered them. The second part examines the parallels Poles drew between their own and other nationalities' migration, and opinions about migration in general. Since the book analyses Poland's transition to migrant receiving country status 'from the bottom up' it is helpful to understand the views of ordinary residents, and particularly to appreciate how they were becoming used to this change in local society. Given that the interviewees in question had a special fund of migration knowledge and expertise, they might serve as representatives of those sections of smaller-city society whose personal migration histories could influence their socialisation into 'receiving society' identity. As mentioned in Chapter 1, for these return and circular migrants, migrants to Poland are both 'them' but – at least in some cases – also 'us'. Moreover, in addition to the pool of return and circular migrants living in each city, there were many other residents who had vicarious migration experience. Like Mariola and Jadwiga, the migrants' mothers in my sample, they had their own views about migration and migrants which they had picked up through visiting and being in contact with friends and family abroad.

Chapters 4–5 have already outlined some aspects of this migration knowledge and expertise, which, taken together, could be labelled 'migration culture'. For instance, it seems that many of this group of Polish returnees were suspicious about employment agencies which recruited Poles to work abroad. They were sympathetic to tales of exploitation of migrants by agencies and they appreciated that migrants might prefer to use their informal networks. Chapter 4 also described cases of discursive hostility towards Poles abroad, as well as, more rarely, cases where interviewees personally had unpleasant experiences with other Polish migrants. They expressed regret that, unlike other nations, Poles did not display solidarity towards other Poles abroad. Poles also had extensive experience of how families were affected by migration, and they could understand why parents would want to bring their children with them – although they also knew how difficult this could be in practice.

On the other hand, Polish migrants are a varied population. In some countries, such as the UK, it makes sense to think of Poles as constituting a kind of microcosm of society in Poland (White 2018c). Hence, as discussed in Chapter 4 with reference to interviewees' opinions about diversity abroad, they displayed a range of attitudes towards migration by non-Poles and dispositions towards openness or the reverse. To some extent this links to socio-demographic characteristics. Many studies, in Poland as elsewhere, have found that higher education, wealth and youth are correlated with greater openness to others (Gołębiowska 2014). However, as qualitative research shows, sometimes this apparent cosmopolitanism can be rather superficial. It seemingly rests on an acceptance that diversity is a normal phenomenon, but not does extend to the speaker being able to think themselves into the shoes of others, or avoid making poorly-founded generalisations about national character or 'mentality' (White 2018a: 179–80). Making a similar distinction, Grzymała-Kazłowska (2021: 246) follows Walzer (1999) in writing about 'passive tolerance'. Conversely, some migrants do display deep cosmopolitanism (or active tolerance). They learn empathy through the process of migrating and can genuinely understand the worldview of migrants from other countries. Moreover, they are not always the people with the highest level of education (Garapich 2016b: 255–7; White 2018a). Chapter 4 presented the examples of Jan and Tomasz forming friendships and acquaintances with Muslims. If they lived abroad for several years, Poles were also conscious of how the ethnic composition of societies could change over time: for instance, as Romanians arrived in increasing numbers in the UK and began to rival the Polish population in size.

As members of the receiving society, Poles who had returned to live in Poland were also subject to the same influences as members of receiving societies everywhere. Chapter 4 mentioned Allport's (1954) contact hypothesis, in accordance with which sustained contact with others, on an equal basis, helps break down barriers and promotes openness and understanding. Similarly, Ager and Strang (2008) emphasise the importance for migrants of social links with the receiving population. These links are often assumed by scholars to be primarily instrumental, 'bridging links', but they can also be links of bonding and friendship. Similarly, and as already illustrated with reference to the Polish interviewees' own careers as migrants, the place attachment literature shows that social ties are of great importance for making migrants feel at home. At a minimum, these can be just nodding acquaintances, but ideally they should be more substantial 'integrative encounters' (Mayblin et al 2016). These can help members of the receiving society learn to take an active role in making their new country of immigration a place where migrants want to settle.

One aspect of receiving societies is that they are characterised by ethnic hierarchies, as is all too evident in countries such as the USA and UK today. Some ethnic groups have more power and status in the receiving countries, and some groups of migrants are more welcome than others.[1] Ford (2011: 1018–9) writes that 'A long line of research on ethnic identity … has shown that there are systematic patterns of preference between ethnic groups in diverse societies. These "ethnic hierarchies" are based on proximity to the majority or dominant group, which is inevitably at the top of the hierarchy'. In fact, as already shown, Polish former migrants do not necessarily rate Poles as superior to other nations. The interesting question is how the 'systematic patterns of preference' arise. One could assume that when a country first acquires a receiving country identity it also acquires ethnic hierarchies, and that whenever a new group of migrants arrives it is allocated a place in the hierarchy. Racial and orientalising stereotypes combine with perceptions of the types of work which migrants do to help determine where they are placed in the hierarchy. It seems to be commonplace, for example, for perceived 'low-skilled' migrants, such as 'East Europeans' in the UK, to be placed lower on the hierarchy (Bulat 2019). Koppel and Jakobson (2023) suggest that migrant hierarchies, at least in populist rhetoric, are based on the idea that some migrants are more moral than others. Hence, for example, refugees might be regarded as more deserving than labour migrants, or vice versa – as seems often to be the case in Poland.

Although ethnic hierarchies are normally studied in the context of social cohesion in receiving societies, no doubt all societies, sending ones included, produce their own ethnic hierarchies. This is illustrated in Poland by CBOS opinion polls over many years about positive and negative attitudes towards various 'peoples' (*narody*). CBOS data to some extent reflects views about settled minorities within Poland, notably Roma (always near the bottom of the hierarchy) and Jews (improving their position over recent years). With regard to peoples living outside

Poland, the data shows a consistent preference for Americans and citizens of West European countries, with 'Arabs' – a catchall term for Muslims from the Middle East and North Africa – regularly at the bottom. After 2015, when the Law and Justice party stoked up hostility towards Syrians, refugees became unwelcome among a large section of the Polish population, though by no means all (Jaskulowski 2019). Right-wing politicians fan Islamophobia and intensify negativity towards 'Arabs'. However, in 2023 Russians replaced Arabs to become the most disliked group. It is unknowable whether respondents are thinking of ordinary citizens or governments when they answer the survey questions. For example, the worsening of attitudes towards 'Belarusians' in 2022–3 could result from hostility to the Lukashenka regime and its support for Putin's war on Ukraine. Ukrainians occupy a place in the middle, although attitudes have improved over time, particularly in response to the Orange Revolution, annexation of Crimea and full-scale invasion. By 2023, 51 per cent of Poles liked Ukrainians and only 17 per cent disliked them (Omyła-Rudzka 2023: 4–5). Considering that Ukrainians and Poles massacred one another in the Second World War, and that many Poles believe the Ukrainians were the sole perpetrators, there is strong potential for negativity towards Ukrainians. Ukrainians' drop in popularity in 2018–9 can be at least partly attributed to the fact that Polish nationalists had been reviving public consciousness of the events of 1943.[2]

The CBOS data shows that, despite being a sending country, Poland already possessed ethnic hierarchies. This raises questions about how, if at all, the construction of hierarchies changed as the result of the transition to receiving country status, when migrants rather than ethnic or national minorities become the most important 'others'. Overall improvement in attitudes towards Ukrainians since the 1990s, and especially since 2018, suggests that perhaps familiarity with Ukrainians in Poland was helping

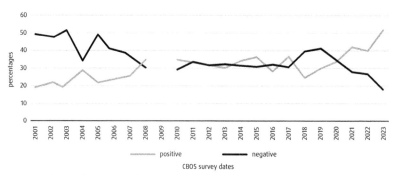

Figure 6.1 Polish attitudes towards Ukrainians, 2001–23 (CBOS)
Data source: Omyła-Rudzka (2023: 4-5) (data missing for 2009)

to induce friendlier attitudes. However, this could be explained by a more general positivity towards labour migration. CBOS conducted surveys between 1992 and 2019 about attitudes towards labour migration which showed that attitudes had become considerably more positive. In 1992, only 9 per cent of respondents stated that foreigners should be able to work freely in Poland, while 39 per cent said that they should have open access to certain jobs. In 2019, 62 per cent of Poles (and over 50 per cent of all social groups) asserted that foreigners should be able to work freely in Poland, with 29 per cent advocating restricted access (Bożewicz and Głowacki 2020: 5). Labour migrants were therefore placed 'above' refugees in terms of acceptability. No doubt some of this approval is based on an instrumental attitude towards labour migration, which is seen as necessary for the Polish economy: a view argued for example by Buchowski (2020). That would be a typical 'receiving society' attitude in the early stages of the migration transition, as mentioned in Chapter 1. However, the evidence from KPP discussed below suggests that positivity towards labour migrants is also founded in a more general, sending-country positivity towards labour migration.

As discussed in Chapter 1, the rapid increase in migration to Poland can be explained largely by employers' perceptions that they need migrant labour. Employers, and the recruitment agencies associated with them, can operate in accordance with their own hierarchies. Friberg and Midtbøen (2018), writing about 'immigrant employment hierarchies', describe how Norwegian employers view the most newly-arrived migrant groups as better than others, because they appear to possess ideal soft skills, such as tractability. Since employers do not want to spend time investigating the suitability of individual employees, they use national identity as a 'shorthand', in the Norwegian case for instance 'Pole = model labourer'. Over time, however, as new migrants settle and become reluctant to accept exploitation, employers revise their opinions in favour of even newer arrivals. Friberg and Midtbøen (2018: 1476) observe that 'the content of group stereotypes change over time as existing groups change behaviour and new groups enter'.

Chapter 4 illustrated that some Poles who have had contact with foreigners through migration become less prejudiced, and disregard common stereotypes about those nationalities, in line with contact hypothesis. Another possibility is that some groups of society and types of migrant and former migrant – particularly manual workers – view migration neutrally, without ethnicisation, rather like neoclassical migration theorists. Their vision is flat, not hierarchical. This was the attitude I usually encountered in small Polish towns which I had previously researched (White 2017). Local people know from the Polish experience that everyone who needs to do so will go to work abroad if they can, and they are not judgmental about this, even if the migrants they describe are from other national groups. As discussed in Chapter 1, this is not necessarily the same as empathy, the capacity to imagine oneself in the shoes of someone else, although it can be the same. No doubt it is relatively easy for Poles to imagine themselves in the shoes of Ukrainian migrants because they are proximate in various respects: they are white, usually speak some Polish and are often encountered in Poland. However, it is also their labour migrant identities which are important. In addition, as my research showed, it was sometimes their identities specifically as members of a wave of labour migrants which appealed to the imagination of my interviewees, because they could connect these features with their own lives abroad.

Visibility and scale of migration

Chapters 11–12 consider the impact of (in)visibility on the experiences of migrants living in KPP. This section of Chapter 6 considers how much, if at all, Poles in KPP noticed that their cities were becoming 'cities of immigration', and discusses why migrants were more visible to some Poles than to others. An interviewee's husband in a white-collar job observed:

> In all my 37 years in Płock, and I was born here and worked here all my life, I've met barely any foreigners, whether working here or just passing through. I even don't see the Ukrainians. They are somewhere, I don't know, in factories or shops, but I don't meet them.

He was expressing his sense that foreigners might be invisible in KPP to people like himself. Several interviewees had heard specifically that Ukrainians worked in local factories, but since they did not go to factories they did not see them at work. Dawid, for example, who had worked on building sites in Piła, had never met any Ukrainian workers there, but associated them with the 'big factories'. Karolina said:

> It's mainly Ukrainians, a few work in kebab bars, as far as I know, perhaps they are Turks, I don't know exactly what nationality … Now there's the war a lot of people have suddenly arrived. It didn't use to be like that. Just individual people. Perhaps Piła simply wasn't a very attractive place for them. But once upon a time you did hear that they were working in the bigger factories.

'Visibility' is a term often used by migration researchers with reference to undocumented migrants, but all migrants – like all social groups – are differently visible to different groups within society. A Ukrainian factory worker in Poland may be visible to other local Ukrainians within their own networks, or to fellow factory-workers and other acquaintances of other nationalities, but not to other Poles. In the smaller city of Pabianice, for example, a survey of 250 Poles in 2018 found that it was the factory workers who personally knew Ukrainians and other foreigners (Jakóbczyk-Gryszkiewicz 2020: 78). In public places, Poles do not always notice Ukrainians, unless they wear their working clothes, or look lost, or speak Ukrainian. Ukrainian women with pushchairs around stations and reception points were also very noticeable in the weeks after the full-scale invasion of Ukraine in Feburary 2022. Conversely, because these smaller cities are overwhelmingly white, Black, Asian and other people who do not outwardly resemble stereotypical Poles are conspicuous in public places.

Wherever they live in Poland, Poles are familiar with certain media images of migrants, so they have an idea of what a migrant should look like. Bielecka-Prus (2020: 195), for example, shows how some categories of migrant are present in the Polish media and others are not. The article, published in 2020, before the 2022 refugee influx, claims that 'nothing is written about students and refugees, nor is there anything about highly-skilled migrants working in their professions' (Bielecka-Prus 2020: 195). Overall, Bielecka-Prus suggests that the stereotypical Ukrainian female migrant, after 2009, was a university graduate working in a menial job and subject to exploitation by Polish employers. Obviously the Poles interviewed in Spring 2022 had also been exposed to media coverage of Ukrainian refugees, including negative stories circulating on social media, probably partly because of Russian trolling. In any case, certain images of what types of Ukrainian prevailed in Poland were present in their imaginations. Similarly, certain preconceptions exist about other foreigners and people of migrant heritage. For instance, many Poles would expect to find Chinese and Vietnamese people in the big cities and also in Wólka Kosowska, a giant wholesale goods centre and village described by Brzozowska and Postuła (2022: 93) as 'the Asian town in Poland'. However, they might not be aware of how widely spread they are across the whole of Poland.

Grzymała-Kazłowska (2021: 250), in a study of Polish attitudes towards ethnic diversity, found that 'growing ethnic diversity … remains rather underestimated in Poland'. Instead, her interviews revealed:

a prevailing vision of the contemporary Polish nation as homogeneous … The lasting self-image of a highly homogenous Polish society, which is striking in the context of recent migration to the country, can be illustrated by the following comment of one of the participants: 'The trouble with Poland is that we have very few foreigners' (IDI 11). Although the same participant subsequently noted the current high numbers of migrants he highlighted the temporariness of this phenomenon: 'There are a lot of Ukrainians at the moment …' (IDI 11)

Similarly, Karol told me 'I'm always surprised when I hear of foreigners in Płock. What fate brings them here?' Many KPP informants seemed to visualise their home city as more or less homogeneously Polish. Most often, they downplayed immigration to KPP, while at the same time acknowledging the scale of migration to big cities in Poland, in order to point the contrast with KPP. Dariusz, for instance, said, 'I haven't noticed them. In Warsaw there are a lot. In taxis and Ubers, or in catering. In Płock I haven't noticed them even in outlets which sell foreign food.' Justyna similarly asserted, 'In big cities there are more of those foreigners than in Kalisz, for example. I'm always curious about how they found themselves in Kalisz.' Regarding Piła, Ewa said that 'I think that Poznań, being a bigger city, is more international than our modest little Piła'. Interviewees justified their comparisons by referring to the soundscape of the big city. For instance, Feliks said, 'You hear various languages spoken in the big cities, especially Warsaw.' It was perhaps noteworthy that interviewees relied on their ears and did not mention the linguistic landscape, a fact which is less surprising if one takes into account that there was very little signage in foreign languages in Poland before February 2022 (Levchuk 2021).

When I asked Polish interviewees or Polish people I met around KPP whether there were many foreigners living in the city, other than Ukrainians, they usually could only think of one or two examples of actual individuals: a half-Polish child in the school where they worked (who might have a Polish name and be almost unidentifiable as a migrant), an engineer or a handful of non-Polish looking people working in kebab shops and other food outlets. These people were sometimes identified as Albanian or Indian, or described as being from an unknown country, although it seems likely that many were Bangladeshi (see Chapter 12). In Kalisz and Piła, several interviewees mentioned Romanians and/or Bulgarians trading at the open-air markets, although I also heard (from an Armenian) that in Kalisz there were some long-established Armenian market traders, so potentially there was also some confusion of nationalities here.

Some interviewees voiced the belief that, as had happened in Western countries, immigrants would eventually spread throughout Poland. Mateusz, for instance, expressed this sense of impending migration transition when he commented in 2019: 'There still aren't a lot, though probably they are to be found on building sites. So far you don't find them in restaurants or cafes. There aren't that many Ukrainians in Płock.' Displaying his migration knowledge, with a reference to 'normal' patterns, Jan too referred to how immigrants would spread throughout Poland:

> There are probably many more in Warsaw because there's more work and higher wages. Like Poles at first went mostly to London and only later to other towns. I think for the moment there are more in Warsaw and other big cities like Wrocław and Kraków, but they will spread. That would be the normal pattern.

However, when they spoke about 'foreigners', the interviewees may have sometimes mentally excluded Ukrainians from that label. For instance, Justyna, quoted above, also said: 'Definitely there are more and more Ukrainians. You can hear them on the street.' Visibility exists on a spectrum, with some foreigners more visible than others. Degree of visibility obviously relates to their numbers and physical appearance, but perceptions that they are visible also link to how much Poles are expecting them to be present. As illustrated in Chapter 12, Poles can often assume that a foreigner is Ukrainian, but be mistaken.

Just a handful of interviewees asserted that there were 'lots' of foreigners now in KPP. In some cases, these were people who encountered them in their everyday lives. Ewa, for instance, said that she had been attending a fitness club in Piła and there had been 'quite a lot' of Ukrainian women in her group, taking advantage of a membership deal organised for them by their factory. Jagoda said in 2019:

> I work in a shopping centre and so you can see there are a lot of Ukrainians [at the tills] … And a great variety of nationalities come to my shop. It's surprising. Płock is a tourist city, so there are lots of foreign visitors. But many foreigners settle here as well. They get married. I have some regular clients where the husband is Italian, and they live in Płock, and someone of some English-speaking nationality, and the husband is dark-skinned, I have a Russian, I don't know if he's from Russia or Ukraine, I can't completely understand the language.

In contrast to these accounts, where Ewa and Jagoda seemingly had conversations with foreigners, other interviewees mentioned noticing Ukrainians while they were out and about. Barbara said about Płock: 'You can tell them [only] by their accent. At petrol stations, in Auschan, in security.' Jadwiga also said with reference to Płock that 'many work in shops, for example in Mila [supermarket], at the checkout. You can hear them. They speak Polish, but the accent is completely different.' Janusz (in 2021) also referred to hearing the Ukrainian language in shops in Kalisz. 'You can notice the Ukrainians, because there are plenty of them. Mostly you meet them in the shops ... On the street you'd be unlikely to notice them, but in the shop where somebody is buying stuff and speaking Ukrainian then you do notice.' Zenon claimed that it was possible to spot Ukrainians by their appearance. 'They stick out. They usually go round in small groups. I can't say exactly how I recognise them ... It's more about their behaviour [than their clothes]. Poles are quite inhibited in public places, but compared with Ukrainians we are relaxed. They behave stiffly, compared to us.'

Janusz explained the extent of his expertise precisely:

> If I see a student from a foreign country, well, let's put it like this, when I was in Ireland there were lots of people from a wide range of countries. I met people from Portugal, Spain, Italy. And for example if I met a Spaniard or an Italian in Kalisz I would know they were Spanish or Italian. By their accent, sometimes by their appearance. But in other cases you can only tell someone is a foreigner by their skin colour, although not to be racist (*nie żeby być rasistą albo coś*). But that's the only way of spotting a foreigner from a distance. In other cases, without talking to someone, I wouldn't be able to identify them. As I say, if I had a conversation with a Spanish person I'd identify them at once.

It was noteworthy that Janusz was uncomfortable with the thought of staring at someone because they were black: a form of racism which black people in Poland do encounter. Also significant here is Janusz's assumption that a black person was necessarily a foreigner, rather than potentially a Polish citizen and/or a Pole with a black parent – an assumption which according to Balogun and Joseph-Salisbury (2021) is widespread in Poland. On the other hand, Feliks acknowledged that Poles were not always white: 'I think the only ethnic community in Kalisz is Vietnamese. But most of them, I'm not sure, but I think they've been here roughly since the early 1990s. So there's already a generation who were born here and are Polish. Otherwise, Kalisz is pretty homogeneous, mainly Poles and Ukrainians.'

Interviewees also reported their own small interactions with foreigners. Agata for instance told me that she had helped a Ukrainian in McDonald's who was struggling with Polish and English. Lech (aged 50) said, 'I know Russian too, I had it in school. I don't know everything, but if I meet a Ukrainian then I can have a normal conversation with them in Russian.' Krystyna told me about a Ukrainian who worked in a local shop. 'I know from her accent, she speaks Polish beautifully, but she has an accent. So I said, "I suppose you are from Ukraine? Are you homesick?" She says, "I've been here for ages." She's not so homesick any more, and her boyfriend is here.' Here Krystyna seemingly displayed the common assumption, in societies not very used to the presence of migrants, that foreigners must also be newcomers. On the other hand, perhaps Krystyna's own migration experience prompted her question about feeling homesick. A small handful of interviewees knew Ukrainians personally. For instance, Feliks in his previous job used to work with about 50 Ukrainian drivers in a managerial capacity. He pointed out that back then, about 2018, only a couple of them wanted to invite their families, and the rest were just temporary workers. Krystyna, as the senior resident in her block of flats, acted as a warden, for example assisting with replacement keys. Hence, she interacted with Ukrainians living in the same building. She also let a flat to a Ukrainian couple, whom she visited once a month. She said she would ask how they were getting on and commiserate (pre-February 2022) about the war. That was the extent of her contact; as she said, 'You shouldn't poke your nose into other people's lives.' A couple of interviewees had also learned some Ukrainian language. Feliks said that 'since we had lots of Ukrainian drivers I needed to be sure that they knew and understood everything'. Edyta, speaking to me after the full-scale invasion, said that she and her fellow sales assistants had learned some Ukrainian words to be able to communicate with refugees.

Interviewees also had acquaintances from other countries, but usually just one, rather than 50. These were children at school, spouses of friends, a neighbouring doctor, regular customers and in one case a tenant. Countries mentioned included Egypt, Turkey, India, France and Cuba; interviewees also referred to unspecified 'black' and 'African' acquaintances. Some interviewees talked about their Polish friends who employed Ukrainians, typically on farms or building sites, but also in a warehouse in Kalisz. One person in Płock had a friend with his own building company who said he found it hard to attract Polish workers. Hence he employed many Ukrainians. However, he was not impressed with most, saying they were lazy and demanded 'lots of money'. In addition, now Ukrainians were able to work in Germany they were departing from Poland. Janusz told a similar tale about a relative who initially employed Polish builders, but found them unreliable.

> One day they'd show up to work, one day not, one day he was expecting five and only three came. So he started to employ Ukrainians and he was very satisfied because they came as expected and worked and everything was good. But after two or three years those Ukrainians started to leave. They found other jobs, very often as lorry-drivers. Because of the money.

This is an illustration of the phenomenon mentioned in the chapter Introduction, whereby employers adjust their mental ethnic hierarchies, becoming disenchanted with one nationality after another as they settle down, become less exploitable, and seem to need to be replaced with newer and cheaper workers.

Attitudes towards migrants and migration

KPP interviewees seemed to view Ukrainians not as a cultural threat or through the prism of historical conflict, but as normal labour migrants, no better or worse than Poles who engaged in the same types of work abroad. However, just as Poles could sometimes self-orientalise (seeing Western Europe as 'better' than Poland) so they could also display a patronising attitude towards people from Ukraine and other countries of the former Soviet Union, who were allotted a lower place because of their countries' economic inferiority to Poland. Grzymała-Kazłowska and Brzozowska (2017: 118) also conclude that in their sample, overall, Ukrainian 'migrants were constructed as ... rather inferior'.

When presenting their views about immigration to Poland, most of my research participants were basing their statements on direct migration experience and expertise. For example, in a conversation about Ukrainians with Polish Cards, Zenon challenged my suggestion that such Ukrainians necessarily had Polish roots. He backed up his point by referencing what he had heard or witnessed about Romanians when living in the UK. 'In Ukraine you can buy a Polish Card. It's like in England, where some Romanians buy their driving licences.' Similarly, remarking on Ukrainian family reunification in Poland, Aneta drew parallels with the migration transition in Ireland. 'There are lots of Ukrainians in Płock – you see them doing their shopping. First it was men, and now I see women and children. It was like when I was in Ireland, that's how it goes'. Alicja's explanation was in effect an exposition of dual labour market theory.

> We didn't use to have so many of those factories around Kalisz. There were fewer, and [Polish] people worked where they could. But now there are more and more factories. The companies are growing, employing more and more people, so the situation has changed. There's a tendency for local people to look for something better, higher status and better work. So those typical manual jobs are normally done by people who come to Poland from other countries … Ukraine is the nearest country to Poland. Germans are unlikely to come, because there is always a trend for people to migrate from poorer countries [to richer ones].

Interviewees pointed out numerous parallels between Poles and Ukrainians. To some extent these were simply illustrations of the 'principle' that people naturally migrated to places where they could earn more. Anita said, 'If someone, for example, grows tomatoes or apples, people will come from Ukraine, like we went from Poland to England. In Poland they earn three times what they could in Ukraine. It's on exactly the same principle.' Jolanta also mentioned:

> [My friend's son] used to worry in Poland about whether he'd have food to put on the table. But he says to me that when he works abroad his only worry is what kind of car he should buy himself. That's the difference between earning money in Poland and anywhere else … On the other hand, a Russian or Ukrainian or Belarusian has bigger earnings in Poland than at home.

They also drew parallels about the scale of migration. Feliks, for instance, stated: 'They come from Ukraine just as we used to do. At one time there was a big wave of migration from Poland, and in the same way now we have people coming here.' Zenon said, 'It will be like England 20 years ago,' although he also thought that the Ukrainian wave was even bigger than the Polish one. Mateusz, thinking back to his problems finding work in Poland after graduation, suggested 'they are having a hard time at the moment, because their economy is in trouble as a result of the war, and they are going through what we experienced 12–15 years ago. They are at that stage. They graduate from university but there is nowhere for them to work in their own country.'

The idea that Ukraine is at one stage of development and that Poland is at another is reminiscent of migration transition theory. Jan, a musician rather than a demographer, provided the most thought-out analysis of Poland's current transition, drawing on his knowledge of Polish migration to the UK. His remarks about migrants spreading out to new destinations were quoted in the previous section. Jan had been part of the EU swell, and since coming back to live in Poland in 2018 had returned for visits to perform in the UK. This ongoing transnational livelihood gave him particular insight into both countries. He said:

> I've noticed that in every state, when it reaches a certain level of economic development, it attracts foreigners. For example, at one time in England Poles were coming to do those simple manual jobs. And now it's the same in Poland … And I think that Poles have the same attitude towards Ukrainians that English people once had towards Poles. Ukrainians come and do the lowest-level jobs, the ones Poles don't want to do. There's plenty of work, but Poles don't want to work for such low wages. It was the same in the UK. British people didn't want to work for that money, but Poles were happy to take the jobs. It's the same here and that's why you can see a bit of, I think, a bit of a patronising attitude. But they'll settle in Poland like Poles did in the UK and those differences will fade, like they have with Poles in England. I think they are gradually disappearing in England.

Anne: So how will it happen? Will Ukrainians learn to speak very good Polish?

> Jan: Not all of them. For example I know Poles who've been in the UK 12 years and don't know the language. You can live in England without knowing the language and I think it will be the same in Poland. There'll be so many people that in some workplaces things will be written in Ukrainian, and there will be Ukrainian shops.

Jan's was the most comprehensive and coherent account, but other interviewees also picked up on similar parallels, particularly about wage differentials and job vacancies as pull factors. For instance, Karol observed, 'At that time there was a great demand for labour in the UK. For that kind of work I did. Now in Poland it's the same, and Ukrainians come to Poland.'

Several interviewees took a moral stance on such behaviour, expressing their approval. Poles and Ukrainians migrated not just in accordance with some law of migration, but because they had a right to migrate. This was perhaps unexpected, considering that Poles, as EU citizens, actually have more rights than Ukrainians, but my informants were not making a point about legal status. It was more that, having been migrants, they were convinced that migration was normal and acceptable human behaviour. Jolanta, for example, stated, 'My view is that you have to understand why a person came. Like Ukrainians, Belarusians, they come to us because they can earn more money.' Jerzy said that 'everyone has the right [to work abroad] and I don't mind it at all.' Andrzej commented, 'I understand and respect that. We [probably meaning his own family] also used to go abroad, to Germany, to England.' Similarly, Justyna asserted, 'I don't have any problem with it at all. Perhaps because I took advantage of the opportunities in another country and went there to earn money. I was helped by another state and I don't see why they shouldn't come here, if things are worse in their own country, if they shouldn't come and improve their finances by working in a different country, like Poland.'

Nonetheless, a few other interviewees appeared to be applying double standards and displaying their ethnic hierarchies. It was notable that a couple of interviewees who also made racist comments about black people and Muslims in countries abroad were ready to state that they understood the motives of Ukrainians coming to Poland. For example, one person said that Ukrainians migrated 'on the same principles as Poles' but also (separately) expressed her objection to Muslims who seemed to make themselves too much at home in Oslo and by implication did not have a right to be there.

> On the street there are lots of Muslim women in headscarves. When I first went, we were walking along and I said, 'I can't see any Norwegians!' It's just Muslims or black people ... Especially in the subway, there's nobody else. They are quite relaxed, and pushy ... They want you to make way. One Muslim woman will be with five or six children.

Her comments, though shocking, are in line with findings by other researchers (for example Gawlewicz 2015 and Nowicka 2019) as well as some of my own. Another interviewee, who had an Indian tenant in KPP, was positive about Indians coming to work in Poland as engineers and commented: 'They somehow assimilate. Don't force other people to be like them.' The same person made hostile remarks about Muslims in the UK.

Many interviewees had specific points to make about how migrants work. For instance, Zenon commented on typical migrant jobs, asserting of Ukrainians that 'they work like Poles in England in warehouses, factories or hotels'. Dariusz said: 'hermetically [sealed] places where you [i.e. most members of the receiving society] wouldn't go. They work on the same principle – just like in England, I worked in warehouses – or shut up in factories.' Ukrainians were said to work hard. For instance, Daniel said he would be happy to employ Ukrainians because 'they work hard. Like we Poles when we are abroad, we do a good job, and I know they also try hard'. Krystyna suggested:

> When they want to earn more money, just like Polish construction workers abroad, they work twelve hours a day instead of eight. And they happily go to work on Saturday and Sunday. Because they need the money … It's like us in the West. I work [long hours as a carer] for so little money that no German woman would ever even consider it.

Although some interviewees, like Krystyna, stressed that migrants were prone to exploit themselves, others highlighted how they were exploited. Edyta, for instance, claimed that it was 'well-known that we don't pay Ukrainians the same rates just the same as we weren't paid the same' (as agency workers in Germany). Tomasz portrayed the situation in Kalisz:

> They've started working in places – like me in Sweden – where Poles don't always want to work. We don't want to work in a factory for 2000 zloties and do some boring factory job for eight hours or something. We have lots of factories around Kalisz, big ones. There are factories supplying IKEA, Komforty, that's a very big factory, and Winiary Nestlé and Kaliszanka [confectionery], and all those. There are lots and lots of factories where Ukrainians come to work. And Poles make money out of them. There are plenty of agencies which exploit them. As far as I know, people also make money out of renting them accommodation, that's what happens, isn't it? And add to that all the tomato farms, and horticulture in general, where not many Poles want to work. It's really heavy work, it's hot in the greenhouses.

Other interviewees pointed out that because Ukrainians will work for lower wages, some Poles say they are driving down wages and/or 'stealing' jobs. For instance, Beata mentioned, 'Some [British people in her small town in England] thought Poles were stealing jobs. People are different, aren't they. Some are nice, and some not so nice. It's the same with Poles. People come from Ukraine and lots of Poles say they are taking jobs.' Several interviewees asserted that this claim was false because – as Tomasz mentioned in the above quotation – members of the receiving country disdained the worst manual jobs. Sylwia spluttered:

> Poles don't want to work at supermarket checkouts [in Poland] because the pay is too low … At one point [in Berlin] I was living in a house with a man called Ernst and he told me 'You come and steal our jobs'. I said, 'Don't complain – you don't want to do that work. And there are plenty of vacancies.' It's the same with Poles who complain there's no work. I say, 'I'll show you.' Off we go. Every second shop has a sign saying they need a sales assistant. But they say, 'And how am I expected to work for a wage like that?'

Justyna similarly observed that 'I don't have the feeling that they are stealing our jobs. Because they often work in sectors and for wages that no Pole would accept.'

On the other hand, Jagoda, who, as described in Chapter 4, had had a negative experience of working with Poles abroad, implied that foreigners did in fact drive down wages. However, it was noteworthy that she seemed not to be speaking from direct experience, but rather from hearsay. She said that 'it's like when we went abroad, we accept lower wages, it's well known [*wiadomo*], everyone complains about us – and it's the same here, isn't it?'.

Several interviewees asserted that racism and hostility existed equally in Poland and abroad. Jolanta, for instance, told a story about her friend's experience while they were working in the Netherlands.

> She was on the street where she lived … and someone told her to cross to the other side because she was a Pole. They said, 'You should be over there.' Well, what do you think of that, you do find unpleasant types, don't you (*rozni są, nie*)? In Poland various stuff happens as well. [Slightly lowering her voice] They don't like Turks. Lots of [bad] things happen.

Some stories were about micro-aggressions, even perhaps imagined micro-aggressions deriving from self-consciousness about speaking a foreign language and a sense of being conspicuous as labour migrants.

> Janusz: When I happen to notice [people speaking Ukrainian] in the shops then I always think about how I was in Ireland and used to do my shopping in Aldi. I'd be there, for example, with my friend and we'd be speaking Polish but I'd be conscious of how people standing behind me in the queue were feeling.
> Anne: How do they feel?
> Janusz: Oh, I don't know. Like 'Oh, they're Ukrainians, they've come here to work'. 'Oh. Poles. They've come here to work.'

Several interviewees said that local people were unfriendly towards migrants. For instance, Anita asserted that 'Kalisz is a not very tolerant city. It's not open towards Ukrainians'. When I asked her where you could see Ukrainians, she said, 'In the factories … They don't come out into the city. No, no. Perhaps you might meet them in a shop. But on the whole they live in their own world. There's not much integration.' One interviewee told a story about a friend with new Ukrainian neighbours who had bought a nice flat.

> Of course he's not completely happy about that, not that he's anti, but I have the feeling he does have a slight antipathy towards immigrants and says they don't always know how to behave … they go to clubs and are a bit rowdy and he doesn't like that. He says, 'They are in Poland, not at home in Ukraine.'

He seemed to believe that such attitudes were inevitable in receiving societies. 'You often hear people muttering about Ukrainians. There is a bit of dislike, unfortunately. But it's the same everywhere. Ukrainians come to us, we go somewhere else.' However, other interviewees reported that they had never seen any hostile behaviour of local people towards Ukrainians and that, in Krystyna's words, they 'generally have a positive attitude to foreigners and try to help them'. Edyta, who had a black neighbour, was particularly adamant that the situation for black people had improved compared with the racism her mother described as existing 'fifteen to twenty years' previously, when black people got beaten up in Piła.

Based on their experiences abroad, other interviewees foresaw more pessimistic trajectories. Unlike Jan, quoted on page 122, with his optimistic 2019 assessment of how Poland would become socialised as an immigration country, Daniel, in 2022, was focused on the part of the migration transition where hostility grew towards migrants. He asserted that this was predetermined, apparently a law of migration transition.

Everywhere you see 'Ukraine, Ukraine', flags, Ukraine, and I know people will begin to be negative about that. It's the same as with us Poles. When we first arrived [in Ireland], everyone said 'Wow! You're Polish! Take this job, take that job!' But three years later it was different. Everyone was hostile to us. That we're newcomers, we steal jobs, drive down wages. That's how it will be in Poland after a while. I think. I hope not. But I know it's inevitable, because everywhere is the same.

So far, the discussion in this section has focused mostly on relations between Poles and Ukrainians, and interviewees' disposition to see equivalences. However, they also mentioned hierarchies between different nations. Tomasz observed that immigrants are despised by the receiving country because they come from poorer countries.

When [Swedes] know [you're Polish] they immediately start treating you differently. Unfortunately, that happens here too. Since I'm sure you will be talking to people from Ukraine. I don't know if they can spot it, but we look at them a bit differently, because they come here to work. We complain about how bad things are here [in Kalisz] so that we need to go abroad to work. And if someone comes from another country to work in Poland that country must be really, really bad.

Krystyna, with long experience of working in Germany, complained that 'Germans sometimes treat us the same way as we treat Ukrainians. Poles think they are from the sticks and don't know anything ... But I don't treat my [Ukrainian] tenants as if they were stupider'.

Poles were also said to be hostile to labour migrants but welcoming to tourists. In Płock, the most touristy of the three cities, Beata said, 'We welcome them with open arms. We like showing them our best side.' I asked whether that meant that not every foreigner was disliked. She said, 'No, it depends why they came. Though obviously I personally have no problem with it.' Sitting in an outdoor café in Kalisz, Anita reflected:

I think people have warmer feelings towards the West than the East. That's my impression ... I see how [Polish] people behave. If they're out and about and hear somebody speaking Ukrainian they look quite offended. But if some people are sitting having a conversation in English they look at them with interest.

In all the interviews conducted in 2019 and 2021, only one interviewee complained about the (perceived) behaviour of Ukrainians. She asserted that Ukrainians behaved in the opposite way to Poles – in effect, that they did migration differently.

> The problem is, as I've discussed with my fiancé, when I went abroad I had the impression that it was up to me to learn to understand. But when Ukrainians come to KPP it's like they are offended that we don't understand them. We have to try and make ourselves understood, a bit in Polish, a bit in Russian – it's hard. That wasn't my approach when I was abroad. I had to cope for myself, and they seem to have exactly the opposite impression.

She also 'othered' Ukrainians in how she referred to them: 'I know there were some big meat factories in KPP which employed lots of Ukrainians – I think it's hard work and a normal person can't afford to work for such low wages. That's probably why there are more and more of that nationality.'

I interviewed Poles in Piła in a different context. The interviews took place after the full-scale Russian invasion of February 2022. Some interviewees expressed relaxed attitudes towards Ukrainian refugees. For instance, Daniel highlighted that there were plenty of available kindergarten places in Piła, including private ones. As mentioned above, Edyta and her colleagues had learned some Ukrainian words, so they were able to 'cope' when refugees came into their shop. An interviewee who worked in local social services said that her colleagues communicated with mothers seeking advice in English. At a school where I interviewed Polish and Ukrainian staff as key informants, they already had a little experience in educating Ukrainian children, and seemed confident that they would be able to manage, thanks to their careful arrangements for receiving more. However, other Polish interviewees expressed concern, mostly with reference to two areas which Ukrainian informants – speaking to me before the invasion – had already tended to identify as weak spots of Piła: the price and scarcity of rented accommodation, and poor access to hospital consultants. The most concerned informant had a child with a health condition and expressed their worry that Ukrainian children would be prioritised. To some extent, however, these (very few) negative interviewees were clearly just repeating complaints they had heard on (social) media about other cities. For example, one expressed annoyance that Ukrainians had free zoo tickets, although Piła has no zoo.

Two interviewees, who were friends, expressed worries about Ukrainian competition for jobs in the West. One person said:

> We don't know how much competition there will be for jobs abroad. My friend in Holland said that lots of Ukrainians had come there and that there was less work ... I heard from some of my friends that they're afraid there'll be less. I know people who go to do seasonal work in Germany and Holland, or work as carers. For example my friend's mother who works as a carer in Germany is afraid that the Ukrainian women will take lower wages.

The other complained:

> If only it wasn't for Russia's conflict with Ukraine. It's spoiled everything [sigh]. Everything. It's even taken away our trips abroad, isn't that right? ... Ukrainians are taking work everywhere. They'll work for pennies. People will take them on because they're cheap labour. They'll be taken on, and we won't be wanted.

Conclusions

The Polish research participants in Płock and Kalisz, interviewed before the 2022 invasion of Ukraine, barely noticed the recent influx of foreigners to Poland, although they had heard that there were plenty of Ukrainians. The fact that they seemed unbothered by this wave of labour migration might back up Arango's (2012) suggestion, reported in Chapter 1, that in the first stage of migration transition the receiving society adopts a neutral or instrumental approach to immigration. A handful of Piła informants expressed alarm at the influx of Ukrainian refugees in spring 2022, and this could corroborate Arango's further argument that in the second stage of transition the receiving society becomes more anxious and hostile. However, there is plenty of counter-evidence to suggest that Arango's framework does not apply very well to the migration transition in KPP. This chapter explained that the majority of Piła informants expressed friendly attitudes towards Ukrainian refugees, like other Poles who participated in nationwide surveys in 2022–3. Moreover, when Orlen's 6,000-capacity container town for international migrants opened in Płock in 2023, as described in Chapter 2, the city's residents seemed to accept the situation. Journalists commented:

> This part of Mazowieckie region is undergoing a lightning lesson in international, intercultural and interfaith tolerance … Men with darker skins can be encountered every day in the city's housing estates and shops. They can even be seen in groups of 100 or more when they come by the busload to Płock's only hypermarket. It seems that week by week they occasion less and less surprise (Burzyńska and Adamkowski 2023)

As also mentioned in Chapter 2, journalists reported that some Poles in Płock mentioned their own migration experiences as a reason to accept the new situation.

The fundamental problem with applying Arango's framework to KPP is that these are not ordinary 'receiving societies' which need to learn about migration, but societies of migrants and former migrants where most people already suppose that they know quite a lot about migration from their own and their friends' and families' experiences. Chapter 1 asked whether Poland's experience of migration transition is influenced by the fact that Poland maintains its identity as a country of emigration. The evidence presented in Chapter 6 suggests strongly that this is the case. The interviewees were able to detect all sorts of parallels between their own migration and that of Ukrainians coming to Poland. Sometimes they also mentioned other foreigners. They applied dual labour market theory (Piore 1979), explaining how – just as in western Europe – some jobs in Poland had become spurned by local people so that gaps in this secondary part of the labour market were filled by migrants. They recognised that Ukrainians were arriving in Poland as a wave, and they knew how it felt to be part of such an exodus. They could see a pattern in how Ukrainians were now spreading out to smaller cities in Poland and bringing over their families, just as Poles had done in the West.

The interviewees were keen to point out that in their opinion labour migration was a completely normal and predictable social phenomenon. They focused on the fact that migrants were behaving as one would expect people to behave – migrating to work where better work was available. This was in keeping with the findings of CBOS opinion polls which showed that most Poles were in favour of unrestricted labour migration, even though after 2015 many were hostile towards refugees. The interviewees did not dwell on ethnic aspects of immigration to Poland, unlike politicians. However, the whiteness and assumed Christianity of Slav migrants in Poland possibly did influence the perceptions of a few, judging by the fact that these people also made hostile comments about Muslim migrants in Western Europe. A number of interviewees also expressed the view that, although they personally did not have objections to foreign workers, they believed that some local people in KPP looked down on Ukrainians and could be hostile towards foreigners, partly because they (inaccurately) supposed that foreign workers might 'steal' Polish jobs.

Notes

1. The theoretical literature is primarily concerned with where and why different social groups or categories are located in hierarchies. It can refer to institutions and existing power structures (such as institutional racism) as well as to how individual people conceptualise ethnic diversity: their hierarchies of preference and feelings about the status of different groups. Here it blends with literature on social distancing (Bogardus 1947).
2. A CBOS study in 2018 suggested that over 10 years the share of Poles who knew nothing about the events had more than halved, from 41 per cent to 19 per cent (Herrmann 2018: 5).

7
Motives for leaving Ukraine

Introduction

As Chapter 1 points out, Poland's migration transition is also the story of Ukraine's transformation as a sending country, with a much increased volume of migration to Poland since 2014. Less often remarked upon is the fact that, in the years before February 2022, a more socio-demographically diverse range of people came to Poland (Górny et al 2019: 55). This was well illustrated by the diversity of my own sample and was both a cause and effect of the increased volume of Ukrainian–Polish migration. The fact that so many types of Ukrainian decided to come to Poland for such a variety of reasons helps explain the size of the exodus. In turn, as existing migrants invited their family and friends to join them, the migration networks came to encompass an increasingly diverse range of people.

My interviews suggested that many Ukrainians were not likely to consider returning permanently to Ukraine. They wanted to be in Poland, either as regular circular visitors, or to settle with their families, at least for the medium term. Like Poles migrating to the UK and Ireland after EU accession, they chose a migration livelihood strategy because it seemed accessible. They had a sense of mobility options, and of being able to treat migration as an experiment, even while often stressing that they were forced by circumstances. They used the same turns of phrase: for example, 'I decided that it would be OK to try it out for three months' (Klara); 'you need to give it a go' (Larysa); 'we decided "let's give it a try"' (Sergei). Having experimented with migration to Poland, most interviewees liked it enough to want to stay for at least a few years.

Interviewees chose international migration as a livelihood strategy in preference to other options. International migration was attractive partly because they were pessimistic about finding sufficiently well-paid jobs in Ukraine, even if they migrated to a big city. The cost of living in the big cities negated any advantages they might possess in terms of greater availability of jobs. Mihaylo, for example, dismissed internal migration as a livelihood by saying, 'It's not realistic for an ordinary worker to work anywhere in Ukraine … not in a single city.' He estimated that if he went to Kyiv, after paying rent and bills he would take home $100 a month to his wife in a central Ukrainian city. Other interviewees made similar comments. It was also difficult to access credit at affordable rates, or subsist on pensions and welfare payments. For instance, Lyudmila, explaining why she went to Poland to earn money for a flat, instead of trying to obtain a mortgage in Ukraine, explained that 'the mortgage would use up all my money and there'd be nothing left even for food … I couldn't pay off a mortgage in Ukraine, and quite possibly my children would be paying it off [after my death]'. There were also certain jobs which interviewees were simply not prepared to undertake, despite the fact that they were comparatively well-paid. Ihor, for example, complained that 'it's very hard to earn the same money in Ukraine as you can in Poland. You would have to go down a mine, work in a coalmine, but that's hellish work'.

Nineteen of the 69 labour migrants whom I interviewed in KPP were from west Ukraine.[1] Their presence was unsurprising, given the longer history of west Ukrainian migration to Poland. However, three-quarters of the interviewees (50 individuals) were from central, eastern and southern Ukraine. Like the west Ukrainians, they were finding economic circumstances difficult in their home cities, towns and villages; some of them had experienced business failures and incurred debts which made them feel 'forced' to migrate; and in a number of cases they were also worried about war and/or pollution. Twenty-six interviewees were university graduates, of whom 16 had been employed in white-collar jobs in Ukraine just before they departed. Forty-three were women and 26 were men. The mean average age was 38.

Chapter 7 is similar in structure to Chapter 4, about why Poles migrated from Poland. The 69 were all labour migrants, and the chapter begins by briefly examining economic reasons why they chose migration as a livelihood strategy. The chapter proceeds by adopting an intersectional approach, to some extent employing rough typologies to separate out sub-groups within the Ukrainian sample. In the chapter's second section, I group the interviewees according to their various stages of progression towards settlement in Poland. The third section considers the diverse motivations of one group who might particularly be expected to settle: interviewees with Polish origins and connections. Each migrant's behaviour is also influenced by their individual migration experience and mobility capital, so the fourth section considers their migratory careers before they came to Poland and KPP. The longest section of the chapter analyses socio-demographic diversity within the sample, identifying sub-groups of interviewees according to features such as age, gender, education and occupational careers in Ukraine. This latter is particularly important, given that working in jobs not commensurate with formal qualifications is a significant part of many migrants' experience, and that downward social mobility can deter migrants from settling in a foreign country. However, this deterrent was hardly mentioned in the interviews. It emerged that a large group of interviewees arrived in Poland already deskilled in Ukraine, in the sense of not making use of their formal qualifications. Finally, Chapter 7 compares the motivations of migrants from west Ukraine with those from other parts of the country.

Economic migration from Ukraine

Oksana claimed that 'today all of Ukraine is travelling somewhere to earn money and feed the family'. Interviewees believed that economic migration was both predictable and widespread. For instance, Viktor, talking about other Ukrainian migrants, commented, 'They're doing the right thing (*vse pravil'no*). People seek out the place where they'll do best.' Mihaylo observed, 'People don't leave their country to run away from the good life. Humans, like other creatures, look for the warmest, most comfortable spot.' The 69 labour migrants could be seen as constituting a single group of people motivated by financial considerations. Almost every interviewee complained about low wages in Ukraine. Researchers agree that 'the main reason for labor migration in Ukraine remains low wages' (Chugaievska and Rusak 2022: 389). Górny et al (2019: 54), on the basis of 2018 survey evidence, suggest 'unsatisfying wage levels' were becoming an increasingly common Ukrainian migration motivation, as opposed to unemployment. For instance, among their interviewees in Bydgoszcz who had arrived after 2017, and who seem in many respects to have resembled those in KPP, 84 per cent cited inadequate wages as their main reason to come to Poland (Górny et al 2019: 32).

KPP interviewees were not satisfied with their Ukrainian wages because they had certain standards of what constituted a normal standard of living, and this inclined them to migrate abroad. Several described themselves as having been 'forced' to migrate. They were not prepared to continue subsisting on Ukrainian wages if they could not buy even what they considered basic goods. For example, Oksana, a nurse in Ukraine, commented that 'to buy a phone in Ukraine I'd have to work for six months not eating or drinking anything. Here I bought myself a phone and I can also send money home'. Even more importantly, a 'normal' life was one in which one did not have to compromise certain life goals, especially children's higher education.

When explaining her migration decision, Alla said, 'It was hard to plan. It was hard to be sure about anything.' Brzozowska (2023: 2378) found that 'what migrants shared in common was searching for stability and a "normal" life'. 'Normal' is a hard-to-translate word found in various Slavonic languages, often used when stating aspirations (Hrckova and Zeller 2021: 114). It implies adhering to certain norms. 'Proper' is sometimes a better translation than 'normal'. The normal standard is the standard that everyone deserves to have. It may have been achievable without migration in the past, but nowadays can only be achieved by working abroad. Poles often use exactly the same terminology (Galasińska and Kozłowska 2009; White 2017: 4–5).

Like Brzozowska (2023), Chugaievska and Rusak (2022: 391) note that Ukrainian 'economic instability' was a key factor driving migration. Inflation after 2014 was often mentioned by my research participants to explain why they had recently migrated to Poland, although previously they had subsisted on Ukrainian wages. Other aspects of instability were linked to unpredictable consumer demand. For example, Ihor, a carpenter, explained that 'there was work, but there was less demand, because of the economic crisis. In my area of work there was very strong wage fluctuation'. Some interviewees, such as Kira, who owned an adult shop, claimed they had been driven out of business because local people had no money to spend on extras. Similarly, Irina's husband, a carpenter who specialised in putting up prefabricated wooden holiday homes, lost his livelihood because fewer Ukrainians were able to afford them. He moved to Poland, where there was ample business.

Other people, who had kept their jobs while their fellow workers had been dismissed, and in some cases seen their wages cut, complained of being unable to cope with the extra workload. For example, Oleksandra, an engineer, had found herself doing the job of five colleagues, for a pay cut. The Covid-19 pandemic exacerbated such problems. Elena explained:

> I was working in a restaurant where there used to be eleven staff, but only four were retained … and I was paid half what I used to get, though I had lots more responsibility. Because of the lockdown, we had no customers and weren't being paid. I was going to work, getting stressed, but not being paid … I realised it was pointless. If I didn't go abroad then, I never would.

Finally, corruption was mentioned by interviewees as a reason to leave Ukraine. Andrejuk (2019b) labels this 'governance-induced migration'. Corruption played a role in making life unpredictable and livelihoods insecure. Boris claimed that it had 'spread out its roots like a tree, into all areas of business'. By comparison, Poland was regarded as a haven of security. Lev, for instance, observed, 'In Poland there's no particular corruption, people are too afraid.' Mihaylo said, 'It's a quiet country. They observe the laws. There's none of that anarchy.'

Stages on the path to settlement

Poland's transition to being a country of immigration (if 'immigration' is understood as migration to settle) was happening in 2019–22 because Ukrainians were beginning to stay for longer periods and apparently settling in Poland. Górny et al (2021) demonstrated that the Covid-19 pandemic did not halt this trend. According to their survey, the share of Ukrainians planning to settle in Poland rose from 45.8 per cent in 2019 to a majority, 54.6 per cent, in 2020. However, judging from my own interviews, 'settlement' may imply settlement for the medium term, rather than necessarily 'for life'. To shed light on the overall migration transition process, it seems useful to distinguish between individuals at different stages of settlement, as well as to identify those who might eventually travel further. Hence any population of Ukrainians in Poland, including those in KPP, could be split into various sub-groups according their position along this continuum. Among my interviewees, only one person (interviewed in 2019) was determined to return soon to Ukraine and remain there.

Yurii, who lived in a migrant workers' hostel in Kalisz, summed up the main types of migrant he observed in the hostel and at his factory. He recognised that 'everyone has different motives' but also divided them into two groups.

> Some are here without a visa. They work very hard for three months every day of the week from dawn to dusk. They know they came for three months, they collect their money and they go home. Either to have a rest or because they'd earned the money for a house, some repairs, a car. But some come to have a look and decide to stay because of the excellent quality of life.

My sample contained no one who was just in Poland for a one-off visit. They had all 'come to have a look' and in that sense practised a strategy of intentional unpredictability. Moreover they were already 'staying' in the sense that everyone I interviewed was making their living chiefly by earning money in Poland. However, they were at different stages of their migration careers. As discussed by Górny (2017), there exist various patterns of Ukrainian temporary migration to Poland, determined by (changing) immigration policies and visa/work permit rules. These patterns also connect to the particular livelihood strategies of individuals.

About one third still considered their main homes to be in Ukraine, and themselves to be circular migrants, even if hardly any of these people could envisage returning soon to live in Ukraine full-time. They were lone mothers with small children; women and men with disabled partners; or men whose wives refused to join them in Poland. The second, largest group were those who seemed to be transitioning towards residence in Poland and who were often at different stages of family reunification. Some were trying to persuade relatives still in Ukraine to come to Poland. Others were in KPP with siblings or parents – ties which might not be strong enough to keep them in KPP, or even in Poland. In other families, parents were living with their school-age children who were already quite well settled. Some of these interviewees transitioning towards residence in Poland already possessed temporary residence cards. In Kalisz and Piła, they tended to live in rented accommodation, not in migrant hostels. Finally, there existed a third group, just a handful of interviewees, consisting mostly of people with several years' experience in Poland and interviewed in 2021–2. They had definitely decided to acquire long-term residence rights. This in turn could lead to citizenship, although at the time that the fieldwork was conducted, only one interviewee was a Polish citizen, on the strength of a Polish Card. On the other hand, acquiring the permanent residence status of 'long-term EU resident' could also lead to migration further west, so that this group of formally most-settled-in-Poland interviewees were also the best placed to move on. In general, it was the younger and better-educated Ukrainians who were more likely to be considering moving further west, as discussed in Chapter 10.

As Ukrainians became more settled in Poland, this had an impact on their transnational practices and ties. Most interviewees, for example, travelled for shorter or longer return visits to Ukraine. The intervals between return visits varied, largely depending on whether interviewees were living with close family members in Poland. At the extreme end was Halyna, whose young son was still in Ukraine, and who reported that there had been periods when she flew back to Ukraine every weekend.

Similarly, Oksana said that she was rarely in Poland for more than a month at a time. However, it was more common to return just once or twice a year. Not surprisingly, there was some tendency among the handful of more senior migrants to return less frequently. Ostap, in Poland for five years, had not been home for the last two and a half. He had paid for his mother to visit him in Poland – a sign that his 'home' had shifted location. However, other senior migrants existed in a state of suspended temporariness, torn between two locations. Lavra had worked in a factory in KPP for three years, but disqualified herself from applying for a Polish residence card by her visits back to Ukraine every couple of months to see her adult daughters. On the other hand, it transpired elsewhere in the interview that her state of suspension in Poland was linked to hopes of moving to Germany once it opened its labour market to Ukrainians.

The frequency of visits was dependent on legal status – how often the interviewee had to renew their visas and work permits, and whether they had acquired a residence permit which would enable them to come and go at their own discretion. Employers also seemed to vary in their willingness to allow short absences. In the factories, permission to be absent depended to some extent on the ebb and flow of orders. For example, when Olha's workshop shut down production for a week, she had gone home to see her children. 'I went just for the day. You travel for two days, have one day at home, and then it's two days back … The children were happy, and so was I.' Covid-19-related redundancies and travel restrictions had also played a role in upsetting plans and restricting mobility in 2020.

In other words, interviewees were at the mercy of structural constraints, but also able to exercise a degree of choice regarding their own mobility. The following quotation from Nina illustrates how her sense of being in control of her livelihood was modified by various emotional and structural factors, and also how the initial strategy of working in both countries had been abandoned. Nina had been working in Poland for six years, in a beauty salon where custom had somewhat declined as a result of the pandemic.

> In the past I would go home to Ukraine, work in the salon there for a month, but somehow I didn't like it. People weren't the same … I go home every two to three months because I miss my family, my children … Recently I was at home for two months waiting for my documents … It all depends on work, if there's enough custom, we stay [in Kalisz] and work. You can always go home later. You can do anything. Of course, I do want to be at home for Christmas and Easter … Last year I was in Poland for Christmas. I was so depressed!

Polish ethnic affinity

Ukrainians with Polish heritage constitute a particular subset of Ukrainian migrants and might be expected to have greater reason to stay in Poland, given their personal ties and also, in many cases, the fact that they hold a Polish Card. The Polish Card is an identity document created in 2007 and available to people living abroad who are not Polish citizens but can prove their Polish family background and pass an examination. It is a tool of Polish diaspora policy which aims to attract such people to live in Poland, offering scholarships for higher education, access to the labour market, and a simplified procedure for obtaining permanent residence and eventually naturalisation as Polish citizens (Gońda and Lesińska 2022).

Like co-ethnic 'return' migrants to different countries around the world (Brubaker 1998; Fox 2003; Hess 2008), partly-Polish Ukrainians have different motivations for migrating to Poland. Some are 'roots migrants' (Wessendorf 2007) who feel a sentimental attachment. In other cases, more pragmatic considerations seem to prevail. Gońda (2016: 113) in his book about student Polish Card holders from various former Soviet countries distinguishes between 'those who, on the one hand, come to a mythologised homeland that is an important source of emotions, common symbols, family narratives or language for co-ethnics, or, on the contrary, those who come to that country only because of educational and professional possibilities being offered there'. Those possibilities include moving further west after graduation. However, as Gońda also shows, there is a continuum rather than a dichotomy between roots migrants and pragmatists. Moreover, there are different ways of feeling 'ethnic affinity' (Brubaker 1998). Co-ethnic return migrants are differently conscious of their ancestry; lived to different extents in their co-ethnic communities (including online communities) before they migrated; speak their ancestral tongue with different levels of competence; and are differently proud of their new citizenship. Among the KPP interviewees with Polish ancestry only one person clearly belonged to the roots migrant type. Nonetheless, the others did feel connected to Poland in various ways. They were not in Poland – to use Gońda's phrase – 'only because' of work opportunities.

Just three interviewees owned a Polish Card at time of interview, despite the fact that it was a useful possession, especially in 2021–2, when other migrants in Poland were waiting months and in some cases more than a year to receive residence permits. If people who are entitled to the Polish Card are not claiming it before they come to Poland, that suggests that it is not doing its job at intensifying Polish Ukrainians' sense of Polish ethnic affinity. As Jirka (2019) also found in his study of Ukrainians of Czech origin, among my small sample there seemed to be considerable ignorance about how to formalise one's Polish connection.

Polishness, for the interviewees, was only partly about roots and family history. It also connected to having relatives currently living in Poland, and, much more importantly, to Polish language knowledge and length of stay in Poland. The most Polonised interviewee was Adam, who had been in Poland since the 1990s, before the Polish Card was introduced. He had made his own life in Poland, where he had bought a flat. He had acquired a permanent residence card both for himself and for his wife, and also deregistered from his Ukrainian address, although his wife still lived there with other family members. Adam had a Polish grandmother and relatives in Poland, who had visited his family in Soviet Ukraine when he was a child, and fired his interest in learning Polish and going to Poland. He spoke fluent Polish. However, he said he had not yet got around to claiming Polish citizenship, although his wife was encouraging him to do so. On one occasion in his interview, Adam referred to Ukrainians as 'they', but then laughed embarrassedly at his use of the pronoun and explained, 'I've already cut myself off.' He said that with his EU resident's card, he could have gone west and earned better money. However, he would stay in KPP because he was a 'Polonophile'.

Anna identified squarely as Polish. Her forebears had lived in Płock, and her husband also had Polish ancestors. In the past, she had visited relatives in the city, but by the time she and her family decided to sell their house in Ukraine and move to Poland, the relatives were dead. Nonetheless, Anna migrated to the place she considered her home city. She claimed, 'Now I've returned to my ancestral homeland.' When her Polish workmates asked when she was going 'home' to Ukraine, she said that she was already at home, in Płock. Anna possessed a Polish Card but said her husband had been too busy at work to apply for one – again suggesting it is not such a significant marker of Polishness. They lived in a hostel with other Ukrainians, so her contact with Poles was limited. She said she was comfortable speaking Polish, but in our interview soon lapsed into Russian, the language she spoke every day.

Milena also claimed to 'always feel at home' in Poland because of her Polish origins, although when we spoke she had not yet acquired a Polish Card and did not write Polish confidently. She had Polish cousins living in a different part of Poland, whom she visited as a child, and she had long hoped to move to Poland. However, when she came to work in Poland she chose not to call on the cousins for help, because she did not want to burden them. She aspired to forge her own local Polish identity and she did this partly by being the pioneer in her family, with her husband and son originally staying in Ukraine.

Olesya was less sentimental about her origins than either Anna or Milena. Her father had been Polish and she knew some Polish language, but got around to applying for the Polish Card only after she had decided to start working in Poland. She had relatives in another part of Poland and had visited them in the past; however, she came to KPP through a recruiter recommended by a friend. She worried that she would be hindered in acquiring citizenship by her problems writing Polish. She also obtained a Card for her teenage son, hoping he would study in Poland, but although he went to school for a year in KPP he decided to go to university in Ukraine, so this part of Olesya's strategy did not work out. Olesya's adult children and second husband were living in Ukraine.

Melaniya, the only Polish citizen among the interviewees, had obtained a Polish Card as part of a household livelihood strategy. When the economy worsened after 2014, her welder husband went to work in Poland, but she stayed behind to study Polish and apply successfully for a Polish Card on the basis of roots. Within a few months after her arrival in Poland she obtained permanent residence, but it took her a few years to improve her Polish language and prepare herself emotionally for taking on citizenship. Subsequently, her husband, who was living in Poland on the strength of Melaniya's citizenship, had applied to the Polish president for his own citizenship, by lottery. Melaniya referred to Poles as 'they'.

Valentin moved to Poland with his family for economic reasons, but, to make their situation easier, his wife, who had a Polish grandmother but barely spoke Polish, had successfully applied for a Polish Card and then for citizenship. She and their two sons now had dual citizenship. Valentin said he had 'given permission' for his wife to apply for the Polish Card, implying it was a serious step emotionally.

Bohdan was among the most ambivalent about his Polishness. He was working in Poland with his stepfather, his Polish birth father having abandoned the family when Bohdan was a small child. He confessed to never having considered seeking Polish citizenship, and when asked whether he felt Polish replied:

> Not consciously. I have a Polish surname and I know that I have some kind of relatives in Poland. I've never met them and don't have much desire to find them. If they'd wanted to contact me they would have done that long ago. What's the point of looking for them? Well, if possible, I would meet up with them sometime. It could work out.

A handful of other interviewees had Polish roots, but were in KPP as regular labour migrants. They did not (yet) possess a Polish Card, for different reasons. Like Czech Ukrainians studied by Jirka (2019), some found obtaining the necessary documents a daunting task. Andrei had a Polish great-grandfather and had tried and failed to obtain documentation which he would need to prove his right to the Card. Halyna wanted the Card but did not want to spend time going back to Ukraine to apply for it. She complained that Ukrainians, unlike Belarusians, could not apply in Poland. Yevhen, a solo circular migrant from southern Ukraine, had a Polish grandmother, but had not grown up speaking Polish. He had not yet got round to applying for a Card, although he thought it might be a good idea. It would lead to permanent residence status in the EU, and increase his options to travel further west and support his family in Ukraine even more efficiently. Hlib, 23, had a Polish great-grandmother but neither he nor his parents, who were well-integrated in Poland through their own efforts, had claimed a Card.

Oksana was not descended from Poles, but had distant Polish cousins living elsewhere in Poland. In fact, despite not having Polish ancestry, of all the interviewees she was the most connected to her Polish relatives. They had invited Oksana and her husband to stay after she first arrived, frequently phoned up, and had invited her to come again. This backed up Oksana's positive impressions of Poland and her overall feeling of having made Poland her new home. Finally, Elena, from west Ukraine but without Polish roots, was engaged to a Pole. She had been informed that she could apply for citizenship two years after her marriage. At that point, the couple hoped to move to Denmark.

To sum up: having Polish origins – in a minority of cases symbolised by the Polish Card – seemed for most interviewees to constitute an 'anchor' rather than 'roots'. It was one of a number of reasons to feel more connected to Poland, but appeared not to be a stand-alone factor. As the examples illustrate, it was not just status which counted, but also practices. There were multiple ways to perform one's Polishness. For Oksana, visiting relatives was important; for Anna, it was asserting to Poles in Płock that she was a local person.

Previous migration experience

Only a few interviewees were in KPP as the continuation of a long career of international migration. Reflecting the well-established tradition of migration to Poland by west Ukrainian women, two interviewees from the far west had worked as carers in Warsaw in the 1990s and early 2000s. Perhaps surprisingly, given that one reason for the increase in Ukrainian labour migration to Poland was the diversion of migrants who hitherto worked in Russia, there were only six such individuals in the sample. Two men from Kherson had done manual work in Moscow and Petersburg, one from Dnipro had driven deliveries of granite from a quarry in southern Russia, and three woman from Kharkiv and Poltava regions had worked in a provincial Russian supermarket (living with a relative) and as servants. As also found by Gerber and Zavisca (2020), their experiences of work in Russia had been mixed, and sometimes quite positive. They had left Russia for various reasons, including the cost of living, falling wages and, most recently, Covid-19 restrictions. Two complained about poor Russian attitudes towards Ukrainians, expressed through not paying their wages on time and not caring about their health and safety. Their experiences were gendered in the sense that all the women had changed their occupation and were now working in factories in Poland, whereas some of the men had performed skilled manual work (welding and lorry driving) in Ukraine, Russia and Poland. Other common Ukrainian destinations include Czechia and Israel. Zlata had recently done seasonal agricultural work in Czechia 'where I felt very uncomfortable … We weren't treated well … So I wouldn't work there again, despite the fact that wages are high'. Artem had worked undocumented in Israel and been deported; he then started migrating to Poland, partly because it was legal.

With regard to length of stay in Poland, although the sample was not representative, the interviewees were typical of Ukrainian migrants to Poland in at least three respects. Most had arrived in Poland since 2016. Secondly, novice migrants continued to arrive in Kalisz and Piła even in the pandemic year of 2020.[2] Thirdly, the newcomers included many migrants from areas other than west Ukraine. In fact, 30 per cent of my interviewees in 2019–22 were from regions identified in 2012 by the International Labour Organization (ILO 2013) as having 'very low' migration.

The fact that new people were constantly arriving in KPP meant that those who had been there only slightly longer could be considered old hands. Artem, for example, was training new recruits and showing people round Płock. 'They say, "Take me here, take me there, show me the way to the zoo, you know where it is. I could get a job as a tour guide!"' More important than introductions to Marta the 89-year-old alligator, however, was the information and advice about jobs and migration practices which Artem and similar senior migrants could pass on to new arrivals.

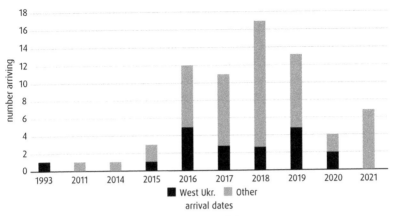

Figure 7.1 Ukrainian interviewees' arrival dates
Source: own data. West Ukraine = Khmel'nitskyi, Rivne and Chernivtsi regions plus all regions west. Columns for 2020 and 2021 are lower because the Płock fieldwork took place in 2019.

Age, life stage and lifestyle aspirations

The mean average age among the interviewees was 38, compared with 36 in Górny et al's (2019: 25) study of Bydgoszcz. Most interviewees were under 50, as seems to be typical for Ukrainians in Poland (ZUS 2022: 14). However, the fact that many were no longer very young indicates that, like Polish target earners discussed in Chapter 4, they encountered some shock to their Ukrainian livelihoods in middle age which made them reorient towards Poland.

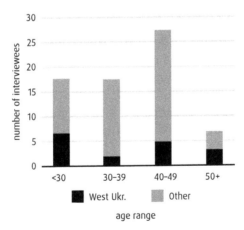

Figure 7.2 Ukrainians' ages when interviewed
Source: own data

MOTIVES FOR LEAVING UKRAINE

The youngest migrants included three who had joined their parents already working in KPP once they had completed secondary school or higher education. They therefore combined a second-generation with a first-generation migrant identity. In no cases had they been pressurised to come to Poland. As discussed in Chapter 8, middle-aged migrants also told many stories of how they had invited their adult or teenage children to be with them in KPP.

A handful of the youngest interviewees displayed some similarities with the Polish EU wave whose stories were told in Chapter 4, and who migrated not just for money but also for love, fun and adventure. Solomiya, for example, came to KPP aged 19. She had studied book-keeping at college in a small town in southwest-central Ukraine, and her mother told her to go to university, but she decided she would rather follow her husband to Poland. Fadei, aged 20, reported:

> I finished secondary school and thought I might go to university. But then I thought that I was too lazy. I didn't feel like it. So I said to myself 'OK, I'll go and work'. But I thought it was better to earn money here than there … In Ukraine, you don't get the same chances as here. Put it like that. I came to Poland and opened up new opportunities for myself.

Fadei wanted to buy a car, had been taking driving lessons, had Polish friends and went clubbing in neighbouring Ostrów Wielkopolski: he had been having fun, despite the pandemic. Artur (19) had just found a well-paid construction job in a bigger city near KPP to support his lifestyle. He said, 'I don't care what kind of job I get. The main thing is that it should make a profit [sic], so that I can comfortably live on that, and buy whatever I like. Not have to deny myself anything.' Finally, Olena (22) was becoming bored of working as a hairdresser in Ukraine and, using the same phrase as many Poles *circa* 2004, told her husband, 'Let's go and try working abroad.'

Curiosity was predictably also a motivating factor in this youngest age group. For instance, Kvitka had tried and failed to set herself up in Lviv, where she had worked as a chef but not been able to afford the rent. She went back to her parents in a west Ukrainian village. Kvitka's parents wanted her to stay with them after she married: incomplete, circular migration was the norm locally, and her husband could migrate alone. However, she wanted to be independent and join her husband in Kalisz. 'I wanted to achieve something in life. I want to travel, I find that interesting, we've travelled around … I'm interested in self-development.'

As I argued with reference to Poles, lifestyle motivations can also be found among older and target-earner migrants, such as Jerzy and Jolanta from Płock. It is not necessary to be a 'lifestyle migrant'. Ukrainian migrants over 30 expressed plenty of curiosity and lifestyle motivations. For instance, 36-year old Pavlo said, 'It's all eye-opening. This is the first time I've been out of Ukraine ... For me it's very important experience, and everything I see is interesting.' Lyudmila, aged 48, a printer's assistant in Ukraine, said, 'I want to learn to drive. Because in Ukraine not many women can drive. I want to learn new skills, not just to work, to earn money.' In my sample, women were somewhat more likely to mention additional, non-economic motivations, but it is hard to generalise further. The women were at different life stages: with small children they could bring to Poland; with teenage children considered old enough to leave behind in Ukraine; or with adult children now independent. Yuliya, who arrived aged 32 to join her husband, after working in a betting shop in Ukraine despite her university degree, said, 'For ages I'd been dreaming of going abroad and experiencing new things.' Nina, who came to Poland aged about 40 after a career as a senior community nurse (*fel'dsher*) in a village in west Ukraine, explained, 'There came a moment when I just got bored with that life. I decided to have a change. I told myself, "I want to go to Poland. Work a bit and see how people live."' Zinaida, who arrived aged 45 from Mariupol, made similar comments:

> I'd simply wanted to work in Poland for a very long time. I always thought that when my daughters grew up I would definitely go. My daughters are grown up. They got their MA degrees, they are independent, 24 years old and I decided that now was the time. To work a bit and see how people live.

Youth might also be connected to ambitions such as learning new skills, setting up one's own business or finding a dream job. To some extent the younger interviewees did express such aspirations. Fadei, aged 20, performed in a band and had already given one concert in Wrocław. He said:

> You have to make your dreams a reality. And if I can perform in Poznań, that will be another of my dreams come true ... I joke to my Polish friends, 'I came here just to work in a factory and I'll become a pop star. And no one in Ukraine will believe it.'

Other aspirations voiced by the youngest interviewees included setting up a Ukrainian restaurant in Kalisz; becoming a florist; and driving forklift trucks. However, middle-aged interviewees also aspired to become entrepreneurs. For instance, Boris (38) wanted to open his own logistics firm; Ostap (36) a car workshop; and Emma (40) a café. She said, 'We want to open a kind of coffee shop with cakes to order, baked goods. I dream about it all the time. It's my aspiration and I know I can achieve it. If you really want something and try to make it happen, you will.'

Some middle-aged interviewees also expressed non-economic aspirations. Tatyana (40) needed to earn money to invest in her daughter's future higher education. However, as an English teacher who had never been abroad before, she also saw Poland as a stepping stone towards a country where she could practise her English and fulfil her own ambitions. Yuliya (36), the betting shop employee, dreamed of training as a teacher in Poland, where she had already been promoted from school cleaner to teaching assistant. Realising her dreams had been dependent on leaving her home city. 'Anyone who wants to really achieve something in life won't be able to do it there. It's a backwater … There came a point when I realised that I had outgrown that city.' Sportsman Valerii (41) was most ambitious of all: 'I want to be champion of Poland. That's what brought me here. Not to earn money, like many Ukrainians.'

One attribute of these ambitious migrants, particularly the women, was that they were perfectionists about their Polish language, which they did not want to remain on a communicative (conversational) level. This was partly instrumental, so they could obtain more interesting and high-status jobs in future. For example, Halyna, a policewoman turned machine operator, said, 'I want to study, I want to develop my talents, I want more high-powered work. I have these goals and I know I can attain them. My current objective is to learn Polish to perfection … Later it will depend on what I choose. Perhaps banking, perhaps my own business.'

Among young migrants of all nationalities, building or buying a house is a common migration aspiration. It was mentioned in connection with Polish migrants in Chapters 4–5. It was curious, however, that most of the Ukrainian interviewees who expressed this ambition were no longer very young. Their ages on arrival in Poland had been 26, 30, 34, 42 and 45. In some cases these were middle-aged people who had lost housing, for example when a spouse had died and the property was inherited by stepchildren.

Interviewees with student children

Interviewees in their mid-to-late 30s and 40s had often migrated to pay for children's higher or further education. Except for those who had brought children to Poland or were planning to do so, practically all parents of older teenagers migrated to help pay for their children to study. There were 13 such interviewees, both men and women. It seemed equally acceptable for mothers and fathers to migrate in such situations. Oleksandra, for example, said:

> I worked in Ukraine for 14 years for a company named X. Since I was divorced, I then had to face the problem of my son's education. Unfortunately my salary couldn't cover the cost of a university education. So I settled my affairs in Ukraine, took my suitcase and went to Poland.

For many, the time when children were close to leaving school seemed to force a change in livelihood strategy. Anzhela, for example, a lone parent and shop assistant, commented that 'I was living my life, working peacefully, but then came the moment when I had to think about my daughter's education. Up to then, it was OK'. Lizaveta, also a shop assistant, commented, 'It was a forced change. I'd got divorced and my daughter went to study at college and I had to migrate.' By contrast, Mihaylo presented his migration as part of a household strategy: 'Living conditions are really bad, and you can't earn enough to put your child through education. So my wife and I discussed it and decided that one of us would have to make a sacrifice.' Since she had two jobs in Ukraine and his business had just failed, he was the spouse who went to Poland.

There is a cultural dimension here. In other societies, children would not expect parents to migrate to finance their university education, whereas in Poland, Ukraine and Russia – among some sections of the population, particularly perhaps in small towns – it seems to be a common practice (White 2022b). Zenon and Jerzy, Polish parents from KPP who went to the UK to support their children at university, were mentioned in Chapter 4. A particular Ukrainian twist (also noted by Dolińska 2019(a): 150–2) was the perceived necessity to pay bribes at every stage of a child's university career. This imposed a financial challenge on a scale which seemed to necessitate earning money abroad. Oksana, interviewed just before the Ukrainian presidential election of 2019, when the media were full of stories about corruption (Wilson 2022: 355–6), claimed apparently on a mix of her own experience and hearsay that:

If a parent pays a bribe it won't be hard for their child to get into university. You can buy anything in Ukraine ... You can buy a doctor, a public prosecutor, a judge ... So the lecturers want money for your child to pass their examinations ... And to graduate, you also need to pay a bribe so your child can graduate with a good degree.

Households and gender roles

Forty of the 69 interviewees were living with family members in Poland. For some men, migration had seemed necessary to maintain their role as chief breadwinner. For example, in Ukraine, Valentin had been working in a low-paid professional job, as well as moonlighting, and he and his wife had borrowed money from their parents. He told the story of how one day he came home after buying a banana, two apples, milk and a couple of other products and realised that, sitting at work for 11 hours, he had earned only enough to buy that bag of shopping. Valentin's sons were growing up and he could not afford to support them. 'As a bloke (*facet*) you have to be able to provide that.' As a consequence, Valentin and his wife decided on a new livelihood strategy: 'we must try out migration.' Similarly, Sergei commented that 'there are no decent wages in Ukraine. But I'm a normal person, a man, I ought to be able to support my family'. Since Sergei now had a highly-paid job as a long-distance lorry driver based in Poland, he had recently told his wife that she did not need to work after she arrived. She should concentrate on improving her language knowledge. (As mentioned in Chapter 4, several Poles I interviewed also mentioned that their wives had initially not worked, but focused on improving their English.) Pavlo, by contrast, told his wife to go home to Ukraine. 'I simply told her it wasn't necessary. She was earning too little here. I was earning twice as much, and our children were in Ukraine.' Emma's husband had also experienced upward mobility as a result of migration, moving from a recycling factory in Ukraine to well-paid construction work in Poland. He had told Emma that she should not work for money until he had earned enough for them to open the café mentioned earlier in this chapter. Ostap was clearly proud that he 'could afford' for his injured girlfriend, living in KPP, not to work. 'I said, "Don't try to find yourself a job. We'll find some work you enjoy."'

Although these male interviewees self-identified as breadwinners, the women were not so obviously homemakers, with the exception of Lizaveta, who commented that her fiancé 'was born with a spanner in his hands and I was born with a frying pan'. The handful of unemployed wives expressed frustration that they were not working. Wives who were working full-time in KPP could also regret their homemaking burden. Nataliya said, 'If I was here on my own I would just drink tea, eat a sandwich, buy a bit of chocolate, have a snack. But, as things are, it's meal after meal [which I have to cook].' Oksana cooked for her husband at weekends, when he was based in company housing in a village, but she had refused to work and live there during the week, on the grounds that she would be lonely. In KPP she had made some good women friends and enjoyed being able to do odds and ends of shopping for herself after work.

Women graduates who had joined partners working in skilled manual occupations often seemed particularly dissatisfied with KPP, but also resigned to staying in the smaller city for the sake of their husbands and sometimes also their children. For example, Irina was a senior accountant from a Ukrainian city, married to a carpenter who had done well in his Polish company and been promoted to manager. Irina had requalified at an adult education college in Piła but struggled to find a suitable job. She explained, 'My husband was working near Piła, which is why we rent a flat here and live in Piła. I would have liked a bigger city, but! … I spent a long time looking for a job and couldn't find one. Perhaps because I'm Ukrainian they didn't want me. I don't know. It's a small city. There were jobs available in Poznań.' Yuliya recalled:

> Usually people go to bigger cites, but it happened that my husband's friend found him work in KPP … We did talk about the fact that there are bigger cities. And he said he really liked the way of life in a smaller place and for example you don't need to commute an hour to work like in a city. So we're different in that way, because I like big cities, where there's lots going on.

Solo women and men

The women who had migrated solo, often as the only breadwinner in their household, might seem to have been particularly forced by circumstances. This group of interviewees included two women who were fleeing violent partners. The fact that they lived in small towns in Ukraine made it hard to hide from their partners, and Poland offered a safe haven. Another group of women had disabled husbands and were the family breadwinners. Olesya, for example, left her poorly-paid job as a security guard to work in Poland as soon as she considered her children old enough to be sufficiently independent. Raisa worked as head of human resources in the local hospital, but despite this apparently senior position her salary seemed far too low. Her husband was ill, she had some responsibility for supporting her mother, and her daughter was about to become a student. She tried working as a servant in Moscow, but was sent back to Ukraine in the Covid-19 pandemic, and felt there was no option but to migrate to Poland. Lone parents were under particular pressure to migrate. In most cases, they left their children with their mothers in Ukraine, although one arrived in KPP with her teenage son. Other women did not have family responsibilities, but had found women's work too insecure and poorly paid in Ukraine. Alla, for instance, had a string of jobs, as fruit machine supervisor, translator in a firm which then shut down, market stall trader, administrator in a warehouse, and finally manicurist. She had come to Poland because she was invited by her former colleague and because she felt her life in Ukraine was too uncertain.

At first glance the eight married men who worked alone in Poland – all in Płock in 2019[3] – might seem to be typical 'incomplete' migrants, fulfilling their breadwinner role while their wives cared for children in Ukraine. However, from the interviews it became apparent that they had not adopted the role of solo breadwinner migrant from choice. Three had already invited their wives to join them, but the latter had refused. Two more had wives with disabilities. The remaining three wives had breadwinner status in Ukraine, thanks to their superior jobs. On economic grounds it made sense for them to stay behind, although they were not averse to working abroad. It was not unlikely that family reunification might happen eventually in some of these cases. In Kalisz and Piła, two to three years later, the married men I interviewed were all living with their families.

Educational level and occupation in Ukraine

Forty-three of the 69 interviewees did not have higher education, making this a less well-educated sample than many Ukrainians previously studied by researchers, but more similar to the profile of workers in Bydgoszcz surveyed by Górny et al (2019). A handful of younger men possessed only a secondary education, and had left school without taking examinations. Like Dawid in the Polish group, these men went straight into migration after school. However, the other non-graduates possessed some kind of vocational training, in a variety of fields. For men, this was mostly construction-related. Women held below university-level healthcare or teaching qualifications; there was also one female metal-worker and vocational college teacher, and several technicians.

The 26 university graduates had degrees in law/policing, engineering and metallurgy, teaching, economics and accounting, administration and management and information technology. Sixteen were working in white-collar jobs before they migrated. Overall, it is difficult to generalise about the graduates, partly because the qualifications and institutions attended were so diverse. A handful of interviewees had completed five-year degree programmes from big city universities; one had worked as a university lecturer and another had turned down a lecturing job to become a journalist. However, most interviewees did not have prestigious qualifications, and they sometimes made disparaging comments about their educational background. For instance, Nataliya, who had completed a part-time extramural degree from a college in a small Russian town, where she was working as a labour migrant, asked rhetorically, 'So what kind of education is that?' Like their Polish counterparts, they tended to complain about how people in graduate-entry jobs were too poorly paid, even in the biggest cities. For instance, after completing a Law BA, Ruslana had worked for three months in Odesa around 2019, earning £100–140 a month.[4] She decided to give up and joined her mother in KPP, where she worked in a factory.

As among the Polish target earners, small business failure was a strong incentive to migrate, particularly when accompanied by debts. The case of Kira and her sex shop was mentioned earlier in this chapter. Former entrepreneurs mentioned high taxes and bribes as particular hazards in Ukraine. For instance, Mihaylo – who also explained his migration decision with reference to his son's need for higher education – complained: 'If you work and pay all the taxes you'll become bankrupt. You have to conceal something. They've created a situation where it's impossible to function. So I shut my business and told my wife, "I'm off to Europe, let's see what it's like there."'

Skilled manual workers who worked using their Ukrainian-gained skills and expertise in Poland constituted a separate and in many ways privileged group. They included welders, carpenters, builders and drivers. Some other interviewees had been trained in welding in the factory where they were employed in Płock and were considering using this skill in their further careers. The five unemployed women in the sample were married to skilled manual workers, who could keep their families on one Polish wage, even though welders and drivers were sometimes said to have not earned much money in Ukraine. Nataliya, who worked in a supermarket in Ukraine and a factory in Poland, pointed out that it was easier for men to migrate abroad, if they had manual skills. 'A man can always find work – as a welder, for example – but what about me?'

The other Ukrainian interviewees had generally not expected to work in Poland using their qualifications. This was partly because so few had done so in Ukraine. Although migrants in many societies cannot work using formal qualifications, this downward social mobility has sometimes already occurred in the sending country, a fact which must influence the migrants' further choices about which country offers the best livelihoods. To return to Ukraine, for these interviewees, would often not imply returning to a congenial, still less a high-status job. Musiyezdov (2019: 41) speculates that many Ukrainian migrants in Poland had not worked according to their qualifications in Ukraine and suggests that 'it is unlikely that professional disqualification abroad is so different from that in Ukraine'. My research confirms this.

This shift of occupation had taken place for numerous reasons. In some cases, interviewees or their parents had been unable to pay the necessary bribe to secure a job commensurate with their qualifications. Some older interviewees were caught out by possessing obsolete qualifications. Anna, for instance, had a Soviet law degree, but spent her life in petty trade and market gardening. A further set of interviewees graduated with particular vocational qualifications which made it impossible for them to find adequate employment. They included several welders who had finished college with a qualification for a skill level which was lower than what was required in most welding jobs. Women were disadvantaged because they tended to follow their husbands, meaning that they could be living in a location where there was no demand for their skills. Not surprisingly, mothers, after maternity leave, were particularly likely to have stopped using their professional and vocational qualifications. For instance, Larysa trained as a nurse, had children, and worked as a florist in Ukraine before losing her job. Emma had worked as a detective inspector but later sold lingerie at her sister's market stall.

The interviewees had found themselves at the mercy of wider structural forces, as Brzozowska's (2023) study of Ukrainians in Poland also indicates. Hence, their livelihood strategies were quite adaptive. This was particularly evident in the stories of women aged 42–60, who were well-represented in my sample. For instance, Tamara had trained as a Russian teacher, in Russia, but that turned out to be unneeded in Ukraine, even though she lived in the Donetsk region. She and her husband became entrepreneurs, but were evacuated to Poland because of the Russian invasion in 2014. Polina had become a candidate member of the Communist Party of Ukraine as part of her livelihood strategy, but with the disintegration of the USSR this turned out to be useless. She

had trained as a jeweller in a college – presumably connected to the local factory – but with the transition to a market economy she was unable to secure a job using her qualifications. She ended up doing heavy manual work in another factory for most of her career, together with some care work in Warsaw, and smuggling, since she lived near the Polish border.

West–east comparisons

In 2012, the Labour Migration Survey organised by the International Labour Organization, with Ukrainian partners, interviewed 45,500 Ukrainians in 23,500 households (ILO 2013). The results showed how migration from Ukraine was overwhelmingly a west Ukrainian phenomenon, involving 10.8 per cent of people between the ages of 15 and 70 in west Ukraine, compared with under two per cent in other regions (ILO 2013: 37). More recent surveys, conducted in Poland, show the mass arrival of labour migrants from non-western regions. Górny et al's (2019: 24) survey of Ukrainians in 2018 in Bydgoszcz, a city of 335,000 near to Piła, and a comparatively recent destination for Ukrainians, presents information most comparable to my own.[5] Their figures suggested that only about a quarter of Ukrainians in Bydgoszcz were from the west. As shown above in Figure 7.1, west Ukrainians, defined to include people from Khmelnytskyi, Rivne and Chernivtsi regions as well as all areas further west, were also the minority among my sample (19/70). Interviewees were conscious of the turn. Kira, from a central Ukrainian city, noted that 'there were people who used to migrate to Russia, but now they don't go on principle. In connection with the conflict. Even though they didn't earn badly there ... So they started going to Poland, Germany, Czechia, and some men went to Latvia and Lithuania.' Others, such as Oksana, who had been in KPP since 2016, noticed that the proportion of Russian-speakers had risen. She commented that 'life in that part of Ukraine used to be good. Now the whole of Ukraine is migrating'.

Górny et al (2019: 25) observed that west Ukrainians in Bydgoszcz were most likely to hail from villages and from towns of up to 50,000 population, whereas over one third of migrants from east Ukraine came from big cities of over 500,000. A similar divide was visible in my own sample: among the west Ukrainians, only 1 of 19 was from Lviv (the only sizeable city in west Ukraine), with a further three from smaller regional capitals of over 200,000 population (Ivano-Frankivsk and Ternopil). By contrast, 39 of 51 of the non-western interviewees were from cities of over 200,000, including the student and one labour migrant from Kyiv.

Western Ukraine

Elena, explaining why she came to KPP from Rivne region, explained 'because I'm from a small little town' (*takoi gorodok nebol'shoi*). West Ukraine contains many small towns and villages with a history of international migration stretching back to Austrian Galicia in the nineteenth century. Kaltenbrunner (2018) writes of the 'globally connected Western Ukrainian village'. Transnational networks and traditions persisted through the twentieth century, despite the Cold War. After the disintegration of the USSR in 1991, west Ukrainians began migrating intensively again, as described for example by Blank (2004: 349) in her account of a 'town on the southwestern border of Ukraine where the collapse of the Soviet system has triggered the disintegration of the political, economic and physical infrastructure, as well as the concomitant departure of almost all those able to obtain visas to emigrate'. The usual livelihood strategy was incomplete migration by just one family member. Geographical proximity and visa-free travel up to 2003 particularly encouraged migration to Poland (Brunarska et al 2016: 116), as did Polish ancestry and connections which were quite common in the region.

In the KPP sample, the longest-established interviewee, Adam (60), was a construction worker who had grown up in a small town near Ivano-Frankivsk with a tradition of chain migration to North America and Europe. During the Soviet period he taught himself Polish with the aid of Polish women's magazines, and had Polish friends working on local oilfields as well as relatives in Poland, who came for visits and later to sell sausage. Adam himself had visited Poland, and when his business failed in 1993 it seemed the obvious livelihood strategy to stay with a friend in KPP and find some building work in the shadow economy.

The other west Ukrainian interviewees arrived after 2014. By this time, incomplete migration was beginning to be succeeded by family reunification. For example, Hlib came from a small town in Lviv region. When he was a child, his parents had taken it in turn to migrate to Poland, while he and his sister remained in Ukraine. His parents then settled in KPP and Hlib joined them when he finished college. Polina, a solo migrant from another small town in Lviv region, told me about her sister, who had recently started working in Poland. 'Her husband had been going to Poland for fifteen years, without her. So she said, "I miss him too much, I'm not the right age any more, I want us to be together."' In another case, Daryna, from a village in Lviv region, had come to KPP first, then invited her parents, whom she worked alongside in a factory. The grandmother remained in Ukraine on the family smallholding.

Some informants emphasised the diversity of migration destinations from west Ukraine. Olesya implied that for many, Poland was just a stepping stone to other countries.

> There was a time, long ago, well perhaps ten years or more, when people used to go to work in Poland … But nowadays from my little town they go further afield. They tried it here in Poland, earned a bit of money, then went further west, to those Jews, to Israel, and to Italy, lots of women went to Italy … Sometimes I come back and the town is practically empty. Everyone is migrating. They go to Poland, to Germany, at one point lots of people went to Portugal. Only those people who can't leave stay.

On the other hand, the stories told above about family reunification by west Ukrainians suggest that, in those families at least, Poland was chosen as a place to settle.

Most interviewees came directly to Poland from their Ukrainian villages and small towns, although, as mentioned already, Kvitka, from a small town near Lviv, had tried and failed to establish a livelihood in the city before going to KPP. Just five interviewees were city-dwellers. Like Kvitka, they complained about the cost of urban living, but, overall, push factors were less noticeable in their stories of why they came to Poland than in the accounts of interviewees from small towns and villages. Milena, from Lviv, emphasised pull factors – her sense of connectedness because of her Polish roots. Zlata, from Ivano-Frankivsk, had been tempted by a friend to start working abroad because she was not enjoying her managerial job. She stayed in Kalisz because of the Covid-19 pandemic, since her perception was that Ivano-Frankivsk had been harder hit by unemployment than Kalisz, then met her future husband, from east Ukraine, and married him in Kalisz. However, she wanted to return if that ever became possible. 'To be honest, I like my city, Ivano-Frankivsk, much better than Kalisz. You say you were there three years ago? It has developed a lot since then. It's so beautiful, I feel really fond of it.'

Yuliya was more ambivalent about Kamianets, a city about the size of Kalisz: 'Although Kamianets-Podilskyi is a beautiful city for tourists, if you look more closely at everyday life then it seems it just has the shops, the market, and that's it.' Oksana and Olena, the two interviewees from Ternopil, depicted their city as livelier and more multicultural than Kalisz or Płock. Olena, for example, practised her English when cutting hair for students she described as 'Afro-American'. She complained, 'In Ternopil there's more going on. Here, at the weekend you don't see anyone out.

There's nowhere to go. Here people are quieter. In Ternopil, there are lots of little cafés, restaurants, shops – when it's a day off, people meet up, while here they hide away.' Both Oksana and Olena had good jobs in Ternopil, as a nurse and a hairdresser. Oksana had left to follow her husband, a highly-skilled technician, while Olena had thought it might be fun to try working in Poland with her boyfriend, escaping her parents. However, even though they gave no impression of feeling forced to migrate from Ternopil, unlike their village and small-town counterparts, Oksana and Olena both suggested that migration from Ternopil was substantial. Oksana (aged 41) said:

> Lots of my friends work abroad. I have a very good friend in Austria, she's been there for years ... My (other) friend was in Italy for six years ... Parents of my son's schoolfriends often go abroad. Sometimes the mother, sometimes the father. There are some parents a bit younger than me whose own parents are still abroad. They just stay in Ukraine with the children and their parents send them money. Grandparents are here, and Mummy and Daddy are in Ukraine.

Oksana's suggestion that younger people were encouraged to make livelihoods in Ternopil because they were subsidised by parents working abroad chimed with comments by Fadei, aged 20, from a town of about 16,000 population near Lviv. He claimed his contemporaries generally preferred to stay and try to set themselves up locally, whereas their parents went to work abroad. Lavra, aged 45, from an industrial town in Lviv region, had done exactly this – migrating originally to buy housing for herself in her home town, but then spending the money on a flat for her daughter. These accounts by interviewees from places which were considerably larger than villages indicate the need to recognise the variety of sending locations within west Ukraine.

Southern, central and eastern Ukraine

Forty-seven of 70 interviewees were from regions which the ILO (2013: 38) had defined as having 'low' or 'very low' intensity of labour migration in 2012. However, even then these regions did include individual places from which people migrated abroad. For example, Anzhela, commenting on her own town, from which no one had migrated five years previously, mentioned that 'my sister lives in a village [near Poltava]. By the way she's in Poland too at the moment. And there are no jobs at all. Practically none. That's why there are a huge number of people from villages like that working abroad.' I interviewed Andrei, who had left Mykolaiv in 2011. He said, 'Life forced me. I had no job. It was hard to find work, and I could see that everyone was migrating. So off I went. On my own.' On the one hand, Andrei's impression that 'everyone was migrating' as long ago as 2011 is intriguing. On the other, the fact that he went on his own, with nothing fixed in advance, hints at the absence of established migration networks with which west Ukraine was already richly endowed.

Interviewees who had arrived in Poland a few years previously often had the sense that they had been at the start of a wave. Kira, from Kropyvnytskyi, already quoted with reference to the turn from Russia, asserted that:

> I wasn't one of the absolute pioneers (in 2016) but it wasn't on the same scale … It didn't often happen that people from central Ukraine went abroad to earn money. Very rarely. And now for the past three years lots of people have started to migrate because the situation in Ukraine is so unstable … I went back for New Year, and I heard that lots of my friends had left … Practically every second person has left.

Ivan, who had also left Kropyvnytskyi in 2016, was the first person he knew to do so, but, like Kira, thought that there were now many. Similarly, when Dmytro left Zaporizhzhia in 2016 he was such an amateur that he tried to find work in Poland through a travel agency. However, when he went back to the city after an absence of just three months he was struck by the increased number of advertisements for work abroad. Anzhela left her town in Poltava region in 2017. She explained how local people had previously lacked both incentives and confidence to migrate, but that since about 2019 they had gathered confidence, as the migration networks evolved.

> People used to joke and call our town Little Hollywood. Everyone felt fine, there were factories, it was OK. So there wasn't that flood of people leaving, specifically from our town. Five years ago, when I left, it was unusual. People were too scared. But over the last two years I've heard about a lot, really a lot of people, and I can see on Facebook that people are leaving.

Varvara, who had been a hairdresser in Kryvyi Rih, and claimed to have a 'large acquaintance', kept track of people she knew on Facebook. She commented on how 'lots of our acquaintances came to Poland after we did. Lots and lots of people are coming.' Other interviewees mentioned Kherson and Sumy as cities where nowadays many Ukrainians were leaving to work abroad.

However, in a paradoxical and, in view of the war, now poignant twist, some interviewees in 2021–2 also had the impression that their home locations had been developing rapidly in their absence. They underlined the infrastructural improvements which had taken place in recent years.

> Halyna: Sometimes I show Polish people my photos of Dnipro. Dnipro is so much better than it used to be. It's really flourishing now. It's so lovely that when you show the photos they don't believe it.
> Anne: Is that because they think Ukraine is a very poor country?
> Halyna: Yes, they think it's all derelict and in ruins.

Similarly, Alla mentioned:

> In summer (2021) I went back home to Chernihiv after a gap of three years. The city had changed dramatically. So much had been built, new homes, new roads, and really up to European urban standards … Such lovely parks, perfect roads and really even pavements. Unfortunately Kalisz isn't like that.

Raisa, from a much smaller town, in Kharkiv region, mentioned that 'it has transformed over the last 10 years. It's a little tiny European town. A lot depends on the mayor'.

In contrast to pretty western and central Ukrainian tourist cities like Chernihiv, Ivano-Frankivsk and Kamianets-Podilskyi, some other cities in central and eastern Ukraine were seen by interviewees as dangerous places because of pollution and the threat of war. Pollution from Soviet-era industry was mentioned by parents from Kryvyi Rih, Mariupol and Zaporizhzhia. Vera, who had left Ukraine in late 2021, and also mentioned the war, said 'Our goal was to leave Kryvyi Rih. Because it's an industrial city … and there is so much pollution that you can't breathe. Particularly closer to the city – the sky is red, there are the factory chimneys, and always that particular smell. Our son has asthma.' Emma, also from Kryvyi Rih, said, 'If you hang clothes on the balcony they'll be covered in smudges within an hour or two. Because our city is a city of mines. It's full of mines. Children are constantly ill with laryngitis.' Lev complained:

> In Zaporizhzhia we have lots of polluting factories. People try to protest about them but there is corruption and nothing gets done. Of course the weather is nice, and the one very good thing is the River Dniepr which runs through the city. But the rest isn't so good. It's a big city, a million inhabitants, lots of cars and factories, so it's very hard.

Exceptionally, Lavra, from west Ukraine, also complained about pollution. She liked Płock because she perceived it to be unpolluted, compared with the mining town where she lived in Ukraine.

Although Andrejuk (2017a: 223–6) found that insecurity about war in Ukraine was already leading some families to migrate to Poland, by late 2021, the threat of full-scale Russian invasion was becoming a more urgent migration motive for people in east Ukraine. Boris said that:

> We left Ukraine very quickly, we'd wanted to get visas and we'd applied for them but because of the situation brewing around Ukraine – the possibility of war, and those incursions, we decided not to wait for the visas ... In three days we had gathered our things, got in the car and drove to Poland.

Similarly, Emma mentioned that 'they were packed and gone in exactly two weeks'.

The war had touched interviewees personally in different ways. Tamara, the refugee, has already been mentioned. Pavlo, who had served in the army, and lived near the front line, said what it was a relief to be in Poland: 'You work your eight hours, and no one is pointing a gun in your face.' Two interviewees were widows of soldiers who had been killed in action, leaving them not just emotionally scarred but also having to support themselves economically. Polina, interviewed in late 2021, was in a state of anxiety about her son, a professional parachutist in the Ukrainian army. Other interviewees also had sons and brothers in the military. Alla, for example, described how she had not felt able to come to Poland the first time she was invited, in 2014, because she was constantly worrying about her brother. 'My brother is a soldier and so I couldn't just leave Ukraine. I was so worried and I couldn't think of making any trips abroad. But time passed, as they say, you can get used to anything. And I realised that I had somehow to earn my living.'

The interviewees from east Ukraine were also worried in more general terms about the situation in their local area. Tatyana, for example, described the terror of experiencing a night of explosions in a local arms depot, while Emma was worried about minefields. Two interviewees from Mariupol both introduced themselves in 2019 as being from 'where the war is' and mentioned how stressed their neighbours had become. Interviewees from Kropyvnytskyi, further from the front line, also felt it had made living in Ukraine a sad experience. Mihaylo said, 'Everything is worse than it was, people are envious, they are embittered because of the war.' Kira complained, 'There used to be some stability, people would paint their houses, touch up the window frames or whatever, and now they don't have any money, everything is grey, grey and faded, you can see life is tough.'

Conclusions

This chapter adopted a livelihood strategy approach to analyse why Ukrainian interviewees decided to migrate, and thereby understand migration to KPP. Hardly any were considering returning permanently to Ukraine. They expected to be in Poland either as circular migrants – mostly in cases where for reasons such as age or disability their family members could not join them – or, increasingly, to settle in KPP for the medium term with their families. As in the case of many post-2004 Polish migrants, the migration culture contained seemingly contradictory elements. Ukrainians had a sense of mobility options and agency, while stressing that they were 'forced' by economic circumstances and in some cases also war and/or pollution. Although they were not officially refugees, even before 2022 war was a prominent *motif* in the narratives of interviewees from east and east-central Ukraine. Adopting an intersectional approach, the chapter identified different sub-groups of Ukrainians, considering the influence of education, age, life-stage, gender and family status on motivations. For example, parents of older teenagers had overwhelmingly migrated wholly or partly to finance their children's education, if those children were still in Ukraine rather than Poland. This seemed to be an expected sacrifice. Another sub-group consisted of women graduates married to skilled manual workers who were in KPP chiefly because it suited their husbands, even though they preferred big cities. Several male interviewees had migrated to maintain their breadwinner roles, which in some cases they had enhanced by migration. However, only one woman mentioned enjoying her homemaker role. Stay-at-home mothers did not seem pleased to be kept by their husbands and expressed frustration that they lacked paid employment.

As in the case of Polish interviewees, age or social status did not predictably link to curiosity or aspirational and lifestyle motives for migration – these were expressed by people of all backgrounds and ages. Aspirations varied widely, from learning to drive to becoming a popstar. However, it was noteworthy that the ambitious women were more likely than the men to highlight the importance of learning Polish perfectly in order to realise their ambitions. The prospect of deskilling in Poland could potentially deter would-be migrants, but this was barely mentioned in the interviews. Most interviewees had already deskilled in Ukraine in the sense that they were not working using their formal qualifications. Location of origin also played a role in shaping motivations. War and pollution in east Ukraine have already been mentioned. East–west differences were also manifest in how interviewees spoke about the scale of migration from their local areas: their own motivations were contextualised within those wider flows. Interviewees from west Ukraine, including cities, were conscious of long-standing and massive international migration to the west, although they also mentioned that nowadays adult children of migrants were quite likely to stay put in Ukraine, partly supported by remittances from their parents. Migrants from other parts of Ukraine did not mention multi-generational migration patterns and in most cases they commented that migration to the EU, especially from cities, was a recent phenomenon. Nonetheless, they reported that over just a few years migration had become normalised as a livelihood strategy and that cultures of migration, in a narrow sense, had sprung up across central, southern and eastern Ukraine.

Notes

1. Defined here as stretching from Ukraine's western border up to and including Chernivtsi, Khmelnytskyi and Rivne regions.
2. For Wielkopolska figures, see USwP (2022) and UdSC (2021).
3. If not for the pandemic, I would have conducted the Kalisz and Piła interviews in 2020, before some of my interviewees' family reunifications had taken place. I would therefore have been more likely to have some of this type of pre-reunification male migrant in my sample.
4. She said 500–700 zl.
5. Ukrstat (https://www.ukrstat.gov.ua/operativ/menu/menu_u/ds.htm) also publishes migration statistics, but these are based on de-registrations from place of residence, so they understate the scale of migration.

8
Migration to Poland: agencies, families and friends

Introduction

Chapter 7 analysed Ukrainian interviewees' migration motives and push factors from Ukraine, including their perceptions that migration had become a normalised livelihood strategy in their local areas. Chapter 8 looks at pull factors: how and why the interviewees had migrated specifically to Poland and, even more specifically, to Kalisz, Piła and Płock. Chapter 8 builds on Chapter 3, which considered why migrants and return migrants sometimes prefer to settle in smaller cities, contributing to the second stage of Poland's migration transition. However, Chapter 8 is largely concerned with the mechanisms of migration: how Ukrainians migrate to these smaller cities, which in turn does much to explain why they end up there in particular. After a short section discussing reasons to prefer Poland over other countries, the chapter looks first at what the interviewees said about employment agencies, and then at their use of family and friendship ties.

Agencies play a large role in facilitating migration to Poland, partly thanks to the simplified procedure for migrants from western countries of the former Soviet Union. Employers declare that they need a certain number of workers who are then recruited by agencies (Górny et al 2018: 28; Kindler and Szulecka 2022: 462–4).[1] These labour brokers can be considered part of the migrants' networks, constituting 'weak ties'. However, as Kindler and Szulecka (2022) also show, in the years before February 2022 many Ukrainians were employing a combination of 'strong' and 'weak' ties. Researchers have also found that Ukrainians moving to the Warsaw agglomeration, where there was a longer history of Ukrainian migration, relied more on their social capital, whereas in provincial cities there was more use of agencies (Górny et al 2019: 40, 58). In Bydgoszcz, near Piła, 40 per cent of respondents found their jobs through agencies and 40 per cent through Ukrainians who had worked for the same employer (Górny et al 2019: 40).

The chapter particularly focuses on personal networks, since they were the main factor determining why the interviewees came to KPP. Networks linking origin and destination countries do much to explain migration routes globally (Boyd 1989; Massey et al 1993). Chapter 4 illustrated that family and friendship ties and networks have been and remain significant in Polish migration. The same proved to be true for the Ukrainian interviewees. This is not surprising, given evidence about Ukrainian migration collected by other scholars, such as Brunarska et al (2016), Górny et al (2019) and Kindler and Szulecka (2022). Family reunification in Poland is a particularly important topic for this book, given that it often consolidates migrant settlement plans and thereby underpins the settlement stage of Poland's migration transition. Writing about Mexican–US migration, Massey and Espinosa (1997: 952) observed, 'Migration tends to become self-perpetuating because each act of migration creates additional social capital that promotes and sustains more migration, which creates more social capital, which produces more movement'. In the twenty-first century, migrants can communicate, persuade one another and share information more easily than in the past, and the dynamism of network formation is impressive. This is as true for the Ukrainian as for the Polish case. Mihaylo, for instance, mentioned how in the central Ukrainian city of Kropyvnytskyi in the last couple of years 'it turned out that everyone was inviting friends and relatives to join them, or bringing over their whole family'.

Nonetheless, family reunification attempts sometimes fail. In this respect, as in many others, the migration transition process is not always smooth. When researching transnational migration networks, questions need to be asked at every stage about how exactly networking takes place: who initiates the process, how widely decisions are consulted, and, in case of disputes, how agreement is reached or objections overridden (White 2017). Dynamics within the family – sometimes the extended family – need to be taken into account (Hondagneu-Sotelo 1994). Families are differentiated according to life stage: children can be young, teenage or adult, and some migrants have caring responsibilities towards their older parents in Ukraine. Moreover, since migration often also takes place within specific mobility cultures, networking should be explained with reference to prevailing norms and conventions.

The 69 Ukrainian labour migrants in KPP comprised 36 'trailing' family members and friends as well as 33 people who had come independently or with their spouses. Forty were living with family members in KPP and

19 were (still) living on their own. The share of migrants living on their own was larger among the 2019 interviewees in Płock than the 2021–2 interviewees in Kalisz and Piła, perhaps by chance (given that I did most of the Płock interviews in a migrant hostel) but more likely partly reflecting the fact that Ukrainian family reunification had become more prevalent in Poland by 2021. The two groups' motivations for being in KPP were different. Individuals who migrated alone were people who had chosen jobs in KPP. The trailing family and friends had come to KPP to join people already there. They in turn might invite others to follow.

Chapter 8 begins by considering general reasons why the pioneers chose Poland, rather than other countries. It then considers the means by which pioneers migrated – through agencies and personal networks. Here personal networks were being used instrumentally, to find jobs. By contrast, for the non-pioneers, personal networks constituted migration motives. Trailing interviewees migrated because they wanted to join someone already abroad, and/or that person wanted them to come. The chapter explores practices in the migration culture concerning the processes and conventions of inviting and reunification. It also analyses instances of refusal, where spouses or adult children could not be persuaded to leave Ukraine. The refugee phase of Poland's migration transition partly constituted a delayed family reunification process, as Ukrainians already living in Poland before the full-scale invasion gathered in their parents, female family members and children – even though some of these family members must have previously resisted joining their Poland-based kin. Finally, the chapter looks at invitations from friends. Chapter 7 mentioned the new waves of migration from locations in eastern, central and southern Ukraine. These waves were possible not just because family members were inviting one another to Poland but also because of rapid networking between migrants and their friends, the potential migrants. In some cases, this was a reunification of close friends abroad. In other cases, the relationship was more distant, but if requested to do so the interviewees often seem to have felt obliged to help people they knew.

Pioneers' reasons for preferring Poland

For half a dozen interviewees, Poland had not been their first choice. They had been put off by the cost of UK visas; failed in their attempts to find people to support them to go abroad to Ireland, the UK and Italy; and in one case been refused a visa. The visa applicant, Sergei, dreamed of moving to Canada, a classic country of emigration from Ukraine. He said that after he was refused, 'I didn't know what to do. It must have been God who pointed me in the right direction. I was considering selling my kidney ... but at Easter, after church, an inner voice told me to open my laptop and look [again] for work in Ukraine or abroad.' This was how Sergei found his dream job in Poland. The other interviewees' reasons for preferring Poland were more conventional, and similar to those uncovered in surveys by other researchers. They included the simplified procedure; language; and (more rarely) perceived geographical proximity.[2] With regard to easy documentation: as Irina put it, 'Only Poland gives us the right to come here and work. Germany doesn't, England doesn't, it's less simple to get into Czechoslovakia [sic] ... That's why there's such an influx of people, everyone is going to Poland.' Varvara also mentioned that you could easily bring children: a reason why families were settling in Poland:

> There's no other country where you could come and get a visa, a residence card. You can be here and work and live with a child. That's important. If I'd gone to another country I wouldn't have been able to bring my son from Ukraine. But as soon as we arrived my son was accepted into a school and I found a job ... Czechia in principle is as good as Poland ... However, you wouldn't be able to bring over your child right away.

A second reason for preferring Poland was the language. This was similar to the case of Poles feeling it might be 'easy' to go to the UK and Ireland because they had learned English at school. As Lyudmila pointed out, 'There are lots of similar words, so you can learn Polish faster, you can understand it faster'. Germany was appealing to several interviewees, especially after it became easier to work there legally from 2020. Nonetheless, they worried that German was harder to learn than Polish. For instance, Nataliya said, 'I'd be interested in Germany, but it's scary. In Poland at least you can understand the language.' Finally, some countries seemed too far away. Olha cited the example of her friend who worked in Finland for very high wages and invited Olha to join her. However, for Olha, being 'close' enough to visit her children, a two day's bus journey, was more important. She commented, 'Everyone has their own priorities.' As mentioned in Chapter 3, Zinaida claimed that Poland was preferable because it was 'near' Mariupol.

Impressions about the downsides of other countries often came from other migrants, a type of information-sharing which can be considered an aspect of social remitting, where ideas picked up abroad were spreading among Ukrainians (White 2024b). For instance, two interviewees had close relatives who had worked in Germany and their experiences put them off. Italy, although tempting to some, and a traditional destination for Ukrainian women migrants (Solari 2017) was also said to have disadvantages. Lyudmila had heard that there were 'lots and lots of immigrants, African refugees, which is why wages are lower, so wages have fallen for Ukrainian labour migrants'. Moreover, she claimed that Poles were considered to be 'more open' to Ukrainians than were Italians. Israel, Italy and Germany were all mentioned as options having been rejected because of the hazards of working in the shadow economy.

Agencies

Granovetter's (1983) distinction between strong and weak ties is helpful for understanding migrants' use of agencies. Strong ties might find you one particular job, and you can trust the person who recommended it. By using a weak tie you gain access to a wide range of jobs, but the agency or informal labour broker may turn out to be untrustworthy. A number of interviewees, mostly in Piła, were convinced that you could not just walk into a job in Poland but would need to be employed by a temporary employment agency, at least for an initial period. This was perceived as a significant limitation on the freedom to move and change jobs. However, others, particularly in Kalisz and Płock, had obtained work in factories and other workplaces directly, simply by contacting the human resources department. Hence, they did manage to bypass agencies.

When the solo interviewees first went to Poland, the exact destination often seems not to have been considered important, except insofar as they had chosen to be in an urban area, in preference to agricultural work; some interviewees also discounted big cities as options. The nature of the job and the working conditions were the most important considerations. In some cases the agency had not even consulted applicants about their destination.

> That was another deception. Because I was going to the Samsung factory and was officially registered in Wronki. But once I'd sat out the quarantine they put us on the bus and took us to Piła. I even thought I was in Wronki! We were taken to Piła, and went to work, and they told us that there were no vacancies in Wronki and we've brought you here instead.

As Elena's reference to 'another deception' indicates, Ukrainians could be the victims of agencies' lack of transparency in various respects – according to Polish labour inspectors, a common phenomenon (Kindler and Szulecka 2022: 464). KPP interviewees complained that agencies, especially in Ukraine, charged a lot of money; were unreliable about meeting migrants when they arrived in Poland; took a big cut out of their wages; and fined them too readily for small infringements of rules. Some interviewees had their own bad experiences, and many heard scare stories on the migrant grapevine.

Liliya was an example of an interviewee with bad experiences. She and her relatives had paid $1,000 to an agency in Ukraine to fix up visas for Poland, but the agency failed to do the work, so Liliya approached an acquaintance instead. Inna and her husband had rushed to KPP because their agency told them they were needed to start work immediately, only to find that the jobs were no longer available. With 50 others, they were out on the snowy streets in an unfamiliar city looking for work. Olha complained that 'the first time, I went through an agency. I paid a huge amount and the work turned out to be different from what was advertised'. Several interviewees had experienced a string of bad luck. Lyudmila, for example, reminisced about a hostel where 'we were expected to sleep two to a bed, the beds were packed together, no furniture, you had your suitcase under the bed, the conditions were awful and you had to pay 250 zloties for the accommodation!' She and her sister decided it was unacceptable and found some work cleaning railway carriages in the freezing cold for 12 hours a day. Then, when their agency lost its tender, they were transferred to a chocolate factory which was unbearably hot. Finally, they gave up on agency work. Another sister had meanwhile gone to KPP, and recommended it, so they decided to be employed directly by the factory where she was working.

Scare stories were not just personal experiences, but also part of migrant lore. Some interviewees took it for granted that agencies would cheat, setting their own experience against this background of general knowledge. Dmytro commented, 'Of course, the work turned out to be completely different from what was advertised.' Alla, who had been invited to KPP directly by her employer and had no direct experience with agencies, referred to stories on the internet:

> To be honest I wouldn't risk it. I think it's a bit unreliable. Because there are lots of online reviews where people write that agencies deceive people. They promise something and when you arrive they more or less place you in barracks. Not in good conditions.

Yurii mentioned that he had gathered stories about unreliable agencies from living in a migrant hostel. Artem thought that the problem was mostly on the Ukrainian side, basing his judgement on a more general conviction about legal culture in the two countries:

> There are agencies in Ukraine which just take your money and that's it. They will forget to process your passport and send you to Poland. So everyone is scared … If it's a Polish agency, it's OK to use it … Ukrainians are greedy, they want to make lots of money fast.

However, interviewees recognised that you might need to use an agency the first time you came to Poland, before you had acquired migration expertise. Yevhen observed:

> Some people don't have friends who can give them tips about how to do things properly. They go through an agency. I did the first time I came to Poland. I didn't like it and I found another job. It's bad to use an agency because they deceive people. They say one thing, and when you arrive it turns out different.

'Tips about how to do things properly' include soliciting recommendations from friends and relatives who have used a particular agency or employer (see also Kindler and Szulecka 2022: 468). For example, Artur waited until a friend had received his first month's pay before following his lead and signing a contract with the same company. He said, 'I think they sometimes write one thing and it turns out to be quite different in reality. But we've already checked it out. My friend who is working there already has been there a month and got his first wage. So I know that I can go there too.' Olha said, 'There are lots of agencies nowadays, many in every city … When it comes to work, I think, if you're looking for it, you should find out from people you trust, who've worked there already, who've been there and are 100 per cent sure they do pay the wages'. Lyudmila explained, 'We ask our acquaintances, if we've found a likely place, whether they would advise it. If they don't, we don't go there.' Four interviewees possessed friends who ran their own agencies, in Ukraine and Poland, so this gave them a certain degree of trust that they would not be cheated.[3]

Kindler and Szulecka (2022: 469) conclude that 'social networks play an important role as safety nets when it comes to labor exploitation'. The KPP interviewees also used their personal networks to mitigate the risks of relying on labour brokers. The consensus seemed to be that personal contacts should be used wherever possible. Interviewees prefaced their comments with the phrase 'of course', indicating that this was self-evident migrant wisdom. Yurii for instance stated, 'It's better through friends. Of course. For the agency, there aren't any individuals, just a workforce.' Solomiya said: 'Of course, it's best not to go through an agency. Because an agency could cheat you, how can you be sure?' The flip side of this automatic distrust of labour brokers was sometimes a readiness to trust ordinary Ukrainian strangers. Solomiya had found her job through a stranger whom her husband happened to meet when travelling back to Ukraine. Kira told a story of how she used an agency when she first came to Poland but the recruiter failed to meet her in Warsaw. She solved her problem by talking with a Ukrainian couple ('of course, you see other Ukrainians') who were waiting for a lift to KPP.

Family reunification

According to migration network (or 'social capital' or 'cumulative causation') theory, pioneers invite family members and friends to join them in the receiving country. Over time, migration becomes less risky for migrants who are weaker in various respects, such as dependent wives and children (Massey and Espinoza 1997: 53). Although it might have been cheaper for the household to remain in the sending country, the incentives such as missing each other and the benefits for children are stronger than economic motives (White 2017). Family reunification abroad also happens because the pioneers, as they form place attachments abroad, want to invite their family members to be with them and to make a new home.

Given the common expectation in Ukraine, as in other countries, that men are the main breadwinners, it would not be surprising if men played the role of pioneer. Fourteen wives in my sample had followed their husbands to Poland. In several cases, they presented this as part of a family strategy, suggesting that they had always intended to move to be with their husbands, but that for practical reasons it made sense for him to go first. In these cases the women should not be viewed as 'trailing' wives. In other cases, the husband had migrated expecting only to be a short time in Poland, or had open-ended plans. Although many female interviewees had followed their husbands, there was only one case where a male interviewee had successfully been joined by his wife, and this was at his second attempt. The processes by which the wife – and sometimes the children – became migrants are discussed below.

In another successful reunification, the woman was the pioneer. As mentioned in Chapter 7, Milena felt strongly Polish. She initiated the family's move to KPP. She said, 'I was the first to come to Poland. My husband doesn't know any Polish but I've understood Polish for years … I always planned to come to Poland … and my husband was fine with it, he always agrees with me.' Among women I interviewed in KPP, several had had arrived together with their husband, and in some of these instances the wife was the instigator. Zinaida and Olena's accounts of how they decided to migrate to Płock – taking their husbands with them – were quoted in Chapter 7. In Płock, hostel accommodation was available in two-bed rooms, facilitating migration by couples. It helped explain why in 2019 at least one of the interviewees had ended up in Płock rather than elsewhere. In September 2019, Nataliya complained that it was hard to find cities where married couples could live together, hence when she joined her husband Płock was one of the few options available. However, by 2021 there were plenty of employment agency advertisements for couples to work in Poland, with accommodation. There had been 'a dramatic increase in demand for vacancies for married couples. According to the Gremi Personal surveys, about 15 per cent of respondents plan to move to Poland with their families' (Zarobitchany.org 2020).

Some KPP couples left their children in Ukraine, and no one expressed surprise at this. Here the Polish case is not parallel, since relatively few parents migrate together without their children, especially for extended periods (Walczak 2014; White 2017). As research in other countries shows, mothers who leave their children in the sending country tend to do so only if they feel confident that they will be well-supported in their absence; usually this means leaving them with female relatives (Parreñas 2008: 62; Urbańska 2009: 78). Kira said, as if it were self-evident, 'Naturally, children are left with their granny, an aunt or a sister.' This was the usual arrangement among my interviewees, backed up by phone calls and internet communication as well as visits back to Ukraine. Zinaida for instance explained how she continued to act as head of her Ukraine-based household even in Poland:

> In the break, I phone my parents and my daughters at work and keep up with all the family matters. I need to know what's going on. I'm the boss (*rukovoditel'*) [laughter] I decide all the complicated questions. All the questions come to me … Not my husband, he's my second husband … My parents and I brought up my daughters on our own. That's why I run everything, know everything, make all the decisions.

Only one interviewee reported a man being entrusted with childcare. Larysa had left her two younger children with her estranged husband. She presented this as being for his own good, saying, 'It's for him to bring them up, to teach them, feed them, clothe them, and understand what it means to be responsible for children.'

Naturally such arrangements raised concerns. On the one hand, interviewees were not always sure their child was being brought up as they would like. Oksana's son, for example, was her mother's only grandchild, but when she tried to persuade her mother to give him more independence she said, 'Oh, you're so far away, it's so hard for him, he's all alone.' On the other hand, there was the possibility that the grandmother would not be able to cope, because she was still employed. For example, Nataliya's mother was still working night shifts, while also being responsible for her two teenage granddaughters, a situation Nataliya described as 'scary'. Larysa had left her two elder children with her mother, but complained that 'when I was at home, they took their schoolwork more seriously. Now they seem to be a bit more casual'.

Anna knew cases where arrangements had broken down and the children had come to Poland.

> We have people at our factory who have put their children into the technical college in KPP ... They want their children to be with them, not granny. Well, you understand, when adult children or teenagers are left with granny and grandad, it won't end well. They're not going to study properly and they simply want to live their own lives. The grandparents can't control them.

Several interviewees mentioned that they decided to migrate only when their child had passed a certain age limit and could understand the situation. The age limit was never younger than 14. Actual maturity of behaviour was also taken into consideration. Lizaveta felt able to leave her teenage daughter because she knew how to keep house; in fact she had consulted her daughter about whether to go to work in Poland. 'She said, "Mum, I'm an independent girl," so I wasn't afraid to leave her. I knew my parents would keep an eye on her.' By contrast, Lizaveta's sister would only come to Poland for summer seasonal work, not leaving her son for longer. He was 'a bit of a spoiled boy, so my sister has to be with him'. Svitlana justified the fact that she and her husband had left their 14-year old son with his grandparents in Mariupol by saying that already he had 'a grown-up way of thinking'. The temporariness of the arrangement was also used in justification. It was only until he finished school in Mariupol, after which he would come to KPP. Svitlana also backed up her argument by saying that '80 per cent of labour migrants (*zarobitchan*) leave their children because they have no other choice'. In other words, she justified her action by presenting it as a recognised if regrettable aspect of the migration culture.

Caring at a distance for older relatives was also a concern for some middle-aged interviewees. As Kordasiewicz et al (2018) found with Polish migrants, people started worrying about how they would care for parents in advanced old age well before the parents had actually reached that stage of dependence. For example, Lizaveta mused about whether or not she should go back to Ukraine. 'My parents are there, you know, in about three, or maximum five years, I ought to be there … I understand I should be there for when they are old.' Lizaveta's sister lived near her parents, who were comparatively young, and Lizaveta's immediate family were based in Poland, so it seemed unlikely that she would return to Ukraine, but she had a sense of guilt and obligation. Several interviewees mentioned how they supported their parents financially and in kind. Oleksandra, for instance, had recently returned to Ukraine to buy her mother's fuel for the whole winter. Only in a very few cases (before 24 February 2022) were interviewees talking about bringing their parents to Poland, and when this was mentioned it was sometimes to complain that the parents – usually young retirees – did not want to come. In other couples, family reunification of wife with husband in Poland did not take place because the wife was prevented from leaving by caring responsibilities towards parents or in-laws.

Parents among the interviewees spoke of how much they missed their children, or had missed them before they were reunited in Poland. Those initially left behind sometimes talked about missing the pioneer. Irina, for example, joined her husband with their children in Poland out of the conviction that 'a family at a distance (*sem'ya na rasstoyanii*) isn't a family'.[4] However, even although missing each other and wanting to be together for emotional reasons was the root cause of family reunification, reunification could only happen once it came to seem possible because acquaintances were behaving this way. Interviewees reported on how they noticed more instances of children coming to Poland with their parents, or to join a parent or parents already working in KPP. Irina, for instance, commented on this phenomenon in Piła: 'There are lots of people coming as families. Particularly because of the situation [in early February 2022]. There could be a war tomorrow. Three years ago there were hardly any families. I knew every one of them. But now there are lots.' Olesya similarly observed: 'Nowadays people are coming to Kalisz from the east, from central Ukraine, from the south – they are simply coming as whole families. The whole family arrives: him, his wife and the children. And the children go to preschool and then to school.' Ruslana, who had joined her own parents in Kalisz, and worked in a different factory from Olesya, said, 'I often meet people where the parents came first and then collected their children. Lots of people who work at my factory have come here to settle, with their children, lots of children are going to preschool, and there are plenty of young people about my age.'

Being aware of the phenomenon led to reflection on whether it might be possible to do it oneself. For example, in Kalisz, Nina commented, 'Recently many people are arriving as whole families, with children. To stay in Poland for good.' She continued, 'I've been here four years and I'm thinking about this as well ... although you have to take into account the child's age. My friend brought over her daughter, who's 14, like my son. She's having a very tough time. A small child adapts more easily.' Nina's comments point to some of the difficulties involved with family reunification. Others include the paperwork. As mentioned in Chapter 1, it is possible for Ukrainians to join family members in Poland through an official family reunification route, but this can be a lengthy process. Yuliya mentioned that she sat at home unemployed for two years waiting for her documents. Childcare was obviously a potential obstacle to reunification with younger children, although, in one case, the interviewee's mother had come to Poland.

War was mostly not mentioned as a motive for family reunification, except by people arriving in 2021–2, and by a few interviewees from east Ukraine with personal experience of the post-2014 conflict (see Chapter 7). Tatyana, interviewed in 2019, was a lone parent from Luhansk region and said that she really understood what war meant. 'It is very scary. It's one reason why I came to Poland. I was afraid that our area would become a war zone again. I thought, it's all the same to me where I live and work, it doesn't have to be as a teacher. I want my family to live in a peaceful place.'

Aspirations for children's education are a common migration motive, and the Ukrainian interviewees were no exception. Brzozowska (2023: 2380) also found that her interviewees aspired to give their children a better start in life. To quote Irina once more: 'To give the children a future, better than I could give them in Ukraine. Here they will be able to choose how they want to live and what to study.' In the context of Poland's migration transition, it is noteworthy that part of the settlement process for some parents with older children consisted of abandoning aspirations for the children to achieve higher education in Ukraine and instead focusing on bringing them to Poland to complete their education. Parents interviewed in Płock in 2019 had mostly not yet managed to bring over their children. However, people who lived in the migrant hostel learned that it might be possible, and began to dream their own dreams. Tatyana, for instance, hoped that her daughter, who wanted to become a translator, could study languages in Poland and have a year abroad during her degree programme. Tatyana's original plan was that her own vacation work in Poland would finance her daughter's higher education in Ukraine. But then she decided to continue working in Poland because she could earn so much more money there, and she became aware that it might be possible for her daughter to join her. At first the daughter had been reluctant, because she did not want to leave her friends in Ukraine, but after reflection she decided that she would try. Tatyana was planning to looking for a school in Płock specialising in English.

Nataliya had recently joined her husband in Poland, on an experimental basis, although she was keen to continue. She was trying to decide what would be the best course of action for their teenage daughters.

> I said to my daughters, 'Let me bring you to Poland. I can work, and you can study.' 'No, no, we want to study in Kharkiv. We're going to stay in Kharkiv' ... My daughters will finish secondary school in two years' time and I won't be able to get them into an institute unless I work in Poland ... But if I leave them there, while they are teenagers, how are they going to study? They need their mother with them. But in Ukraine I can't earn enough money ... I say, 'Why don't you come to Poland, get your education here, and the whole world will be open to you.'

Larysa had heard stories about older Ukrainian children attending school in Płock, and this prompted her to wonder whether she might be able to bring over her four children in descending order of age. 'My son is about to finish Year 9 and I'm trying to decide about his education. Now the snow has thawed a bit, I can go and make enquiries, if they would take a child after Year 9, whether they need to know Polish in advance.' Oksana had already tried to persuade her 15-year old son to come to finish his education in a technical college in Płock, but he refused on the grounds that he wanted to study a different subject.

In Kalisz and Piła, many parents I interviewed in 2021–2 had already brought over their children, mostly within the last couple of years. These included not just older children but also children of preschool and primary-school age, although only in families where there were two parents who had both migrated. Mostly these parents made use of their friendship networks and social capital to help them settle with the children, as discussed in the section on friendship networks below. There were also some pioneers in this group. Lev and his wife had worked temporarily in Poland before the pandemic, then used their enforced absence from Poland for a period of reflection. They had decided to try migrating as a family. A major consideration had been the son's education. 'Here they have European degrees and you can use that degree the world over. Our Ukrainian degrees are worthless in Europe. If you get a Polish qualification you could work anywhere in Europe.'

I also interviewed one Ukrainian student, Antin, who was the son of migrants living in Poland. His parents were divorced and he had grown up with his mother in a big city in Ukraine, but come to KPP to study because his father was working there. Since Antin also worked at a variety of jobs during his studies, some of his comments are included in other chapters of this book. As a student, he integrated very successfully. Although he did not have Polish origins or a Polish card, he had attended Polish cultural events in Ukraine and dreamed of coming to Poland since he was a child. His Polish language, which he learned in KPP, was excellent;[5] he was doing well at his studies; and he was an active volunteer. He intended to apply for a permanent residence card after five years of living in Poland. As an information technology specialist, he felt confident about his future career, and he already had an online part-time job. After graduating, he wanted to set up his own business. His girlfriend was from KPP and they aspired to buy a plot of land, build a house and bring up a family in KPP. On the other hand, I was told several stories of children who had attempted to study in Poland but not succeeded academically.

The process of family reunification sometimes includes an inspection visit. For example, Bohdan's stepfather checked out work in a factory in KPP before deciding that it would be all right for Bohdan to join him and work there. For migrants already living abroad, place attachment plays a role: they invite their families to visit partly because they want to show off the place where they now live. For instance, Olha said, 'I would really like the children to see how I live here, my work, what it's like here.' Yevhen said that he wanted to invite his wife, show her Poland and walk round Płock. In some instances these holidays also plant seeds in the minds of the invitees, and there can be a fine line between a holiday and an inspection visit (White 2017). For instance, Inna reported, 'We'd been here for a year and my daughter came to see us in the school holidays.

It was her first time abroad and she wanted to see what it was like here. And then she stayed.' Liza said of her own daughter, whom she had left in Ukraine when she first migrated:

> She's in Poland now and she's 22, she's already grown-up. She visited me once for my birthday and since she was finishing college then [in Ukraine] we were thinking about higher education [in Ukraine]. But she liked it here, and after two weeks she was saying she wanted to live in Poland. So I said 'Give it a go' … She tried to study here but it didn't work out … So she got a job.

Family reunifications were sometimes planned in stages. Anna, as mentioned in Chapter 7, had a Polish Card and considered Płock her home city. She and her husband had paid a brief inspection visit to check out the options for education and employment. Her children then completed their secondary education at a technical college, living in student accommodation intended for Polish children from surrounding villages. Meanwhile their father lived in the factory hostel and Anna sold their property in Ukraine before coming to join him. Now the whole family lived in the hostel and worked at the factory. As also mentioned in Chapter 7, Melaniya's husband came to Poland two years before she did, as a labour migrant. Meanwhile she had been studying Polish in Kyiv and getting her Polish Card.

Anna and Melaniya, despite moving later than their husbands, were actually the chief migrants, since it was thanks to their Polish Cards that their families gained residence rights in Poland. They presented the household strategy as one which belonged equally to the two spouses. In other cases, however, husbands would persuade or even pressurise their wives to join them. For instance, Kseniya said 'My job was quite creative … it was a shame to leave it. But my husband [a long-distance lorry driver based in KPP] likes it here, and he was the initiator. He wanted it. That's why I came to Poland.' Oksana said that her husband did not like being alone in Poland and 'called her' (*pozval*) to join him. In fact, Oksana then lived separately from her husband during the week. Nina also resisted living with her husband who was working in a different city in Poland. Nina had a great deal of self-confidence and enjoyment from her new career in a beauty salon. Among the interviewees, she was unusual in distancing herself from the migration culture and highlighting that she was flouting convention. 'Some envious people in Ukraine tell me I ought to stay at home. But it depends. I don't have to do what they say. I do what's best for me. It's my life, isn't it? I only live once.'

It seemed to be universal to consult children's opinion, a practice rarely mentioned to me by Polish mothers in connection with their own family's migration but which has also been discovered in other Ukrainian migration research (Krakhmalova and Kloc-Nowak 2023). The need to consult was mentioned both by adult children, who had joined their parents, and parents who were thinking about or trying to persuade their children to join them. For instance, Hlib said, 'They said it was better in Poland, but they didn't try to make me come. I decided for myself. I could have stayed in Ukraine.' Olha said about her elder son: 'He should only come if he really wants to. First he needs to come and have a look, and then the child will make his own decision.' In cases of whole-family migration the choice of country sometimes had to be agreed between family members. Olesya told the story of a fellow factory-worker who had come to KPP with her daughter, wanting to give her a better life, and had originally been hesitating between Germany, Czechia and Poland. The daughter had chosen Poland and was now happily settled in school.

Family reunification did not just concern husbands and wives, or parents inviting children. It seemed normal for invitations also to be extended in other directions. Children could invite their working parents, as in the case of Daryna who had invited her parents to join her at the same Polish factory. Moreover, extended families also arrived through the process of chain migration: siblings, aunts and uncles, and other family members could be involved. Viktor and his sister had both been working in Russia but then she tried out Poland and invited both him and later his father. All three, together with the sister's husband, were now working at the same factory. Svitlana had been invited by her son and was now working at a factory in KPP with not only her son but also her husband, her brother and his wife, as well as her niece. In a distant relationship: Polina had been working in Lviv and commuting from a small town in Lviv region. Her son's girlfriend's mother worked in KPP. 'She invited me to come here to work. She said it would be easier. "You can sleep at home [sic]. You won't be doing night work." And so I came here.'

As Ryan (2023: 63–4) points out, despite the 'lure of strong ties', for each pull towards the receiving country there are usually competing ties to family and friends in the sending country. I found in my book about family reunification from Poland to western Europe (White 2017) that reunification also has a reverse side, a kind of invisible dark matter. This is constituted by non-reunification, or attempts at reunification which fail. Among my interviewees, several had unsuccessfully invited their wives. They refused usually because they had good jobs in Ukraine, which they were reluctant to leave. In a few cases, the woman invited already had migration experience, and preferred to stop being mobile. Artem, a long-term circular migrant, explained why his wife refused to join him in Poland by saying, 'We have a proverb that moving house twice is as stressful as experiencing a fire ... In Soviet days, that's what people said.' One interviewee described his wife, who refused to budge, as being the type of person who prefers to 'sit like a cat in one spot'. There were also several cases of children who refused to join parents in Poland, including some already mentioned in this chapter. Married children or siblings with their own children were often said to be too settled in Ukraine to want to migrate. It generally did not seem expected, and sometimes perhaps was not considered acceptable, to try to invite these settled families to come to Poland. This changed after the Russian full-scale invasion of February 2022.

Exceptionally, some interviewees had refused to invite their family member even when that relative was keen to come. One woman described how she was holding out against her pensioner husband's requests that she either come home or that he join her in Poland. In his opinion, they were not a proper family if they were not together. In her opinion, he needed to mind their flat, and she needed to earn money in Poland to support him and their children and grandchild. A possible compromise – that he should come as a tourist – had recently been scuppered by the pandemic restrictions.

Finally, there was a category of reunifications where the invitee came, but returned to Ukraine. For example, Polina's disabled husband had come to KPP and tried working as a taxi driver for two months. However, the cost of hiring the car and renting the flat made it financially not worthwhile. Olesya had obtained a Polish Card for her son, and he had worked for a year in KPP, living with her. However, he decided he wanted to go to university in Ukraine and at the time of interview she was supporting him there, although he was hoping to be able to work in Poland in the vacations. Andrei had come to Poland 10 years previously and continued working in Poland. He reported:

> At one point my son did work in Poland. He worked for six months and said, 'Dad, I don't want to do this.' The work was too heavy! Now he's [in Ukraine], something to do with computers. And he has just started driving a taxi. He does have a job and an income, but so it wouldn't get boring at home I thought up the idea of the taxi.

One interviewee had tried moving from KPP to Poznań and persuaded his wife and son to join him. However, they had a difficult time and she began to suffer mental health problems. Hence she told the interviewee, 'I'm leaving, because I'll go mad here, and it's bad for our son,' and returned to Ukraine.

Migrating to KPP with the help of friends

Migrants are important in providing information about locations abroad for their contacts back in the sending country. Nataliya, from Kharkiv, had been one of the first people she knew to move to Poland. She said, 'I was one of the first. And as soon as I went everyone started phoning me and asking how it was going – was it working out? They're keen as well.' However, unlike in previous periods of history (even the Polish migration wave of 2004–7) potential migrants did not necessarily need to contact their personal acquaintances if they wanted information about how to migrate; social media was to some extent a substitute. When I interviewed Liliya in KPP and our conversation turned to family reunification, Liliya took out her phone and showed me a YouTube video where a Ukrainian family in Gdańsk described their experiences of settling in Poland. She took this to be an authentic experience which provided sufficient guidance for Ukrainian people considering taking the same step, whatever the proposed Polish destination. Hence, the mobility culture is being reinforced by social media. Ivan similarly remarked:

> There are lots of Ukrainians here in Poland, so [at home in central Ukraine] we don't particularly talk about Poland. You know, when I used to go home, when very few Ukrainians migrated, then people were really interested. 'What's it like, how is it in Poland?' And now there are heaps of Ukrainians in Poland, so everyone knows about everyone else and when you come home they don't even bother to ask. 'So, you came home. So what. It's good you're back.' No special questions. Well, they might ask 'How was your job? How much did you earn?' But actually people already know for themselves. There are lots of YouTube videos, they show everything. About prices, living conditions, etc.

For some interviewees, friendship ties had been a strong migration motive. Reunifications abroad take place not just between relatives but also between close friends. In my sample, Margarita and her daughter followed her husband to KPP, and then, as part of the plan, her close friend Varvara came with her son. Hence both women's families were reunited in KPP. Klara, aged 25, was in KPP because she had been persuaded by her best friend. Her first attempt failed when Klara changed her mind and decided she could not leave her small children in Ukraine. However, on a second attempt the friend succeeded. Lizaveta told me how she was persuaded by a friend based in Poland – later her fiancé – who was visiting Ukraine on holiday. At the time, Lizaveta was working in a shop and feeling exploited.

> He said 'Don't you want to come to Poland?' So I said 'Poland? No! I'm never leaving home.' So he said 'Well, think it over.' The next time he dropped into the shop he goes on at me again: 'So how are things?' I say 'Worse and worse.' So I think – perhaps I should take the risk? And I asked my daughter what she thought.

Possessing transnational ties with trusted close friends helps explain why the alternative option of internal migration is often not regarded as a viable strategy. Klara, for example, had come to Poland from her small town apparently without even considering whether she might work in a Ukrainian city. She commented that you would need to fix up a job and accommodation – on your own – and it would be too expensive. However, just as there exists a 'dark matter' of unsuccessful family reunifications alongside successful ones, so too there are cases of unsuccessful persuasion by friends. Nataliya told me about a friend, who, with Nataliya, had earned 'kopecks' in a Kharkiv supermarket. The friend had been spending the summer working seven days a week in a restaurant in Bulgaria, and would earn 3,000 euros. Nataliya said, 'She was constantly telling me, "Come on, Nataliya!"' Lizaveta mentioned how her own woman friend had tried to persuade her to switch from Poland to Germany.

Simply knowing people does not constitute social capital: for a friendship to constitute a resource, the friend has to be ready to help. They may be more likely to do so in locations where there exists a culture of migration, including a general expectation that friends will help each other migrate. This is true in some small Polish towns (White 2017). As so often, west Ukraine seems to present a parallel case. Yeva, for instance, who lived in a village in west Ukraine, said that she would always invite someone who asked her, although she had personal misgivings. I was interested in finding out whether interviewees from parts of Ukraine with less well-established migration traditions felt under obligation to invite their friends. I asked Yevhen, for example, if there was an ethos of helping people to migrate from his village in southern Ukraine. He said that some people helped, while others viewed the would-be migrants as 'competition' and refused. On the whole, however, people did invite one another. Svitlana, reporting on how they had invited a female friend to join them from Mariupol, simply said: 'that's normal.' There were some interviewees who had made a definite habit of inviting others, although sometimes these were people they met in Poland. Ostap, from east-central Ukraine, said:

> On my shift there are six of us from Ukraine. They're my friends. I was the first. I was the only Ukrainian working in logistics. I gathered together the rest of them. I recommended them to my boss. I told him I had some friends who would do a good job and were keen to work. They want to live in KPP and to stay for the long term. First one, then a second, then the second brought over his son, then another person, and I had collected a whole team. One was from my home town and the rest were friends I'd made in Poland.

Margarita and Varvara, the friends mentioned earlier in this chapter, were prolific inviters of friends from their home city in eastern Ukraine, but Margarita's husband was not. Margarita said, 'They say, "Help me with a job," or "Help me find a flat." So we help … My husband says, "Rita, stop it." But if I can help, why not?'

Other people prefer not to help, but will do so if asked. I asked Ivan whether he had invited people to Poland. He said, 'On purpose, no, but when they asked me, yes. I've already explained to you. I love Ukraine and want to return to Ukraine. I don't want to bring people to Poland! I want to live in Ukraine, I don't want my friends to come and live here.' Some interviewees refused to invite others. Artem, who was exceptionally negative about KPP, said: 'No. Probably because I work tremendously hard, and I don't want someone to come here and then complain that they did such a heavy job and earned peanuts.'

Other interviewees had themselves been refused help by friends, and felt betrayed. Valerii, for instance, was in KPP unintentionally. He expected his friend, who was well-established in a big Polish city, to help him in some way, at least for the first week when he knew no Polish at all. When this friend changed his mind Valerii phoned another friend who was based in KPP. The story illustrates how members of the wave can be so well-networked that they can survive being let down by one acquaintance. Lyudmila had also been let down, by her son's partner's mother, who worked in Italy.

> We once had a conversation about it, and I asked her, but she shied away, I could see she didn't want the responsibility, so I didn't ask her again. I don't like being a burden on anyone. So if I go there I will look for myself, not through my friends. Of course back then I was in dire straits and I needed to go abroad as fast as I could, but she didn't help. And I stopped asking.

Lyudmila seemed to think that the (informal) in-law relationship carried some level of obligation beyond that of a mere acquaintance, but clearly the other woman did not. On the other hand, as mentioned above, Polina was in Poland because her son's (informal) mother-in-law took the initiative.

Conclusions

Asked why they chose Poland, the Ukrainian pioneer and solo migrants mentioned similar reasons to those given by Ukrainians in other studies. Poland was 'easier', both linguistically and in terms of access to the labour market. Some also mentioned an additional reason: the possibility of bringing one's children with one. Agencies play a considerable role in recruiting foreign workers to Poland, much greater than they did in recruiting Poles to work in countries such as Ireland and the UK after 2004. The pioneer and solo migrants had tended to use agencies for their first trip to Poland, and some were in KPP in particular because an agency had sent them there. They had been attracted by the advertised pay and conditions. However, the chapter also showed that for subsequent trips interviewees often tried to reduce their use of agencies. There was a culture of relying on personal networks wherever possible, either to bypass agencies or to check their reliability. In a number of cases, interviewees had originally gone to a different city in Poland through an agency, had bad experiences, and then used informal networks to find the KPP employment. In other words, as they became more experienced migrants, they became more embedded in social networks. Yevhen, a welder in Płock, was quoted as asserting, 'Some people don't have friends who can give them tips about how to do things properly. They go through an agency.' By implication, 'doing things properly' meant relying on friends and family, in accordance with the prevailing migration culture.

Migration culture was changing apace over the years 2019–22. Many individuals were changing their strategies – no longer migrating to support children's education in Ukraine, but bringing them to Poland and educating them there. This happened because family members were unhappy to be parted, and because of dissatisfaction with arrangements whereby children were left with grandparents. Migrants also felt that older children would obtain a more useful education in Poland. However, another factor was that the pioneers realised – after living in KPP – that it would be possible to emulate members of their migrant networks in KPP. Bringing children to KPP and settling in those cities was an achievable aspiration. The pioneers were also putting down anchors in Poland, and becoming attached to KPP. Hence they wanted to invite their family members and sometimes also their close friends to be with them and make a new home. Just as in Poland after EU accession, the migration culture was evolving to encourage whole-family migration. Thus it helped consolidate Poland's migration transition.

Continuing on the theme of migration culture, various conventions attached to the practice of family reunification. Generally, in my sample, men were the pioneers and initiators. However, there were cases where this role fell to the wife. Children were always consulted about whether they wanted to move to Poland. Chains of extended families were also quite common, as siblings, aunts, uncles and other relatives relocated to the same Polish city and often the same workplace. However, the background to this dynamic process of family reunification was a 'dark matter' of failed reunification attempts. Although this family settlement phase of Poland's migration transition was impressively rapid, it was not as rapid as it might have been had these failures not occurred. Migrants also invited their friends and provided information to potential migrants from their places of origin. Generally the information-providing role of existing migrants was decreasing, thanks to social media such as YouTube. However, friends still had a strong supporting role, notably in helping newcomers find schools for their children. Although many locations in Ukraine have a very short migration tradition, it seemed that there was already a culture of existing migrants helping potential migrants, if asked for support. However, it is possible that this sense of obligation to help was partly or largely engendered within the populations of Ukrainian migrants living in KPP: in other words, the migration culture was in the receiving country, rather than the individual sending locations in Ukraine.

Notes

1. By 2017, the peak year, almost 9,000 agencies were registered in Poland (Kindler and Szulecka 2022: 464).
2. In a 2022 survey, language similarity was named by 30 per cent of labour migrants and 40 per cent of refugees as an important reason for choosing Poland (Jarosz and Klaus 2023: 19).
3. A phenomenon also discussed by Kindler and Szulecka (2022: 468).
4. For similar Polish cases, see White (2017), Chapter 7: 'The emotional impact of migration on communities in Poland'.
5. I interviewed him in Polish, unlike the other student interviewees, who preferred to speak Russian.

9
Ukrainian jobs and integration

Introduction

Ukrainians were increasingly settling in Poland, but there were several strands to the settlement process, which are explored in Chapters 9–11. Chapter 9 uses integration as a framework of analysis to consider how interviewees improved their legal status and labour market and cultural integration. They had to apply for visas and residence permits; choose work (insofar as they had choice); seek better work, or promotion; and come to terms with feelings about deskilling in Poland and dissatisfaction with their current occupations. The chapter also considers their language acquisition and reflections on cultural differences which they perceived to exist between Ukraine and Poland. These included positive Ukrainian auto-stereotypes circulating as part of the Ukrainian migration culture abroad. Applying Ager and Strang's (2008) indicators of integration, the chapter therefore considers how interviewees were integrated in the domains of citizenship (in this case, residence status); employment; language; and culture. Ager and Strang's model is particularly suitable for this chapter since it 'displays a sensitivity to the relationship between the specifics of the places into which … [migrants] settle and the particulars of the integration process' (Platts-Fowler and Robinson 2015: 480).

Given that interviewees were unevenly integrated in different domains, and also that many of them were not sure whether they wanted to stay in Poland or move further west, the chapter also invokes Grzymała-Kazłowska's metaphor of 'anchoring' to help understand how a sense of being securely anchored in some respects was superimposed on the actual temporariness of formal status possessed by most interviewees. Chapter 10 applies a different conceptual lens, place attachment, to consider more closely the emotional dimension of integration. It looks at why some Ukrainian interviewees seemed likely to stay in KPP, while others would move on, and investigates how interviewees talked about their process of attachment and settlement. Overall, Chapters 9 and 10 illustrate how grassroots processes contribute towards Poland's transition to becoming a country of immigration. However, as in the case of family reunification processes analysed in Chapter 8, Chapters 9 and 10 also show that integration and place attachment paths are often far from smooth, and are marked by stops, starts and changes of direction. As in previous chapters, I apply an intersectional approach to understand how different combinations of identities and competences resulted in different experiences. Unsurprisingly, the extent of each person's language confidence and exposure to Polish native speakers turned out to be particularly significant in facilitating or impeding integration. However, there were also common denominators, including, in 2021–2, near universal frustration with long waits for residence permits, which undermined interviewees' sense of making progress in settling.

The Covid-19 pandemic might have been expected to affect the labour market experiences of Ukrainians interviewed in 2021–2. It had particularly hit Ukrainians working in feminised sections of the Polish labour market, such as hospitality and cleaning (Górny et al 2021: 60). Lizaveta, for example, worked in a bar in Kalisz. She said, 'There was less work, so we went home … We were stuck in Ukraine for three months because they shut the border and didn't let us back. But the Polish girls went on working … They still had a little bit of work.' Most of the KPP interviewees were doing other jobs, in less gendered sectors, but the pandemic still caused a certain amount of disruption, for both women and men. It resulted in several interviewees' not having their contracts renewed, although in most cases they later returned to the same factory. In some cases, they were replaced by Polish female workers who had been made redundant. Oleksandra recalled in 2021:

> They shut the shopping centres, and the young Polish women lost their jobs. And in our [feminised] factory they didn't want Ukrainian workers because they were scared of coronavirus. There were more Polish women looking for work. Workplaces were shutting down … The bars and pubs were closed. So people came looking for work and now there are Polish girls working here.

There was also a domino effect from Polish migrants returning to KPP. For example, Milena explained, 'When coronavirus began, Ukrainians went back to Ukraine and Poles to Poland. When I finally managed to get another visa and returned to the factory [near Kalisz] there were no spare jobs because it was only Poles working. But afterwards they all rushed back to Germany.'

Finally: the chapter demonstrates once again that making money was by no means the only marker of achievement for many interviewees. Quality of life in Poland was also very significant. Dolińska (2019a: 157), writing about Ukrainian university graduates in Poland, suggests the need

> to look beyond the economic migration motivations ... as the primary incentive to relocate abroad. It was rather the overall better working conditions, the lack of the ubiquitous corruption, the flexibility of travel resulting from their regulated legal status, the developed infrastructure, and the transparency of the social system allowing for greater self-realisation and for assuming agency, which in general translates into the capacity to actively take control of their decision-making.

Although most KPP interviewees were not university graduates, they seemed to display a similar set of motivations, particularly as their stay in Poland extended, and their original 'target-earner' motives were overlaid with other considerations. Hence working conditions, for example, were very important when choosing and staying with a job.

Residence permits

Ager and Strang (2008) claim that 'rights and citizenship' is fundamental to achieving integration in other domains. This does not mean that migrants have to become naturalised as citizens. As denizens in a foreign country, they have rights and can become integrated in many regards, as long as they possess secure legal status. Like other Ukrainians in Poland, the interviewees mostly began their stay with a permit on the basis of an employer's declaration of intent to employ a foreigner, or a work permit granted to a specific individual. A few had arrived in Poland 'on their biometric passport', taking advantage of their entitlement to spend three months in Poland without a visa or work permit, after which they either went back to Ukraine or regularised their stay. A handful had joined their spouse through the family reunification route.[1] By the time of their interview, in 2021–2, my informants in Kalisz and Piła had generally progressed to the stage of extending their stay by obtaining a temporary residence permit. Some had set their sights on long-term EU resident status, for which they could apply after five years in Poland and passing a language examination.[2]

Logically, obtaining official resident status should make a migrant feel more anchored in Poland. However, the process of obtaining the residence card from the regional (*wojewoda*) offices in Poznań was often so lengthy and difficult that it had the opposite effect. Applicants felt alienated and unwanted. These were not just individuals' private experiences, but shared with other Ukrainians on social media and in everyday conversation. Boris, for example, mentioned that 'I met a guy at a petrol station who told me he waited a year and eight months for his first card. It's a nightmare. We have a friend in Zielona Góra who waited five years'. The delays with residence documentation dented interviewees' impression that Poland was an efficient country with a good legal culture, despite their better experiences with officialdom in other areas. This was not just an experience particular to Ukrainians in KPP. Szaban and Michalak (2020: 191) cite the fact that it took so long to obtain a residence permit as the chief frustration mentioned by their 36 Ukrainian interviewees in Wielkopolska in 2019–20. Brzozowska (2023: 2384) writes that for her interviewees living in and around Warsaw 'acquiring a residence status was a demanding and challenging task even for informants with relatively long experience in the Polish labour market … In 2018, the legalisation of temporary residence took more than six months on average'. The time limit on working in Poland without a temporary residence permit was extended in January 2022, and then suspended altogether by the March 2022 decree on provisions for Ukrainian refugees. However, Ukrainian interviewees in Piła in February 2022 had applied for residence permits under the old regulations, so this was what they complained about in their interviews.

The interviews revealed at least six different types of problem with applications for residence rights. The first problem was the long waiting time. Interviewees had often waited over a year. The second problem was the difficulty of influencing the outcome. Decisions were made at regional capital level, exacerbating the sense of helplessness in people based in the smaller city. Just one interviewee had in fact managed to obtain a short-term, stopgap permit after visiting the office in Poznań. Moreover, during periods of Covid-19 restrictions offices were closed for face-to-face visits. The third frustration was having to refrain from visits to Ukraine while waiting for permission to remain in Poland.[3] Nina, for example, as quoted in Chapter 7, complained, 'Last year I was in KPP for Christmas. I was so depressed that I was here, and my family was at home … It was because I was waiting for my documents.'

A further grievance was arbitrariness. Other people who applied later or seemed less worthy in some respect of a residence card sometimes had better luck. This rankled, for example, with Oleksii.

> Oleksii: I waited 15 months. It's a very long time. Because my parents and everyone are at home, sometimes you want to go back for a week, don't you? You have to wait because to get a visa from Ukraine [the alternative] also takes a long time. You have to wait about two months. But now I have my residence card I can go where I like.
> Anne: It's not connected to the pandemic?
> Oleksii: No, it's connected to Kalisz. It's difficult to get documents. Well, for example, just to compare, my colleague who is completely uninterested in Poland or anything, and just worked here, she came to Kalisz and got her card in four months. How can that happen?

Oleksii was already negatively disposed towards Kalisz, so perhaps it was not surprising that he particularly blamed the city, although this is not where decisions are made. The fifth grievance was that officials made mistakes. Tamara, for instance, mentioned that 'we've been living in Poland for four years already and still not got our residence cards. They got lost, then the process was started again, then they wrote that I was Ukrainian, not Russian, they got mixed up – that's the sort of thing that happens'.

There was also the fear of being refused and having to return to Ukraine. Elena told a story about a former colleague who had been refused a card, apparently in error, after waiting two years. Another case resulted from the malice – as Elena saw it – of the Ukrainian agency representatives (*koordinatory*) in the factory.

> There was a Ukrainian who got pregnant and when the *koordinator* found out that she was pregnant – and she had applied for a residence card – they sent some document to Poznań, for her file, saying that the agency did not want to support her application. So she was refused and went back to Ukraine with a tiny baby... Whereas if she'd stayed in Poland she could have gone back to her job after five months.

Hardly any interviewees had reached the next stage, of applying for a permanent residence permit. Those few longer-term migrants who mentioned wanting to apply displayed different levels of confidence about passing the language examination. It was also possible to avoid taking the examination by acquiring a Polish educational qualification, and several interviewees had studied or were studying Polish language or courses such as floristry and cosmetology for free at an adult education college, partly for the purpose of securing their residence rights.

Workplaces and occupational mobility

Chapter 3 mentioned that registered unemployment in 2021 in Piła, Kalisz and Płock was 3, 3.2 and 6.1 per cent respectively; in 2019, the Płock figure had also been 6.1.[4] There was plenty of work available. Improving labour markets in Poland are connected to overall economic growth more than emigration (Kaczmarczyk 2018). One example of such development is the construction of new factories around Kalisz. However, local media and officials sometimes ascribed job vacancies to emigration, claiming that emigration and immigration were interlinked. For instance, Artur Szymczak, the head of the Kalisz Job Office, had observed in 2016 that 'many Poles go abroad when faced with the choice of working for 1,800 zloties a month here, or 4,000, for example, in Germany or Holland. Our eastern neighbours come to work in their stead' (AW 2016). In 2021, the local media (MS 2021) was still making the same point, referring to:

> the influx of workers from eastern Europe, especially Ukrainians, who are employed in horticulture, agriculture and construction, as well as other areas, including those sectors where Poles don't want to work … Polish standards of living and aspirations are increasing. It's harder and harder to find people to do simple manual jobs. Workers today want a good, well-paid job – those same people who ten years ago would have been glad to take anything.

Ukrainian interviewees were impressed by the availability of work which local people did not want to do. Yurii, for example, commented, 'You see beggars, local people, and you think why on earth? If I can find a job, so can you. Here you have plenty of choice (*rabota po zhelaniyu*). If you don't like one job, go and find another. There are enough jobs for everyone.' Dmytro, another Kalisz interviewee, referred to labour-hungry factories taking in Ukrainians 'by the parcel' to work on assembly lines. The sense that it was possible to change jobs, at least between factories, seemed to be important to some interviewees, and contributed to their feeling of a basic level of security in KPP, similar to that of Poles who arrived in the UK and

Ireland during the economic boom at the start of the twenty-first century. Several interviewees had taken advantage of this opportunity to move horizontally between factories. On the other hand, interviewees seeking non-factory jobs could find their choice restricted. They complained, for instance, about not being able to get work in bakeries or café kitchens. As the chapters on Polish migrants mentioned, white-collar work was particularly in short supply in KPP, and interviewees had struggled to find clerical or accounting jobs, even when they were qualified to do them. Personal contacts were helpful here, as in the case of Elena, who was dismissed from her factory because she was pregnant, but was given a job in her boyfriend's sister's business, dealing with Ukrainian clients.

Parutis (2014) found that Lithuanian and Polish young people in London after 2004 often thought of progressing from 'any job' to a 'better job' and finally, perhaps, their 'dream job'. This imagined trajectory helped them put up with doing menial work when they first arrived, although in many cases they did not mind spending time 'drifting' (Trevena 2013: 182) and doing easy manual jobs. Chapter 7 mentioned Ukrainian interviewees who had a vision of their ideal job, whether as a florist, forklift truck driver or popstar. Yuliya, for instance, dreamed of becoming a special needs teacher. She had started her career in Poland as a cleaner in a special needs school, and then been offered the better job of teaching assistant. She was being encouraged by the school to train as a teacher.

Some middle-aged interviewees seemed to feel they had already arrived at their dream job. Andrei, aged 45, had performed seven different jobs in Poland before landing his dream job as a railway mechanic. He said he could not imagine a job he would prefer to do. Women working in beauty and hairdressing salons and restaurants, using their skills and qualifications, also seemed particularly satisfied with their work. This was partly because they were using their skills, but also because of the social side of their jobs. In some cases, the women had worked in factories after they first arrived in KPP, so they had progressed from 'any job' to 'better job', and in some cases 'dream job'. Ukrainian long-distance lorry-drivers were employed for companies based in Kalisz and Piła. They earned more than many Poles, so this was a 'dream job' for some. For all the discomforts, Sergei, who was quoted at the very beginning of this book, treasured the opportunity to travel round Europe, socialising with drivers from many countries. He also enthused about the perks and conditions offered by his employer. Similarly, Margarita's husband had always dreamed of being a long-distance lorry driver, and when he retired from the police in Ukraine he became happily employed in a company based in KPP. On the other hand, the process of place attachment in KPP could involve transitioning to a Polish lorry driver's contract. Sergei valued this because it enabled him to spend more time at home in KPP. Another interviewee, Ostap, had recently qualified as a lorry driver with a view to leaving his factory job in KPP, but changed his mind, because he did not want to be absent from his home in KPP and his girlfriend. He said, 'I don't want to leave my family. Money is less important than being with the person you love.'

Forty-one of the 69 interviewees currently worked in factories: 26 women and 15 men. Some viewed it as a temporary stage in their careers. Bohdan, aged 28, said for example, 'To start with of course I'll work a bit in a factory, but then I'll look for something better.' Zlata, also 28, and in her third factory job in KPP, commented, 'I can't say I'm wildly enthusiastic about the work, that I really enjoy it. But for the time being it's the only option.' Yeva (34) commented, 'Even if you work in a factory, you have work, you get paid – there is a kind of foundation.' Tamara was a little older, but in her case factory work was only intended as a temporary expedient ('stability and a wage') – somewhere to go after the pandemic forced the closure of the family business. Filipek and Polkowska (2020: 215) found that 'for some unknown reasons, Ukrainian workers in Poland avoid difficult topics and conceal negative job experiences'. This was not the case with my interviewees. However, like Filipek and Polkowska (2020: 216), I heard claims that 'it would be worse in Ukraine' to justify poor pay and conditions in Poland, a form of 'downward social comparison' which the authors claim is used by informants to reassure themselves and salvage their self-esteem. For example, when I asked Yevhen, a factory worker, 'Do you like your job?' he replied, perhaps evasively, 'It's better than in Ukraine.'

It was not the case that the interviewees would take absolutely 'any job'. As illustrated by Duszczyk and Matuszczyk (2022), it is not just the wage which matters to Ukrainian labour migrants. Conditions are also taken into account when they choose their jobs in Poland. My interviewees were often not prepared to do those 4D jobs which across the globe are often the fate of migrants because they are dirty, difficult, dangerous and dull. For example, only one person had worked in an abattoir (not in KPP), and he left after two days. Some interviewees had already rejected a succession of jobs in other cities. Their rejection of very poor jobs in these other locations helped explain why they ended up in KPP, where they arrived at their 'better' jobs. Olha was one of these interviewees, and she commented about her job in Płock: 'You're constantly breathing in paint fumes, but never mind. I've had harder jobs.' Yurii's point about the availability of a 'choice' of work (as evidenced by the huge websites of the recruitment agencies) is the context in which the interviewees shaped their livelihoods, even if visa restrictions sometimes made it inconvenient to change from one job to another. The interviewees were in KPP partly because they had chosen not to work in the countryside, where the hardest work and conditions are often to be found. Some would only do so in extreme circumstances. For instance, two men who had arrived relatively early in Poland (before and after 2014) mentioned that towards the end of their first trip to Poland they were ashamed of returning to Ukraine empty-handed, and this was why they took agricultural work as a short-term expedient. Halyna, who was intent on earning extra money on top of her factory wage, had tried working in greenhouses at weekends. She left after she developed an allergic reaction. 'The worst thing is that your hands are always damp, even if you wear gloves. And there are particles from the cucumbers and tomatoes, it flies in your face and makes you sneeze.'

In keeping with stories of Polish return migrant interviewees, for example about working in industrial laundries in the UK and Ireland, it seemed that simple manual work was not always perceived as a problem if your friends were all in the same boat. There was a certain collegiality linked to being part of a wave of Ukrainians doing manual work, especially since it provided opportunities to meet a diverse range of people. For instance, Raisa said that she found it interesting to share her room in a migrant hostel with a midwife, a historian and a shop assistant. Often, a shift from a skilled manual job in Ukraine to a different manual job in Poland was considered acceptable. This was sometimes because the social side of work was enjoyable. Varvara, a hairdresser by profession, was looking for 'any' job to regularise her status when she came to KPP just on her passport, without a visa. She became a cook, something which she initially found 'scary' but which she came to enjoy. Elena, who switched from sushi chef to assembly line worker, put up with this partly because she liked her Polish colleagues and enjoyed the coffee breaks. Like some Poles in the UK, she also found it something of a relief to do a dull but not stressful manual job. 'I simply had my workplace and got on with my work … For instance, I'd spend a whole night just making one chandelier.'

Although some interviewees complained about the boredom of working on an assembly line, others valued the predictability of factory work in Poland. Olesya said, 'I've been working in the same factory almost five years … It's simply that there's a kind of stability here. The way it is, you go to work, and you get paid. You work, you get your money, and you can buy what you like.' Some manual workers also viewed the shift to new work in Poland as an opportunity to extend their skills. For instance, Ihor said, 'I made furniture myself, and I was also the sales manager. So I had two positions. Then I came to Poland as a builder. So we'll be learning something new.' Hlib had gone to a vocational college in Ukraine but then acquired an entirely new vocation in KPP. He said, rather proudly, 'It's turned out that I've become a professional baker. I've been working in that profession for three years now.'

Interviewees also justified their choice of livelihood strategy in KPP by presenting themselves as people who were not afraid of hard work. Nina, who worked in a beauty salon, pointed out: 'Here, if you want to earn a good wage, you do need to slave away, to be honest'. Factory workers in Płock, many of whom were doing particularly heavy and unpleasant work, lifting metal parts weighing up to 25 kilograms or working with paint, made comments such as 'We came here to work and earn money', 'We didn't come here to have a rest', 'I was never afraid of hard work' and 'We're not afraid of physical work'. They seemed to have no qualms about applying to themselves the colloquial word for labour migrant (*zarobitchanin, zarobitchanka*), which is rejected as humiliating by some university-educated Ukrainians (Kindler 2021: 520–21). Some interviewees referred to childhoods in the Ukrainian countryside to back up their claims that they were familiar with manual labour. This was the approach taken by Vera, an accountant who had recently arrived in KPP to join her husband, and was still seeking work. As a child, she had often been sent to stay with her grandparents in the village.

> For the time being, I don't know, perhaps I will need to do some manual job while I'm learning the ropes here. I know some people are scared of manual work, but I'm not. I feel brave about it. I know what it's like to work in the village, with acres of vegetables … Once they went off to sell their potatoes and left me alone to look after it all, not just minor items like hens and geese, but pigs, a horse and a cow.

Belief in one's own capacity for hard work could be extended to assumptions about all Ukrainians. Ostap for instance said that 'my friends help me and I help them [with repairs]. Like me, they can do anything. That's the kind of nation Ukrainans are. And if someone is from a village then he really can do anything'. Garapich observed with regard to Poles in London that negative and positive auto-stereotypes existed side by side. On the one hand is the image of the Polish 'conman', the Pole who cheats and is selfish and generally ill-intentioned, disappointing expectations of co-ethnic solidarity. On the other hand, Poles are conceptualised as clever in a good way: resourceful and adaptable, as well as hardworking (Garapich 2016c). The same auto-stereotypes are met among Ukrainians. Svitlana said, 'Ukrainian people are adaptable, it's no problem for them to pick up a new occupation.' She also stated, 'We Ukrainians are not afraid of hard work. As long as it's properly paid. We're not afraid of any work.' Margarita similarly said that 'Ukrainians know how to work'. Resourcefulness and adaptability were also emphasised.

> Mihaylo: It's bad our families aren't with us, they're at home in Ukraine, but we are getting used to it. That's the kind of nation we are!
>
> Vadym: As adaptable as rats, we can get used to new conditions, that's what Ukrainians are like. Life forces them to be like that.

As is probably common among migrants *vis-à-vis* natives in receiving countries with well-demarcated migrant sections of the labour market, there was a conviction that Ukrainians worked harder than Poles. Why else would Poles refuse to do the heavy jobs? Filipek and Polkowska (2020: 212) quote a Ukrainian worker who asserted: 'I've heard Poland needs Ukrainian workers. Ukrainians are more hard-working than Poles'. Konieczna-Salamatin (2015) and Brzozowska (2018: 91) also found Poles referred to as lazy. Similar sentiments were expressed by the KPP interviewees. Andrei, for example, recounted how he worked digging ditches alongside a road.

> Andrei: We worked with spades and the Poles worked with excavators and finished off the ditches neatly.
> Anne: Why did you work with spades?
> Andrei: Because we're Ukrainians. Ukrainians always work with spades. And Poles work with technology. But so what? We don't mind that. That's the sort of nation we are. To be honest, Poles don't want to work like Ukrainians. You know that perfectly well. When we Ukrainians work, we work properly, if we start a job we'll finish it off. Poles aren't like that. To be honest, Poles are lazy.

The following quotation is from my interview with a Ukrainian couple which was also attended by another interviewee, Liliya. She was a more experienced migrant, who was tempted to join in the conversation. The extract illustrates how migrants pass on wisdom and stereotypes from their own experience to other migrants.

Liliya: We Ukrainians know more.

Boris: Yes, just comparing the warehouses where I worked in Ukraine with Poland, the Polish one needs plenty of development…

Liliya: But the Poles are happy with it as it is.

Boris: They don't mind the dirt and dust …

Liliya: I've noticed that Poles are lazy. For example someone just goes to an Institute and does his job, but we're not like that, we always want to do better, do something extra, out of sheer enthusiasm.

Veronika: It's because we get bored. If we finish one job we're not going to sit idle until the end of the working day.

Liliya: But Poles will drag out that boring job so they aren't given some other task to do.

However, some interviewees did not seem convinced that awareness of one's Ukrainian or individual work ethic was sufficient motivation to put up with heavy work. As it happened, the cases mentioned here all concern people with university degrees or sub-degree level medical qualifications. Nataliya, for instance, asserted that 'after all, we came here to work' but also showed me her burns and bruises and complained about dust levels in the factory. She was used to manual work, but in a spick and span supermarket: it was the 'dangerous and dirty' aspects of factory work which were off-putting. Oksana was clearly torn. 'I came from working in a doctor's surgery to a factory. Dirt on my face and hands. I found it very tough. But now some time has gone by, I know more people, I socialise with more people, I have good friends (*druz'ya*).' Several women voiced doubts about whether they should be doing heavy factory work by framing the work as 'not suitable for women' (*nezhenskaya*, in Lavra's term). For instance, Nataliya expressed surprise that most of the workers in her section of the factory were women – both Polish and Ukrainian – considering that they put in so many hours of heavy labour. Anna complained about the heat and heavy lifting, commenting: 'it's not for women'. Anna (60) and Leonid (48) additionally made the point that they felt too old to do heavy manual work. On the other hand, some lighter factory work was considered especially suitable for women, something which became important with the influx of female refugees seeking work in 2022.

A sub-group of interviewees had felt humiliated by their downward mobility in Poland. However, in each case they also mentioned compensating factors. Tatyana, a teacher, was horrified by her transformation from 'a teacher, in a blouse and skirt' to a factory worker.

She hoped to address this problem by moving to an English-speaking country where, even if she did manual work, at least she could use her language skills. Valentin, working as a printer, commented that as a journalist in Ukraine he had been able to have a coffee with the mayor. 'And now suddenly [making a downward gesture] you are nobody.' However, he engaged in voluntary work. Boris complained: 'You can't find a job using your professional qualifications if you don't know the language ... So you have to overcome your pride ... and because you don't understand and can't always perform the [humble] tasks you're asked to do you get the impression they think you're stupid.' Nonetheless, he was conscious that, once he improved his Polish, his boss intended to promote him to a managerial position more consistent with his status in Ukraine.

The term 'migration culture' used in this book implies that migrants act according to certain norms. However, not everyone complies with norms. Unsurprisingly, it seemed typical of the most educated interviewees to avoid networks and their conventions, and plan their migration strategies as individuals. They no doubt felt they had enough cultural capital to exercise their own agency and not adopt common practices, insofar as they were even aware of these. For example, both Valentin, the journalist, and Liliya, a university lecturer, had come to KPP without any job fixed in advance. University graduates sometimes preferred to be temporarily unemployed while they looked for white-collar jobs, or at least better-paid manual jobs in Poland. For Liliya this strategy was linked to a friend's experience. She concluded, 'I know that if I go to wash floors I will never raise myself from that.' She was still working online for her university in Ukraine, so she had some means of support. Similarly, Melaniya had spent three months unemployed, presumably dependent on her husband, rather than working on an assembly line, which seemed to be the only option in the small town outside KPP where they were living at the time. The couple then decided to move to KPP. When interviewed, Leonid was subsisting on savings while trying hard to find a job which would pay more than the minimum wage, but becoming discouraged. As Liliya's example illustrates, it was possible to create a transitional period while looking for a 'better' job – rather than accepting 'any job' – if one could keep one's livelihood based in Ukraine. Artur, who had also arrived quite recently and was hunting around for a well-paid job in construction, in the meantime lived with friends of his parents and supported himself by running the online business which he had established while he was still at school in Ukraine. Emma, although she was supported by her husband and had been told by him that she was not to go out to work, was occupying herself with online fundraising for charity, just as she had done in Ukraine.

Promotion could constitute moving to a 'better job'. Transferring to a permanent contract, with regular hours and holiday and sick pay, was naturally seen as a milestone. Ostap, for example, was proud of having achieved this after 18 months at his factory, in comparison with other Ukrainians who had been waiting for years. Some interviewees at other factories had received permanent contracts more quickly. Moreover, five interviewees, all graduates working in Kalisz, had been promoted to the role of machine operator, as well as *brigadir* or *lider*, in three separate factories. A different interviewee claimed this was factory policy, to retain talented Ukrainians by offering them promotion. The move removed them from the assembly line: they were responsible for running the computer programme which controlled their section of the factory, along with associated responsibility for a team of workers. Since these workers were Polish as well as Ukrainian, and in some cases also Venezuelan and Mexican, this could be a linguistic challenge. The interviewees liked the fact that they had permanent contracts and presumably also better pay, but they did not perceive being a line manager as satisfying work in its own right. A partial exception was Oleksandra (aged 50), who was responsible for managing 15 women on three production lines and had the sense that she was well-respected. She was not looking for other employment. For the time being, the four younger interviewees (all aged under 35) who had been thus promoted put up with the situation, although in Dmytro's case he was only persuaded to stay by having a new role of 'senior operator' created just for him. Yeva, a trained teacher, had escaped from her managerial job at one factory, where she found the paperwork overwhelming, moved as a manual worker to another factory with better conditions, but then found herself promoted again. A sixth interviewee, Ruslana, also a graduate, was hoping to be transferred to the factory's human resources department, as a Russian and Ukrainian speaker.

So far, the concept of 'good' work has been discussed mostly in terms of the quality of the work itself. However, of course the pay and hours were of crucial importance. Interviewees who considered themselves to be temporary migrants – or regular circular migrants, who did not plan to work during periods spent resting in Ukraine – were prepared to put up with low hourly wages as long as they could work plenty of hours and earn a sufficient sum overall. Labour migrants employed according to the simplified procedure are said by employers to work longer hours than Poles (Górny et al 2018: 115). For example, Zinaida, echoing the words of my Polish interviewee Wojciech, quoted in Chapter 4, said that she had been happy during the summer to be able to work long hours: 'you work [hard], but your work is properly paid'. Other more settled interviewees preferred to work eight hours, usually because they wanted time with their families, although sometimes, in the case of solo women, because they wanted time for themselves. Occasionally, such settled interviewees complained that they were expected to do more than they wanted. Anzhela, for instance, left one factory when they told her to do night shifts: her daughter had come to join her in KPP, and she wanted a normal family life. She also felt it was unjust that Polish workers were not expected to take night shifts. She said:

> There was such unequal treatment. The Polish workers worked the first and second shifts[5] and the Ukrainians worked the second and third, always the second and third. If I'd come to Poland to work for three or four months I might have agreed to those conditions. But I came here to live. With my child. I don't want to spend my whole time at work and do nothing else. So I refused to do night shifts and left the job.

A more common cause for dissatisfaction was that the employer offered fewer hours than originally promised. Filipek and Polkowska (2020: 215) mention the same complaint, on the part of a Ukrainian warehouse operator in 2018. 'They promised me to work about 10 hours a day and have overtime. But I work only 8 hours a day… Only Christmas time was busy here and I had a chance to work long shifts including Saturdays and Sundays.' This was a frequent grievance among interviewees in KPP. In 2021–2, it was partly as a result of the pandemic resulting in factories receiving fewer orders – far fewer, according to some informants. However, even in Płock in 2019 there was a sense of opportunities contracting. Yevhen, a welder, commented that three years ago 'it was *very* good. There was lots of work. Now there isn't. You do one job for four hours, then the parts run out, so you go to a different place in the factory and work for four hours'.

Dissatisfaction was exacerbated by the impression that overtime was not available to everyone. Interviewees consoled themselves by remembering that working for eight hours in Poland was still better than working in Ukraine, but the unfairness rankled. Olha, keen to provide for her two children in Ukraine, was one of the 'lucky' ones who received extra hours when they were available.

> Before the New Year I worked 16 hours a day. Now I've come back from my holidays I'm working eight, sometimes 16 … I work 16 if the work is available. Usually eight, but last week there was 16,

because there were plenty of orders. They let some people do 16, me for example, but not everyone, only people who work well and can last out for 16 hours. If the manager sees that someone can't manage of course they don't get permission.

Olha also mentioned that she had gone to work with a temperature because she was afraid that if she missed a day she might not receive a bonus. At this same factory, some welders seemed to be a privileged category: if there was extra work, they would be offered overtime. One even claimed to have worked 24 hours in a row. Other welders did not have this access. Viktor, for instance, complained that ideally he would like to work 12 hours. A thousand euros would be a 'normal' amount – a good sum to send home for his wife and children. Kira, not a welder, blamed Polish co-workers for the eight-hour shifts in her section of the factory. They had previously worked two 12-hour shifts, but the Poles had not been happy about this and the work was organised into the standard three shifts per 24 hours. Hence, the Ukrainians were working either eight, which was too little, or 16, which Kira found exhausting.

Wages were a cause of dissatisfaction, particularly when they stayed fixed for years, despite steep inflation in Ukraine, and by 2021 also in Poland. Again, there was a perception of arbitrariness, for example because different workers were employed at the same factory through different agencies and received different wages. Górny et al (2018: 109) found that employers perceived Ukrainians to be becoming more demanding, an opinion also expressed to me by one of my key informants, who recruited foreign workers from different countries. Olha reported on how she and her co-workers had protested to the factory management in 2019 about the fact that some Ukrainians were earning two zloties (about 40p) an hour more than others. 'We went and asked, "Why is this happening?" But they didn't give us an answer. We are a bit annoyed.' In some factories, the perceived arbitrary behaviour of agency representatives in docking pay from workers who had infringed apparently unreasonable regulations was also much disliked. Melaniya, with an office job, complained:

> It was a long time before they raised my salary to the same level as other people I know at the same level. Now I do get that salary after two years. For two years I had no salary increase, it was just above the minimum wage. It was only last autumn they raised it. I think it's connected [with discrimination]. There's an opinion that if you came from Ukraine you should work harder, for less money.

One response to disappointing wages at one's main workplace was to seek additional earnings elsewhere. Halyna and her husband were saving up as much money as possible in advance of their small son coming to join them in KPP. She said:

> Before the pandemic there was more work. Much more. Now there's less. But I've found a second job! In the kitchen at McDonald's. They let you work four or five hours, on a flexible timetable, so I can work eight hours at my basic job and four to five at McDonald's. I'm holding up for the moment. I try to work every day, except Sunday.

A few other interviewees mentioned cleaning and doing repair and maintenance jobs for Poles, discussed in Chapter 12. In some cases this work was on a regular basis. Brzozowska (2023: 2379) found that in Warsaw doing additional work was commonplace and 'working extra part-time or at weekends allowed labour migrants to make intensive use of several months of stay'. However, presumably there is less such work available in KPP. Artem, who had a second job every evening and Saturday, claimed it was uncommon. An alternative was to do odd jobs for Ukrainian migrants. One interviewee, for example, mended cars in an informal workshop.

Some factory jobs came with tied accommodation, which was particularly convenient for Ukrainians on their first trip to Poland. In Płock, factory workers returned multiple times to one student hostel used by the factory where most of my informants worked. The accommodation constituted an important anchor. In at least one case the interviewee returned to Płock just for the sake of the hostel, having tried to find a better-paid job in another city. Another interviewee, Oksana, said she could have afforded to rent a flat in Płock, but she always came back to the hostel because it was a pleasant place to live and she liked the warden. Yevhen said that he liked the fact that the warden made sure inmates did not drink alcohol. A sign on the door in Russian stated 'No admittance to drunks'. Rowdy behaviour was not allowed, the common spaces were clean and there were monthly inspections. Each room had only two beds, making it suitable for couples, siblings and parents with their children. This was one of the hostel's chief draws. Inmates also liked the friendly atmosphere created by the energetic, Polish but Russian-speaking warden. In Kalisz, interviewees also mentioned satisfaction with both a hostel and factory-rented flats. However, other hostels were more cramped, and in Piła hostel accommodation was considered a stop-gap arrangement.

Language and culture

Apart from a couple of temporary circular migrants, interviewees were convinced that it was important to learn Polish. Other researchers, such as Grzymała-Kazłowska and Brzozowska (2017: 110), found the same attitude among their own respondents. Many KPP interviewees had studied Polish informally or formally, including taking courses before they left, in big cities like Dnipro and Kyiv. Online teaching made Polish tuition more accessible, so in some cases they continued studying with the same teacher in Ukraine even when they were in Poland. For the more ambitious interviewees, the goal was to sit the State Certificate in Polish as a Foreign Language, which was necessary for a permanent residence permit unless a foreigner had a qualification from a Polish educational institution, which for Ukrainians tended to mean taking a Polish course in an adult education college.

Interviewees perceived language learning as a journey. Although – like Ukrainians surveyed by other researchers – they chose Poland as a destination partly because the language was 'easy', their accounts of language learning tended to highlight the difficulties along the way. This is consistent with the findings of other scholars such as Janicki (2015: 244) who point out that it should not be taken for granted that Ukrainians will integrate easily thanks to their linguistic competence. Like many labour migrants, the Ukrainians in my own sample often lacked time to work on their formal language. Anzhela, for example, said her written Polish 'could be better, let's put it like that. I did understand that I would need it, if I wanted to stay in Poland and get a proper job. I went to classes for a year, but somehow it happened that I had lots of overtime, it got quite hard, I was doing two shifts a day.' Self-confidence was also a problem for some. Pronunciation put them off – for instance, Lizaveta complained, 'All this prz, prz, prz, I can't do it!' It seemed that Ukrainians could become stuck once they had been in Poland a few years, especially if they did not mix much with Poles. Yeva had a degree in Ukrainian philology and had lived in Poland for five years, so she should seemingly have had a linguistic head-start. However, she complained:

> I did have a close Polish friend but she emigrated to Germany to be with her sister. I mix with Poles at work but there is a language barrier and I can't express everything. I speak, but not much. I don't feel very free when I speak. I worry about saying the wrong thing.

Writing was the main difficulty. Varvara had been in KPP over three years and spoke Polish all the time at work, but lamented, 'I still can't write ... It's a problem for me because wherever you go you need to write ... My son can write of course so he writes stuff for me and I copy it.'

Apart from language, the interviewees did not mention many cultural adjustments, in the sense of changes to their behaviour they had needed to make in KPP. Larysa mentioned that she had to learn to stop herself jaywalking. Lyudmila said that she had lost the habit of expecting to be rudely treated by shop assistants. Although they could not always access food of the standard they enjoyed in Ukraine – Olena for instance complained of 'peaches like cotton wool' – in general, they found KPP comfortable and easy places to live, an impression of Poland noted for example by Andrejuk (2017a); Brzozowska (2018); and Dolińska (2019b). Like Ukrainians interviewed by other researchers, they singled out the reliable and uncrowded public transport, well-maintained roads, smaller quantity of litter and vandalism, efficiently-functioning government offices, scrupulous attention to health and safety at work, a more relaxed and less showy dress code, and smiles and politeness in public places. In all these aspects they contrasted Poland with Ukraine.[6] Larysa, for instance, asserted that:

> In Ukraine older people can be quite irritable and impatient. They don't like to stand in queues and you need to make way for them and be respectful. Here they are beautifully dressed – ours go round in headscarves – and they wear little hats, and they're polite. If you try to give them your seat on the bus they sometimes refuse.

Lavra claimed:

> Poles behave calmly, and in fact so do their dogs! I'm amazed. My daughter has a dog in Ukraine. We take him for a walk and he's running all over the place. I keep telling her, 'What sort of training is that? In Poland dogs walk along quietly ...' In Ukraine, they rush around, and here they walk quietly. It's the same with people. They go along quietly, in one direction.

For parents, it was particularly important that children were treated with respect at school. Emma had fought a long battle to call a teacher to account for hitting her son at his Ukrainian school. She explained how much she appreciated the different educational philosophy and practices at the Polish school.

When he comes home from school he's happy and he wants to go to school in the morning, unlike in Ukraine, where it was impossible to drag him out of bed, because the teachers were so unpleasant … Here all the teachers smile and whenever you phone up his class teacher she will always explain what do do, listen to what you have to say, give you advice. They explain everything calmly and don't make a fuss. You can phone the headteacher or another teacher and they will always help.

Yuliya similarly observed:

I found out that [in Poland] it's not allowed, for example at a parents' evening the teacher will never discuss your child with someone else or in their presence. Only with you separately. And no one else has the right to know. But in Ukraine it's still the case that, at parents' evenings, the teacher sits down with all the parents in the class and she can complain that some child is being naughty and everyone hears it. Now, I find that totally uncivilised.

This was a clear example of cultural diffusion and of how a migrant can change their views as a result of living abroad: 'acquiring' a social remittance, in the words of Grabowska and Garapich (2016). Since Yuliya was a teaching assistant, she was in a position to diffuse such norms among other Ukrainian migrants living in KPP.

Conclusions

The chapter discussed how interviewees were becoming integrated in the domains of citizenship (residence status); employment; language; and culture. Although Poland was an attractive destination for Ukrainians because of the simplified procedure for accessing work, informants were not made to feel welcome when they wanted to update their legal status and stay longer. Acquiring a residence permit should have made them feel they belonged in KPP, but they found the process alienating. They complained bitterly about lengthy procedures; being unable to visit Ukraine during the process; helplessness in influencing the outcome; officials' arbitrariness and mistakes; and their fear of refusal and deportation.

Some slightly longer-established migrants had already progressed along the integration trajectory 'any job – better job – dream job'. The most satisfied included cooks, hairdressers and beauticians (all women) and welders and lorry-drivers (all men). They possessed a sense of being integrated into the normal labour market, typically working alongside Poles. Their jobs constituted an important motivation to settle in KPP. However, most interviewees saw their jobs more as temporary anchors, which kept them in KPP, but did not constitute the main incentives for staying there. As in Górny et al's (2019) study of Bydgoszcz, most Ukrainians I interviewed were employed in factories. They had not yet progressed to 'better work', except insofar as factory work was better than previous Polish jobs in greenhouses or abattoirs, or factories in other cities with more unpleasant working conditions. In Kalisz, some factories seemed to have a policy of promoting Ukrainian university graduates to lower-level managerial positions, so this also constituted 'better work'. However, except in the case of one late middle-aged interviewee it did not seem to be something which might permanently tie them to Kalisz.

From interviewees' accounts, it seemed many factories in KPP were highly dependent on migrant labour, except during the Covid-19 pandemic. As also found in other studies, many Ukrainians were anxious to work as many hours as they could, and this also distinguished them from local Polish people and contributed to their segregation. In my sample, these were typically people who had recently arrived and were without their family members. However, these informants tended to claim that the factories did not offer as much overtime as previously and as they would have liked. Nor was casual part-time evening and weekend work as available as it would have been in a larger city. However, despite this reduction in their earning powers, the interviewees preferred to stay in KPP rather than moving on; as discussed in Chapter 10, the fact that they had circles of Ukrainian friends does much to explain their behaviour and growing place attachment. On the other hand, many Ukrainians were in KPP with their families, and these migrants were naturally more focused on living and less on earning. These priorities meant that they were less ambitious to work long hours. It should also be mentioned that all interviewees, including those most focused on earning money quickly, had high expectations about their work conditions and accommodation, and complained loudly when these fell short. This bears out the findings of other scholars, and of a recruiter I interviewed as a key informant, that Ukrainians were 'demanding' and not susceptible to exploitation.

It is often assumed, by both Ukrainians and Poles, that Ukrainians have an integration head start when it comes to learning Polish. This is expected to be easy because of the similarities between Polish and Ukrainian and, to a lesser degree, Polish and Russian. However, my interviewees typically did not seem to rely on picking up Polish effortlessly and instead worked hard at learning the language, including studying it in Ukraine before they arrived. Moreover, they were often dissatisfied with their progress once they were living in KPP, particularly when it came to written Polish. Writing accurately would be essential if they later tried to apply for a white-collar job or to pass the examination to secure long-term residence in Poland. Young women university graduates seemed particularly frustrated in this regard. They would have benefited from advanced-level courses which were not always accessible. Aside from language, the participants tended not to comment on any cultural barriers, and they voiced their appreciation of many aspects of Polish behaviour which helped them feel relaxed and at home in KPP. These included courtesy on the street and in public offices, and careful attention to health and safety at the workplace. On the other hand, they expressed pride and a sense of superiority with reference to Ukrainians' supposedly superior work ethic and adaptability – an aspect of the migration culture similar to the positive auto-stereotypes mentioned by Poles abroad.

Notes

1. For regulations, see https://www.mos.cudzoziemcy.gov.pl/en/informacje/zwiazek-mal/wprowadzenie_EN (last accessed 10 October 2023)
2. For regulations, see https://www.gov.pl/web/uw-lodzki/zezwolenie-na-pobyt-rezydenta-dlugoterminowego-ue (last accessed 7 August 2023)
3. Either an extension of an employer's declaration of intent, or a residence permit.
4. https://svs.stat.gov.pl/
5. 06.00–14.00 and 14.00–22.00.
6. For discussion of the similarities between their observations and those of Poles in Western Europe after 2004, see White (2021). For more details on different social remittances, see e.g. Duszczyk and Matuszczyk (2022: 938) on health and safety, or Dolińska (2019b) on dress.

10
Ukrainian place attachment in Kalisz, Piła and Płock and likelihood of moving on

Introduction

Chapter 9 considered Ukrainians' experiences over time in KPP, using integration as the organising framework. However, the integration concept is not generally used to analyse emotions, although emotions are important in helping migrants decide where to make their home. Hence the concept of place attachment can also be used to understand why some Ukrainians were increasingly coming to feel that KPP was where they wanted to be. Those interviewees who had not become so attached were likely to consider moving on to a third country, or potentially back to Ukraine. Place attachment is an umbrella term (Smith 2017: 2; Trąbka 2019: 67) which is used in many disciplines. Quantitative researchers employ it to measure characteristics of settled populations (Lewicka 2011). However, there is some research which is more processual and qualitative, and which explores the process of place attachment among migrants (Kohlbacher et al 2015; Lynnebakke 2021; Trąbka 2019).

Smith (2017) proposes an (overlapping) typology of functions performed by places. These include 'secure', 'restorative', 'socialising' and 'transformative'. Each migrant appreciates their new location as it fulfils these various roles. For Ukrainians in KPP, processes relevant to these four types of place attachment are making a safe home; seeing KPP and surrounding nature as a place to recover from the stresses of life in Ukraine; making friends with other Ukrainians and with Poles; and coming to associate the smaller city with biographical milestones such as the birth of children or acquisition of a dream job. Trąbka (2019) identifies slightly different aspects of place attachment from those suggested by Smith. Her list consists of: 'place dependence', based on instrumental attachment, for instance because the location provides the migrant with a job; 'place discovered': making efforts to get to know the place and engage actively in local events and affairs; place identity, a deep emotional bond and self-identification with the place, as expressed for example by Sergei in the quotation about taking his grandsons fishing which opens Chapter 1 of this book; and 'place inherited', which Trąbka points out is similar to Hummon (1992)'s 'everyday rootedness'. 'Place inherited' also somewhat corresponds to Smith's idea of the 'transformative' place – somewhere where significant life-shaping events have taken place. As you live in a place and put down roots, so you build up an accumulation of experiences which can also attach you to that particular location. Although studies show that attachment usually grows over time, this is not an automatic process. Therefore, for place attachment to develop, the instrumental connection with the place needs to be supplemented with more active engagement and a greater range of experiences and associations. These aspects 'often coexist and may emerge gradually in the process of adaptation to a new urban setting', although place discovery can take place quite quickly (Trąbka 2019: 67, 69, 71). Lewicka (2011: 244) claimed that 'we still know very little about the processes through which people become attached to places'.

Place attachment is sometimes conflated by sociologists with 'sense of community' (Scannell and Gifford 2010: 4). The process of becoming embedded in networks facilitated place attachment and integration, thereby helping to explain why Ukrainians increasingly seemed to be settling in the three cities. This sense of community was beginning to emerge before the full-scale Russian invasion of Ukraine in 2022, though not through formal institutions. As in the case of the Polish wave, the Ukrainians took pleasure in their often extensive and expanding informal friendship networks, and this helped tie them to their new city of residence. Zielińska and Szaban (2021) in their article about Ukrainians in Wielkopolska region show how, even if economic motives caused their migration to Poland, they wanted either to stay in Poland, or to return to Ukraine, because of their emotional ties to family and friends, a finding which is consistent with the return migration literature discussed in Chapter 5. Ukrainians were forming ties to both Ukrainians and Poles. This chapter considers the Ukrainian networks, while Chapter 11 considers their friendships with Poles.

The chapter examines how Ukrainian interviewees were thrown together with other Ukrainians by their situation; even in the smaller cities they developed networks sufficiently extensive for them to be able to pick and choose their friends. As already discussed in Chapter 4 with reference to Poles abroad, Ager and Strang (2004) emphasise that migrants need to be able to identify with some community of people who can provide support, but that these do not have to be members of the receiving society. Migrants should be 'socially connected with members of a (national, ethnic, cultural, religious or other) community with which they identify' (Ager and Strang 2004: 5). Co-ethnic networks provide not just emotional and practical help, but also information and training in migration practices. Belonging to these networks in KPP consolidated interviewees' sense of belonging to a migration wave, which possessed a certain migration culture. This sense of membership in turn helped give them the confidence to settle. Altogether, there were many parallels with the situation of Poles in countries such as the UK and Ireland, Iceland and Norway after 2004. However, just as in the case of Poles abroad, the presence of co-ethnic migrants could also be a factor deterring place attachment to the new location.

The remainder of Chapter 10 examines individuals' processes of attachment to the place, rather than the people. As mentioned in the chapter about Polish experiences abroad, migration scholars writing about place attachment have highlighted the significance of social ties, even weak ties such as with people encountered in passing around the neighbourhood (Kohlbacher et al 2015) and, for some migrants more than others, lifestyle factors, such as bonding with nature (Lynnebakke 2021). Life-stage is significant in place attachment. 'Migrating in early adulthood makes it more likely to gain life-shaping experiences in the destination country and thus facilitates deeper bonds with this place' (Trąbka 2019: 71). Lewicka (2011: 226) refers to the significance of everyday routine for place attachment. She cites 'Seamon (1980) who suggested that sense of place is created through formation of a "body-ballet" and "time-space routines", i.e., a set of automatized everyday activities performed in the place'. Different types of place attachment were leading a large number of Ukrainian interviewees to become attached to KPP, and influencing them to stay.

Nonetheless, some interviewees were less attached, and would probably move on somewhere else, either in Poland or abroad. The final section discusses their motivations to do so, and suggests what characterised this type of potential transit migrant. However, although I make some attempt to categorise the interviewees into the more and the less settled in KPP, it is important to recognise that they often felt torn, and wavering about the future. Alla, for example, with a flat and friends in both Ukraine and KPP, said, 'Man proposes, but God disposes… I can't say that I feel completely that I am coming home [when I return from Ukraine]. But I have got used to it, and I feel comfortable.'

The people: co-ethnic networks and place attachment

Kindler and Wójcikowska-Baniak (2019: 106–7) suggest that Ukrainians rely on each other for support and manifest co-ethnic solidarity mostly during their early days in Poland. However, over time, the Ukrainians they interviewed in 2017 in Warsaw, working in care, construction and cleaning, became more wary of forming ties to fellow Ukrainians, who were regarded as competitors for the same jobs. There was no evidence of such transition among the KPP interviewees. Those who had been in the cities the longest were equally as embedded in Ukrainian networks as the new arrivals, although sometimes they were different networks. Perhaps this connectedness partly linked to the nature of their work (not in such competitive sectors) or to the greater opportunities for socialising offered by life in the smaller city. Given the absence of formal Ukrainian institutions and organisations in KPP, it might be premature to speak of a 'community'. However, many interviewees commented that they enjoyed socialising with other Ukrainians and had made new friends, contributing to their place attachment.

Chapter 7 discussed how interviewees from non-western parts of Ukraine had a sense of the origins and gathering pace of the migration wave to Poland over the last few years. Correspondingly, Ukrainians living in KPP were impressed by how the local Ukrainian populations had grown in these destinations, as well as in Poland overall. Having migrated, they possessed triple networks: people they knew from their location of origin, Ukrainians they met face-to-face in Poland, and Poland-based contacts from social media. This gave them a sense of the scale of Ukrainian migration. In addition, in 2021–2, several interviewees made assertions about statistics they had read in the local Polish media. They claimed that there were 10,000 Ukrainians in Kalisz, or 2,000 in Piła – numbers which seemed too big, but indicate their impressions that there was a very large number of Ukrainians. Adam, who had lived in Płock since the 1990s, pointed to the proliferation of new bus routes as evidence of the scale of Ukrainian migration.

> There used to be just one bus route, so people had to come by train, which was very hard, through Przemyśl. Later there were three buses from Ivano-Frankivsk plus buses from Lviv. Now in the bus station you see Kharkiv, Odesa, Zhytomyr. All Ukraine is in Poland. Wherever you go – Ukrainians everywhere.

Olesya referred to her friend who had been in Kalisz since about 2013:

> She said that when she came there were just three Ukrainians. Practically no one in Kalisz at all. Then, after she'd been working here for about six months she went into the supermarket and heard Ukrainian spoken. She was amazed back then. And now wherever you go there are lots of Ukrainians. Lots and lots.

Kvitka measured the influx by its effects on rents. She commented in 2021 that their rent had gone up and she thought it was because there were more foreigners in Kalisz and therefore more pressure on rented flats. When her husband came in 2017 rents had been lower. In Piła, too, interviewees who had lived in the city slightly longer had noticed how the Ukrainian population had grown. One interviewee even claimed there was a Ukrainian district in the city, which if true, would make it different from Warsaw, where, according to Kindler and Wójcichowska-Baniak (2019) there are no separate Ukrainian neighbourhoods. Vera said:

> There are lots of Ukrainians. Especially in Górne, where we're renting, I have the impression there are really a lot of Ukrainians. You just have to go into the supermarket and everyone is speaking Ukrainian or Russian. And the checkouts are staffed by Ukrainians. If I'm talking to my son and then say 'Goodbye' in Polish the cashier replies [in Russian or Ukrainian].

Ukrainian friends can constitute anchors in the new location (Grzymała-Kazłowska and Brzozowska 2017: 116). Senior migrants, those who had been in KPP slightly longer, had particular responsibilities for supporting newcomers. As I argued in Chapter 1, such practices can also be seen as part of a migration culture existing among migrants in the receiving country: the practice of giving and receiving advice about migration. Chapter 8 mentioned for example Yevhen's assertion that migrants provided one another with 'tips' about how to avoid using agencies. Such advice could also take the form of emotional support. For example, Boris reported, 'Everyone always said that the first three months would be really hard.' His experience then backed this up. 'We didn't believe it, we thought it was a fairy tale. But actually that's how it is. The first three months are really hard.' Similarly, Polina said that 'I was always told that the first time you come is hard. But the second time will be easier. And then even easier. That's just how it was. Next time I came it was like I was coming home.'

Tamara listed situations in which she and her extensive network of friends would help each other out:

> They say 'Toma, where do you buy such-and-such?' 'We get it here.' 'You have a grown-up daughter, how did you do such-and-such?' Or something about cars. Or residence permits. That was a big thing. Legalising our stay ... Also, child benefits, choosing a bank, getting a mortgage. 'Where did you get your mortgage? How did you buy your flat?' Those are the sorts of questions. We support each other. 'Which doctor is best? Which hairdresser? Who do you recommend?'

Family reunification was facilitated by friends helping the new arrivals, particularly with finding schools. There were several examples in Kalisz and Piła in 2021–2 where friends sorted out these problems for the new arrivals, a situation which contrasted with the expectations of interviewees in Płock in 2019 that they would have to traipse around the city from school to school making their own enquiries. Veronika said, for instance, 'We came to KPP because we have more friends here, they helped us bring our children, it's not so easy to bring a child from Ukraine, they got us invitations from the school, and from the kindergarten. Confirmation that they would accept them in the new school year.' Varvara said:

> When my son and I arrived we went with Rita, who'd been here a year already, we went to the school with her. I didn't speak any Polish but we came and she explained how it was. The mother has come to earn money, the child needs to go to school, and they accepted him without any problem.

Similarly, Emma reported, 'Our friends met us. I'm very grateful to them. They helped us settle in, they helped us find the school and kindergarten. They didn't leave us to our own devices.'

Kindler (2021: 515) points out that homophily, being drawn to spend time with people like oneself, may be the result of institutional and other structural factors, implying that it is not necessarily a matter of choice. In fact, my Ukrainian informants, thanks to their membership of a large migration wave, had some choice about with whom to associate. It was easier to become attached to the place when you could be selective about your friends. Alla said:

> Most of my Ukrainian friends are girls I met through work, when they came to get their nails done … Somehow we help each other out, and we feel close because we are all foreigners together. But I don't feel that way about all Ukrainians. I have a selective approach. I only socialise with people I really like … Although I'm not saying I only want to be friends with Ukrainians. I'm very happy spending time with Poles.

Living in KPP also presented an opportunity to extend one's social networks to other places in Poland, as former co-workers moved on to different destinations. A couple of recent arrivals asserted that people tended to lose touch after they moved on. However, longer-established migrants explained how they stayed in touch through social media. For instance, Olha mentioned that she knew Ukrainians who lived in other hostels in KPP through social media and that she also had friends from other towns where she used to work. 'Of course, we're always on Facebook, we send holiday greetings, sometimes we phone each other with questions.' Some interviewees also mentioned visiting their Ukrainian friends who lived elsewhere in Poland. Such friends sometimes help each other migrate to new locations. For instance, Raisa said, 'I would like to go to a big city in Poland, Wrocław, Warsaw, Łódź … I heard about them from other girls who'd worked there. We share information and experiences. Who'd been where, seen what, knows what.'

Kindler (2021: 514) observes that 'networking may be deliberate, with actors consciously forming ties or refusing to do so, but it may also be an unintended outcome of situational or structural settings'. She suggests that the latter was common among her own Ukrainian interviewees. In KPP, there were examples of both. Deliberate networking – reaching out to local Ukrainian strangers – took place on social media. For instance, Yuliya mentioned that they used the Facebook site *Nashi v Pile* to ask for advice about where to buy goods and services, although she did not think that it was a good way to find a job. My own observation, before February 2022, was that these requests were varied, with people writing in search of everything from dill to a Russian-speaking tattoo artist. After February 2022 the websites became even livelier. Another form of local networking took place in churches. Religious interviewees were mostly Greek Catholic, but one was a Protestant and one a Jehovah's Witness. Churches were places to meet, but also to help one another. Nina, for instance, mentioned that she had been helping a Ukrainian labour migrant bedridden with back pains and no money for medical care. She commented, 'It's a problem for Ukrainians. So we try to help each other... Lots of Ukrainians go to [Greek Catholic] services [in Kalisz Cathedral]. We pray, meet each other, get to know one another, help.' On the other hand, as Kindler pointed out, there are also situations where Ukrainians are simply thrown together. These include Ukrainianised workplaces such as factories, but also migrant hostels and adult education colleges. One interviewee claimed that in her own class (floristry) they were of various ages, from their 20s to 56, and there were whole families, even including some men. One interviewee in Piła said that most of her new close friends were young Ukrainian women whom she had met when their children went to preschool.

The migration turn from Russia to Poland threw together Ukrainians from different parts of the country. Kindler and Wójcikowska-Baniak (2019: 110) found that east and west Ukrainians in their sample were not associating much with one another. This was definitely not the case in KPP. In fact, being in Poland seemed to enhance interviewees' sense of pan-Ukrainian belonging, as they gained more knowledge of different places in Ukraine. Olha said, 'It's interesting. You can socialise with people from all different towns, we may all come from Ukraine, but we haven't been to those places, I've seen more of Poland than Ukraine.' One mixed west-east couple had met and married in KPP, and there were also cases of people from different parts of Ukraine sharing accommodation and becoming fast friends. Anzhela described her own new friends: 'You make friends at work. Also from west Ukraine. Very good people. When I was on my way home to Ukraine I stopped off and paid them a visit at home. They're really very nice. The world is full of nice people, but you wouldn't go to visit just anyone.'

Some interviewees also highlighted that they spoke a Ukrainian-Russian-*surzhik* mix with their co-workers and fellow hostel inmates. Olha said, 'Whatever language anyone speaks it seems to me that everyone understands each other.' Marina mentioned that 'I live with a girl, Oksana, from Ternopil. We've known each other over two years. She talks Ukrainian to me, I speak Russian to her, and we understand each other with no problem'. Marina also mentioned trips out in KPP with her new Ukrainian-speaking friends. However, the youngest interviewees did not always understand Russian. Olena and her husband, a young couple who had recently arrived in KPP, went out in the evening with their Ukrainian-speaking friends, rather than socialising with the east-west mix in the migrant hostel.

Although my interviewees very rarely expressed hostility towards people from other parts of Ukraine, it did surface in a few interviews, intertwining with other factors, such as worries about recruitment agencies, and snobbishness about small towns. Kira, from a city on the Dnipro, commented that

> It's really a shame that Ukrainian agencies deceive other Ukrainians, although that's only the case with agencies from west Ukraine. Because after the dissolution of the Soviet Union people from west Ukraine were the first to go to work abroad. Central and southern Ukraine didn't migrate, but west Ukraine always did. So they know everything and, hmm, some began to make money out of that.

In another interview, someone from a big city in the east displayed a patronising attitude towards west Ukraine, equated with small-town Ukraine.

> The bigger the city, the more outgoing the population. For instance, my room mate doesn't like Poland much – he likes his own city, Ternopil [population 300,000]. It seems so tiny to me [small dismissive chuckle]. Well, each to their own. We make friends with everyone, we're really friendly, because we're all in the same boat.

Among the west Ukrainians, there were a couple of manifestations of impatience with Ukrainians who could not understand Ukrainian language. Oksana, now living happily with Marina (see above) was annoyed with a previous roommate. 'I used to live with a girl, I would say something to her, and she would just stare at me. "My God, you're from Ukraine as well. Can't you understand a single word?"'

As Ukrainian society in KPP grows and becomes more complex, dividing lines become more apparent. The east/west fault-line seemed barely visible, but social class divides were potentially significant. Stratification could be reported neutrally. Tamara mentioned her observation that the majority of Ukrainians in Kalisz 'didn't put their children into sixth-form college (*liceum*) – they prefer a vocational college, so they quickly get some skills and earning power'. She agreed with me that they could be labelled working-class, whereas her family (with its teacher/business background) was *intelligentsia*. Zlata referred to the class divide with regret: 'You can't say that all Ukrainians who come to Poland are perfect. You meet all sorts, both in Poland and Ukraine. Sometimes when you look [at Ukrainians in Poland] you do wish that more educated and cultivated people would come here.'

In some cases, migrants distance themselves from others seen as inferior. Kindler (2021) mentions how networks of university-educated Ukrainians distance themselves from working-class people. There were few graduates in my own sample. However, like Polish migrants, non-graduates sometimes distanced themselves from migrants whom they perceived to be poorly behaved and therefore shaming the majority of 'good' Ukrainians. Ostap, for instance, complained, though not with specific reference to KPP, 'There are lots of Ukrainians, including some who aren't very good people. I see from watching the news. For example, they drink and drive. You feel ashamed, because after accidents like that Poles might think all Ukrainians behave the same.' Valerii had personal experiences to put him off.

> Ukrainians who come to Poland, well, I don't know how to put it, they are people who couldn't make anything of their lives ... After two weeks I stopped spending time with them [his housemates] because they drink vodka and so forth ... In my room now it's all neat and cosy but when I first came there were empty vodka and beer bottles and cigarette stubs ... They just drink beer, etc., and they never wash their clothes.

Another fault-line was settlement status and intentions, with more settled migrants socialising with each other and not associating except at work with temporary migrants. Anzhela, for instance, said that she and her daughter 'have lots of friends at the moment, including Ukrainians. The Ukrainians who are here with their families, with children. They've all come to KPP, normal, good, very good people'. Tamara complained:

> It's very hard to make friends with Ukrainians in Poland. Because most are here temporarily. You get used to someone and then their visa expires and they leave. You stay behind. That's why those of us who are here long-term are friends and keep in touch with each other. We celebrate birthdays together, invite them to parties, those are people who've been in Poland for five, six, seven years. Some are already Polish citizens, some have bought a flat here. But making friends quickly is more complicated. We've tried. That's my experience. They never come back, and you've already become attached ... We're living here long-term and that's why we have a different network of friends.

Chapter 4 discussed the quite frequently encountered discursive hostility of Poles towards other Polish migrants. Brzozowska (2018: 94) suggests that 'Ukrainian migrants, unlike Poles in the UK, don't engage in discursive practices of distancing themselves from co-ethics based on stories of mutual enmity and dishonest behaviour abroad. Such opinions, even if they are to be found among [Ukrainian] migrants, are not evident among forum and discussion group members.' Nonetheless, among Ukrainian KPP interviewees, despite all the examples above of actual collaboration, there did exist a certain amount of migration lore that Ukrainians abroad were not to be trusted. Halyna commented on perceived Polish-Ukrainian similarities in this regard.

> I find it hard to work with Ukrainians. I'm Ukrainian and I find it hard to work with Ukrainians. It's easier for me to work with Poles. But Poles say it was easier for them to work with English people than with other Poles. Both Poles and Ukrainians like to put their compatriots down and humiliate each other … They treat each other like enemies.

Inna, married to someone from the Caucasus, contrasted Ukrainians with other supposedly more solidaristic groups. She thought the Ukrainians lived 'more in their family circles'. Ukrainians also compared themselves unfavourably with Poles. Lev said: 'We Ukrainians don't particularly have any sense of solidarity. It seems that's the case, at least that's what I've been told, but all the same it's true, that when you're abroad a Pole is more likely to help you than a Ukrainian … He [a Ukrainian] will be glad if he's OK and you're not.' Anzhela complained:

> To my great regret, whenever I meet people who aren't so nice they turn out to be Ukrainians. That's my experience. I don't know why – I can't explain it. You would think, if people have travelled a thousand kilometres, from a different country, they should treat each other like friends and help each other.

The place: different types of attachment to KPP

Interviewees were at different stages in the process of becoming attached to KPP, and differently able to reflect on how that attachment had proceeded. In general, however, they were at the early stages. The day they arrived was a milestone for some: a 'transformative' occasion and memory which helped shape their attachment to KPP.

> I didn't know I would be coming to Płock. We arrived in the evening, it was a summer evening … and they brought us to the hostel from the railway station. I looked out at the city, it was my first time abroad and in Poland, and I thought how clean it was, how nicely-kept. We came to the hostel and got out of the taxi, here in the yard. It looked so beautiful. Lots of greenery, and so very quiet and peaceful. (Marina)

> It is a beautiful, impressive city. When I first saw the Vistula, what a river, and such a lovely embankment. We first arrived in June, and it was a holiday, we had four days off, so we didn't have to go to work, and we went to the Vistula. Although we were wondering why people don't swim in it. (Nataliya)

Forms of attachment in the early stages of life abroad include establishing a routine, an 'everyday rootedness' or 'body-ballet'. Bielewska (2023: 10) for example writes that 'the familiarity that comes from everyday unreflexively repeated routines allows migrants to call Wrocław "home"'. Interviewees had already built up a set of everyday routines. In fact, given the nature of their work, routine was a marked element of their daily lives. Oksana, for instance, described her routine in KPP:

> I've been here three years, and everything is familiar, all the different places, I know my way round the shops. We went home for Christmas, and as soon as I came back I thought 'Where shall I go, which shop should I go to?' I get up early and think 'Ah, I need to go to this shop or that shop.' It's the same every day, so it's familiar now.

Lev, who had been six months in Kalisz, commented that:

> It seems to me now that I've been living here for a very long time. That's so odd, that you feel you've been here for ages, you know everything about it. Now I feel more or less relaxed, not so self-conscious, I've got used to Poles, and everything else.

Going for walks was part of the routine, but also 'restorative' and linked to exploring and 'place discovery'. Olha commented, for instance, 'You don't get time for proper exercise. But Płock is a nice city, it's good on the Vistula embankment. It's nice just to stroll about the centre.' Viktor also mentioned walks into the Old Town and commented that Płock was 'a beautiful city, especially along the Vistula. It makes you feel at peace'. Similarly, interviewees spoke fondly about the restorative aspects of life in Piła. Melaniya, for example, mentioned, 'There's a nice atmosphere. When I came I liked it, on the whole. It's interesting to walk around, perhaps there aren't that many parks, but still there are places to go.' Veronika echoed the common opinion when she said, 'Piła is a green city. There are lots of places where you can go with children, including parks.' Other interviewees enjoyed simply wandering through local housing estates. Larysa, echoing Hirt's (2012) observations about 'privatisation of space in the post-socialist city', commented that:

> In Ukraine there are high walls, everything is closed off. You can't see much. But here, yesterday my sister and I took a walk, and it was very pretty. Even the blocks of flats, each one is different, they are painted brightly, and they have nice tiles and little pavements. We go for walks on Sundays and just look about.

She also described how they had visited a church and a cemetery:

> We went to see a Catholic church. It was lovely – we really liked it. We walk around, comparing things. My sister and I even went to a cemetery. At first I didn't want to go, but it was beautiful and so tidy. In Ukraine there are all those artificial wreaths and various rubbish, but here it was lovely. We lit some candles.

A smaller number of interviewees mentioned activities such as swimming and mushroom-picking which also helped them feel attached, especially when they involved bonding with nature. Ostap, for example, described outings with male friends from the factory, together with some Ukrainian lorry drivers. 'There are forests and lakes [around Piła]. Egypt is nice for a holiday but it would be too hot for living. I like walking in the forest. We go fishing together.'[1]

Place discovery could consist of becoming informed about KPP. For some, this included reading the news. Olha said, for instance, 'There's a Facebook page. You don't understand every word but since we live here we're interested in what's going on.' Others looked up local history on the internet. For example, Alla, who lived in a picturesque street in central Kalisz, mentioned, 'I was interested to read about the history of the street on the internet. The House of Culture and Arts is on my street. And I found out about its history.'

For some, being able to have short casual conversations with local people on the street and in the shops constituted important steps in their attachment to the place. Glick Schiller and Çağlar (2016) refer to 'urban sociabilities' to describe small acts of friendliness which can characterise city life. Interviewees who worked in beauty salons and hairdressers mentioned, for example, how they liked chatting to clients. Marina opened our conversation by declaring that she had 'fallen in love with Płock' and that 'I feel at home, I know how to find places here'. It turned out that she had no friends outside the factory and hostel. However, she was becoming attached to the city thanks to her small interactions with strangers. In the following extract, Marina explained how her progress in speaking Polish was parallelled by her increasing interactions with local people and feeling of being accepted and belonging. We were speaking Russian, but she quoted the Poles in Polish, mimicking their intonation.

> I walk around the city and people ask me in Polish for directions, which I can give them, with details. For example … someone asked me the way to the post office. I explained to him, in Polish, and afterwards I thought 'Wow! I managed to do that!'. That's nice, of course. Of course it wasn't the same when I first came to KPP. If I went into a shop. I can compare my first stay in KPP and my next one. I could only ask in broken Polish and they found it hard to understand. But everywhere I went, I listened out to what people said, how they said it, to make it sound friendly … It was lovely when a shop assistant asked me, 'What would you like, darling?' That was super.

> Another nice thing that happened was on my first stay in KPP. I was coming back from work … and there were boys aged about seven and nine on bikes who said hello to me. I felt it wasn't just a greeting but as if they'd paid me a compliment. Another time, last year, I was in a shop and there was a woman with a girl of about five and the child asked, 'Mummy, can I say "Hi" to auntie?' She said, 'Go on.' So the little girl says 'Hi' and I say, 'Hi, darling!' It's that interaction with strangers, unknown children, that 'Hi!' and 'Hello!' I was in Kaufland and a Polish woman started telling me how she'd bought a saucepan and didn't think it was very good, so I recommended a different shop. I like those trivial conversations with strangers. It makes me feel good, very secure. That someone decided to share something with me.

Unlike the Polish interviewees discussed in Chapter 4, who had spent up to 20 years abroad and often became parents in the process, Ukrainians in KPP had rarely experienced significant biographical milestones. A few had met their current partners and one couple had married. However, for most, the important family-related events such as parental death, or births of children and grandchildren, had happened in Ukraine. Nonetheless, they did refer to certain milestones during their lives in KPP which made them feel that they were becoming increasingly at home.

Progress in place attachment could include overcoming initial alienation caused by homesickness and mental health problems. Fadei reminisced: 'When I first came people used to ask how I felt and whether I liked it. So I said, "I don't like it. I want to go home.' I had depression … because you know that if you depart from your comfort zone you don't feel that good.' Fadei then made plenty of friends and the second time he came to KPP he already felt more comfortable. Children's academic achievements represented milestones not just for themselves but also for their parents, who had often reproached themselves for uprooting the children and were upset by their problems adjusting to life in Poland. Anzhela, for example, was delighted when her daughter, who came to KPP as a teenager and had problems at first with studying online, finished the year top of her class. Tamara was very proud of the fact that her daughter had been accepted at one of the best schools in the city.

Progress in place attachment also links to the migrant's 'appropriation' (Boccagni 2022) of their new housing. They make homes more homely, for example by keeping pets. Some interviewees brought their cats and dogs, which constituted a symbol of commitment to stay. Varvara, for example, mentioned, 'We brought our dog with us, a little chihuahua. We knew that we weren't just coming on a visa, we were here to stay.' Inviting people from Ukraine to one's home in Poland could also contribute to the sense of being in control of one's own space. Ostap said, 'I don't feel homesick any more. I don't miss Ukraine. I used to really miss it and want to go home. Now I don't. It's easier for me to invite my friends to visit me here, than to go to Ukraine.'[2] Homemaking was also about beautifying one's living space. Valerii, as previously mentioned, had moved into a room strewn with empty bottles in a house in multiple occupancy. He continued his story: 'I have a normal room, not with five people, I live on my own. All the home comforts … I painted, tidied up, washed, put up lines for drying, did everything that was needed to make it comfortable. That's how I'm used to living, not any old how.' Most interviewees in Kalisz and Piła preferred not to live in shared accommodation, where it was hard to 'appropriate' the space and feel at home. Instead, they rented flats with their families. However, the high price of rents could be a disincentive, particularly in Piła, as discussed in Chapter 3. Boris mentioned that when he and his family first arrived in the city he spent 80 per cent of his wage on rent. Tamara, whose husband worked in a big city and whose family probably had a higher income than most, explained the household's priorities.

> We're planning to live in Kalisz for a long time, so we've rented a good flat. A place where you can return after work and really relax. It's not so expensive, we're paying 1,600 for a three-room flat. It's in [estate name] and everything is near at hand. So we're staying there, it's a good flat, we have good relations with the landlord and neighbours … We've done all we can so that we can feel at home.

By contrast, interviewees in Płock who were circular migrants were in one case building a house in Ukraine and in another hoping to buy housing there. More often – like many Poles working abroad – the Ukrainian interviewees already owned, and maintained, a Ukrainian home while simultaneously becoming more attached to homes in KPP. Only one person told me that the family had sold their Ukrainian housing. Some interviewees were hesitating about whether to sell up, because it was too expensive to keep up two flats; others were more possessive. Margarita said of her empty flat, 'I don't want strangers living there.' Keeping housing in the country of origin might be seen as a rational strategy for a migrant, in case they decided to return, but in fact this was not how it was presented to me in the interviews. In some cases it seemed to be more of a transnational emotional tie.

The final stage of attachment and commitment would be to buy property in Poland. Of the interviewees, only Sergei had so far succeeded in this ambition. Brzozowska (2023: 2385) suggests that 'high prices for renting and buying a flat in the biggest Polish cities, low credit worthiness and the tight housing market made it difficult for circulants to settle and realise the aspiration of owning an apartment'. Several interviewees, including two unemployed women, mentioned that they dreamed of buying housing, but this was unrealistic at the moment. However, in Kalisz at least some Ukrainians did manage to buy property, as I confirmed for example in a bank located in central Kalisz which advertised its mortgage services around the city, in Ukrainian. Solomiya told me, 'We really want to buy a flat here. A two-roomed flat. I know lots of us Ukrainians are buying flats and living here. We calculated that it's better not to pay for rent. We want to stay here to live. We've already made enquiries.' Yeva, who had a managerial role at her factory, said, 'I have an idea of getting a mortgage for my own flat [in Kalisz]. I've been to discuss it with the bank. I'm scared, because it's lots of money. But a lot of my [Ukrainian] friends already have flats. And they have a mortgage for 20 or 30 years.'

As Bielewska (2023: 10) discovered with her interviewees from different countries working for international companies in Lower Silesia, returning to Poland was often remembered as a moment of truth when you defined your identity in relation to where you lived abroad. Sergei, a lorry-driver, said, 'For five years now, whenever I cross the River Odra into Poland, I have the feeling I'm coming home. A warm feeling of being at home. Poland has become a second home to me, it opened its heart, its gates, I don't know how to put it. I feel very comfortable.' Similarly, Anzhela said:

> I feel at home, I have my job, my circle of friends, my daughter. I feel good ... When we went abroad for our summer holiday I felt most comfortable when I came back to KPP. I had the feeling of coming home. Somehow I didn't like it there, some places were dirty, or other things weren't right, but here I feel I'm at home.

Margarita, however, began to weep when she admitted to the same feeling. She said, 'The scariest thing is that I feel that when I go back to Poland I'm coming home. For me that's frightening, strange and incomprehensible.' She attributed her reaction to her Soviet upbringing and instilled sense of patriotism.

Place alienation and ambivalence

There were also some interviewees whom place attachment researchers might describe as 'alienated' (Hummon 1992, cited by Trąbka (2019: 72)). Living in a deprived area can inhibit place attachment (Kohlbacher et al 2015: 458). This had happened to two interviewees who separately rented flats in a poor area of Kalisz city centre, where corner shops sold alcohol late into the evening. Lev complained, 'The whole neighbourhood where I live is full of people who drink. It's the first time I've seen such people. More lower-class it seems. People who don't behave very nicely.' Zlata complained about being woken by shouting in the middle of the night and said, 'It's scary to walk along the street – there's no streetlight, and scary people.' Both Lev and Zlata were unhappy in Kalisz for other reasons, so living in this neighbourhood intensified their alienation.

In other cases, 'ambivalent' would be a more accurate label for the less enthusiastic interviewees. Usually they expected to stay in KPP because other family members wanted to do so. For instance, I asked Kseniya if she saw her future in Poland, and she said, 'Half-in-half, but my husband one hundred per cent.' Oksana, mentioned earlier as a 'trailing' wife, seemed to enjoy living in Poland, where she had friends and relatives. However, when asked if she would consider moving to Germany or Italy, where her friends were working, she did not deny that she might want to do this. The reason she gave for not moving was that her husband had a good job in Poland and was used to it. Most often, it was children who kept these interviewees in KPP. Irina said, 'I was considering moving about three years ago, but the children said, "No, we have friends here, and we really like school." It would be stressful for them to move to another city. You don't know what it would be like, they don't have good attitudes towards Ukrainians everywhere.' Similarly, Margarita reported, 'When we'd been living here for two years we felt we had to choose. What should we do? Should we return home, or buy a flat here? Our daughter begged us to stay. She said she didn't want to go home.' At the same time, Margarita experienced conflicting emotions. She said that Poland was convenient because they could easily get back to Ukraine to see her mother, but she also mentioned that she and her husband had long searched for a way to work in the UK, and that she regretted passing up the opportunity to go to the USA 20 years previously. Tamara, though well-integrated and attached to Kalisz in many respects, would have liked to find a better job in another city, but their teenage daughter 'begged us, "Please don't change to a different city – all my friends are here now."'

Some interviewees also reported inertia as a reason for staying. Having taken the trouble to learn Polish, they were unenthusiastic about learning other foreign languages, which would be more difficult. Age was construed as a barrier, at least by interviewees from outside west Ukraine. For middle-aged and older west Ukrainian women, it had been normal for decades to migrate abroad (Brunarska et al 2016). However, Artem (56) from central Ukraine claimed he was 'too old' and Svitlana (47) suggested that for middle-aged people (implicitly, people in her home city of Mariupol), other countries were too far: young people, such as her son, a welder already in Poland, might be more adventurous. Several other interviewees made the point that even though they personally would stay in KPP, their adult children would go further. Lizaveta reminisced about how when her daughter came to KPP 'right away she began saying, "Mama, let's go further, to Poznań or Warsaw." But that's not for us. Me and my husband are homebodies'. Anzhela said:

My daughter wants to go somewhere further for her university education. For some reason she's been dreaming for ages of studying in America. That's why she's doing [extra] English classes, she's moving towards her goal, or at least making an effort. I don't know about myself. To be honest, I like it here.

Return to Ukraine or migration to third countries

Zielińska and Szaban (2020: 53–4), in their interviews with Ukrainians in Wielkopolska region in 2019–20, found several interviewees intending to return to Ukraine because they were lonely in Poland and missed their family and friends. However, although there were plenty of people in KPP who missed family and friends, they did not want to return to Ukraine. They tended to dream about visiting their family members, or bringing them to Poland. Only one interviewee was determined to return soon to Ukraine and live there permanently, and he did not have a partner, children or other caring responsibilities. Ivan ascribed his desire to patriotism. 'I want to live in Ukraine. I was born and grew up in Ukraine. I love Ukraine.' Another reason was that he had been building himself a house in Ukraine all three years of his stay in Poland, and had almost completed his project.

Among my interviewees, about one quarter – mostly not from west Ukraine – expressed some aspiration to move to a third country. Presumably the west Ukrainians, being networked with more people in Western countries, often had had more options to go further than Poland on their first attempt at international migration. Olesya, aged 53, exemplified this group of interviewees. She said: 'People from west Ukraine have already tried Poland and gone on further. But some [west Ukrainian] people, I don't know, like me, have stayed.' Olesya struggled to define 'like me', but she seemed to typify a group of middle-aged women interviewees, often without university education, who emphasised that they did not have the energy or desire to move further on. The same group also highlighted as reasons to stay in KPP their sense of security; their social contacts; the convenience and cleanliness of their accommodation; the city's attractiveness; and the geographical 'closeness', as they perceived it, of KPP to Ukraine.

By contrast, the interviewees most determined to move on from KPP included male solo migrants who had already accumulated a certain amount of migration experience and who were not particularly anchored in Poland. They were tempted mostly by higher earnings as well as inspired by the example of Polish migrants who had worked in Western Europe.

Ihor: Poland's only the start.

Nikolai: Germany's next.

Ihor: Perhaps yes. You have to aim higher! … Though it doesn't have to be Germany. We could try Holland or Belgium. People, I mean Poles, go there a lot, to earn money, so why not? Poland's only the start. While we're young.

Another small category of potential westward migrants consisted of ambitious university graduates, mostly single, motivated by curiosity and adventure. Tatyana, as a teacher of English, was determined to go to an English-speaking country to perfect her language skills, and so her daughter could also do the same. However, possibly this was also because she was tempted by other migrants. Although Tatyana was from east Ukraine, she had an aunt and uncle living in west Ukraine whom she visited on her way home from KPP. The visit had obviously made an impression. The relatives had 'seen the world' by working in both Poland and Ireland, and were able to pass on information about Ireland to Tatyana. Young men such as Fadei, Artur and Yurii also expressed interest in seeing the wider world, but these were rather vague thoughts about the future rather than concrete plans. However, some middle-aged people also expressed a desire to try out new migration options. Zinaida, for instance, had heard stories from acquaintances in her village of origin near Mariupol about working in Italy. 'Girls from the village have been working for years in Italy and they're happy with it. I want to give it a try.'

Interviewees could express contradictory aspirations in the same interview. Olha, who was mentioned in Chapter 8 as previously choosing Poland rather than Finland, because Finland was too far, and then expressed a strong wish to bring her children to be with her in Poland, later in the interview said that she was now thinking about Germany. Halyna was similarly self-contradictory:

Halyna: My goal was to earn some money. But after living here a bit, I didn't want to go back …

Anne: Although it's hard to say 100 per cent.

Halyna: I see my future in Poland one million per cent.

Later in the interview:

Halyna: Somehow I like Germany better.

Anne: So why don't you like Poland?

Halyna: Perhaps it's just become ordinary for me. I don't have a sense any more of a dividing line between Ukraine and Poland … It's all one space, but Germany is something different.

Conclusions

Explaining why she stayed in Kalisz, Nina said, 'I have lots and lots of friends and acquaintances. And somehow I have put down roots.' For very many interviewees, friends and family ties were a strong reason to feel attached to KPP and want to remain. Hlib was another example of an interviewee who made the direct connection, when he said, 'I have friends and acquaintances. [So] I would prefer to stay here.' Interviewees were struck by the fact that 'wherever you go there are lots of Ukrainians' and this made it possible to find congenial company and 'only socialise with people you really like'. In these dense and extensive networks, friends could provide practical support and advice drawing on a wide range of experiences in KPP. They could also offer tips specifically about how to do migration – in other words, they were busy creating and reproducing migration culture. The sense of being part of a wave of migration from the whole of Ukraine also contributed to a feeling of pan-Ukrainian identity, including through close friendships between migrants from west and east, and in one case an east-west marriage. Very few interviewees expressed hostility towards compatriots from other parts of Ukraine. Insofar as they commented on stratification within the KPP Ukrainian population, this was usually framed in terms of the more settled *vis-à-vis* the temporary migrants, or else those who manifested 'good' or 'bad' behaviour – the badly-behaved being the heavy drinkers, who were probably also more likely to be the temporary migrants. A few informants made generalisations about the untrustworthiness of Ukrainians abroad, nearly identical to remarks made by Poles about one another, as mentioned in Chapter 4. Sometimes these complaints were based on personal experience but in others they seemed to stem from migration lore ('I've heard that …').

Chapter 10 also illustrated the truth of Trąbka's (2019) observation that migrants can become attached to places quite rapidly, at least in certain regards. Most interviewees no longer treated KPP instrumentally, as a place where they had found a suitable job. Instead, they had passed certain emotional milestones during their lives in KPP, such as overcoming initial feelings of depression; making the place their own by having small encounters with Poles around the city and finding favourite spots where they could relax and bond with nature; 'appropriating' their new housing by making it comfortable and inviting guests; seeing their children make friends and succeed at school; or coming back to Poland from holidays in Ukraine or third countries and feeling that they had returned home. Just a few people articulated lack of attachment, such as two informants who lived (separately) in a rundown inner-city neighbourhood and were keen to move to another Polish city.

It was striking that only one interviewee was determined to return in the near future to Ukraine. A number of people were toying with the idea of treating Poland as a stepping-stone to the west, although in their interviews they often expressed contradictory or ambivalent thoughts about their future plans. It seemed likely that the habitual circular migrants might move on to a third country, just as the circular migrants in the Polish sample had typically worked in more than one country. Ambitious university graduates who did not have husbands or children to keep them in KPP also seemed likely to go, although perhaps in some cases only to another Polish city. Younger men also expressed hopes to move on elsewhere, although they were also sometimes the people who seemed to have the strongest friendship ties in KPP. Probably the group most likely to stay were middle-aged parents, especially women, who had been in KPP for a few years, were well-embedded, and felt unwilling to uproot themselves again. This illustrates the truth of Trąbka's (2019: 71) observation about the significance of life-stage in migrant place attachment, although in this case the migrants concerned were not transitioning to adulthood but making new lives and livelihoods in middle age.

Notes

1 As Ostap's comment indicated, foreign holidays were also part of some migrants' experiences. Poland was therefore 'discovered' as a gateway to Europe and the wider world. Some interviewees went on package holidays, while others visited Ukrainian friends working in different countries. Such travels helped motivate them to continue their often humdrum work in Poland, but also made them still more conscious of the scale of Ukrainian migration and Ukrainianisation. For instance, Varvara recalled: 'I got out of the bus in Prague and realised that everyone around me was speaking Russian. And I said to my son, "Where have we landed – in Czechia or Ukraine?"'
2 For discussion of similar hosting behaviour by Poles in the UK, see White (2017: 180).

11
Ukrainian–Polish networks and relations

Introduction

The quality of inter-ethnic relations helps make a city attractive or otherwise to migrants. For migrants wanting to settle for the medium term in smaller cities in Poland, this factor is particularly significant. Chapter 11 analyses the opinions and experiences of the 70 Ukrainian interviewees regarding their relations with Poles. It complements the Polish interviewees' accounts as reported in Chapter 6. The Polish interviewees were a self-selecting group who had chosen to participate in the research project and who might be expected to hold sympathetic attitudes towards migrants. However, Ukrainians in their everyday lives encountered a broader spectrum of local Poles. Hence their accounts are essential for understanding how Poles in smaller cities have been adjusting to the migrants in their midst. Chapter 11 considers both emotional and instrumental functions of links to the Polish majority population, usually described in scholarly literature as 'bonding' and 'bridging' ties. It continues by considering street and workplace interactions with Polish strangers, and interviewees' reflections upon and interpretations of those encounters. It discusses what the interviewees gleaned about Polish people's experiences of migration, and the conclusions they drew from that knowledge. The chapter considers both the types of conversations interviewees reported having with Poles and the overall impressions they formed about local Poles' attitudes to foreigners. The chapter uses the same conceptual lenses applied to understanding the Polish interviews, such as visibility and contact hypothesis. It tries to isolate the specifically 'smaller-city' character of Ukrainians' opinions and experiences.

Life-stage and family responsibilities influenced the time available for socialising with Poles. Living in a flat with one's spouse and children took up time and energy and – as with non-migrants – could limit networking.[1] On the other hand, younger and single middle-aged interviewees were often the best networked. Significant contacts were particularly likely to be formed at the workplace (as Grabowska (2018) also argues with reference to Poles working abroad) and some workplaces are more 'migrantised' than others. However, as migrants come to feel more attached to their new place of residence they extend their networks into other spheres of local society.

Sustained contact – in accordance with Allport's (1954) 'contact hypothesis' – is important for building friendship and trust. Better networks partly resulted from having lived longer in Poland, but this correlation was not to be taken for granted. Nor did longer experience of Poland necessarily lead to migrants forming better impressions. On the one hand, some newcomers had worse experiences because they were more dependent on help from Polish strangers. If they asked questions on the street these could be met with impatience. Longer-established migrants knew where they were going and felt more at home because they 'blended in'. On the other hand, people who had been in KPP longer had had time to collect experience of both good and bad encounters. Just one bad encounter could be bruising, and cancel out many good impressions. Ukrainians with more Polish acquaintances – living in flats rather than migrant hostels, working side-by-side with Poles, and/or interacting with Polish clients – often did articulate more mixed impressions. They were more likely to have encountered real hostility, not just casual unhelpfulness on the street, but in some cases they had also met with kindness in situations where they needed serious help. Moreover, they were better able to see things from the point of view of their Polish acquaintances, partly because they knew something about the latter's own migration backgrounds. Overall, they were more likely to be in equal relationships with Poles, which – again according to Allport (1954) – is important for creating understanding and openness to difference, as well as opportunities for conviviality (Rzepnikowska 2019).

By contrast, recently-arrived Ukrainians often had little time to meet local Poles. Particularly when they first arrived, labour migrants typically worked very long hours. For instance, Olha, a lone parent supporting two children in Ukraine, who had been doing two jobs when she first came to KPP, reminisced, 'There was no time and no one to socialise with, because it was just work, work, work, work, you sleep three hours and then it's work, work all over again.' Solomiya said, 'We haven't been invited to anyone's home yet – there just isn't time. But we do make friends, at work, and we exchange telephone numbers, so we can chat.' Svitlana, living in a hostel with her husband, mentioned her domestic chores: either she was at work, or cooking and doing housework.

Family and friends

Among the Ukrainian interviewees, four Ukrainian speakers (mostly from west Ukraine) said they had Polish partners, and another claimed that binational partnerships were common among Ukrainians and Poles of her acquaintance. With one exception, these were very young people. Migrants who were young and/or without Ukrainian partners in KPP were also much more likely than others to report having close Polish friends. These were people they described in Polish or Russian by terms such as *koleżanka*[2] or *drug*, meaning a closer friend, rather than *znajomy* or *znakomyi*, a less close friend, or acquaintance. Bonding ties helped interviewees feel more attached to the city. Their friends were neighbours, work colleagues, clients and friends of friends. For example, Yurii, 30 and apparently unattached, was a gregarious person living in a hostel, with friends of all nationalities, including Poles. Oksana, living in KPP without her husband, described her Polish line manager as a friend (*koleżanka* in Polish). She had invited Oksana to her home twice, as well as to her daughter's wedding. Oksana said she missed her when she was in Ukraine. Although two visits in three years might not seem very much, this was a relationship which Oksana found important. Women working in hairdressing and beauty salons, especially solo migrants such as Nina and Alla, made friends among their customers. One of Nina's clients, for instance, had made the friendly gesture of trying to persuade Nina to migrate with her to Germany. 'I said, "Why do you go to Germany?" "Because the money is good". And she said, "Learn some German and you can come with me." I said, "It's hard for me to learn languages." She said, "It can be learned."' Another marker of friendship was going on holidays together. For instance, Alla and her Ukrainian friend from KPP spent a week holidaying in Sopot with a Polish woman whom they had met on holiday in Croatia. Fadei, one of the youngest interviewees, was planning to buy a package holiday to Croatia with some Polish friends and they also wanted to go together to visit Chernobyl. These interviewees also sometimes claimed to feel 'at home' in KPP because of their Polish friends.

By contrast, Ukrainians living with their spouses and children, even if they were gregarious and good at speaking Polish, sometimes found it difficult to form close friendships with Poles. Tamara said 'We know people we can talk to, have a chat with, go for a walk. Poles who live in Kalisz ... But not friends in the sense of going to their houses for a birthday or some other celebration. Those friends are all Ukrainians.' Yuliya said:

> I have Polish womenfriends/acquaintances. Perhaps not so many, but some. But it wasn't always like that. Of course it takes a while to happen. The first steps aren't easy ... You have to make your own way. Put it like this, if you knock on every door, one of them will open.

She had the impression that at the weekends her work colleagues were busy with their families and extended families, for example if their siblings lived in KPP.

The Ukrainian interviewees almost all named work colleagues as their main Polish contacts. They mentioned chatting to their colleagues in breaks – for example, swapping Polish and Ukrainian recipes. However, some of them – as it happened, all younger women working in factories – refused to distinguish between different nationalities. They were equally friends. For instance, when asked whether she socialised with Poles in the factory, Kira downplayed the significance of ethnic difference, saying, 'We're all people, we socialise, chat'. Solomiya said, 'I socialise with Ukrainians, Belarusians and Poles, and I don't notice any differences.' I asked Halyna, 'Do you mix with Poles during the lunch break?' She replied – unusually among the interviewees – with reference to Slav identity, although also to shared humanity.

> It makes no difference. It's exactly the same. We're very alike. We are similar in being Christians. We think the same way. We are Slavs ... There are situations like, well, I say I did such and such, and she says, 'So did I.' So I can't see any fundamental difference, no real gulf. I have a very easy time. Insofar as I have any problems, I have them with Ukrainians as much as Poles. I don't attribute it to the fact that they are Poles, they are just people.

By far the largest share of Ukrainians were working in factories: 26 women and 15 men. From their accounts it was clear that different factories, and different sections within a single factory, employed different proportions of Poles and foreign workers. Some interviewees – those with very good Polish – were the only Ukrainians in their section. More often, interviewees reported a mix of nationalities. In this situation, Poles were picking up some Ukrainian language. It was perhaps noteworthy that the only interviewee who claimed to work entirely alongside Ukrainians was also the only one to voice doubts about whether Poles in the factory were friendly. She said:

> There are people like that. 'I'm a Pole, and you're nobody.' Especially at the factory it's the men. Not the women, they're OK with us. But there are some men who take the line 'You should know your place'. The managers are fine. They come up to you and ask how you are. But the average welder, when he says 'girls', I don't know, you get that impression.

Generally, relations were said to be cordial. Elena, for example, who had worked exclusively with Poles, reported:

> There are six people on each assembly line, and the line managers, I got to know everyone, it was a very friendly environment, you go with the other people on your line to drink coffee, and it's really friendly. Of course there are a few unpleasant types but that's true everywhere.

Interviewees from different factories in different cities made similar comments about how they were treated equally at work. Yeva, for example, said, 'Nobody refers to the fact that we're Ukrainian. We're treated as workers.' Fadei reported:

> I feel good working there. The attitudes are good. I really liked it that there was one situation when someone made a bad comment about Ukraine and he was fined. Yes, he was even fined for harassment on the basis of nationality. I really like the fact that there's equality. That everyone is equal, Ukrainians and Poles are equal.

Zinaida generalised about a more relaxed and democratic management style in Poland to explain why she preferred to work at her Polish factory.

> I also worked in a factory with metal [in Mariupol] and the management here is much more modest, their offices are simply furnished … The factory director can be seen just wandering around

the factory. It's not like that in Ukraine. If you want to see the director you have to get past the security, the secretaries, and their super-offices ... They think it's cool to work in a beautiful office and they don't care if the workers earn kopecks. That's why I like it here.

However, there were also a few negative comments. Polina, who worked alongside Fadei and similarly had friendly relations with her Polish co-workers, said of the bosses: 'There are Poles who like Ukrainians and others who don't. At the factory they watch us like hawks. If they catch us standing doing nothing they find some work for us to do, if only taking a cloth and doing some cleaning. You have to *arbeiten* [said in German] non-stop.'

For these Ukrainians, socialising with Poles mostly took place at work. Some interviewees attributed this to the fact that Polish factory workers did not live locally, but were commuting from surrounding villages. Workplaces had different traditions when it came to socialising and conviviality. For instance, Lavra mentioned her disappointment that – unlike when she had worked as a teacher in Ukraine – her factory colleagues in Poland did not celebrate each other's birthdays at work. The tradition did however hold in Polina's factory. She clearly considered the ritual important, since after our interview she went to spend the interview fee on sweets for co-workers celebrating her own birthday. Some Polish workmates were said to be people who had worked in the factory for decades, so age was perhaps a barrier to close friendships with Ukrainians in their 30s and 40s. More often, Ukrainians highlighted that there was a high turnover of Polish workers, partly because they were leaving to work abroad. Lyudmila said, for example, 'Very few Poles have worked there for a long time. Very few. They keep on changing all the time. Young people and older ones. They're always changing.' Yeva, as mentioned in a previous chapter, had had one close Polish friend, but the friend then left KPP to go to Germany.

Several interviewees, especially in Płock, stated that having a good Polish line manager was a reason to feel at home in Poland, and even to return persistently to Płock. One manager was praised for how well she understood Ukrainian, as a result of her experience of working with Ukrainians. As mentioned in Chapter 8, several Ukrainian interviewees with university degrees in Kalisz had been promoted to line managerial roles and had responsibility for Polish workers. In general, the Ukrainians did not seem to feel that this difference in nationality hindered cordial relations. It was more important that the line manager needed to be of a certain age in order to wield authority. Oleksandra (aged 50) commented:

When I went home to Ukraine they had trouble finding someone to take my place. They put in a younger person but the girls didn't accept her. Some of them are older people, some are middle-aged, some are young. And the woman who substituted for me was quite young and they wouldn't take orders from her … The Polish women can understand me, I've been with them two years and they seem to be happy. When I went to Ukraine they wrote asking me to come back

Dmytro, aged 28, mentioned that it was the older Poles with whom he sometimes needed to use his diplomatic skills.

Non-factory workers were almost always the only Ukrainians at their workplace, even if they were working in settings such as restaurant kitchens which in a big city would very likely have been staffed by other Ukrainians. The size of the workplace seemed to be important. In small restaurants, workshops, hairdressing salons and a specialised primary school, relations were said to be very friendly. For example, Margarita, a hairdresser, said (using the diminutive form of her boss's name): 'I have a really good boss, my friend Dorotka. She helps me, explains stuff, gives me advice. If I need to miss work to do some errand she says, "Off you go, then."' Varvara, who worked in a kitchen, was pleased that her workmates called her 'our Varvara'. Antin, the Ukrainian student, had experienced different attitudes at work. Nowadays he felt he was treated with respect by his boss, because he was working (remotely) with computers. However, when he had previously worked in bigger companies he had not felt that respect. This was particularly a problem working in greenhouses. He claimed that 'often I saw that a Pole who picked a third of what I picked was paid more'. He had better experiences at McDonald's, though he still sensed hostility. His opinion was that all workers from the former Soviet Union could expect to meet unfriendly attitudes in such workplaces. Four construction workers were not integrated into any workplace. They were only in KPP for a single period of employment, so they had little place attachment. They were highly mobile and transnational, and barely integrated in Poland. Mihaylo said, 'We don't have any acquaintances, people have a different culture, well, home is always best, isn't it? … And all that chopping and changing, and learning the language … so you don't feel like trying to make friends.'

Friendships could also be made or maintained via social media. One interviewee from the hostel in Płock said that they used Facebook to socialise after work with their Polish colleagues who lived outside the city. Another interviewee, who had been through a serious illness, had made Polish friends through an online support group. It was my observation that the Ukrainian Facebook groups before 2022 were not used by Poles, and that the Facebook groups for Polish residents of each city were not used by Ukrainians. This seemed like a missed opportunity for positive contact, although it also helped protect the Ukrainians from knowing about anti-Ukrainian sentiments expressed online. For example, the Płock interviewees in 2019 were almost uniformly glowing in their assessments of local friendliness, but Płock Polish-language social media showed that some local people were less than welcoming. However, in 2022, after the full-scale invasion, this social-media segregation changed in Piła. The new group, 'Piła residents in support of Ukraine', was set up by Poles but then attracted many Ukrainian posts and became a site for Polish–Ukrainian dialogue. This was evidence that Ukrainians trusted Poles who had expressed goodwill towards Ukrainian refugees.

Neighbours

In Płock, some factory workers acquired Polish networks as soon as they arrived, since a few Poles who lived outside the city shared their hostel accommodation. As already mentioned, this particular hostel was a pleasant place to live and socialise, without hard drinking and rowdiness. Larysa said:

> We do know some people who live here all the time, they work at our factory, and sometimes we socialise together ... They listen and learn our language. If we gather on the street, we're having a chat outside, we start laughing and telling stories, they ask us to repeat what we said, they're drawn into the conversation, and if necessary we explain to them in Polish (*na ikhnem*).

It seems that Ukrainians benefit from being the largest group in the hostel, not just the majority minority, but the actual majority. Consequently, the handful of Polish inmates was learning Ukrainian. In Kalisz and Piła, almost all Ukrainian interviewees were living in rented flats. Several mentioned cordial relationships with landladies. To some extent they also knew their neighbours and in some cases these included parents of children at the same school. In just a couple of cases, cited in Chapter 10, interviewees who lived in a run-down part of Kalisz city centre complained about rowdy Poles. However, they were exceptional. Most interviewees either did not mention their neighbours, or made positive comments. Kohlbacher et al (2015: 449) cite research which suggests that 'families with children have significantly more neighbour contacts than those without children'. For example, when Yuliya first arrived and was caring for her son at home, she made friends, though not close friends, when she took him out for walks in the neighbourhood. She said this helped her improve her confidence at speaking Polish. Tamara, with a child at school, similarly had a wide network of Polish acquaintances, and also walked a dog. She claimed, 'I know a big group of Poles from going dog walking.' They talked about Polish migration, among other topics. In Sergei's case, the roles were reversed, since he had just bought a house and was able to play the host. He said, 'We have great neighbours, Poles. They're all fine with us. On Friday we invited them to supper [said in Polish] and had a barbecue and drank whisky. We got to know each other, it was good. We feel completely accepted.'

Sport could also bring foreigners and Poles together and promote conviviality. Valerii, a keen sportsperson, said, 'I came here and I already have Polish friends, I socialise with them and they invite me to visit them at home. That's the sort of person I am.' Oleksii reported: 'We've been playing football with Poles … We play all the time … with friends from work, from various places, it depends on who people know and bring with them to join the match … We agree among ourselves [on the internet] when to meet.'

Bridging ties

Migration researchers, following Granovetter (1983), tend to emphasise the usefulness of bridging ties – contacts with people unlike oneself, who can help in ways which friends and family might not be able to do. Usually researchers assume that, for migrants, these bridging contacts will be members of the receiving society, rather than co-nationals. However, Ryan (2016: 952) convincingly challenges the assumed 'dichotomy between strong, intra-ethnic, bonding ties versus weak, inter-ethnic, bridging ties'. Ukrainians in Kalisz, for example, could make use of their acquaintance with the Ukrainian Greek Catholic priest, or Ukrainian line managers. Nonetheless, it did seem that Ukrainians often utilised their informal ties with Poles for instrumental purposes. Societies in countries formerly under communist rule are typically characterised by quite high reliance on informal relations and practices. Ukrainian migrants left Ukraine partly to escape extensive corruption, and they were also often wary of undocumented work. However, they valued other forms of informal exchange. Kvitka, for example, mentioned, 'We are good friends (*khoroshie znakomye*) with lots of Poles. Who can help me in any situation, that's a big plus.' As mentioned in Chapter 8, many interviewees preferred to trust in friends rather than agencies to find work in Poland. The same applied when they were already in Poland and looking for extra jobs. Kira, for instance, said:

> I work with Poles, we socialise, and they have their own friends. They invited us, for example, someone's father-in-law lives on his own in a two-storey house and it needed cleaning but the children didn't have time so they asked us to come and clean it. We wanted [to find some casual work] through an agency here, there is a little agency, but we read the reviews and they weren't good. We were afraid. At work they know us – Poles are good people. They're constantly helping us, and if something needs doing, they call. They say [to their friends] 'We have Ukrainians', they contact us to go and clear up someone's country cottage, mow the lawn, whatever. 'We know people who can do it at the weekend.' So they sometimes get us work through their friends. Or cleaning up some flat, the same way, through people they know.

Poles were also consulted about finding regular jobs. Lyudmila, for example, said:

> We already know lots of Poles. Through the internet, through Facebook, that's how we hunt of course. We ask people we know. If we find a possible job, we ask their advice, and if they advise not then we decide not to go there. That's how it works.

Poles could offer informal solutions to Ukrainians' problems. Elena, for instance, explained how her Polish line managers unsuccessfully attempted to help her when she was pregnant and threatened by the Ukrainian agency representative with deportation. The Poles tried to get Elena accepted as a worker for the Polish agency, on the exceptional basis that she was a good worker. Her conclusion was that 'Poles really help, more than Ukrainians'. Liliya told a story of how she had viewed the flat which she eventually rented, but at first decided it was too expensive. However, after she left and had said goodbye to the estate agent, the Polish landlady ran and caught up with her and offered to rent the flat to her for a lower rate, bypassing the agency. Halyna similarly praised Polish helpfulness:

> Sometimes our co-workers come to our flat and do repairs together with us … It was hard when we first arrived. But now there's no problem … I can always go and ask a workmate for help, no problem. They give us any advice we need.

Helping Ukrainians migrate further west constituted a special kind of bridge. Mihaylo referred to the informality of such arrangements. Before Germany opened its labour market to Ukrainians, Ukrainians who wanted to work in Germany had to 'come to Poland and find some good or not so good ways through somebody to get to Germany'. On the other hand, sometimes Poles suggested informal solutions which Ukrainians found unwelcome. One interviewee said she was being taught Polish by the Polish wife of her husband's friend. Since this woman was not a trained teacher she was not learning much. Another interviewee had been befriended by a Polish border guard, who invited her to jump the queue at passport control. She found this extremely embarrassing.

Contacts with strangers

Chapter 3 argued that some foreigners preferred smaller cities because they were perceived to be friendlier than big ones. Although smaller towns and cities are stereotypically considered to be conservative and unwelcoming, this is not necessarily the case. As mentioned in Chapter 1, for example, in 2015 residents of smaller cities and towns seemed to be more favourably disposed to Ukrainians than people living in the biggest cities (Boguszewski 2015: 5). Jakóbczyk-Gryszkiewicz, on the basis of survey evidence from 250 Poles in Pabianice, a slightly smaller city than Piła, found that 'generally, their attitude to foreigners has been positive' (Jakóbczyk-Gryszkiewicz 2020: 71). Seventy foreign respondents, mostly Ukrainians and Indians, agreed with this assessment (Jakóbczyk-Gryszkiewicz 2020: 79). Interviewees living in KPP made comparisons between those cities and bigger ones on the basis of personal experiences, but also from stories told by other Ukrainian migrants.

With regard to encounters on the street, Nina for instance said:

> On the whole I meet nice, normal people … It's the people I like in Kalisz. Because when I worked near Zakopane, and a bit in Warsaw, there were some who weren't so pleasant. But here they are kind … When I first came to Poland I didn't speak Polish as well as I do now. [They said] 'I don't understand'. There are others who try to

understand, and ask, 'Can you tell me again what you wanted to know?' But some say, 'I don't understand' and have done with it. Off they go. When I needed to ask about something. That happened in Warsaw, for example. 'I don't understand,' and she turns away and walks off. But here people are kinder. They try to find out what you want, they repeat your question if necessary.

Halyna said, 'Lots of my friends who went to work in cities like Wrocław or Poznań returned [to Kalisz]. Because of the attitude ... towards Ukrainians. They were cheated there.' Irina gave as a reason for not moving away from Piła the fact that, elsewhere, 'some people have bad attitudes towards Ukrainians'. Ostap referred to Piła as a 'peaceful, clean town with good attitudes towards newcomers, towards foreigners. I never had any problems. I've heard they happen in other cities'. Anzhela attributed this happy state of affairs to the low numbers of Ukrainians. This accords with Arango's migration transition theory discussed in Chapter 1. She said:

> Piła is the sort of city where there still aren't that many Ukrainians. It isn't yet like cities where there are lots of factories and lots of people come to work. They seem to be saturated with immigrants, and that's why people feel angry at Ukrainians. It's like that. I've often heard that people don't like them.

However, Lyudmila suggested the opposite explanation, more in keeping with the contact hypothesis: 'They behave towards us in a good way (*normal'no*). I think [it's because] in Płock they've already got used to Ukrainians, there are so many of them.'

Like Nina and Lyudmila, interviewees often used the word 'normal', in the normative meaning discussed in Chapter 7, to characterise Polish people and their attitudes. With reference to Polish attitudes towards Ukrainians, Lyudmila for instance used the term again when she said, 'All my acquaintances are properly-behaved people, with nice manners, welcoming and friendly. If you are friendly to them, they are friendly back.' Svitlana said, 'People are friendly ... Most people treat us properly and with respect.' Kvitka said, 'Most people are nice. Of course there are others, but most Poles are nice. There's no such thing as "You're Ukrainian and you're a so-and-so." No. They're nice. Even when I didn't know the language, they treated me properly.' Yurii, after an initial bad impression of Poles gained when working at a factory in Wrocław, said when he came to Kalisz and began talking to local Poles he realised that they had a good/unbiased (*normal'noe*) attitude towards Ukrainians. 'It's just that people are people. Some are nicer and more patient than others.'

As the above examples suggest, the Ukrainian interviewees liked KPP because local Poles lived up to the standard they expected. Hence their comfort in KPP was not just thanks to the quality of life and livelihoods, but also to standards of behaviour. Poles were found to be welcoming and kind towards strangers. Even more importantly – judging from the Ukrainians' remarks – they appreciated that they were being treated as equals. As Allport (1954) suggests, this is a prerequisite for positive contact. For instance, Lavra asked rhetorically, 'Why am I in Płock? Because I haven't seen any difference here in how I'm treated, between me as a Ukrainian and the Poles.' She had previously done seasonal work elsewhere in Poland and had some bad experiences. Inna said, 'The Poles we met here received us very warmly, as one of their own. There was no sense that we were foreigners and that we were being treated badly. They just treated us as if we were at home, and that was an important reason to stay in KPP.' Halyna agreed. 'I've never been badly treated. Usually when we talk about the fact that there are lots of Ukrainians and Belarusians [in Poland] they say that there are all sorts in Poland as much as in Ukraine. It's not connected to nationality.' Likewise, Andrei asserted, 'If you go into a shop, everything is fine (*normal'no*), you don't get any "Oh, so you're from Ukraine"' [said in an accusing tone of voice]. Varvara also said, 'They don't distinguish us from Poles. We're just the same as Poles here.'

The quotations in the previous paragraph are from Ukrainians with different socio-demographic features, working in different occupations. What united them was that they had all lived in KPP for several years, and spoke Polish confidently. Hence they had been able to engage with local Poles in a meaningful way. There would seem to be a virtuous circle where they were becoming attached to KPP and simultaneously facilitating their own integration by initiating contacts and conversations. Nonetheless, even interviewees who had arrived more recently could make the same judgements. Nataliya said:

> I was very surprised when we first came [to KPP]. The sales assistants are friendly, and they do try to understand. They give us advice and they explain things to us. Really a lot. I think that, in general, people in Płock are very friendly towards strangers, I feel that's the case.

Chapter 6 mentioned that Lech, a manual worker aged 50, was able to chat to Ukrainians in Russian. Many Ukrainian interviewees mentioned their surprise but also gratitude that Polish strangers used Russian to help them out. I personally was also surprised to learn this, given my memories of Poland in the 1980s and attitudes towards being forced to learn Russian at school. It transpired that Russian in KPP was a *lingua franca*. Numerous interviewees, in all three cities, commented on the fact. For instance Lyudmila said, 'Old people studied Russian and it happens that they come up to you and want to chat, they're being friendly.' Varvara said, 'In Soviet days they all learned Russian. If they hear you're Ukrainian, they immediately produce a few words of Russian. Lots of Poles know Russian.' Lizaveta reported that when she first came to KPP, and was working in a factory, other Ukrainians used to give her the advice: 'If you get lost, look for an older person and ask them. They used to study Russian … Start asking your question in Russian and they will tell you everything.' Ivan, who was a circular migrant without much Polish, said that when he was in the bank he tried to find an older person to help him, or a younger clerk would call an older one. On the other hand, Svitlana, herself a Russian speaker, thought it better to use Ukrainian. She said that at the bank they would start off in Polish and usually have no problems, though sometimes they would use sign language and Ukrainian. They used Ukrainian in preference to Russian because Ukrainian was more similar to Polish. However, 'if I go to the bank or the travel agency [to buy tickets back home to Mariupol] I choose people who are a bit older, who learned Russian in their time'.

Overall, however, the interviewees seemed to believe that it was up to them to learn Polish. Russian or Ukrainian might be used, but only in emergencies, or if a Polish person initiated the conversation in Russian, not as a matter of course. Oleksii for instance said, 'When you come to a different country, like to Poland, it's up to you to learn the language.' Valentin said, 'Sometimes people behave dismissively … but it's normal. If you can't speak Polish, why should a Pole want to talk to you?'

Nataliya was quoted above expressing her surprise when she first arrived in KPP that sales assistants were so friendly and willing to help. Her surprise might have derived from the fact that her husband, in his previous job elsewhere in Poland, had gathered the impression that they should expect hostility – telling Nataliya not to speak Russian on the street. The fact that so many interviewees quoted above chose to stress the aspect of equality in their interactions hints that they too had been prepared to meet discrimination, which of course to some extent they had done in cases where they were exploited at work. Insofar as they had bad experiences on the street – mentioned by just a few interviewees – these seem to have been the 'dismissiveness' mentioned by Valentin. They explained that they had occurred during their tongue-tied early days in Poland. Usually, if they complained, they also added that the majority of encounters were friendly. Lyudmila adopted the approach, saying 'it takes all sorts'. She continued, 'Of course there are people who avoid us. I understand that perhaps they have their own problems, or there's something they don't like, but they don't say anything, there's no verbal abuse. Nothing like that.' Dmytro suggested that things would improve once they saw the person behind the Ukrainian: 'There were moments [of hostility] but when they got to know me better they changed their minds.'

Yurii attributed unhelpfulness to impatience. He said, 'Some are nicer and more patient than others. Sometimes you use sign language and the Pole tries to put themselves into your position and work out for themselves what you mean.' Lizaveta thought that young people were less friendly. She said:

> I try to ask grannies and grandads and they understand me. Young people don't particularly want to understand. They say 'I don't know' and pass on. But older people will stop, tell you what you need to know and understand what you want. They'll tell you to go right, left, 200 metres, 100 metres or whatever.

Irina used the stronger term 'discrimination'.

> Sometimes you do see discrimination. In the shop, or at the hospital. If a person can't speak Polish they answer 'I don't understand'. Well, alright. Perhaps I do make a few language mistakes, but we can't be expected to speak as well as Poles do. Some people simply don't want to understand.

Vera, a recently-arrived interviewee, attributed such attitudes to nationalism.

> Of course there are some who are nationalists, but what can you do? They sort of splutter at us ... When you go up and talk to them, in broken Polish of course, they start pretending they don't understand what you're saying. And they begin speaking aggressively, not that they shout, but you can feel the aggression ... I don't pay any attention but my husband flares up ... It's happened in the shop, at the chemists.

Halyna, despite her overall good impressions, had been frustrated by the unhelpfulness of doctors. She said: 'There are problems here with doctors. As soon as they find out you're Ukrainian they freak out. Because they're afraid to talk to us. They're afraid we won't understand, that we won't be able to explain ourselves. That's why they have that first reaction.'

The only interviewees who suggested that their city (Kalisz) was less friendly than bigger cities were Lev and Taras, interviewed together. Both had previously worked in or near Warsaw and wanted to return. Here there seemed to be a vicious circle in operation, since they were not going out of their way to make Ukrainian or Polish friends in Kalisz.

> Taras: Poles in Kalisz are less friendly to Ukrainians, from what I saw … In Warsaw they seem to have a different attitude to us, there are more of us Ukrainians …
>
> Lev: [In Kalisz] they are a tiny bit prejudiced.
>
> Anne: Do people say anything?
>
> Lev: You can tell by their behaviour, that they seem displeased, when we start talking Ukrainian or Russian, they begin behaving like that.
>
> Taras: They think since we came to Poland we should speak Polish.
>
> Anne: Do they tell you that?
>
> Taras: No, no, no.
>
> Lev: You just have the feeling.

In fact, the few Ukrainians who had been the victims of racist treatment in KPP were, unlike Lev and Taras, mostly well-embedded and attached in the cities. They referred to their experiences as exceptions which proved the rule, but they left a bitter taste. Nina said:

> There are some people who don't like foreigners. I must admit that there are some. Once I was walking to church on Sunday and talking quietly to my daughter. And there was a man sitting there, not very well-dressed, and he heard me talking Ukrainian, and he said, hm, he swore, 'Fxxx off to Ukraine.' But you can't judge everyone by people like him. I have lots of Polish friends including close friends. So you can't say that. That's what I like in Kalisz, the people.

Fadei referred to his accuser as 'stupid' for not realising that it was normal to migrate to another country for work:

> I remember that soon after I came to Kalisz I was in a shop and I said something in Ukrainian, because I didn't know the language yet. And someone said – may I use bad language? – he said, let me say it in Polish, 'Fxxx off home.' I didn't say anything, I just went on my way, because even if I'd hit him it wouldn't have done any good. I just passed by and said nothing. Because I know that you can meet, well, stupid people. Because only stupid people would blame another person for coming here to seek a better life. He wouldn't be in Poland if he'd had a good life in Ukraine ... It was the only time, but still it was imprinted on my memory. And then I even began to hate Poles a bit, because I thought they were all like that. Then I met other people and got very fond of them. We call each other 'brother' ... I will probably remember that incident for a long time. Because it wounded me to the heart. I should try to forget it and move on.

Margarita, a hairdresser in Piła, commented:

> There are many very good people. But during my five years of working here there have been three people, and one of them even said, 'I don't want a Ukrainian even to touch my hair.' They were all grannies, well over 80. Real old women. I don't understand why. Young people no. They are chatty and helpful. People my age or yours [middle-aged] are all friendly. But those grannies and grandads. It's incomprehensible why ... It was very upsetting. I cried every time.'

A couple of other interviewees mentioned in passing that they had been told to go back to Ukraine (in one case with the usual swear word), but they did not associate such abuse with attitudes specifically in KPP. In fact one had had her worst experience (being shouted at and told she ought to speak Polish) on a train. Finally, Tamara mentioned her daughter's hurtful experience:

> Personally I've never had any problems. But Katya did. The teenage world is different, more cruel ... She was afraid to speak because they'd make fun of her. She only spoke to the teacher. We went to extra Polish classes every day. Then she fell in love for the first time, with a Pole, and he said, 'Katya, you're a very nice girl, but you're Ukrainian, and I don't want to be your friend.' So we booked a few sessions with a psychologist and overcame that stage.

With the possible exception of Margarita's encounters at the hairdressing salon – located in Piła, where many Polish people from what became Soviet Ukraine had been re-settled after the Second World War – only one interviewee mentioned being on the receiving end of hostility connected to historical enmities. Melaniya was very unusual in the sample in that she had a white-collar job, so she presumably had a more educated circle of acquaintance. She said:

> I've noticed a trend that older people say more discriminatory things. Young people aren't bothered. Ukraine, Belarus, it's all the same. Estonia. They don't particularly understand that they are different countries. They're just foreigners. But older people are under the influence of the Soviet past. Those wars, or not wars, conflicts between Ukrainians and Poles, they immediately start talking about the [1943] massacres in Volhynia, you know. That's why there's a negative attitude. To Banderovtsy. We're Bandera's descendants. But young people simply don't know about that history.

In contrast, several interviewees mentioned that Poles were interested in the current situation in Ukraine. In December 2021 Alla commented:

> All the stuff that's going on in Ukraine, you want to talk about it to someone … I've never heard a Polish person take the side of You-Know-Who, against the Ukrainians. Seemingly, Polish people have negative views about that person. Perhaps that's one reason why I feel comfortable here. I feel surrounded by people who think like me. Of course, in general I try not to talk about politics. But on the other hand many clients have been coming to me for quite a long time … so we can talk as friends.

Unusually, Melaniya mentioned that she knew Poles with relatives in Ukraine:

> There are lots of people with relations in Ukraine, I often get talking with people and they say right away that they have some relative living in Ukraine, in Kharkiv, in Kyiv, in Lviv. And people who have been to Ukraine and spent time with their relatives are better at understanding the situation in Ukraine. If someone got married to a Ukrainian … It's a question of being better-informed.

Several interviewees also mentioned knowing Poles who had visited different destinations in Ukraine as tourists. My informants were pleased that the Poles had been impressed by Ukraine, though Irina commented tartly, 'There's a difference between living in a place and coming to have a look. And between making a living in Ukraine and travelling there as someone earning a Polish salary.' Varvara, a cook, provided the most detailed account:

> Lots of people have told me they'd been. Mostly to west Ukraine, to Lviv. They say that they liked it – it's beautiful, particularly the mountains … You get talking to somebody and if they've been to Ukraine they say at once, 'I've been to Ukraine, I've been to this place and that.' My son's teacher said she had been to Rivne and described it in a really interesting way. They like to travel. And the feedback is always positive.

Reflections on Polish attitudes

When reflecting on their experiences with Poles, the Ukrainian interviewees very occasionally expressed the idea that Poles and Ukrainians might behave differently from one another. One belief was that Poles could afford to be nicer. Yuliya said:

> People's mentality is different. I like Poles because they are kind and helpful. Even when they don't know someone well, if you're a neighbour or just an acquaintance. At least I have always met helpful and kind people. Perhaps it links to the fact that people feel happier here. Financially as well … There's none of that anger and envy.

Raisa, who had spent less time than Yuliya in Poland, was more critical and suspicious. She said, 'People in Poland are less open [than Ukrainians]. When they seem to show friendliness I think it's more because they were brought up that way. A well brought-up person will smile just out of politeness.' However, much the most common conclusion, already evident in many of the remarks quoted earlier in this chapter, was that human nature was the same everywhere. Hence one should not make generalisations on the basis of nationality. My interlocutors usually based their comments on their own experience, in other words, their migration wisdom. The following are just two examples.

> It seems to me that any problems [between Poles and Ukrainains] aren't connected with whether Poles in general behave well or badly towards Ukrainians. They depend on who you meet. Because there's a mix of people, whether they are Polish or Ukrainian. It's an individual matter. You can't say that Poles are bad or good. There are some irresponsible employers who don't treat their workers well, but it's the same in Ukraine. You can't generalise. (Alla)

> It depends on the individual person, because he can [be tolerant if he wants]. For example, I don't have anything against anyone, well, only Russians (laughs), but apart from them. I don't pay any attention to people's skin colour or race … There are lots of good people in Poland, but, as they say, you can meet hooligans anywhere. Even where you live, in the United Kingdom. The world is full of them. (Fadei)

Reflections on Polish migration

Like the Poles I interviewed in KPP, the Ukrainians drew parallels between Polish and Ukrainian migration, often quite spontaneously.[3] This too was part of their migration wisdom. Sometimes they made normative comments expressing their approval of migration. For instance, Emma said, 'They [Poles] go to Germany, or to other cities … If he thinks he needs to go because the money he gets here isn't enough, and he goes abroad, I think he's doing the right thing. Because *he's* just the same as we are.' In most cases, however, the approval was implied rather than overt.

Some interviewees based their parallels on what they had heard about Poland, rather than their personal experience. For example, Sergei attributed the troubling shortage of senior doctors in Piła to emigration, apparently basing his comments on general knowledge. 'They're short of specialists. They're all in the UK, the Netherlands and Germany because the pay is higher. We came here because it's better than in Ukraine and we're happy with everything. But there are Polish doctors who are less satisfied.' Nina, pouring ridicule on Polish xenophobes, exclaimed:

> Ukrainians come to Poland and some Poles get indignant and say 'Poland for the Poles'. What can you do? We're all free people. We can live and work where we want. Poles go abroad themselves, to Germany and other countries, and no Poles want Germany only to be for Germans, or England only for English people.

Others made connections between Ukrainian and Polish migration based on their interactions with Poles elsewhere in Poland. Yuliya mentioned that they had been on holiday in the Mazurian lakes – an area of high emigration – and the hotelier had commented that 'it's so good that you decided to live in Poland, because lots of young [Polish] families go abroad'. Olha had previously cleaned for a rich Polish woman in a big city suburb.

> She said, 'I worked abroad to provide for my family, I left my children too [like Olha] and went abroad and worked and worked. And now I've made my fortune. But the children didn't appreciate it … They lived so long without me. Now I have cancer and it's hard. My daughters do help, but all the same … They don't really understand that everything was for their sake.'

Olha concluded, 'And now when I come here to Poland, and my children are growing up, from one point of view I think perhaps I shouldn't do that, but on the other I know that I couldn't provide for them properly if I didn't work abroad.' Kira reported:

> We were in Warsaw and this Polish woman said to us, 'I know what it's like to be a labour migrant (*zarobitchanin*),' and she said, 'I really feel for you, leaving your family. Because I tried going to Germany too.' It was hard for her, the work, not knowing the language, and she said, 'You're in the same position here.' It's good that people sympathise and understand. Because they were in the same situation themselves, or they simply understand.

Despite these examples of conversations elsewhere in Poland, more often the interviewees referred to personal acquaintance from KPP who had told them their own migration stories. Sometimes they mentioned the number of Poles they knew who worked abroad, as well as their various destinations. In Płock, for instance, Lyudmila said:

> At our factory I know about 10 people who worked abroad, men. They went to Holland, Belgium, Germany … There are all types, young, old, different ages … They just work in KPP in between, it's convenient like that, they work in the factory so they're not sitting at home, work a bit and then go off. There's a kind of rotation of workers. We come here and they go there. Of course a Polish wage is very small compared to wages in Germany or England, but our

> Ukrainian wages are even lower. Of course I understand that here they have to pay taxes, and for their housing, and so on. So it's expensive for them to keep a family.

Viktor, in the same factory, mentioned that some local people working in his section had recently left. 'They go abroad themselves, to Germany or England. They're tempted by the West. I understand them ... They get paid twice as much.'

Some Ukrainians only found out about Polish migration when they first started working in a Polish factory. For instance, one young factory worker in Kalisz said:

> I have a Polish friend from work who was telling me how she was planning to go to Germany. So I asked her, 'Why's that? We Ukrainians come to work in Poland, and you want to go to Germany.' So she said, 'You come to Poland because the wages are higher than in Ukraine, and in Germany the wages are higher than in Poland.' I didn't realise that – that was how I found out. She used to travel to Germany and come back home. She'd been working there six years.

Nina was well-informed about KPP migration patterns through clients who came to her salon for massages. Presumably they had the money to spend on this luxury. In one case she also mentioned injuries as the result of heavy work abroad. Nina thought that there was a steady flow of target-earning migration to Germany and the UK. The latter destination was favoured by Roma who lived in the vicinity of her salon.

Poles complained to Ukrainians that they found life tough in KPP, and this was why they migrated. Valerii said:

> It's not so good here, Poles themselves tell me that. It's not so good. Why do they all go off to Germany, Bulgaria, Holland, Belgium? They all go there to work. They're all sitting out there. Only the ones who are a bit older return, they've eaten, they've slept, they aren't rushing after things.

Poles also complained to Ukrainians about their lives abroad. Anzhela observed:

> I've not heard them say anything good [about their lives abroad]. They complain that they had to work a huge amount. I hear comments like, 'You came to Poland, and you work. When we

went abroad, we worked twelve hours a day. We lived in really bad conditions.' And they sort of say, 'Now it's your turn.' That's what I sometimes hear. Because, when you go away, you leave your family and try to work flat out. Well, how can they say good things? That they worked non-stop? That's usually how it is. I've yet to hear that someone went abroad and had a good time. They go and work hard. So that they can come back to Poland and be with their families.

Another interviewee said:

I haven't been to Germany but I've heard a lot for example from Poles who migrate to Germany, it's not brilliant, not everyone is welcoming ... 'You're a Pole, we'll work with you but we don't want to make friends' ... And I've heard – which is really shocking – that some Poles live in the UK twenty years and don't speak English. That's why I say ... you have to study, you simply must learn the language. Integration is very important, everywhere. Take France. Poles say that a white Pole can be out and about and simply be afraid to go to some areas because the Arabs could attack you and that's considered normal.

Here, it is not the parallel, but the contrast which is important: Poles' shocking behaviour in not learning English, something upon which several other interviewees also commented. It was very different from the conviction, near universal among my Ukrainian informants, that as a migrant you had to learn the local language. It was also noteworthy that the speaker had picked up on Polish instances of Islamophobia, although it is not clear whether his sources were local Poles or social media.

Sometimes interviewees simply conveyed a string of facts about specific aspects of Polish migration. Yurii, who was able to test his Kalisz acquaintances' accounts against those of his own brother, a migrant in the UK, reported on a Pole he met in Kalisz.

I found out that he'd worked in a furniture factory in England so I asked if he knew English, and he didn't. So I asked how he managed to work there without knowing English and he said, 'When I was there there were a lot of Poles.' Although, my brother works [six months at a time] in England and he says there are lots of Poles who have learned English and just live there ... Poles go to Germany mostly because it's close and they work as circular migrants (*vakhtovym metodom*). They work let's say two weeks in Germany and then they are at home in Poland ... Mostly they go abroad with the help of their friends, or some relative, their brother or brother-in-law, he'd been to the same place, they discussed it together.

Ruslana, who worked at the same factory as Yurii – with many male colleagues – had also met numerous return migrants. She said:

They tell about how they went to Germany or Holland and they didn't know the language and how hard it was and how they had to do manual work. It was hard. They didn't see their families for a year at a time. They came to Poland for a month and had to return to work. But they said that they had to go abroad to have a better life.

At the same factory, Halyna claimed that '95 per cent of Poles among people I know' had at one time worked abroad. She thought they had usually intended to go and return, but some had come back unexpectedly because of the pandemic.

Olesya, at a different factory in Kalisz, was well-informed specifically about women workers. She said that many women had husbands working abroad but that in the previous (Covid) year a large number had gone to join their husbands and not returned. She thought that they often used agencies. This might be because they were doing care work in Germany, like my interviewees Sylwia and Krystyna. Fadei, at the same factory, mentioned an older man who had worked abroad who had told them about what he had managed to achieve. He reported that the man 'said it was necessary to earn some money, so it was necessary to migrate'. In other words, at the factory, migration was a near-compulsory livelihood strategy. Here, the figure of the senior migrant was invoked to give authority to the sentiment that migration was sometimes unavoidable, whether one was Polish or Ukrainian. Raisa, working at a factory in Piła, had a slightly different impression: her workmates did work abroad, but not on the same scale as Ukrainians. They only went when they wanted to make some kind of larger purchase.

The factory workers had a particularly high degree of exposure to circular and return migrants. The women who worked in salons, with a presumably somewhat prosperous clientele, probably saw a different cross-section of local Polish society. Hence Alla, for example, talked instead about the frequency with which local stayers maintained ties to Polish migrants still abroad.

Lots of women who come to my salon tell me about how their children are living abroad, they've got their education and they are working there, and so on, they have their families. That migration process happens everywhere. Lots of clients talk about different ways they're connected with places abroad. One person has children, someone else has their sisters and brothers, someone is going there on holiday. Lots of Poles go abroad. I hear about that.

Margarita, who was a hairdresser, had clients who worked abroad, in Germany, the UK and the Netherlands, but came back to KPP for holidays to visit their parents. Her impression was that they had a good life abroad, but they got homesick – a not surprising topic of conversation at the hairdressers if they were back to visit their families. Several other interviewees commented on how the Poles who returned were pleased with their earnings and enjoyed a good standard of living abroad. One interviewee, Irina, also reported that Poles had said German bosses treated employees better than their Polish equivalents. Such positivity often seemed to be mentioned in the cases of Polish acquaintances with higher-status jobs in Poland. Ostap, who had a particularly good factory job with a permanent contract and was emotionally attached to KPP, reported his colleagues' experiences positively, like his own. 'Some [male colleagues] worked abroad for five, some for ten years but then they came back. [They say] it was interesting being abroad – their work, their new friends.' It was noteworthy that Ostap worked at the same factory as Anzhela, quoted above, who had not heard 'anything good' about migration from her own less privileged female co-workers.

In other cases, the Ukrainian pointed out specific aspects of Polish migration behaviour which were similar to those of Ukrainians. When I commented to Olha for instance that her story of avoiding medical treatment in Poland reminded me of Poles' behaviour in the UK she immediately agreed, and said she had a Polish work colleague who told her about how she had come back from working abroad to go to her doctor in KPP. Halyna's discovery of Polish suspicion towards other Poles was mentioned in Chapter 10. They also pointed out parallel motivations. Andrei for example said, 'They think it's bad here so they go to England. They act just like us.'

Did Poles' own experiences of migration translate into empathy towards Ukrainians? Yurii denied that emotions were relevant. The important thing was to accept that migration was normal. 'Respect or sympathy aren't really the issue here. We are all people, grown-up, properly behaved adults. You came to [a foreign country] to work, so go to work.' However, several other Ukrainians asserted that Polish migration experience could translate into good attitudes towards Ukrainian migrants. Irina, who had quite a wide circle of Polish acquaintance from different walks of life, said:

> I think that people who have relatives and friends working in Germany or England, they treat us fine. Because [they believe like I do that] people have the right to choose wherever they want to live, in whatever country. And where to work. That's my opinion. But people who don't go abroad think we have invaded their country and taken away their jobs, etc., they have negative attitudes towards us ... [Return migrants] are more communicative, I don't know, they are friendlier towards Ukrainians, nicer, more understanding, perhaps you can put it like that. They've experienced it for themselves.

Some interviewees mentioned specific examples of empathy on the part of Poles. Alla, for instance, reported that she had a kindhearted client who 'is always very considerate, and once when I'd been ill she said, "You should have phoned me, please do contact me any time, because I know what it's like to be foreigner in a strange country. I used to work in a foreign country once as well."' Margarita had just one friend who was a return migrant. She mentioned that 'he has a very good attitude to Ukrainians. Because he knows what it's like to live in a foreign country'. Naturally enough, Poles were able to empathise with the situation of Ukrainians who were sad because they were missing close family members. Tamara mentioned:

> One Polish woman I know has children who went to England and stayed. They went to work and stayed. She's here and her children are there. So this is the conversation. [I said] 'How are you?' [She said] 'But how are you? Your own mother stayed in Ukraine. Do you feel miserable?' I say, 'Yes, I am miserable.' She says, 'I can't bear it. I miss my grandchildren so badly' ... [I say] 'Every day I think about my mother, I talk to her every day, do you do the same? Don't be sad, it's OK. They have their own life there.' So we have a good relationship.

Oleksii said of his co-workers who had returned from Ireland and America that 'they know how we feel'. However, he also pointed out the differences he perceived, which meant that they were not really in the same position. 'I think that mostly they go there to earn something and then return to Poland. But lots of Ukrainians come to Poland to settle.' In Tamara's account of multiple such conversations, her Polish interlocutors seem to have been tactless, making false assumptions based on their own experiences of being temporary migrants.

> They know I'm from Ukraine, they hear my accent, and they say things like 'I was in Germany, I worked there for two years' or 'I went to pick blueberries in Holland' or 'I did this and that'. They say, 'Tamara, there's no place like home.' I say [sounding doubtful] 'Yes.' They say, 'Is it tough?' I say, 'Well, yes.' [They say] 'When we came back I bought a house' or 'I bought a flat'. They show understanding … They say, 'I lived in one room with someone else, how about you?' 'We're here as a family.' 'But I lived apart from my family, I really wanted to go home to Poland' … A woman was telling me about how she went to pick blueberries. 'Tamara, I understand how hard it is for you. You don't understand the language.' 'But I do understand!' 'Home is home. There's no place like home.'

Here, the Poles were showing misplaced empathy in their desire to tell their own stories and not enquire too closely into Tamara's. Tamara was assumed to be a labour migrant earning money to save to build a house in Ukraine, where she would be safely 'at home', whereas she was a forced migrant from a warzone. Moreover, she was assumed not to speak Polish, even though she was holding the conversation in that language.

Melaniya, who worked in an office where she said that 'half' her co-workers had been migrants in the UK, the Netherlands or Germany, pointed out that different people had different capacities for empathy.

> You'd suppose that Poles who'd worked in different countries, like England or Germany, or Norway, would understand other migrants better. But actually, it depends on the person. There are people whose experiences remain just their own experiences and they don't see parallels with migrants who are here in Poland … The fact that people migrate to Poland from different countries is seen in an abstract way, it's compartmentalised, so they still think they are superior to the immigrants … On the other hand, there are people who say, 'We understand you, we were in the same situation ourselves.'

Nikolai asserted that Poles were quick to forget that they had been socially inferior when they were abroad.

> Ihor: They go as posted workers and have a tough time. In Germany, Norway, the Netherlands. They are just like us. The only thing which matters is that they can get work.
>
> Anne: Is that what they tell you at the factory?
>
> Nikolai: Yes, we work with them. But not every Pole will admit that, abroad, he's exactly the same as we are here.

Based on such conversations and observations, some Ukrainian interviewees made observations about apparent laws of migration. They saw the Ukrainian and Polish parallels, and often expressed their view that this demonstrated natural behaviour. Anna said pithily: 'The whole world emigrates – Poles included.' Larysa said, 'Poles also want to experiment with working abroad. That's why you get exchange in the world. Except that no one comes to work in Ukraine.' Lyudmila claimed that 'everyone is searching for a better life. If everything was fine they wouldn't go abroad to earn money. I can understand why Poles go abroad to work.' Klara said, 'It's normal. You can earn more there [in western Europe]. Poles don't like it here in Poland so they go there. It's better there. And we don't like it in Ukraine so we come here.' Raisa said, 'Labour migration is everywhere. People come to Poland, people go further afield. Everyone is searching for something better. And you have to go abroad to find it.' Solomiya, having told me about a young Polish man at her factory who had earned a lot of money in the Netherlands, returned to KPP, then gone off again, commented fatalistically:

> They're searching for a better life somewhere. Just the same as us. There is a kind of circulation of migrants. Because everyone is searching for something better. That's normal. Once upon a time no doubt people just stayed in their own country and thought it was OK. And then people began to migrate, more and more and that's how it went. I can understand them because they want something better: it's normal. Because we came here because we want something we don't have at home. And they're the same. You can't change that.

Although the older interviewees were usually very serious when they told me about these parallels and laws of migration, Artur, who was only 19 and had recently arrived in KPP, found the situation amusing.

> Yes, I've heard about that. Ukrainians come to Poland and Poles go to Germany or further afield. I don't know, I suppose you have to see it from their point of view. Perhaps they don't like wages here, the same as we don't like them in Ukraine. The same situation. They don't like their pay, and we don't like ours. But we like their wages! That's the way it is: it's quite funny really.

Interviewees also drew historical parallels: either that history was repeating itself and/or that now the shoe was on the other foot. For example, Valerii mentioned, 'Today at work I was talking with a Pole who told me how "nowadays Poland has become a bit better but in the 90s we had hard times too."' He also said, 'My parents said that Polish friends came to Ukraine to work, in the past. To build the roads. And now times have changed and we're the ones who come to work.' Artem had his own personal experience. Again, the conclusion was that migration was unavoidable.

> [Around the time of the collapse of communism] I was in the Soviet army ... 400 metres on the Czech side of the Polish border, and Poles came to us to trade watches and various Chinese trifles. We talked to lots of them and they told us their stories, some had been doctors. You Poles[4] have simply got through that stage, and we're still at it. All those doctors and teachers were migrating, because they had to make ends meet. Like us. My workmate here is a (Ukrainian) primary school teacher. There's nothing to be done about it.

Conclusions

The Ukrainians interviewed for this book tended to believe that Kalisz, Piła and Płock did indeed remain 'cities of emigration'. Most Ukrainian interviewees were factory workers and this brought them into contact with return and circular migrants, who told them about their experiences living abroad. From their accounts, several factories could be considered 'migration hotspots'. Polish migrants were visible in their everyday lives and their impressions were quite different from those of some middle-class Polish residents whose views were reported in Chapter 6 and who were not sure how much Polish migration still occurred. In addition, Ukrainian women who worked as hairdressers and beauticians interacted directly with Polish migrants when the latter were visiting KPP for holidays, and also had time and opportunity for conversations with their 'stayer' clients about the latter's' transnational family ties. These workplaces could constitute 'schools of migration', where Polish migration culture, for example warnings against leaving one's children behind, was transferred to Ukrainians. On the other hand, some Poles seemed to be rather insensitive and patronising, assuming for example that Ukrainians, like them, would be anxious to return to their country of origin, or would not try to learn the local language. Ukrainians drew parallels between their own experiences and those of the Poles and derived from them some general laws of migration. Overall, based on their conversations with Poles, the Ukrainians' assessment was the same as that of Poles reported in Chapter 6: migration was regarded as an acceptable livelihood strategy, a normal social phenomenon.

The chapter considered the emotional and instrumental functions of Ukrainian–Polish networks as well as Ukrainian experiences of interactions with Polish strangers and more distant acquaintances. Several had been sworn at on the street and told to go back to Ukraine; others reported strangers being unwilling to try to understand their broken Polish, although often these tales concerned other cities, and the interviewee was making the point that KPP were friendlier. Overall, the Ukrainian interviewees had the impression that migrants were not disliked in KPP. They were said to have 'normal' attitudes, meaning that they lived up to the standard Ukrainians hoped to encounter. Many interviewees highlighted instances of Polish friendliness on the street, particularly a willingness to talk to Ukrainians in Russian, as well as their sense that they were treated as equals with Poles in the workplace. Polish acquaintances provided practical advice and direct assistance with sorting out everyday problems. Despite the fact that Polish interviewees reported few close contacts with foreigners, interviews with Ukrainians revealed that some, particularly younger migrants, as well as middle-aged solo women, were forming friendships with Poles. These friendly relations helped anchor the interviewees in KPP even though in other respects one might suppose the younger and unattached migrants were more likely than migrants living with their families to move on from KPP to other cities or to third countries.

Notes

1. This was not always the case. For example, one Ukrainian couple with children were active in KPP civil society and had plenty of Polish friends.
2. The word also means a female colleague, but it was usually clear from the context whether colleague or friend was implied.
3. For fuller analysis, see the section 'Shared Ukrainian and Polish migranthood as viewed by (former) migrants' in White (2022a: 25–8).
4. Like several others, he seemed to forget I was not Polish.

12
Minority minorities

Introduction

This chapter discusses the experiences and opinions of non-Ukrainian foreigners living in Kalisz, Piła and Płock, and considers their contribution to Poland's migration transition. It considers how they are becoming visible to local Poles, and how, if at all, Polish attitudes towards their presence are evolving. Are they, like Ukrainians, treated as 'migrants like us', or othered and regarded in more 'ethnicised' terms? After considering the non-Ukrainians' motivations to come to KPP, together with their experiences of integration and place attachment in the cities, it speculates on whether they are likely to stay in KPP, contributing more permanently to the cities' identities as 'cities of immigration'. The chapter argues that in many respects the interviewees' experiences were shaped by their doubly minoritised position. They were minorities vis-à-vis the Poles, but also vis-à-vis Ukrainians. This is why I use the term 'minority minorities'.

Even before the refugees arrived en masse in 2022, Ukrainians were the most visible foreigners. Compared with individuals from other countries, they constituted the majority minority, not just numerically, but also in Polish perceptions. Ukrainians themselves had a sense of collective, 'wave' identity; some were beginning feel they belonged to a local Ukrainian community; they constituted an increasingly diverse cross-section of Ukrainian society; and many displayed a propensity to settle in Poland, in most cases probably in KPP. Their presence in KPP seemed significant to themselves, as well as to many Poles. Non-Ukrainian foreigners possessed few or none of these attributes. A few were visible to the public because they worked in cafés and restaurants or traded at the market, but even then local Poles sometimes seemed unsure of their nationalities. They could guess if a foreigner might be Ukrainian, but, as Chapter 12 reveals, their guesses were not necessarily correct. When I talked to Poles about non-Ukrainians, they were often surprised to hear of their presence in KPP, particularly labour migrants from Asia and Latin America. The non-Ukrainians' lack of 'critical mass' and community identity also did much to shape their own experiences. These minority minority interviewees were mostly making their way through life in KPP as individuals, without local co-ethnic support.

The 17 interviewees included 8 women and 9 men; 7 with university degrees and 10 without; 8 from the former Soviet Union and 9 from other countries. Excluding the students, they were aged 24–55. Countries of origin were Armenia, Australia (2), Bangladesh, Belarus (5), Italy, Kazakhstan, Nigeria, Russia, Taiwan, Turkey, Uruguay and Venezuela. Some might be considered 'immigrants light', to use Wallinder's (2019: 42) label for Swedish migrants in Germany. They had an integration head start thanks to some or all of various factors, such as well-paid, high-status work; Polish networks; linguistic confidence; and white skin. The Italian, Armenian and Belarusians also enjoyed privileged access to employment by virtue of their EU citizenship or western ex-USSR identity (thanks to the 'simplified procedure', humanitarian visas for Belarusians, and in some cases possession of Polish Cards). Nationals of other countries were less well-placed to integrate in KPP and to settle.

I also had conversations about the minority minorities with three key informants: Eskan Darwich, a Syrian city councillor in Kalisz; 'Martin', an English language lecturer from East Africa; and a Pole who ran an agency recruiting non-Ukrainian workers. Mr Darwich and Martin both represent a category of foreigners discussed by Andrejuk (2017b: 570): people who came to Poland to study but stayed to marry and set up businesses.[1] Mr Darwich spoke warmly about the respect he enjoyed in Kalisz and asked me to emphasise that even during the humanitarian crisis of 2015 he had never felt discriminated against because of his Syrian origins.

Although I collected statistics about foreign students at local higher education institutions, my project was not intended to map the minority minority population of each city. However, the contours were clear. It is hard to speak of any 'communities' of non-Ukrainians. By contrast, researchers based in Warsaw and other big cities regularly refer to certain non-Ukrainian nationals such as Vietnamese or Chinese people as living within 'communities'. For example, Andrejuk (2017b: 562) reports that 'research on new migrant communities in Poland indicates that economic integration of various ethnic groups is diversified and may depend on social and cultural capital within each community.' However, migrants of some nationalities do not constitute communities even in the bigger cities. Bielewska (2021: 620–21) in her analysis of highly-skilled migrants from a range of nationalities living in the Wrocław area found that they tended to identify with 'small groups' – a tiny handful of co-nationals living locally. In KPP, 'small groups' is a better concept than 'communities' to describe all the minority minorities. Occasionally, there were two or three people from the same country coincidentally living in the same city. In other cases, isolated individuals did not know a single local co-national. Individuals from a range of countries had married local Poles. This is reflected in the school population, although Nowosielski et al (2021) in their study of schools in Płock discovered that information about children of bi-national background was hard to obtain, presumably because many children are Polish citizens. As mentioned in Chapter 6, some Polish interviewees were able to identify one Cuban, one Egyptian, one French person, one Czech, and so forth, married to Poles among their acquaintance in KPP. Hardly anyone knew more than one non-Ukrainian foreigner.

Apart from marriage migrants, there are some ethnic entrepreneurs in KPP. However, ethnic catering outlets are few and far between, compared with bigger cities. Moreover, as I discovered, some restaurants labelled 'Italian' or 'Chinese' turned out to be run and staffed by Poles, or Ukrainians. I was told about foreign engineers working for local factories, who presumably tend to live in KPP temporarily. However, I failed to access them through my networks, Facebook or factory human resources departments. Almost certainly the largest population of non-Ukrainian foreigners in Kalisz and the surrounding area was composed of factory workers from a range of countries and continents, including Latin America and Asia. When I conducted my fieldwork, they did not seem to be employed in Piła (2022) and only to a limited extent in Płock (2019).

Despite the enormous increase in the foreign student population in Poland over recent years, international students were few in number. According to key informants at the universities, less than a dozen foreign undergraduates (including Ukrainians) were studying for degree programmes in each city. There were more temporary exchange students on Erasmus programmes. One category of migrant almost certainly absent in KPP is that of West Europeans motivated primarily by lifestyle considerations, distinguishing the smaller cities from places like Kraków, Warsaw and Wrocław (Andrejuk 2017b: 563). Native-speaker foreign-language teachers, insofar as there were any – I could find none in Piła – appreciated aspects of the local lifestyle but were not lifestyle migrants. They were in KPP because they happened to be married to local people. As one Australian interviewee said, 'We're all here for love.'

The chapter considers in turn the case of students, economic migrants, and family migrants. However, it is sometimes difficult to separate these categories, for instance in the case of a Kazakh student who had joined her mother, or an Italian entrepreneur working with his Polish wife. The chapter looks at why the interviewees were in Poland, and in KPP in particular; their integration and place attachment; and their plans either to settle or move on to a different city or country. The chapter then considers how these migrants felt they were regarded by Poles, before turning to relationships between migrants of different nationalities living in KPP. This is a topic nearly untouched in Polish scholarship. However, the quality of such relationships can help explain how much the minority minorities felt at home, and whether they were likely to settle. Finally, the chapter conclusions point to some parallels between different individuals within this very diverse group, highlighting the particular importance of networks and life-stage, as well as the more obvious factor of visa status, in determining whether representatives of the minority minorities were likely to stay.

Students

University administrators contacted international students on my behalf and asked them to message me if they wanted to participate. Three responded. The Belarusians, Aksana and Ivana, had come to KPP because of a particular degree programme offered in the city. Ivana was the pioneer, while Aksana, studying at the same school on the Polish border, followed in her footsteps on the recommendation of teachers. The Kazakh, Karina, had joined her mother, who had recently married a Pole. The Belarusians held Polish Cards, which their mothers obtained for them as children, and had studied Polish in Belarus. Karina, despite some Polish roots, did not possess a Polish Card and was in Poland on a student visa. None of the students self-identified as Polish, and they did not fall into the category of 'roots migrants', unlike some Polish Card-holding students researched by Gońda (2016, 2020). Their approach was more instrumental. For example, Aksana claimed, 'Everyone is going to Poland because it gives you more opportunities.'

Karina's story was in some respects similar to those of many Ukrainian interviewees. She already had a vocational diploma but she had not found work in Kazakhstan using her qualification. Hence, when her mother suggested coming to Poland, her reaction was 'Why not? I should give it a go'. On the other hand, there was no wave of migration from Kazakhstan to Poland and it never previously occurred to Karina that she would migrate. By contrast, Ivana and Aksana were consciously part of a wave of student migration to Poland. Ivana claimed that half her class were studying in Polish universities, while Aksana said that about a fifth had applied. Both students came from intensely mobile families, where other members were also migrants or cross-border traders. In fact Aksana's study abroad seemed to be part of a family livelihood strategy of reunification in Europe. Both Ivana and Aksana had been on foreign holidays, and Ivana also mentioned regular shopping trips to Warsaw and a school visit to Poland.

Długosz (2018) shows how Ukrainian students, despite good Polish language and other advantages, can be disappointed at not being able to form friendships with Poles – a disappointment experienced by international students in many countries (see for example Cena et al 2021; Jones 2013). Długosz conducted his surveys in Kraków, Rzeszów and Przemyśl, where there were higher concentrations of international students. In KPP, there were so few foreign students that during periods of face-to-face teaching they almost inevitably associated with Poles in class. Ivana, the only international student on her course, experienced almost a year of 'normal' university, which allowed her to form friendships with Poles. By contrast, Aksana had started in the pandemic year 2020/21. She was studying online from Belarus for the whole of Semester 1, and this had limited her networking and Polish language confidence. When interviewed in KPP in November 2021 she was again studying remotely. Karina, living at home, also complained about isolation from her Polish peers.

Karina spoke five languages and was linguistically curious. She tried to improve her Polish partly by engaging in casual conversations around the city (similarly to the Ukrainian factory worker Marina, quoted in Chapter 10). She said, for example, 'At the bus stop, I managed to help a woman with her bus … and I was surprised that I could answer her in Polish, and help her. It was nice. I like those situations. It makes you feel more capable and confident.' Despite her student status, Karina also possessed the advantages of a family migrant: she spoke Polish at home, and had Polish step-relatives. This gave her entrance to the family gatherings which other foreign migrants often identified as being how Poles in KPP preferred to spend their leisure time. Karina said:

> It's somehow more family-oriented in Poland. In the sense that at weekends they tend to spend time with their families. They don't particularly go anywhere, and the shops are often shut, unlike in

> Alma-Ata where they are open 24 hours … And here there is more focus on holidays, more attention to tradition. You go and see relatives, dress up, make food, sit round the table together, it's very sweet.

International students also have to integrate academically. Ukraine, Belarus and Kazakhstan follow the old Soviet pattern, whereby secondary school is completed at age 17, and this can pose problems for students in Poland. Karina complained:

> At uni, the lecturers often remark, 'You'll be familiar with this topic from school.' And I sit and think, 'Unfortunately, no, I'm not familiar with it – sorry!' I suppose the education is different. I heard that they have 12 years of school here, while we have 11. So I'm still trying to catch up with my classmates.

By contrast, Aksana thought the school curriculum was more demanding in Belarus: school leavers knew more than their Polish counterparts. On the other hand, aged 17 she was definitely the baby in her class, and this created an extra barrier between her and the Polish students. She mentioned enviously that her Belarusian friend in Poznań was in an academic group where four of the 10 students were from Belarus.

Of the three, only Ivana seemed well-attached locally and likely to remain in KPP. She had a boyfriend, and was planning to do her MA in the city. Her sister was also coming to KPP for her undergraduate degree. She rented her own flat and owned a car. She liked the fact that KPP was traffic-free and cheap compared with big cities. All her Polish friends were students, but she had always found Polish strangers patient and helpful. On the other hand, she also commented that 'with a Polish degree, the whole of Europe is accessible'. Aksana and Karina found local people friendly, but overall were less positive about the cities. They repeated the complaints of Polish interviewees, as reported in Chapter 3, about the shortage of cultural activities. Aksana said, 'There's nowhere to go out. You could take a bus to the shopping centre, that's all.' When asked if she would recommend KPP to other Belarusians hoping to study in Poland, she said, 'The university is very good, and the lecturers, and the classes. But for everyday life – the city is too small and dull.' At weekends she went to see her Belarusian friends studying in bigger cities, and she was hoping to transfer to Poznań for her MA, with a view eventually to joining relatives who were inviting her to the USA. Karina complained: 'There aren't many entertainments for students, places to go – no interesting cafés. There should be more cinemas, a theatre.' She too was hoping to transfer to Poznań.

Economic migrants

The three student interviewees constituted a high share of KPP's tiny international student population. Non-Ukrainian economic migrants (including entrepreneurs) were more numerous, but the six interviewees at least illustrated the diversity within this category of foreign residents. In keeping with the overall Polish trend of a sudden recent diversification of migrants' countries of origin, most were recent arrivals. A Bangladeshi, Venezuelan and Ukraine-based Armenian had come to Poland in 2018–9. Two Belarusians arrived in 2021 as part of the wave of Belarusian migration to Poland which intensified after the 2020 presidential elections and protests. One held a 'humanitarian visa' as a refugee, although he was an economic migrant. Exceptionally, Emre, a Turk, had been living in Poland for over 10 years. Labour migration from Turkey to Poland had intensified after 2004 (Andrejuk 2019a: 164) and Emre came to join his father, who was already working in Poland. Co-ethnic transnational migration networks also explain the choice of Poland from Bangladesh and Venezuela, while the Armenian and the two Belarusians happened to be in Poland, and KPP, for more individualised reasons. Like Ukrainians, they enjoyed privileged access to the labour market, which facilitated their migration.

Emre had come to Poland from Turkey after leaving school, because his father invited him. He then worked in restaurants in different cities. He was currently in KPP because his friend opened a new restaurant and invited Emre to join him there. Turks in Poland often work in food outlets (Andrejuk 2019a), so Emre seemed to be following a typical livelihood strategy. Gor and his Ukrainian wife came to KPP as factory workers through a recruitment agency. Their motivation for being in Poland was that they wanted to set up their own business, something they felt unable to do in Ukraine. They had looked at other cities after they arrived, but decided they liked KPP best, partly because they quickly made friends and found support among the very small but long-established Armenian population. (They had originally located this community by going to the market and speaking loudly in Armenian to one another, in the hope that someone would come up to them.) Here the ethnic dimension helped account for their entrepreneurial success. The 'community', despite being tiny, helped them realise their livelihood strategy and make it viable. Conversely, since theirs was the only Armenian restaurant in the city, it could acquire popularity through seeming exotic to the non-Armenian population.

Recent Belarusian migrants to Poland tend to be young or young middle-aged and middle-class (Homel et al 2023); Zoya and Matvei both fitted this categorisation. Previously, they had been quite well-off and in good jobs, but they asserted that their standard of living had fallen dramatically in 2020–1, just before they left Belarus for Poland. Matvei had run his own business with 15 employees, but found that people in his provincial home city were decreasingly able to afford tattoos, except on credit. Costs were also rising, because of inflation. Moreover, Matvei had previous experience of working abroad, in Russia and Sweden, and this enhanced his self-confidence and ambition to try his hand at working in Warsaw. It was an unsuccessful strategy since Matvei was unhappy in his job and his wife, a university graduate, was unable to find even manual work. Matvei then posted his CV on Facebook and waited for offers. A studio in KPP contacted him, suggesting he work for them for two weeks on a trial basis. Matvei took some holiday from his job in Warsaw and came on an inspection visit. He liked the employer and the city and the couple decided to move to KPP. Zoya, a university graduate, had managed a large restaurant in Minsk. However, 'the pandemic really messed things up for everyone. Last year the restaurants were shutting down, people were afraid to go out, no banquets, no weddings, so our restaurant completely collapsed … And rents are astronomical in Minsk nowadays … There are no prospects'. She also had personal reasons for moving from Belarus. Zoya was not in KPP by intention. She originally chose a factory job in Wrocław, but once she arrived the factory decided not to take on foreign workers because of Covid-19, so the agency offered her KPP; she accepted it without knowing anything about the city.

As already noted, before 2022 Ukrainians were becoming less attractive to some Polish employers, largely because they were more assertive in defence of their rights (Górny et al 2018: 110–115).[2] This made it tempting to hire nationals from countries which did not enjoy special privileges regarding work in Poland, whose workers could expect to be less able to change jobs, more dependent on their employers, and grateful to work for the minimum wage. Malik and Pablo were recruited to work in Poland from Bangladesh and Venezuela as part of this exploitable workforce, although their stories illustrate how it is possible – but only to a limited extent – to resist exploitation, and change workplaces after arrival in Poland.

Malik – speaking in English, a language he had learned from customers in Poland – said: 'Small country, lot of people, no work. That's why every people looking work. This is why every people came and moved to abroad because there is a lot of money and I send money for my family.

And they will better life in Bangladesh.' He had considered working in an Arab country, but been put off by the prospect of 'a lot of work and small money' and because he would have to return to Bangladesh at the end of his stay. He wanted to be in Europe partly because it offered a better chance for family reunification and settlement. Malik chose Poland in particular because his sister in the UK recommended it, and his nephew was already working there. Having paid his agency several thousand dollars[3] and travelled to New Delhi for a visa – since there was no Polish consulate in Bangladesh – he arrived in Poland to find himself assigned to a fish factory. He escaped from this unpleasant work, and found a succession of jobs, in different cities, through the Bangladeshi community in Poland (25,000 strong, according to the Facebook page which Malik showed me on his phone). Malik manifested a high level of trust in his co-ethnics. 'Everybody writing here [on Facebook] if you need work if you need anything you can ask and they will help you … I chose another shop [i.e. kebab café] and called him and asked about salary about how much and then I satisfied. Then I am here in KPP.'

Pablo's story was similar. He said, 'I decided come to Poland because I have a new opportunity and the situation in my country is very, very hard.' He had worked for six months in Colombia, like many Venezuelans, but found Colombians hostile and sometimes violent. His uncle suggested Poland as a destination and explained the procedure.

> He call me and I speak with my wife, with my mum. And I'm maybe scared. And my wife say, 'Don't think about this. Only go.' And I say, 'But how about you? My son? My mum?' And she say, 'Don't think about this. Because people have only one opportunity in their life.'

Pablo's agency sent him to a factory in a small town, where he and his fellow Venezuelans were not paid the wages they were due. He knew people working in KPP who were paid more reliably, hence he and his friends moved there. At the time of interview, their recruiter in KPP was trying to help the group obtain redress from the small-town factory.

Interviewees were conscious of belonging to waves of migration.[4] For instance, Pablo said he received many phone calls from friends asking him how to get to Poland; he encouraged them and provided advice. However, he also commented that 'I don't have many friends in Venezuela now. I have friends maybe in the whole world. I have friend in United States, in Chile, in Korea, yes, many friends, in France, in Spain, Italy, England, many friends'. Malik explained:

> Maybe in Poland, 500 kebab shop, all Bangladeshi owners… When first settled down in Poland they're working in kebab shop. In Turkish kebab. And they are learning how to make kebab … Then they're starting a kebab shop in Poland. First time in big city, then small city, then finally, like village. 5000 people lives in village, there's kebab.

Explaining migration from their countries to Poland, Malik and Pablo argued that, even if wages were lower in Poland, the lower cost of living made it preferable to western Europe or North America. However, Malik noted that, in Spring 2022, inflation was making that strategy less sustainable. He said, 'Now Poland very expensive, everything very expensive. That's the problem for us. Everything was cheap and good for us. But now it's a problem.'

With regard to social integration, Emre stood out from the rest. He had many Polish friends, including a girlfriend, who in typical KPP fashion happened to be in the UK at the time of our conversation. Emre said, 'I left my culture behind in Turkey.' Perhaps partly because he mixed with many young Polish people anxious to escape the small city, Emre was not particularly attached to KPP, and felt it offered too few opportunities. On the other hand, he had found working in Warsaw too tiring. He belonged to the category of interviewees, including both Poles and Ukrainians, who seemed (largely) resigned to living in the smaller city. This was partly because it constituted a base from which to explore the world. Emre's favourite pursuit was travelling in Asia, where he astonished Polish travellers by his fluency in Polish, and where he had also picked up some English language.

By contrast, Matvei, though a recent arrival, was happily settled in KPP and was positive about its lifestyle advantages. He felt he was held in high regard as a tattoo artist among both Poles and Russian-speaking migrants and said that he did not earn less than he would have done in Warsaw. Instead of a one-room flat, as in Warsaw, he and his Belarusian colleagues shared a house in a green outer suburb. His wife had found a manual job to provide an income while she improved her Polish and looked for a job commensurate with her qualifications. Matvei claimed to prefer smaller cities, being from a similarly-sized place in Belarus. Hence, economic and lifestyle reasons combined in his account. He expected to be in Poland for at least six years, since his strategy was to obtain citizenship of an EU state before examining his further options. Given his age, it seemed likely that he and his wife might start a family in Poland.

Pablo was the least well-integrated of the six, either into Polish society, or the regular Polish labour market. He had little opportunity to form any place attachment. He seemed not to mix with Poles at all, since he worked alongside Ukrainians and Latin Americans and shared his house with Mexicans and Venezuelans. He often worked seven days a week: when we met, he had just worked 23 consecutive days. Even though he was a strong 30-year-old trying to save as much money as possible, this regime was too tiring. He said the factory management was very reluctant to accede to requests for days off, a story I also heard from a Ukrainian who (having more options to change work) had left the same factory for this same reason. His integration was therefore into the small world of other Latin American workers in KPP. Pablo maintained strong transnational ties, sending home about 80 per cent of his wage. He had been away for two years and mentioned that some of his Venezuelan friends had been absent for up to five. He said, 'I miss my food, I miss my city, I miss my house, I miss my wife and my son, my friends.' He was dreaming about inviting his wife and son to join him in Poland, but not sure how that could be arranged.

Malik was in a somewhat similar predicament, working long hours for six days a week. He sent remittances back to his family in Bangladesh and had also been saving for his wedding. Like Pablo, his friends were co-ethnics: he knew five Bangladeshis in KPP, four of whom were co-workers. However, unlike Pablo, he had contact with local Polish people, to the extent that he had taught himself English from conversations with customers. His Polish was rudimentary and he said it was 'too difficult'. Since Malik had been in Poland nearly five years, without a break, he could have applied for a permanent residence card, which would have given him access to the EU labour market. He wanted to be able to move to another European country with his wife, since it was important for him to live somewhere with a mosque, where he could properly practise his faith. However, his strategy seemed to be on the brink of failure, since he had neither time nor energy to study for the language exam required to obtain the residence card, or take a course at a local college which would have exempted him from that requirement.

The other two interviewees fell somewhere between these extremes – less at home than Emre or Matvei, but 'immigrants light' compared with Pablo and Malik. Gor, in his mid-50s and with a successful business, did not speak much Polish but could depend on his wife and daughter. He was unlikely to move from KPP, where his restaurant was doing well even despite the pandemic. Zoya's situation was hard to assess, since she had arrived very recently and also had a strong sense of pausing at a crossroads in life. She was pleased with what she saw so far, and her remarks echoed those of many Ukrainian interviewees.

> I like Poland. It's so peaceful and civilised. You notice at once that people are very polite, that they talk to each other on the street, stop at zebra crossings. You've hardly reached the crossing and the car has already stopped … And all that constant 'please' and 'excuse me'. People make way to let you pass, men let women go first. It's a small city, but it's quiet and peaceful, the centre is beautiful and you have everything you need. The X Shopping Centre. You can buy everything you need.

However, she had a West European partner, hence it seemed probable that working in KPP might turn out to be a stepping stone to western Europe. She said, 'Poland is just the beginning of the journey.'

Family migrants

Since Poles migrate abroad from all corners of Poland, and marriage migrants often meet their Polish partners abroad, they could potentially meet Poles from anywhere in Poland. They later move to those places, so it is not surprising to find them spread across different locations in Poland, including smaller cities. This group of interviewees had mostly arrived between 2004 and 2018, so they were better established than the economic migrants and students. Since they were usually living close to their in-laws, they had a very different experience. There was considerable diversity within the sample, but a common feature in some cases was that they had come to Poland as the result of other people's migration experiences. One act of migration led to another. For instance, Sofiya met her future husband while she was in KPP visiting her friend from Russia who had married someone local. Belinda's husband was a welder, a professional circular migrant posted by his company to different countries, including Uruguay, where the couple met. Bob's father had migrated from Poland to Australia in the communist period, and it was when Bob was on a holiday in Poland staying with cousins that he met his future wife. No doubt the most commonplace story was that of Mario and his wife, who met while she was working in Italy before EU accession, like many Polish women.

One interviewee, Nadya, had migrated as a teenager to join her mother in the 1990s. Thanks to Nadya's stepfather, who was a taxi driver, her mother had become friendly with Poles from KPP who were trading in Minsk. They persuaded her first to come and trade in Poland, and then to work in her own profession in KPP. Nadya had taken a degree in Russian at a Polish university and married a local man. As a 1.5 generation migrant, and despite her lack of Polish citizenship, she was the most integrated and least transnationally-minded of all my non-Polish interviewees, several times contrasting herself with her mother who was still not completely confident in Polish and continued to be interested in Russian and Belarusian affairs. Nadya said, 'I'm more interested in Poland, what we can expect in our old age. In my mind, I live here more than there.'

It was clear why these family migrants were in KPP rather than elsewhere in Poland. They either married someone already based in KPP, or else their spouse, a Polish migrant from KPP, returned from abroad to be with her or his extended family. However, it was sometimes more complicated for the interviewees to explain why they were in Poland, rather than in their country of origin. In several cases the main reason seemed to be that the Polish spouse had the better job, but this combined with lifestyle preferences for Poland. For example, it was said to be safer than Uruguay, and to have a more child-friendly, less intensive school system than Taiwan. Bob said: 'There were many times we could have gone back to Australia. My wife's been back there four times. She knows what it's like there. And we've agree to raise our children here because it seems better for us.' James, the Nigerian, was an asylum seeker, so he had no option of going back. Mario, running a restaurant and small hotel in Italy with his Polish wife, had decided that Poland (even KPP) was more attractive economically than Calabria, so they were economic migrants.

Considering that they were living in KPP as families, their own integration was influenced by the choices each couple had made about what language(s) to speak at home, the 'family language policies' (Kozminska and Hua 2021). The different possible outcomes were illustrated by the cases of two Russian-speaking interviewees who were also stay-at-home mothers and had not worked in KPP. Nadya was completely assimilated into a Polish-speaking environment, although she had a slight Belarusian accent. She and her husband spoke Polish at home and had never taught their children Russian, on the grounds that it would be better for them to have English as their second language. Nadya's mother lived in KPP and she had little contact with her father in Belarus, so there were no transnational ties to be maintained in Russian. By contrast, Sofiya, despite having lived for years in Poland, was not completely confident in Polish. She spoke to her daughters in Russian and her husband in a mixture of Russian and Polish. She reported that even her Polish husband sometimes became muddled when speaking Polish. Sofiya's mother visited every year from Russia and her younger daughter spent extended periods with the grandmother, so it was important for the children to know Russian.

Bob and Belinda spoke a mixture of languages at home. Bob was privileged to be a native English speaker; his wife – who had worked in the UK – and friends spoke English. His father was Polish, but he had not been brought up speaking Polish. He said, 'I speak English to my wife and daughter and I speak Polish to my son. I speak Polish to him because he doesn't like English. He tells me, "Dad, not English." And it's a big mistake, I should talk nothing but English to him.' Belinda, by contrast, had no choice. Her Polish husband – despite having been a posted worker in Uruguay – spoke little Spanish. The couple had communicated in English. However, after two years in Poland Belinda began speaking Polish to him. The children spoke Spanish, English and Polish. Judging by her interview, Belinda's Polish was reasonably fluent. The other households seemed to be monolingual. Mario and his family spoke Italian. Leo, an English teacher on a mission to spread English language skills in KPP, consistent with this approach spoke only English to his wife and children. Sue's household was different because the family language, English, was no one's native tongue. Despite having lived in Poland for over 10 years, Sue admitted her Polish remained 'very basic'. She said of life in KPP that 'everything for me is like a puzzle, it's like pieces of puzzles' and confessed to guessing half the words when talking to her husband's family. However, despite – or perhaps partly because of – this disengagement from some details of everyday life, Sue claimed that compared to her life in stressful Taipei, 'I feel much freer [in Poland]. It's like I have a second life …'

Sue's poor command of spoken Polish clearly impeded her integration into family networks. On the whole, however, this group was well-embedded in networks and possessed associated social capital. For instance, one interviewee's mother-in-law had found her her job in KPP. Belinda was in a slightly different situation because her husband still worked abroad. She said, 'I'm always alone … I already have experience [in Montivideo] of living with in-laws, with [my two elder children]'s granny. No, no, no! They live on the same street. So they can keep an eye on the children if necessary. But I like my privacy.' Although Karina, the student migrant, had enthused about Polish family-centredness, Belinda complained about it. 'KPP is a bit closed. Each person lives just within their family circle.'

Most interviewees were married to people with professional, well-paid jobs, so this was an incentive to stay in KPP. On the other hand, Sue was the breadwinner, since her husband was unemployed. As a return migrant he had found it impossible to integrate into the local labour market. The family migrants were all attached to KPP to some extent by their children, particularly if they were born in KPP or came when they were young and were embedded in local networks and fluent in Polish. The integration process had been more difficult when a family relocated with teenagers, or the interviewee had remarried and brought children by a first marriage to Poland. Sofiya, who was Russian, complained about 'othering' towards herself and her daughter. However, like the Ukrainians, the non-Ukrainian interviewees uniformly praised teachers for helping support their children to integrate academically and learn Polish. Like the Ukrainians, they were delighted by their subsequent academic achievements. These constituted milestones in their place attachment journey in KPP. There were also some complaints about bullying at school. Sue was the most ambivalent. She said, 'They are happier now in a way but also disappointed in another way. They have a mixed feeling.' They had also removed their photographs from their Facebook profiles to diminish their visibility as Asians: an example of practising of 'strategic invisibility' (Amer and Leung 2023: 6–7).

Interviewees were forced to engage with Polish healthcare, given that they had children. Moreover, they usually did not return often to their countries of origin, so that, unlike the Ukrainians, or EU migrants in the UK, they did not expect to be treated there. Sofiya was exceptional in this regard, since she did mention visiting a doctor in Russia. The interviewees' main complaints about KPP concerned the health service. They did not criticise the quality of the care but were mostly concerned about waiting times and the perception that for prompt treatment they needed to use private healthcare. Other problems were the cost of medicines and perceived unfriendliness of receptionists and doctors. Reservations about local healthcare therefore impeded place attachment. On the other hand, perhaps their readiness to complain was evidence of their embeddedness in Polish circles – given that (in my experience) Poles often complain about Polish healthcare themselves and this is likely to have been a common topic of conversation in their family circles. As mentioned in Chapter 3, the family migrants based in Płock also expressed worries about pollution from the Orlen oil refinery. Most of the Ukrainians had not experienced health care in Poland and in some cases they claimed it must be better than in Ukraine. Nor did they worry about Orlen. In other words, better integration in the sense of embedding into local networks could also partly alienate the migrants from the place.

With regard to their integration into the labour market, the family migrants divided into two groups. On the one hand were the better integrated Mario, the restaurateur, and the four language teachers, Sue, Belinda, Leo and Bob. On the other were James, Sofiya and Nadya. James was now married to a Pole but he had come to Europe as an asylum seeker; his residence status was still undetermined and he was precariously employed. Sofiya and Nadya were stay-at-home mothers, although Sofiya was also an artist. In other words, there was a gap in fortunes between the first group, with the valuable ethnic-based skills (language, cooking), and the two Russian-speakers, whose skills were less in demand. James, as a native English speaker, had yet to make use of that cultural capital. The next section looks in turn at each of these sub-groups.

Language teaching is a popular occupation among foreigners in Poland, primarily west Europeans (Andrejuk 2017b: 567). Native language teachers can be quite visible in KPP, if they have a large number of pupils. They seemed to feel that the job was prestigious, especially given that native speakers were in such short supply.[5] Sue taught English and Chinese, in a language school and privately. She said, 'They show me respect because I am a native speaker.' Belinda did not have a university degree. Her move to KPP entailed upward social mobility, since she now taught Spanish and dance. In Uruguay, she worked in a hotel, a restaurant and a tollbooth. Bob had experienced downward social mobility by moving from Australia to Poland, but did not regret the move.

> [I left] a good job – a very good job. Very well-paid. It's unfortunate I didn't go back to it, but! … I can read Polish, OK, I cannot write it at all. I've never been to school to learn it. I can speak it, you know, after seven years. Hopefully. I know I make mistakes but it doesn't bother me. If I had Polish education behind me, and … the language, I'm sure I could get a better job. But teaching English is satisfying. It's really what most native speakers do here. They teach.

He had fallen into language teaching almost by chance, while he was a stay-at-home father:

> One day on Facebook I've seen this guy is looking for a native English speaker. So I wrote to him. Said I'd be interested in working. And he came the next day, we had a beer, he said, 'Would you like to work?' I said, 'Sure.' He showed me the ropes and things. But I did also additional studies to get this additional diploma [online].

However, apart from prestige and access to Polish networks, being a language teacher did not necessarily confer an integration headstart. Some interviewees considered the pay to be unsatisfactory. Belinda, for instance, felt she was underpaid. She said she would earn up to twice as much in another language school, or in Warsaw. Like other teachers, the interviewees often supplemented their salaries by tutoring.

Being immersed in one's native language at work precludes immersion in Polish which would be necessary in a different workplace. This situation was exacerbated when the interviewees could depend on their spouses to help them out with written Polish – as in Bob's case quoted above. On the other hand, since Belinda's husband was often working abroad, she had been forced to become self-reliant, though she complained that 'Polish is a really hard language'. The interviewees had different opinions about whether they could conduct everyday business in English in KPP. Someone in Płock was able to sort out their business at the city hall, whereas an interviewee in Kalisz complained that this was impossible. Curiously, two interviewees in the same workplace had opposite impressions. One said he could do all the paperwork in English, but since he also read Polish perhaps he simply did not notice that some forms were in Polish. His colleague asserted that documentation at work was mostly in Polish and 'most of the times I feel like I'm in the dark'.

These interviewees seemed quite settled in KPP, mentioning similar reasons for place attachment to those named by the Ukrainians. Mario, for example, thought that there would be more crime in a bigger city, so there was no point moving within Poland. KPP felt safe, and the police did a good job. He found the architecture 'pretty' and his business was doing well. Mario was pursuing a transnational livelihood, since he still owned a small business in Calabria, but he was considering shutting it down. For the time being, as an EU citizen, he was privileged to be able to keep options open and to have a foot in two countries – a situation which definitely helped him feel comfortable and therefore attached in KPP. Belinda was in a less comfortable position. She had not seen her mother in Uruguay for five years, and if she did not engage in transnational mobility it was because she could not afford to do so. Like Mario and Belinda, Bob emphasised the lifestyle advantages of KPP. He said, 'Coming to a town like this, it's much more peaceful. It's much more quiet. It's got a nice community I would say.' The family's plans for the future were to live 'in KPP or on the outskirts of KPP. The dream is to build a house near the forest, near a lake. More peace and quiet. Because where we live now is a very nice area, very family-orientated area, but … you can't just walk out the back door and into the garden.' His parents visited regularly and planned to spend their time in retirement half-in-half in Poland and Australia.

Leo, the second Australian, was happy to be in Europe, especially since he had relatives in Portugal. However, he was critical of KPP and his opinions were quite the opposite to those expressed by most Ukrainian interviewees. He distinguished between big cities ('in Warsaw and Poznań you can assume that people will speak English) and KPP, which in his view was annoyingly monolinguistic and underdeveloped. However, he also felt attached and at home. His comments intertwined positivity and negativity:

> You know sometimes I drive and I see people working and I'm like, Oh wow. What's happening here, where's the safety, there's no helmet, there's no vest, things like that. It reminds me of when I was in Portugal 20 years ago. It's a funny thing, what I see here in KPP, and Poland in general, sometimes it's like a *déjà vu* ... Because in Portugal 20 years ago, about 20 years ago, it was in the same route. Everything was happening slowly ... The city itself is quite easy to navigate. Everything is very easy ... People ask me 'Would you leave Poland?' No, not really. I wouldn't ... I'm quite happy here ... We had opportunities to go to Warsaw or Poznań but we decided to stay here. Unless something drastic happens. For now we're quite happy. The kids are happy at school, I'm happy that, you know, the education is good.

The three remaining interviewees, Sofiya, Nadya and James, were either unemployed or integrated only into the worst-paid sector of the KPP labour market. There were similarities between the stories of the two women but Nadya (partly because she was a 1.5 generation migrant) was much better embedded and less transnationally oriented than Sofiya.

Both Sofiya and Nadya regretted that they were not living in a city where there would be more opportunities for Sofiya to sell her artwork and Nadya to find a job using her Russian degree. Nadya also blamed the particular difficulties of the labour market in Płock; as mentioned several times in earlier chapters, it was considered by many informants to be a hard place to find work. Nadya had become pregnant in her final year at university in Poland and never had any paid work. Her opinion was that it was hard for women in their 30s returning to work to find a job in Płock – including at Orlen – unless they had the right connections. Warsaw she construed as being too near – if someone needed a specialised translation service, for example Polish translations of Belarusian documents, they could easily get it done in Warsaw. Sofiya however did not have a sense that Warsaw was on the doorstep: she construed it as being a bit too far. In Petersburg, she had been surrounded by cultural opportunities, whereas Warsaw was not very accessible. Both women made positive comments about how infrastructure had improved in Płock since the 1990s.

With regard to citizenship and residence status: Nadya had the impression that her Belarusian citizenship was a barrier on the labour market. Unlike her daughters, who had Polish and Belarusian nationality because they were born in Poland, she would need to surrender her Belarusian citizenship if she naturalised as a Pole. On the one hand, she would like to vote in Poland. On the other, because her elderly father was alone and without any family in Belarus she wanted to be able to go to Belarus in case of emergencies without having to obtain a visa. Sofiya found her long-term residency status in Poland sufficient for her needs. 'For the time being' she was not planning to naturalise.

James was deskilled in Poland. He had been an office manager in Nigeria, a gardener in Berlin, and a factory worker in KPP. His wife had been trying to find him better work but this was impeded by his visa status. He said, 'I aim to get a good job. This bakery job that I'm doing is draining my energy. It's affecting me too. I'm in my 40s. I don't have much power. So what I need to do is to integrate into the society, into the system.' He was still waiting for the residence permit to which he was entitled on the basis of being married to a Pole. He and his wife suspected that a racist official in Poznań was holding up the process: she seemed to be trying to show that their marriage was fictitious.

> I am mentally derailed. Sorry to say that. If I was to describe the situation right now. My wife is complaining about my status. Because I think, 'You are not in a prison [but] you don't know when you will gain your freedom.' I have for the past three years plus, here, no movement, you can't travel, you can't go anywhere alone.

James was keen to improve his Polish language skills so he could do a course and get an office job in Poland. He practised Polish with his in-laws. However, like Leo, he also took the line that Poles in KPP needed to practise their English. He was teaching his bakery colleagues, and was under the impression that most people locally did not speak the language.

> Sometimes, if I go to the park, I see three or four young, teenage, I try to encourage them. Polish is only for Poland. The Polish language. English is universal. When you travel, out of Poland, to Germany, if

> you cannot speak German but at least when you try to speak English someone will be able to [help]. I try to encourage them. So some of them see me as a friend. They say, 'Hello, James! How are you?'

Like some of the Ukrainians, James seemed torn about where he wanted to be. On the one hand, it would be better to live in a country with more ethnic diversity, and he and his wife were looking at jobs in western Europe. On other, the couple considered that they ought to stay in Kalisz for the sake of his mother-in-law, and James had identified a vocational degree course which his daughter would like, and was hoping to bring her to Poland once his own status was sorted out.

Polish networks and attitudes towards minority minorities

The chapter has shown that family and student migrants were mostly well-embedded in Polish networks. However, this does not necessarily mean that they had bridging ties to Poles. Students in all societies can be isolated from the non-student world, and some of the family migrants were also isolated in that they depended heavily on their spouses to deal with the household's paperwork. For example, it was Bob's wife who found him an accountant to do his tax return – Bob did not need to make this contact himself.

Non-Ukrainian foreigners contended with considerable ignorance. Bob the Australian was tired of being asked about spiders and snakes. The Belarusians (even in 2022) found that the Poles they met did not know much about Belarus, except that it was poor. Sue, from Taiwan, attracted the most attention on the street. She said:

> I'm often stopped on the street by people, they are curious where I'm from. Mostly men they stop me on the street. Middle-aged. They give me a lot of nationalities, Vietnam, Japan, Korea, Thailand, China, it never occurred to them it was Taiwan. How old I am, what am I doing in KPP, if I like it.

She was also frustrated by the ignorance she encountered. Even her colleagues of 12 years standing kept saying she was from Thailand. And when she mentioned 'Taiwan' many people 'right away they say China'. She had been touched to meet a man in a shop who asked her nationality and then mentioned Chiang Kai-Shek.

The non-Ukrainian Slavs were often assumed to be Ukrainian. This included Bob, the half-Polish Australian. He said, 'Often when I catch a taxi they say I'm Ukrainian. I always joke with people, I speak in Polish, I say, "Guess where I'm from." "Ukraine?" "No, try again!" Eventually I tell them the other side of the world.' However, he was also identified as a West European. He also said, 'Sometimes they think I am from Austria. Polish people always say, "You look Swedish." Oh! [exasperated sigh] I look like me.'

Inna and Gor, who ran an Armenian restaurant, felt obliged to educate local Poles.

> Inna: Many people don't know anything about Armenia, so we decorated the restaurant with different things which we can use to tell them about the country … They can see our photos, listen to the stories, look at various interesting books. Many Poles for example don't know that Armenia is Christian. They think it's a Muslim country, so we tell them the historical facts. We explain, so that those Poles are informed about Armenia.
>
> Gor (pointing to a mural opposite the door): As soon as you come in the restaurant, there's a cross. So that proves we're not Muslims.

Emre and Malik, who were Muslims, worked in different restaurants but had identical experiences. During the daytime, Polish customers were polite and friendly. In the evening, drunken and abusive Islamophobic Polish men could come and make trouble.

Bielewska (2021: 625) found that foreign university graduates working in Lower Silesia perceived Poles as 'closed and cold' and some of the KPP interviewees had the same impression. Mario said they were 'cold' and Belinda referred to them as 'grey' (*szarzy*). Bob did not have such a poor impression, but he did object to what he saw as Polish prejudice against Ukrainians. 'Polish people don't like Ukrainians. Polish people they think they're better than them. They are on a lower level. I don't like that.' He also noted a *caché* apparently attached to speaking English: 'If you walk on the street here and someone hears you speaking English they stare and they look. Wow!'

Martin, a Kenyan key informant who had lived in Poland on and off since the 1980s, remembered that racism had been fiercer and more open in the past. His children had found it very hard. He considered that nowadays things were somewhat improved. James, the Nigerian interviewee, had been in KPP for three years and had mixed experiences, including plenty of unpleasant ones. He tried to rationalise this by blaming the small city identity, although he also felt that racism was universal in Poland. In fact one of his biggest problems, as discussed earlier in this chapter, was with the apparent racism and obstructionism of an official in Poznań. James said:

> Let me say, based on my ethnicity, I'm a black man, not everybody will like you. You understand. And then you cannot compare KPP with a city like Poznań, Łódź, Wrocław, Kraków or Warsaw. Because these are multi-ethnic cities. Where you have a lot of different ethnicities. While here in KPP there is only a few … Somehow the white people still look down at me. You know? But it's everywhere. Even in bigger cities. So people who are: 'What are you doing in my city? What are you doing in my city? You fxxxing go back to your fxxxing Africa' … I think it's ignorance … All the big cities they are just like other European big cities. Everybody mind their business. But in KPP the majority of people they know each other. They know who is who.

On the other hand, James also felt that his Polish neighbours and acquaintances were friendly.

> James: Some Polish people I don't know around this area, when they see me they say 'hello' … The old people living I think up from this apartment, the top apartment, they always say very [enthusiastically], 'Oh, hello!' … Why do they like me? Because whenever I see them I say the respect for them. Because where I grow up from Africa when somebody was elderly he was accorded, afforded, he was getting the love and the respect.
>
> Anne: So the neighbours *are* friendly?
>
> James: They're very friendly.
>
> Anne: And the people in your workplace are friendly?
>
> James: Yeah, yeah. Very friendly. No racism or whatever.

Sue considered that things had improved since her first visit in 1994: 'Even in summer people made me feel it was so chilly, no one smiled, and they just stared at me, like a glare. It was like they were suspicious, some even made feel they were hostile because I didn't speak Polish.' Now, although she was visible, it was in a good way.

My students say, 'I saw you marching again'. Because I walk very fast. 'Are you sure it was me?' 'Yes, no one walk that fast like you and you was wearing yellow boots.' A lot of people, I think it must be they like me, because they hoot or they stop and wave to me. So I think that's nice and they even cross the street. My two sons didn't know I was so popular in KPP … It's nice to be recognised.

Nadya also mentioned having a hard time when she first arrived in KPP in the mid-1990s, because of prejudice against Belarusians. Her teachers were generally supportive, but she was nicknamed 'the Russian' and she sensed that her particularly anti-Russian history teacher disliked her. Sofiya, who was Russian, had felt ostracised because of her nationality when she arrived in a village near KPP. However, both women were more positive about contemporary local attitudes. Sofiya said for example that now she had moved to the city people 'talk [Russian] to me with pleasure, and they invite me to their houses. They are ones who make the friendly approaches. Not just "hello", but "come and visit us, let's meet up". I've made some good womenfriends and I didn't feel any negative attitudes.' Nadya felt that the situation had improved because there were so many different people from the former Soviet Union living in KPP. She said, 'People hear my voice and say, "You're not from Poland." Now I have no problems saying, "I'm from Belarus."' Karina, who had arrived in Poland as late as 2021, and who would presumably be assumed to be Ukrainian, had never encountered any negativity on the street. People were very helpful and would respond if she asked them questions.

These stories of recently increased local friendliness raise the question of whether the improved attitudes could be partly attributed to Poles' own migration experiences. In general, the family migrants did not comment on the migration experiences of their Polish contacts. Bob was an exception. Through his wife, a member of the EU wave, Bob had local Polish friends who had returned from working in Western Europe. He thought that return migrants were more open. 'The biggest factor for me is if they've left Poland or not. If they've been abroad they should know a little bit about the world.' Nadya, who was thoroughly embedded in local Polish society, participated in spreading the migration culture. She explained how she gave advice, as one migrant to another, to a Polish friend who had gone to Sweden. 'She writes that she really wants to come back. I advise her to stick it out, it's only the first year, it's very hard, but gradually you make contacts, friends appear … Sometimes you want to return, but if the crisis passes everything will start going better.'

Relations between different non-Polish nationalities

Ukrainians in Kalisz mentioned working alongside people of different nationalities: Nepalese, Thai, Indonesian, Filipino, Venezuelan and Mexican. Płock Ukrainians had Vietnamese co-workers, who did not speak Polish and were apparently recently arrived from Vietnam. However, to a large extent the Ukrainians and others seemed to lead lives which did not intersect. Ukrainians had problems communicating with non-Slavs, especially when one party did not speak English. Two interviewees mentioned that Polish co-workers who had learned English in the UK and Ireland acted as interpreters, so in these situations English did seem to be a *lingua franca*. Interviewees assumed that the workers from other continents were in Poland only temporarily. For example, I was told that they changed every six months. The implication was that it was not worthwhile to become acquainted. However, as my interview with Pablo the Venezuelan showed, non-Ukrainians also found ways to extend their stays in Poland.

For foreign factory workers, Ukrainians sometimes formed the majority of their workmates, with consequences for their experiences of living in Poland. Venezuelans had to integrate into a Ukrainian world.

> Pablo: I don't speak Polish, I think it's very hard ... I try to learn but I work with Ukraine people. I understand, hm [searching for English word] ...
>
> Anne: A bit of Ukrainian?
>
> Pablo: Yes. And Polish people sometimes listen me speak Ukraine and they say, 'You don't stayed in Ukraine. You stayed in Poland.' And I say, 'Yes, but I work with Ukraine people. Not with Polish people.'

Adult education colleges are places where Ukrainians, Poles and other nationalities sometimes become friendly.

> Karina: I used to go to the Cosinus School ... Everyone in the group was from Ukraine. I was the only person from Kazakhstan! So it was interesting. There was a nice atmosphere, we studied Polish together, chatted to one another ... we helped each other learn the language.
>
> Anne: Are you still in touch with those Ukrainians?

> Karina: No, somehow, we were friendly at the time, helping each other with the language. But we didn't swap contact details. They already knew each other, probably they were there as friends, they knew one another already. But I was somehow not from their world, well, I didn't completely fit in.

The Armenian restaurant was also a meeting place. Inna said:

> Recently a lot of people came to Kalisz from Mexico. They never used to be here before. And from other countries, some places from which people are in Kalisz for the first time. And they all come here [to the Armenian-Ukrainian restaurant] … Kalisz seems to be a small town, but there are lots of nationalities.

Polish-Ukrainian football was mentioned in Chapter 11. Matches happened in all three cities. However, in both Kalisz and Piła there were multinational matches and in Kalisz even competitions between Ukrainians, Venezuelans and Poles.[6] Some migrant hostels were also meeting places for many nationalities. For example, Yurii in Kalisz mentioned a neighbour from the Philippines. However, the hostel in Płock where I did interviews in 2019 was home only to Slavs and Georgians. Russian functioned as the *lingua franca*, although some Ukrainians claimed that the Georgians did not speak it very well.

There was also evidence of ethnic hierarchies. Some interviewees expressed patronising attitudes towards Ukrainians. Sofiya, the Russian, said, 'I hear they have a very difficult economic situation nowadays. That's why it's not only conmen and criminals, prostitutes, but just people coming for normal work.' Zoya, a Belarusian factory worker, mentioned, 'I was amazed to meet a woman at work with four children at home in the Ukraine.[7] She came here to work – what can have happened that she abandoned her little children and came here to work? What can the situation be like?' In turn, the Ukrainians expressed pity for other nationalities, often intermingled with confusion about their countries of origin. Tamara, for instance, said, 'It seems things are completely dreadful there [in the Philippines].' Oleksiy commented, 'They are from Venezuela, and now there are lots of people coming from Taiwan, hmm, no, Thailand … I've heard they work twelve hours a day and earn very little. It's convenient for the employers.' Several interviewees also made remarks about the small build of Asian co-workers. Zlata, for example, explained:

> I don't know if they are Indonesians but they are from a Muslim country ... They're not used to the work and they find it very tough. They are small, and the mattresses are big and heavy, and they work ten or twelve hours. Because they need to pay back for their travel documents. I think they all work for an agency and they have to pay the agency back.

Ukrainians in Płock also commented on the height of their Asian co-workers – described variously as Chinese and (more convincingly) Vietnamese – and sometimes referred to them as 'kittens', mocking their accents.

Sometimes, however, there was a sense of competition between different nationalities. Alla, who worked in a Ukrainian-run nail salon, said of a Chinese nail salon: 'Some of my clients went there when I was away [in Ukraine]. They work continuously, they are very quick. And their average level of skill is a bit lower than in my salon.' In June 2022, Matvei, from Belarus, expressed concern about Ukrainians.

> When we lived in Warsaw my wife couldn't find a job [in 2021] because so many people from Ukraine had come, and all the jobs, even the simple work like in warehouses, they were all taken ... Life [in Piła] is cheaper and more peaceful than in Warsaw, because [in Warsaw] lots of people have come from Ukraine and they go to the big city to earn big money ... So there is a problem with housing, a problem with work.

Matvei had had a sequence of bad experiences with Ukrainians which perhaps explain his attitude. He was angry at the Ukrainian agency which he used to obtain his first job in Warsaw – considering that they cheated him by taking some of his wages – and regretted working for a Ukrainian tattoo parlour in Warsaw when he first arrived. In his analysis, resentment at Ukrainians – as the more senior and better-placed migrants – seemed to mingle with a certain patronising attitude towards Ukrainians as inferior to Belarusians.

Some interviewees also pointed to parallels and connections between migration by different nationalities, mostly drawing parallels between Polish migration to the west. Nadya, for example, said, 'Nowadays you hear Ukrainian a lot ... You can understand it. Poles also migrate for work, they also migrated. Each does what they can.' Sofiya mentioned, 'In the UK there's a shortage of working hands and it's the same here. I've noticed when we drive to Warsaw there are fields of strawberries.

They used to be well looked after and now there are weeds growing there. Because there is no one to work on them.' Dmytro, a Ukrainian factory worker in KPP, observed that 'there aren't enough workers because Polish people go abroad to work. I think that if more Poles worked here there'd be fewer gaps and it wouldn't be necessary to bring people from the ends of the earth', by which he meant Indonesia.

Conclusions

These 17 stories display the diversity of the non-Ukrainian foreign population in KPP. They also testify to the significance of factors discussed many times in earlier chapters of this book. One such factor is family and friendship networks. Apart from the obvious cases of people married to Poles, several economic migrants were also in Poland thanks to recommendations or persuasion by family members. Malik's transnational family networks, for example, stretched between Poland, the UK and Bangladesh. When asked why they were in KPP rather than other cities, the interviewees' accounts matched those of the Ukrainians. Pablo and Malik had been dissatisfied with their jobs elsewhere in Poland and come to KPP on the recommendation of co-ethnics; Emre was persuaded by a co-ethnic friend; while Zoya the Belarusian had been let down by her agency and shipped to KPP when her promised factory job turned out to be no longer available in Wrocław. The family migrants were in Poland because they had decided to be in KPP in preference to locations abroad; there was no prospect of them moving within Poland. Although being with extended family was often their main motive, the quality of life in the smaller city was also a major incentive. KPP were described as peaceful and relaxing, compared for example with Montivideo or Taipei. At the same time, no doubt because they were embedded in Polish networks, these informants voiced the same complaints as local Poles about pollution and the health service. All categories of minority minority interviewee commented on local friendliness in KPP, in some cases asserting that Poles had become more open to foreigners since the 1990s, a trend which could be connected to their migration experience. However, the black and Asian informants mostly referred here to the friendliness of their personal acquaintances, such as neighbours and co-workers. Sometimes it was a different story on the street, where they were stared at and sometimes harassed and racially abused. Both Muslim interviewees complained about abuse from drunken customers.

With regard to the labour market, KPP differ from big cities in Poland in that there exist very few ethnic bars and restaurants. This can be linked to the absence of migrant 'communities'.[8] However, it seemed that the presence of just a handful of co-ethnics was sufficient to encourage this type of business. Kalisz and Płock (though possibly not Piła) also offered factory work to migrants from Asia and Latin America. Insofar as one can speak of labour market integration, these workers seem sometimes to have been integrated into one of that market's most exploitative sections – truly the jobs which most Poles do not want to do. Several interviewees were teaching languages, and therefore belonged to a generally more privileged section of the local labour market, especially given that native speakers were like gold dust in the smaller cities.

The interviews illustrated once again how language acquisition is fundamental for integration. At one extreme, Pablo the factory worker was learning Ukrainian rather than Polish because he had practically no exposure to Polish. At the other, many minority minority interviewees were either living in Polish families and/or working all day with Polish customers and might seem to have an immense linguistic head start. However, this was no guarantee that they could read or, still less, write – even after years of life in Poland. This constituted a barrier to their career progression or, in the case of people like Malik, to acquiring long-term residence status in Poland.

The interviews also provided some evidence about contacts and relations between Ukrainians and minority minorities. They engaged in ethnic hierarchisation and stereotyping vis-à-vis one another, but sometimes also tried to communicate and recognise parallels between their situations. Some had less contact than others. For example, Ukrainian factory workers associated with Ukrainians and Poles at work and hardly seemed to interact with other migrants; their attitudes towards these nationalities often appeared patronising. On the other, there were a few settings, such as migrant hostels, where migrants of different nationalities were thrown together, as equals, and this could promote friendliness. Adult colleges were another such setting, as shown by Karina the Kazakh's enthusiastic account of learning Polish alongside Ukrainians. However, Karina's story shows that other identity differences – such as age – could constitute barriers to more long-lasting relations. It also illustrates how members of the minority minorities could envy the Ukrainians, as the majority minority, assuming that their critical mass meant they did not need to include non-Ukrainians within their social circles.

Notes

1. This part of my study was limited by the fact that I interviewed only in Polish, Russian and English. I conducted the interviews myself, without an interpreter, and regretted that I could not speak Vietnamese, Chinese or Spanish.
2. The full-scale Russian invasion of Ukraine in 2022 led to a shortfall of Ukrainian male workers in Poland and would constitute an additional reason to seek employees from further afield. See for example Kowalczyk (2023) and Sobolak (2022).
3. I was surprised by the sum, but reports from the Polish cash-for-accelerated-visas scandal which erupted in summer 2023 confirmed that this was not unusual. See e.g. Kowalczyk (2023).
4. In Gor's case, this wave was from Ukraine, where he had been living before coming to Poland.
5. Płock was the only city with several language schools employing native speakers, and one of these was run by Orlen for its employees, again testifying to the city's Orlen-linked exceptionalism. I spoke to two native-speaker teachers in Kalisz and heard of one other. There may have been none at all in Piła. I walked around language schools making enquiries and also combed the internet (particularly looking at tutoring advertisements) but could find nothing more. Leo reported that one of his students had been hunting unsuccessfully for a native speaker to teach her English in Kalisz.
6. https://calisia.pl/miedzynarodowy-turniej-pilki-noznej-konveyor-2021-duzo-zdjec,51463
7. She used the preposition *na*, which is considered patronising – equivalent to English 'in the Ukraine'.
8. There were also no Ukrainian restaurants in KPP when I did the research, though one had closed in Kalisz.

13
Conclusions

Polish Cities of Migration told the story of three cities during the years 2019–22, just after Poland became a country with net immigration. Poland presents an intriguing case of migration transition, because of its strong identity as a 'country of emigration'. Migration transitions have been studied more by demographers and economists than by sociologists. However, as suggested for example by Arango (2012), they should also be studied sociologically, to understand how the majority population in such countries learns to adapt to its new role as a receiving society. *Polish Cities* presents an original, 'bottom-up' account of migration transition. Through interviews with Poles living in ordinary Polish cities, it examines this process of learning to be a receiving society, but with a twist: it recognises that Poles are not migration novices, and that the transformation into an established receiving society is influenced by Poles' own migration expertise and transnational ties.

The book examines this process at sub-national level, recognising that there is no singular, uniform 'Poland'. The migration transition is much further advanced in the biggest cities, such as Warsaw, Poznań and Wrocław. In the eyes of most residents, they no longer seem to be 'cities of emigration'. On the other hand, working abroad still constitutes an everyday livelihood strategy in Polish small towns and villages. *Polish Cities of Migration* looks between these extremes, considering the migration transition in three cities of around 100,000 population. Cities like these are not normally studied by Polish migration scholars. Kalisz, Płock and Piła are located in Poland's wealthier regions and, in 2019–22, they were attracting increasing numbers of foreign workers. However, they preserved their identities as cities of emigration, particularly in the eyes of working-class residents. One of the main contributions of the research is that it revealed the importance of taking into account social stratification within receiving countries when analysing the out-migration component of migration transition. For Polish people without university degrees, migration to western Europe, often temporary, is still a common livelihood strategy. If they worked in factories in Kalisz, Płock and Piła, they were also likely to associate with Ukrainians. By contrast, interviewees in white-collar jobs did not usually work alongside Ukrainians and, unlike middle-class Poles in the biggest cities, they did not employ them as domestic workers. They themselves were less likely to migrate abroad than 10 years previously. Nonetheless, they maintained many ties with relatives and friends living in foreign countries. In that respect, migration remained relevant to their everyday lives. All interviewees, even the most settled, could still see migration as something done by 'us', not just 'them'. The book used the concept of migration culture to understand how a local population, with its own well-developed ideas about how to practise migration, reflected upon migration by newly-arrived people from other countries.

Polish Cities addressed two sets of questions. The first was whether and, if so how, local Poles' self-identification as migrants coloured their thoughts about migration to Poland, and whether this made them more welcoming to migrants in their home cities. The answers to these questions provided insight into how the overlapping emigration–immigration identities of the three cities shape the nature of Poland's migration transition. The book presented a 'bottom-up' perspective, drawing on local foreigners' stories of their interactions with Poles and on Polish residents' accounts of their own opinions and behaviour. Since the new migrants were overwhelmingly Ukrainian, the book's other main research goals were to understand why migration from Ukraine to Poland was taking place on such a scale and why, as the population of Ukrainians in Poland increased, they were spreading out to new destinations beyond the biggest cities. Part of the answer to this question lies in thousands of individual Ukrainian decisions to base themselves in smaller cities. These decisions, as it emerged from the interview material, linked to their growing place attachment in Kalisz, Piła and Płock. Place attachment, the emotional dimension of integration, therefore turned out to be a key concept for understanding migration transition. The cities were attractive in numerous respects, partly because local Polish people were perceived to be patient and helpful, and to understand what migration entailed. Indeed, some interviewees had the impression that in bigger cities they would meet more impatience and anti-Ukrainian nationalism.

Attitudes towards Ukrainian labour migrants also linked to opinions about labour migration in general. Survey data shows that by 2019, 62 per cent of Poles believed that migrants should be allowed to undertake any work in Poland, with 29 per cent favouring access with some limitations (Bożewicz and Głowacki 2020: 5). This support for labour migration was equally evident from the Polish interviews in Kalisz, Piła and Płock. The interviewees did not present migration in instrumental terms, from a typical receiving society perspective, as beneficial to the Polish economy. Instead, they drew numerous parallels between their own and other nationalities' migration. They observed certain patterns, such as trends over time towards more family reunification. They asserted that international migration was a normal social phenomenon and an understandable livelihood strategy. In some cases, they reminisced about how it had felt to be a migrant, and speculated that Ukrainians would feel the same. Ukrainian interviewees, impressed by the friendly attitudes of local Poles, sometimes attributed this directly to their migration experience. However, they could also point to cases where Poles overstated similarities, for example assuming that Ukrainians would want to return 'home' to Ukraine whereas in fact they often hoped to settle in Poland. The majority of Ukrainian interviewees worked in factories and this gave them special insights into Polish migration. They tended to know plenty of Polish circular migrants. From their accounts it seemed that some factory settings functioned as 'schools of migration' where Poles offered information and advice to Ukrainians. In other words, the Ukrainians participated in the lively Polish migration culture which still typified certain social and workplace settings in the smaller cities.

Poland's migration transition is the story of Ukrainian migration to Poland, and the book explored why this migration was taking place even before the 2022 refugee influx. My interviews with Ukrainians showed that the wave of Ukrainian labour migration was typical of much twenty-first century mobility, with parallels to the Polish exodus after EU accession. Potential migrants in both Poland and Ukraine sensed that many mobility options were available, and spoke of migration as an experiment: it was 'worth having a go'. Moreover, they rejected internal migration as a livelihood strategy in favour of international migration. Both types of behaviour can be explained by the fact that they possessed extensive international networks. The fundamental parallel was that Ukrainians were moving to Poland through, and to some extent because of their family and friendship networks. Scholars have long noted this as a phenomenon in west Ukrainian migration. However, my interviews showed that dependence on networks was becoming marked in central and eastern Ukraine, where migration to Poland only began after Russia attacked Ukraine in 2014. Most interviewees kept in close contact with family members and friends in Ukraine, and this explains the dynamism of the transnational networks. (Poignantly, in view of later events, when they described visits back to Ukraine some interviewees mentioned being impressed by the newly smart appearance of their towns and cities of origin, thanks to redevelopment while they were away in Poland.)

Like Poles moving to Western Europe after EU accession, Ukrainian parents quickly began to change their migration strategies in favour of family reunification. Parents already working abroad saw that Ukrainian friends were bringing their children to Poland and this prompted them to do the same. Family migration became normalised within the migration culture. This is turn promoted settlement in smaller Polish cities, which were often seen as more family-friendly: prized for being safe, quiet, compact and green, especially compared with polluted large Ukrainian cities like Mariupol and Kryvyi Rih. These quality-of-life factors compensated for restricted labour markets. As it happened, Poles returning from abroad to Kalisz, Płock and Piła made similar judgements, placing family and quality of life above economic considerations.

The book uncovered many instances in which the size of the waves – which impressed the Poles and Ukrainians themselves – significantly influenced their experiences. The scale of Ukrainians' Ukrainian networks in Poland was an advantage which helped them integrate and become attached to Kalisz, Piła and Płock, just as embeddedness in Polish networks helped many Polish people become attached to their new homes in countries like the UK and Ireland. As one Ukrainian interviewee remarked, migrants needed 'friends who can give them tips about how to do things properly', for example how to avoid over-dependence on agencies, and find new jobs with more decent conditions. (The research confirmed the findings of other scholars that Ukrainians were reluctant to accept exploitation, particularly if they had committed to settling in Poland.) Through their networks, Ukrainians from all parts of Ukraine were brought together, enhancing a sense of pan-Ukrainian identity. Both Ukrainians and Poles expressed pride in their work ethic and contribution to the economies of the receiving countries. On the other hand, the scale of migration meant that the migrant population also contained people who were perceived as being less well-behaved. Just like Poles, Ukrainians engaged in discursive hostility towards co-ethnics and believed stories about co-ethnics who cheated one another. This constituted part of the lore in both migration cultures. As *Polish Cities* illustrates, migration culture is not just a feature of sending communities – as commonly presented in scholarly literature – but is constantly produced and modified among migrants living abroad. Although social remitting is a concept usually used to understand how migrants pick up ideas from the majority population, it was clear from the interview evidence that migrants also learn from one another. This is part of the learning process inherent in the migration transition.

The book applied an intersectional approach to understand the different integration and place attachment trajectories of my informants. For instance, as mentioned in the first paragraph, Polish cities are socially diverse places and nowadays (though not *circa* 2004) some socio-demographic groups are more touched by migration than others. Chapter 4 distinguished between a steady stream of Polish target-earners working all over western Europe up to the present day, and the wave of university graduates and students, followed by what I have termed a 'swell' of friends and family members, who departed for the UK and Ireland around the time of EU accession. Similarly, Chapter 7 illustrated the diversity within the Ukrainian sample. Overall, they were more working-class than the Ukrainian migrants commonly studied in and around Warsaw. However, working-class identities were also diverse. On the one hand were skilled workers in highly gendered occupations, such as lorry-drivers, welders, hairdressers and beauticians. Typically they were satisfied with their labour market integration and also well-embedded in Ukrainian and/or Polish networks. Many of the remaining interviewees had made such unsatisfactory livelihoods in Ukraine that they had nothing to lose by moving to Poland. They had typically been deskilled in Ukraine before moving on to factory work in Poland. Sometimes they had taken a string of unsatisfactory jobs in different Polish cities before they found something tolerable in Kalisz, Piła or Płock, where they began to integrate in various domains. A few had already progressed to better jobs, and in a few cases to their 'dream job'.

An intersectional approach sheds light on the question of whether Ukrainians were likely to stay in Kalisz, Piła and Płock. Poland's immigration country identity will not be maintained if the new migrants decide to move on to Germany, Sweden and the UK. Chapter 10 suggested that construction workers in Poland without their families were particularly likely to move on, as were some of the university graduates and youngest interviewees. By contrast, middle-aged women seemed particularly likely to stay. The book also applied a critical livelihood strategy approach, trying to understand decision-making within family units, and not taking for granted that all family members shared the same assumptions. It emerged, for example, that some women were unhappy about being stuck in the smaller city, but were sacrificing their own interests for the sake of their children and husbands, typically skilled manual workers. The research also revealed cases of failed family reunification, where spouses or children had refused to join family members in Poland, or came to Poland only to return to Ukraine.

Chapter 12 presented vignettes of 17 migrants from other countries, whom I have labelled 'minority minorities'. As mentioned in Chapter 1, increasing ethnic diversity can also be a hallmark of migration transition, but it seemed that non-Ukrainians were represented only by single individuals or tiny groups, at least until Płock spectacularly transformed in 2023 into a city expecting thousands of construction workers from around the world. There were no 'communities' of non-Ukrainian foreigners in the three cities. However, an increasing range of nationalities was represented, as employers recruited factory workers from different countries – apparently partly from a perception that they would be more exploitable than Ukrainians – and as Poles working abroad married people from different countries and brought their spouses back to their cities of origin in Poland. Family networks also explained the presence of some economic migrants, for example a Bangladeshi informant who was recommended to come to Poland by his sister in the UK.

Some of the 17 were anchored in Kalisz, Piła and Płock by their family ties, and had made the same decision as Ukrainian parents that these were safe, convenient and attractive places to bring up children. Others seemed likely to move on. In general, their opinions of the cities were more mixed than those of many Ukrainians. They could often make a wider range of transnational comparisons, and the smaller city did not necessarily meet their aspirations. Black and Asian residents – both family and economic migrants – were conspicuous by their skin colour, which made them targets for some harassment and racist abuse. Factory workers from Latin America and Asia as well as some migrants employed in ethnic eateries were working such long hours that they had little time to form attachments to the cities. On the other hand, foreigners married to Poles knew more than most Ukrainians about local problems like pollution and deficiencies in the health service, and their attitudes to the cities were often more critical as a result.

Local Poles usually had no personal contacts with foreigners other than Ukrainians. There were some exceptions. The handful of international students – strikingly few in comparison to the numbers in Poland's bigger cities – mixed perforce with their Polish classmates. Spouses of local Poles had their extended families and sometimes also a circle of friends, although their stories often revealed that they did not feel well-integrated into local society in various respects, particularly because they tended to lack confidence in written Polish. Foreign factory workers could find themselves associating primarily with Ukrainians, not Poles, as in the case of the Venezuelan interviewee who was learning to speak Ukrainian. However, it seemed that often the Ukrainians and other workers did not mix: the Ukrainians were such a large group that they were self-sufficient and perhaps felt they had no particular reason to engage with other foreign workers.

When they reflected on whether Kalisz, Piła and Płock were already cities of immigration, local Poles always began to talk about Ukrainians. The Ukrainians overshadowed other foreigners in their perceptions, and white non-Ukrainian interviewees reported that Poles often assumed they were Ukrainians themselves. The Poles did not see Piła, Płock and Kalisz as cities of immigration in a broader sense. However, even Poles living in the biggest cities could be ignorant of how quickly Poland was acquiring an ethnically diverse population. Chapter 6 quoted Grzymała-Kazłowska's statement (2021: 250) that 'growing ethnic diversity … remains rather underestimated in Poland'. In 2019–22, many Poles seem to have been unaware of the scale of labour migration and the range of nationalities newly represented in Poland's cities. This was partly because the media seldom presented stories about non-Ukrainian labour migrants.

The arrival of millions of refugees from Ukraine in 2022 intensified impressions that migration to Poland was Ukrainian migration. Even the word 'foreigner', as in the newly opened 'Centres for Integrating Foreigners' in Kalisz and Piła, became shorthand for 'Ukrainian'. However, labour migration from elsewhere continued apace. In fact, the diminished pool of Ukrainian working-age men enhanced Polish employers' desire to source migrants from other countries. Their lack of visibility hitherto was highlighted when they suddenly emerged as a political issue in summer 2023, thrust into the limelight during the general election campaign and cash for visas scandal, coinciding with exposés about the gigantic 'migrant town' under construction outside Płock.

Although individual Ukrainians found their worlds turned upside down in February 2022, it is also possible – from the vantage point of 2024 – to observe the continuing relevance of some overall trends which had emerged over the previous few years. Just as the Covid-19 pandemic made visible and exacerbated already existing global phenomena, particularly social inequalities, so too the full-scale invasion of Ukraine highlighted and reinforced trends which had begun several years before. As illustrated in earlier chapters of this book, Ukrainian migration to Poland had been gathering pace since Russia's first invasion in 2014, and numerous interviewees mentioned in passing how the ongoing war in east Ukraine, whether directly or through economic instability, had influenced their lives and migration strategies. I never asked about the war in my interviews with labour migrants, but when I re-read the transcripts looking for mentions of war I noticed it in many contexts. Moreover, the trends which were a central focus of this book continued to be relevant after February 2022. A main argument of the book is that intensification of the trend towards family reunification led to more Ukrainian settlement outside the big cities in 2019–22. After the full-scale invasion, relatives previously based in Ukraine were gathered in by labour migrants already in Poland. For example, they drove to the Polish–Ukrainian border to collect their older parents, or sisters and their children who had previously seemed comfortably settled in Ukraine. Ukrainian chain migration helps explain why some refugees found themselves in smaller Polish cities in 2022. The warm Polish welcome to refugees from Ukraine can also be seen as an extension of earlier attitudes. I agree with Buchowski (2020) that Ukrainians were the familiar Significant Other, and less stigmatised than refugees from other countries. However, whereas many authors suggest that Ukrainians were favoured because of their perceived cultural closeness to Poles, *Polish Cities* shows that positivity towards Ukrainian refugees can also partly be explained by the fact that Poles already accepted Ukrainians as 'normal' labour migrants, people like themselves.

References

Abella, M. and Ducanes, G. (2014) 'Migration transition in Asia: revisiting theories in the light of recent evidence', in G. Battistella (ed.) *Global and Asian Perspectives on International Migration*. Cham: Springer, pp. 247–66.
Ager, A. and Strang, A. (2004) *Indicators of Integration: Final report*. London: Home Office.
Ager, A. and Strang, A. (2008) 'Understanding integration: a conceptual framework', *Journal of Refugee Studies*, 21(2): 166–91.
Alexander, M. (2003) 'Local policies toward migrants as an expression of host-stranger relations: a proposed typology', *Journal of Ethnic and Migration Studies*, 29(3): 411–30.
Allport, G. (1954) *The Nature of Prejudice*. Reading, Massachusetts: Addison-Wesley.
Amer, A. and Leung, M. (2023) 'Not-so-subtle subtleties: undocumented migrant (in)visibility, (im)mobility and Dutch public spaces as sites of embodied racialization', *Journal of Ethnic and Migration Studies*, 49(15): 3940–57.
Amin, A. (2006) 'The good city', *Urban Studies*, 43(5/6): 1009–23.
Anacka, M. Jaźwińska, E., Kaczmarczyk, P., Kopczyńska, J., Łukowski, W., Mostowska, M., Napierała, J., and Okólski, M. (2011) 'Etnosondażowe podejście do badania migracji jako procesu społecznego', in P. Kaczmarczyk (ed.) *Mobilność i migracje w dobie transformacji: wyzwania metodologiczne*. Warsaw: Scholar, pp. 68–154.
Anacka, M. and Okólski, M (2010) 'Direct demographic consequences of post-accession migration for Poland', in R. Black, G. Engbersen, M. Okólski and C. Panţîru (eds.) *A Continent Moving West? EU enlargement and labour migration from Central and Eastern Europe*. Amsterdam: Amsterdam University and IMISCOE, pp. 141–63.
Anderson, B. (2013) *Us and Them: The dangerous politics of immigration control*. Oxford: Oxford University Press.
Andrejuk, K. (2017a) *Przedsiębiorcy ukraińscy w Polsce. Struktura i sprawstwo w procesie osiedlenia*. Warsaw: Wydawnictwo IFiS PAN.
Andrejuk, K. (2017b) 'Self-employed migrants from EU member states in Poland: differentiated professional trajectories and explanations of entrepreneurial success', *Journal of Ethnic and Migration Studies*, 43(4): 560–77.
Andrejuk, K. (2019a) 'Strategizing integration in the labor market: Turkish immigrants in Poland and the new dimensions of south-to-north migration', *Polish Sociological Review*, 2(206): 157–76.
Andrejuk, K. (2019b) 'Ukrainian immigrants and entrepreneurship drain: towards a concept of governance-induced migration', *East European Politics and Societies*, 33(4): 899–916.
Anon (2021a) 'Członkowie niemieckiego towarzystwa społeczno-kulturalnego na stadionie powiatowym', 20 July. Available at: https://powiat.pila.pl/aktualnosci/4736,spotkanie-niemieckiego-towarzystwa-spoleczno-kulturalnego-na-stadionie-powiatowym (Accessed 25 May 2022).
Anon (2021b) 'Grupa Rozmówki Kaliskie zaprasza do wspólnego gotowania', *Calisia.pl*, 30 September. Available at: https://calisia.pl/grupa-rozmowki-kaliskie-zaprasza-do-wspolnego-gotowania,52894 (Accessed 4 July 2023).
Anon (2021c) 'Piła: Spotkanie Niemieckiego Towarzystwa Społeczno-Kulturalnego', *Nowiny Pilskie*, 9 December. Available at: https://nowinypilskie.pl/20211209448708/pila-spotkanie-niemieckiego-towarzystwa-spoleczno-kulturalnego1639014364 (Accessed 4 July 2023).
Anthias, F. (2012) 'Transnational mobilities, migration research and intersectionality', *Nordic Journal of Migration Research*, 2(2): 102–110.

Arango, J. (2012) 'Early starters and latecomers: comparing countries of immigration and immigration regimes in Europe', in M. Okólski, (ed.) *European Immigrations: Trends, structures and policy implications*. Amsterdam: Amsterdam University Press and IMISCOE, pp. 45–64.

AW (2016) 'Obcokrajowcy na kaliskim rynku pracy', *Fakty kaliskie*, 8 January. Available at: https://www.faktykaliskie.info/artykul/8244,obcokrajowcy-na-kaliskim-rynku-pracy (Accessed 17 August 2021).

Balogun, B. and Joseph-Salisbury, R. (2021) 'Black/white mixed-race experiences of race and racism in Poland', *Ethnic and Racial Studies*, 44(2): 234–51.

Bastia, T. (2014) 'Intersectionality, migration and development', *Progress in Development Studies*, 14(3): 237–48.

Baszczak, Ł., Kiełczewska, A., Kukołowicz, P., Wincewicz, A. and Zyzik, R. (2022) *Pomoc polskiego społeczeństwa dla uchodźców z Ukrainy*. Warsaw: Polski Instytut Ekonomiczny.

Bauere, V., Densham, P., Millar, J. and Salt, J. (2007) 'Migrants from Central and Eastern Europe: local geographies', *Population Trends*, 129: 7–19.

Bell, J. (2016) 'Migrants: keeping a foot in both worlds or losing the ground beneath them? Transnationalism and integration as experienced in the everyday lives of Polish migrants in Belfast, Northern Ireland', *Social Identities*, 22(1): 80–94.

Berriane, M., de Haas, H. and Natter, K. (2015) 'Introduction: revisiting Moroccan migrations', *The Journal of North African Studies*, 20(4): 503–521.

Bielecka-Prus, J. (2020) 'Obraz imigrantek z Ukrainy w polskim dyskursie prasowym', *Studia Migracyjne – Przegląd Polonijny*, 2(176): 177–200.

Bielewska, A. (2021) 'Game of labels: identification of highly skilled migrants', *Identities*, 28(5): 615–33.

Bielewska, A. (2023) 'Place relations of mobile people: national and local identification of highly skilled migrants in Wrocław, Poland', *Nationalities Papers*, 51(6): 1302–1318.

Bierwiaczonek, K. (2016) 'Miasto jako przestrzeń identyfikacji jego mieszkańców', *Górnośląskie Studia Socjologiczne. Seria Nowa*, 7: 102–16.

Blank, D. (2004) 'Fairytale cynicism in the "kingdom of plastic bags": the powerlessness of place in a Ukrainian border town', *Ethnography*, 5(3): 349–78.

Błaszczyk, M. and Pluta, J. (2015) 'Wprowadzenie', in M. Błaszczyk and J. Pluta (eds) *Uczestnicy, Konsumenci, Mieszkańcy: Wrocławianie i ich miasto w oglądzie socjologicznym*. Warsaw: Scholar.

Blum, A. and O. Malynovska (2023) 'Les migrations ukrainiennes, d'un système migratoire à l'autre', *Hommes et Migrations* 2023/2 (1341): 15–27.

Boccagni, P. (2022) 'Homing: a category for research on space appropriation and "home-oriented" mobilities', *Mobilities*, 17(4): 585–601.

Boyd, M. (1989) 'Family and personal networks in international migration', *International Migration Review*, 23(3): 638–70.

Bogardus, E. (1947) 'Measurement of personal-group relations', *Sociometry*, 10(4): 306–11.

Boguszewski, R. (2015) *Regionalne zróżnicowanie sympatii i antypatii do innych narodów*. Warsaw: CBOS.

Borkowski, M., Brzozowski, J., Vershinina, N. and Rodgers, P. (2021) 'Networks and migrant entrepreneurship: Ukrainian entrepreneurs in Poland', *Contemporary Issues in Entrepreneurship Research*, 13: 161–76.

Bożewicz, M. and Głowacki, A. (2020) *Praca obcokrajowców w Polsce*. Warsaw: CBOS.

Brubaker, R. (1998) 'Migrations of ethnic unmixing in the "New Europe"', *The International Migration Review*, 32(4): 1047–65.

Brubaker, R. (2004) *Ethnicity without Groups*. Cambridge, MA: Harvard University Press.

Brunarska, Z., Kindler, M., Szulecka, M. and Toruńczyk-Ruiz, S. (2016) 'Ukrainian migration to Poland: a "local" mobility?', in O. Fedyuk and M. Kindler (eds) *Ukrainian Migration to the European Union: lessons from migration studies*. Cham: Springer, pp. 115–132.

Brzozowska, A. (2015) *Dobór małżeński i integracja imigrantów w małżeństwach mieszanych – stan badań*. Warsaw CMR Working Paper No. 81/139.

Brzozowska, A. (2018) 'Społeczne zakotwiczenie w klasowo-etnicznych formach tożsamości a integracja polskich i ukraińskich migrantów', *Studia Migracyjne – Przegląd Polonijny*, 1(167): 69–99.

Brzozowska, A. and Postuła, A. (2022) 'Feel at Home. Vietnamese Immigrants in Poland', *Space and Culture*, 25 (1): 90–104.

Brzozowska, A. (2023) '"All is not yet lost here": the role of aspirations and capabilities in migration projects of Ukrainian migrants in Poland', *Journal of Ethnic and Migration Studies*, 49(9): 2373–90.

Buchowski, M. (2020) 'Distant vs. Familiar Significant Others: attitudes towards absent Muslim refugees and extant labor migrants in Poland', *Asian Journal of Peacebuilding*, 8(1): 73–91.

Bukowski, M. and Duszczyk, M. (eds) (2022) *Gościnna Polska 2022*. Warsaw: WISE Europa (also available in English as *Hospitable Poland*).

Bulat, A. (2019) '"High-skilled good, low-skilled bad?" British, Polish and Romanian attitudes towards low-skilled EU migration', *National Institute Economic Review*, 248 (1): R49–R57.

Burrell, K. (2011) 'Opportunity and uncertainty: young people's narratives of "double transition" in post-socialist Poland', *Area*, 43(4): 413–19.

Burzyńska, K. and Adamkowski, A. (2023) '10 pytań do prezesa Kaczyńskiego', *Gazeta Wyborcza*, 21 June. Available at: https://plock.wyborcza.pl/plock/7,35681,29886818,10-1-pytan-do-prezesa-kaczynskiego-czy-wie-pan-ze-w-miasteczku.html#S.embed_link-K.C-B.1-L.1.zw (Accessed 21 August 2023).

Bygnes, S. and Erdal, M. (2017) 'Liquid migration, grounded lives: considerations about future mobility and settlement among Polish and Spanish migrants in Norway', *Journal of Ethnic and Migration Studies*, 43(1): 102–18.

Carling, J. and Erdal, M. (2014) 'Return migration and transnationalism: how are the two connected?' *International Migration*, 52(6): 2–12.

Cassarino, J.-P. (2004) 'Theorising return migration: the conceptual approach to return migrants revisited', *International Journal on Multicultural Societies*, 6(2): 253–79.

Castles, S., de Haas, H. and Miller, M (5th ed.) (2014) *The Age of Migration: international population movements in the modern world*. Basingstoke: Palgrave Macmillan.

Cekiera, R., Kijonka, J. and Żak, M. (2022) *Emigracja jako doświadczenie. Studium na przykładzie migrantów powrotnych do województwa śląskiego*. Katowice: Uniwersytet Śląski.

Cena, E., Burns, S. and Wilson, P. (2021) 'Sense of belonging and the intercultural and academic experiences among international students at a university in Northern Ireland', *Journal of International Students*, 11(4): 812–31.

Cerase, F. (1974) 'Expectations and reality: a case study of return migration from the United States to southern Italy', *International Migration Review*, 8(2): 245–62.

Chugaievska, S. and Rusak, O. (2022) 'Labor migration of the rural population of Ukraine: statistical aspect', *Management Theory and Studies for Rural Business and Infrastructure Development*, 44(3): 385–36.

Churski, P., Kroczak, H., Łuczak, M., Shelest-Szumilas, O., and Woźniak, M.(2021) 'Adaptation strategies of migrant workers from Ukraine during the Covid-19 pandemic', *Sustainability*, 13(15), article 8337.

Cohen, J. and Sirkeci, I. (2011) *Cultures of Migration: the global nature of contemporary mobility*. Austin: University of Texas Press.

Connell, J. (2008) 'Niue: embracing a culture of migration', *Journal of Ethnic and Migration Studies*, 34(6): 1021–40.

Cylka, T. (2021) 'A może województwo środkowopolskie? "Żeby Kalisz nie był na marginesie"', *Gazeta Wyborcza*, 27 October. Available at: https://kalisz.wyborcza.pl/kalisz/7,181359,27730518,chca-wojewodztwa-srodkowopolskiego-bo-kalisz-jest-marginalizowany.html?_ga=2.111445252.1422303560.1635150118-1365677934.1526055562#S.DT-K.C-B.1-L.1.duzy (Accessed 27 October 2021).

Denis, M., Cysek-Pawlak, M., Krzysztofik, S. and Majewska, A. (2021) 'Sustainable and vibrant cities. Opportunities and threats to the development of Polish cities', *Cities*, 109: 1–9.

Długosz, P. (2018) 'Integracja ukraińskich studentów podejmujących naukę w Polsce', *Studia Migracyjne – Przegląd Polonijny*, 2: 67–92.

Długosz, P., Kryvachuk, L., and Izdebska-Długosz, D. (2022) *Problemy ukraińskich uchodźców przebywających w Polsce*. Kraków: Uniwersytet Pedagogiczny.

Dolińska, A. (2019a) 'Socio-economic costs of systemic transformation in Ukraine in the lens of the biographical experiences of Ukrainian female migrants to Poland', *Qualitative Sociology Review*, 15(4): 140–60.

Dolińska, A. (2019b) 'The gender-related lifestyle changes and choices of female white-collar migrants from Ukraine, Belarus and Russia in Poland', *Central and Eastern European Migration Review*, 8(2): 123–44.

Drbohlav, D. (2003) 'Immigration and the Czech Republic (with a special focus on the foreign labor force)', *The International Migration Review*, 37(1): 194–224.

Duszczyk, M. and Matuszczyk, K. (2018) 'The employment of foreigners in Poland and the labour market situation', *Central and Eastern European Migration Review,* 7(2): 53–68.

Duszczyk, M. and Matuszczyk, K (2022) 'Non-salary employment conditions as a factor shaping migration decision-making: an example of workers from Ukraine in Poland', *Migration Letters,* 19(6): 933–42.

Duszczyk, M. and Kaczmarczyk, P. (2022) 'The war in Ukraine and migration to Poland: outlook and challenges', *Intereconomics*, 57(3): 164–70.

Dzięglewski, M. (2020) *Coming Home to (Un)familiar Country: the strategies of returning migrants.* Basingstoke: Palgrave Macmillan.

Dziekońska, M. (2023) '"There is time to leave, and there is time to come back." Polish migrants' decisions about returning from international migration', *Journal of Ethnic and Migration Studies,* (online):1–17.

Eade, J., Drinkwater, S., and Garapich, M. P. (2007) 'Class and ethnicity – Polish migrants in London'. Guildford: Universities of Surrey and Roehampton.

Elrick, T. (2008) 'The influence of migration on origin communities: insights from Polish migrations to the West', *Europe-Asia Studies*, 60(9): 150–17.

ESA (2021) 'Rozmówki kaliskie, czyli zaproszenie na spotkanie w Parku Miejskim', *Kalisz Nasze Miasto*, 21 August. Available at: https://kalisz.naszemiasto.pl/rozmowki-kaliskie-czyli-zaproszenie-na-spotkanie-w-parku/ar/c1-8428075 (Accessed 4 July 2023).

European Commission (2022) *Annual Report on Intra-EU Labour Mobility 2021*. Brussels: European Commission.

Fassmann, H. and Reeger, U. (2012) '"Old" immigration countries in Europe: the concept and empirical examples', in M. Okólski(ed.) *European Immigrations: trends, structures and policy implications*. Amsterdam: Amsterdam University Press and IMISCOE, pp. 65–90.

Fazlagić, J., Romanowski, R., Sarrazin, H. , Przybył S. and Krajnik, M. (2021) *Diagnoza strategiczna miasta Kalisza*. Poznań: Metafor Sp.

Feischmidt, M., and Zakariás, I. (2020) 'How migration experience affects the acceptance and active support of refugees? Philanthropy and paid work of Hungarian migrants in the German immigrant service', *Journal of Immigrant and Refugee Studies*, 18(4): 481–97.

Fihel, A. and Kaczmarczyk, P. (2009) 'Migration: a threat or a chance? Recent migration of Poles and its impact on the Polish labour market', in K. Burrell (ed.) *Polish Migration to the UK in the 'New' European Union: after 2004*. Farnham: Ashgate.

Filipek, K. and Polkowska, D. (2020) 'The latent precariousness of migrant workers: a study of Ukrainians legally employed in Poland', *Journal of International Migration and Integration*, 21(1): 205–20.

Fonseca, M. and McGarrigle, J. (2012) *'Policy recommendations: promoting interethnic coexistence, social cohesion and reducing anti-immigrant attitudes'* Lisbon CEGm Migrare Working Paper No. 7.

Ford, R. (2011) 'Acceptable and unacceptable immigrants: how opposition to immigration in Britain is affected by migrants' region of origin', *Journal of Ethnic and Migration Studies*, 37(7): 1017–37.

Fox, J. (2003) 'National identities on the move: Transylvanian Hungarian labour migrants in Hungary', *Journal of Ethnic and Migration Studies*, 29(3): 449–66.

Franceschelli, M. (2022) 'Imagined mobilities and the materiality of migration: the search for "anchored lives" in post-recession Europe', *Journal of Ethnic and Migration Studies*, 48 (3): 773–89.

Friberg, J-H., and Midtbøen, A. (2018) 'Ethnicity as skill: immigrant employment hierarchies in Norwegian low-wage labour markets', *Journal of Ethnic and Migration Studies*, 44 (9): 1463–78.

Fundacja Nobiscum (2021) 'Płock w zasięgu ręki #6. Zabytki płockiego prawosławia'. Available at: https://www.youtube.com/watch?v=x2eeYPiXHyw, June 2021 (Accessed 13 July 2023).

Galasińska, A., and Kozłowska, O. (2009) 'Discourses of a "normal" life among post-accession migrants from Poland to Britain', in K. Burrell (ed.) *Polish Migration to the UK in the 'New' European Union: after 2004*. Farnham: Ashgate, pp. 87–105.

Garapich M. (2013) 'Polska kultura migracyjna po 2004 roku – między zmianą a tradycją', in M. Lesińska and M. Okólski (eds) *Współczesne polskie migracje: strategie – skutki społeczne – reakcja państwa*. Warsaw: Warsaw University Centre of Migration Research, pp. 17–34.

Garapich, M. (2016a) '"I don't want this town to change": resistance, bifocality and the infra-politics of social remittances', *Central and Eastern European Migration Review*, 5(2): 155–66.

Garapich, M. (2016b) *London's Polish Borders: transnationalizing class and identity among Polish Migrants in London*. Stuttgart: Ibidem.

Garapich, M. (2016c) 'Zaradni indywidualiści czy anomiczni egoiści? Stereotypy i autostereotypy polskich migrantów w Wielkiej Brytanii w ujęciu antropologicznym' *Studia Migracyjne – Przegląd Polonijny*, 2: 5–21.

Garapich, M. (2019) 'Migracje z Polski do Wielkiej Brytanii: geneza, stan dzisiejszy, wyzwania na przyszłość', *Studia BAS*, 4(60): 13–30.

Garapich, M., Grabowska, I., Jaźwińska, E. and White, A. (2023) 'Koniec fenomenu migracji poakcesyjnych?', in M. Lesińska and M. Okólski (eds), *30 wykładów o migracjach*. Warsaw: Scholar, pp. 277–92.

Gawlewicz, A. (2015) '"We inspire each other, subconsciously": the circulation of attitudes towards difference between Polish migrants in the UK and their significant others in the sending society', *Journal of Ethnic and Migration Studies*, 41(13): 2215–34.

Gerber, T. and Zavisca, J. (2020) 'Experiences in Russia of Kyrgyz and Ukrainian Labor Migrants: ethnic hierarchies, geopolitical remittances, and the relevance of migration theory', *Post-Soviet Affairs*, 36(1): 61–82.

Gill, N. (2010) 'Pathologies of migrant place-making: Polish migration to the UK', *Environment and Planning A*, 42: 1157–73.

Glick Schiller, N. and Çağlar, A. (2009) 'Towards a comparative theory of locality in migration studies: migrant incorporation and city scale', *Journal of Ethnic and Migration Studies*, 35(2): 177–202.

Glick Schiller, N. and Çağlar, A. (2016) 'Displacement, emplacement and migrant newcomers: rethinking urban sociabilities within multiscalar power', *Identities*, 23(1): 17–34.

Glynn I. (2011) 'Emigration memories and immigration realities in Ireland and Italy', in B. Fanning and R. Munck (eds), *Globalization, Migration and Social Transformation: Ireland in Europe and the world*. Farnham: Ashgate, pp. 65–77.

Gołębiowska, E. (2014) *The Many Faces of Tolerance: attitudes towards diversity in Poland*. London: Routledge.

Gońda, M. and Lesińska, M. (2022) 'Ewolucja Karty Polaka jako instrumentu polityki państwa'. Warsaw: Warsaw University Centre of Migration Research, Working Paper No. 129/187.

Gońda, M. (2016) 'Educational mobility as a means of return migration: young Polish diaspora members from the former USSR', *EthnoAnthropoZoom*, 15: 111–147.

Gońda, M. (2020) *Migracje do korzeni: wybory tożsamościowe Polaków ze Wschodu na studiach w kraju przodków*. Łódź: Wydawnictwo Uniwersytetu Łódzkiego.

Gońda, M. (2021) 'Waiting for immigration to come. The case of Lodz', *Studia Migracyjne – Przegląd Polonijny*, 3(181): 293–317.

Górny, A. (2017) 'All circular but different: variation in patterns of Ukraine-to-Poland migration', *Population, Space and Place*, 23(8): 1–10.

Górny, A. and Jaźwińska, E. (2019) 'Ukraińskie migrantki i migranci w aglomeracji Warszawskiej: cechy społeczno-demograficzne i relacje społeczne. Raport z badań'. Warsaw: Warsaw University Centre of Migration Research, Working Paper No. 115/173.

Górny, A. and Kaczmarczyk, P. (2021) 'Temporary farmworkers and migration transition: on a changing role of the agricultural sector in international labour migration to Poland', in K. O'Reilly and J. Rye (eds) *International Labour Migration to Europe's Rural Regions*. London: Routledge, pp. 86–103.

Górny, A. and Kaczmarczyk, P. (2023) 'Between Ukraine and Poland: Ukrainian migrants in Poland during the war', *Spotlight*. Warsaw: Warsaw University Centre of Migration Research.

Górny, A, Kaczmarczyk, P., Szulecka, M., Bitner, M., Okólski, M., Siedlecka, U. and Stefańczyk, A. (2018) *Imigranci w Polsce w kontekscie uproszczonej procedury zatrudniania cudzoziemców*. Warsaw: Wise Europa and Warsaw University Centre of Migration Research.

Górny, A. and Kindler, M. (2018) 'Cudzoziemcy w Polsce na przełomie XX i XXI wieku', in M. Lesińska and M. Okólski (eds), *25 wykładów o migracjach*. Warsaw: Scholar, pp. 221–34.

Górny, A., Kołodziejczyk, K., Madej, K. and Kaczmarczyk, P. (2019) 'Nowe obszary docelowe w migracji z Ukrainy do Polski. Przypadek Bydgoszczy i Wrocławia na tle innych miast'. Warsaw: Warsaw University Centre of Migration Research, Working Paper No. 118/176.

Górny, A., Porwit, K. and Madej, K. (2021) *Imigranci z Ukrainy w aglomeracji warszawskiej w czasie pandemii covid-19. Wyniki badania panelowego*. Warsaw: Warsaw University Centre of Migration Research.

Górny, A. and Śleszyński, P. (2019) 'Exploring the spatial concentration of foreign employment in Poland under the simplified procedure', *Geographia Polonica* 92(3): 331–45.

Grabowska, I. (2018) 'Social remittances: channels of diffusion', in A. White, I. Grabowska, P. Kaczmarczyk and K. Slany, *The Impact of Migration on Poland: EU mobility and social change*. London: UCL Press, pp. 68–89.

Grabowska, I. (2023) 'Societal dangers of migrant crisis narratives with a special focus on Belarussian and Ukrainian borders with Poland', *Frontiers in Sociology*. Migration and Society section, 8.

Grabowska, I. and Garapich, M. (2016) 'Social remittances and intra-EU mobility: non-financial transfers between U.K. and Poland', *Journal of Ethnic and Migration Studies*, 42(13): 2146–62.

Grabowska, I., Garapich, M., Jaźwińska, E. and Radziwinowiczówna, A. (2017) *Migrants as Agents of Change: social remittances in an enlarged European Union*. Basingstoke: Palgrave Macmillan.

Grabowska-Lusińska, I. and Okólski, M. (2009) *Emigracja ostatnia?* Warsaw: Scholar.

Granovetter, M. (1983) 'The strength of weak ties: a network theory revisited', *Sociological Theory*, 1: 201–233.

Grzymała-Kazłowska, A. (2016) 'Social anchoring: immigrant identity, security and integration reconnected?', *Sociology* 50(6): 1123–39.

Grzymała-Kazłowska, A. (2021) 'Attitudes to the new ethnic diversity in Poland: understanding contradictions and variations in a context of uncertainty and insecurity', *Polish Sociological Review*, 2(214): 241–60.

Grzymała-Kazłowska, A. and Brzozowska, A. (2017) 'From drifting to anchoring: capturing the experience of Ukrainian migrants in Poland', *Central and Eastern European Migration Review*, 6(2): 103–122.

Grzymała-Kazłowska, A. and Ryan, L. (2022) 'Bringing anchoring and embedding together: theorising migrants' lives overtime', *Comparative Migration Studies*, 10(46): 1–19.

GUS (Główny Urząd Statystyczny) *Rocznik Demograficzny 2021*. Warsaw: GUS.

GUS (Główny Urząd Statystyczny) *Rocznik Demograficzny 2022*. Warsaw: GUS.

Gustafson, P. (2001) 'Meanings of place: everyday experience and theoretical conceptualizations', *Journal of Environmental Psychology*, 21: 5–16.

Gwosdz, K., Sobala-Gwosdz, A., Górecki, J., Jarzębiński, M., Rotter-Jarzębińska, K. and Fiedeń, Ł. (2019) *Potencjał miast średnich w Polsce dla lokalizacji inwestycji BPO/SSC/IT/R&D. Analiza, ocena i rekomendacje*. Warsaw: Association of Business Service Leaders.

Hajduga, P. and Rogowska, M. (2020) 'Quality of life in the Polish urban centres. An attempt to evaluate large cities', *Baltic Journal of Economic Studies*, 6(4): 17–27.

Harris, C., Moran, D. and Bryson, J. (2012) 'EU accession migration: national insurance number allocations and the geographies of Polish labour migration to the UK', *Tijdschrift voor economische en sociale geografie*, 103(2): 209–221.

Herrmann, M. (2018) 'Wołyń 1943 – pamięć przywracana'. Warsaw: CBOS.

Hess, C. (2008) 'The contested terrain of the parallel society: the other natives in contemporary Greece and Germany', *Europe-Asia Studies*, 60(9): 1519–37.

Hirt, S. (2012) *Iron Curtains: gates, suburbs and privatization of space in the post-socialist city*. Chichester: Wiley-Blackwell.

Hoły-Łuczaj, M. (2022) 'Granice języka polskiego. Postawy wykładowców akademickich wobec kompetencji językowych studentów ukraińskich w kontekście migracji edukacyjnych do Polski', *Studia Migracyjne–Przegląd Polonijny*, 1(183): 157–180.

Homel, K., Jaroszewicz, M. and Lesińska, M. (2023) 'New permanent residents? Belarusians in Poland after 2020', *Spotlight*. Warsaw: Warsaw University Centre of Migration Research.

Hondagneu-Sotelo, P. (1994) *Gendered Transitions: Mexican experiences of immigration*. Berkeley: University of California Press.

Horolets, A. (2014) 'Finding one's way: recreational mobility of post-2004 Polish migrants in West Midlands, UK', *Leisure Studies*, 34(1): 5–18.

Horolets, A., Mica, S., Pawlak, M. and Kubicki, P. (2020) 'Ignorance as an outcome of categorizations: the "refugees" in the Polish academic discourse before and after the 2015 refugee crisis', *East European Politics and Societies*, 34(3): 730–51.

Horváth, I. (2008) 'The culture of migration of rural Romanian youth', *Journal of Ethnic and Migration Studies*, 34(5): 771–86.

Hrckova, J. and Zeller, M. (2021) 'The everyday abnormal and the quest for normalcy: how Polish equality marches build protester resilience', *Intersections*, 7(4): 104–23.

Iglicka, K. (2010) *Powroty Polaków po 2004 roku: w pętli pułapki migracji*. Warsaw: Scholar.

ILO (International Labour Organization) (2013) *Report on the Methodology, Organization and Results of a Modular Sample Survey on Labour Migration in Ukraine*. Geneva: ILO.

Incaltaurau, C. and Simionov, L. (2017) 'Is Eastern Europe following the same transition model as the South? A regional analysis of the main migration transition drivers', in A. Duarte and G. Pascariu (eds) *Core-Periphery Patterns across the European Union: case studies and lessons from Eastern and Southern Europe*. Bingley: Emerald, pp. 199–232.

Jakóbczyk-Gryszkiewicz, J. (2018) 'Czy imigracja jest szansą dla wyludniających się polskich miast? Wybrane rodzaje ruchów migracyjnych', *Przegląd Geograficzny*, 90(2): 291–308.

Jakóbczyk-Gryszkiewicz, J. (2020) 'Imigranci w polskich miastach: Przykład Pabianic w regionie łódzkim', *Konwersatorium Wiedzy o Mieście* 5(33): 71–80.

Jałowiecki, B. (2008) 'Gminy restrukturyzowane', in G. Gorzelak (ed.) *Polska lokalna 2007*. Warsaw: Scholar, pp. 85–106.

Janicki, W. (2015) *Migracje kompensacyjne jako czynnik wzrostu obszarów peryferyjnych. Rola ukrytego kapitału ludzkiego*. Lublin: UMCS Press.

Janská, E., Čermak, Z. and Wright, R. (2014) 'New immigrant destination in a new country of immigration: settlement patterns of non-natives in the Czech Republic', *Population Space and Place*, 20: 680–93.

Jarosz, S. and Klaus, W. (eds.) (2023) *Polska szkoła pomagania: Przyjęcie osób uchodźczych z Ukrainy w Polsce w 2022 roku*. Warsaw: KM, OBMF, CeBaM.

Jaskułowski, K. (2019) *The Everyday Politics of Migration Crisis in Poland: between nationalism, fear and empathy*. Basingstoke: Palgrave Macmillan.

Jaźwińska, E. and Grabowska, I. (2017) 'Efekty społecznych przekazów migracyjnych (social remittances) w polskich społecznościach lokalnych', *Studia Socjologiczne*, 1: 139–65.

Jirka, L. (2019) 'Nationality and rationality: ancestors, "diaspora" and the impact of ethnic policy in the country of emigration on ethnic return migration from western Ukraine to the Czech Republic', *Central and Eastern European Migration Review*, 8(1): 117–34.

Jivraj, D., Simpson, L. and Marquis, N. (2012) 'Local distribution and subsequent mobility of immigrants measured from the school census in England', *Environment and Planning A*, 44:491–505.

Johnson, K. (2020) 'International migration, development, and policy: reconsidering migration transition theory – a way forward', *Hatfield Graduate Journal of Public Affairs*, 4:1, Article 5 [no pagination].

Jones, D. (2013) 'Cosmopolitans and "cliques": everyday socialisation amongst Tamil student and young professional migrants to the UK', *Ethnicities*, 13 (4): 420-37.

Józefiak, B. (2021) 'Powiedz panu Hienowi, że w Polsce już nic nie ma, zimą można umrzeć. Wietnamczycy na polskim szlaku', oko.press, 26 December. Available at: https://oko.press/wi etnamczycy-na-polskim-szlaku (Accessed 10 March 2023).

Józefiak, B. and Wójcik, M. (2022) 'Skrzywdzeni robotnicy z Ameryki Łacińskiej. Lázaro z Gwatemali: Gdybym wiedział, co mnie czeka, w życiu bym do Polski nie pojechał', *Gazeta Wyborcza*, 25.11.22.

Jóźwiak, I. and Piechowska, M. (2017) '*Crisis-driven mobility between Ukraine and Poland. what does the available data (not) tell us*'. Warsaw: Warsaw University Centre of Migration Research, Working Paper No. 99/157.

Kaczmarczyk, P. (2018) 'Post-accession migration and the Polish labour market: expected and unexpected effects', in A. White, I. Grabowska, P. Kaczmarczyk and K. Slany, *The Impact of Migration on Poland: EU mobility and social change*. London: UCL Press, pp. 90–107.

Kaltenbrunner, M. (2018) 'The globally connected western Ukrainian village', *European Review of History: Revue européenne d'histoire*, 25(6): 885–908.

Kałuża-Kopias, D. (2023) 'The spatial distribution of economic immigrants from Ukraine and Belarus and the socio-economic development of Polish counties', *Studia Migracyjne – Przegląd Polonijny*, 1(187): 163–86.

Kandel, W. and Massey, D. (2002) 'The culture of Mexican migration: a theoretical and empirical analysis', *Social Forces* 80(3): 981–1004.

Kardaszewicz, K. (2018) '*Migrant ties and integration – a case of Chinese community in Poland*'. Warsaw: Warsaw University Centre of Migration Research, Working Paper No. 106/164.

Karolak, M. (2016) 'From potential to actual social remittances? Exploring how Polish return migrants cope with difficult employment conditions', *Central and Eastern European Migration Review*, 5(2): 21–39.

Karolak, M. (2020) 'Returning for (dis)integration in the labour market? The careers of labour migrants returning to Poland from the United Kingdom', in S. Hinger and R. Schweitzer (eds), *Politics of (Dis)Integration*. Cham: Springer, pp. 101–20.

Kędzierski, M. and Musiałek, P. (2018) 'Słowo wstępne', in P. Śleszyński, *Polska średnich miast. Założenia i koncepcja deglomeracji w Polsce*. Warsaw: Klub Jagielloński, pp. 10–12.

Kijonka, J. and Żak, M. (2020) 'Polish return migrants. Analysis of selected decision-making processes', *Studia Migracyjne – Przegląd Polonijny*, 4(178): 115–136.

Kindler, M. (2021) 'Networking in contexts: qualitative social network analysis insights into migration processes', *Global Networks*, 21(3): 513–528.

Kindler, M. and Szulecka, M. (2022) 'Messy arrangements? A social networks perspective on migrant labor brokerage: the case of Ukrainian migration to Poland', *Polish Sociological Review*, 220: 457–84.

Kindler, M. and Wójcikowska-Baniak, K. (2019) '(Missing) bridging ties and social capital? The creation and reproduction of migrants' social network advantages: the case of Ukrainian migrants in Poland', *Central and Eastern European Migration Review*, 8(1): 95–116.

King, R. (2000) 'Generalizations from the history of return migration', in B. Ghosh (ed) *Return Migration: Journey of hope or despair?* Geneva: International Organisation for Migration and United Nations, pp. 7–55.

King, R., Fielding, A. and Black, R. (1997) 'The international migration turnaround in southern Europe', in R. King and R. Black (eds) *Southern Europe and the New Immigrations*. Brighton: Sussex Academic Press, pp. 1–25.

King, R. and Gëdeshi, I. (2022) 'New trends in potential migration from Albania: the migration transition postponed?', *Migration and Development*, 9(2): 131–51.

King R. and Skeldon, R. (2010) 'Mind the gap!' Integrating approaches to internal and international migration', *Journal of Ethnic and Migration Studies*, 36(10): 1619–46.

Kisiała, W. (2017) 'Wpływ utraty statusu ośrodka wojewódzkiego na rozwój miast. The influence of the loss of the state of a provincial capital on the development of cities', *Prace Naukowe Uniwersytetu Ekonomicznego We Wrocławiu, Research Paper of Wrocław University of Economics*, 477:117–26.

Klaus, W. (2020) 'Between closing borders to refugees and welcoming Ukrainian workers: Polish migration law at the crossroads', in E. Goździak, I. Main and B. Suter (eds) *Europe and the Refugee Response: a crisis of values?* London: Routledge, pp. 74–90.

Kohlbacher, J., Reeger, U. and Schnell, P. (2015) 'Place attachment and social ties – migrants and natives in three urban settings in Vienna', *Population, Space and Place*, 21: 446–62.

Kolańczuk, A. (2006) 'Uchodźcy i ich życie w Kaliszu w latach 1920–39', in K. Walczak and E. Andrysiak (eds) *Mniejszości narodowe i religijne w dziejach Kalisza i Ziemi Kaliskiej*. Kalisz: Kaliskie Towarzystwo Przyjaciół Nauki, pp. 80–101.

Kolasa-Nowak, A. and Bucholc, M. (2023) 'Historical sociology in Poland: transformations of the uses of the past', *East European Politics and Societies*, 37(1): 3–29.

Koleva, D. (2013) 'Rural, urban and rurban: everyday perceptions and practices', in G. Duijzings (ed.), *Global Villages: rural and urban transformations in contemporary Bulgaria*. London: Anthem Press, pp. 137–52.

Konieczna-Sałamatin, J. (2015) 'Polacy i Ukraińcy – wzajemne postrzeganie w trudnych czasach', in T. Horbowski and P. Kosiewski (eds), *Polityka bezpieczeństwa. Polska. Ukraina*. Warsaw: Fundacja im. Stefana Batorego, pp. 137–153.

Koppel, K. and Jakobson, M.-L. (2023) 'Who is the worst migrant? Migrant hierarchies in populist radical-right rhetoric in Estonia', in M.-L. Jakobson, R. King, L. Moroşanu and R. Vetik (eds) *Anxieties of Migration and Integration in Turbulent Times*. Cham: Springer, pp. 225–41.

Kordasiewicz, A., Radziwinowiczówna, A. and Kloc-Nowak, W. (2018) 'Ethnomoralities of care in transnational families: care intentions as a missing link between norms and arrangements', *Family Studies*, 24(1): 76–93.

Kotowska-Rasiak, E. (2021) 'Kalisz: modlitwa za uchodźców w katedrze', *eKai*, 26 September. Available at: https://www.ekai.pl/kalisz-modlitwa-za-uchodzcow-w-katedrze-d607236/ (Accessed 25 November 2021).

Kowalczyk, G. (2023) 'Tak afera wizowa już niszczy gospodarkę. Biznes alarmuje o potężnych problemach', *Business Insider*, 27 September. Available at: https://businessinsider.com.pl/gospodarka/afera-wizowa-juz-niszczy-gospodarke-biznes-alarmuje-o-poteznych-problemach/zhcmynv (Accessed 29 September 2023).

Kozminska, K. and Hua, Zh. (2021) 'The promise and resilience of multilingualism: language ideologies and practices of Polish-speaking migrants in the UK post the Brexit vote', *Journal of Multilingual and Multicultural Development*, 42(5): 444–61.

Krakhmalova, K. and Kloc-Nowak, W. (2023) '(Lack of) the space to choose? Post-February 24, 2022 decisions of the forced migrants from Ukraine in Poland in relation to their family life'. KBnM conference *Migracje w obliczu wielkich zmian społecznych – wyzwania dla teorii i praktyki*. Białystok, 20-22 September.

Krings, T., Moriarty, E., Wickham, J., Bobek. A. and Salamońska, J. (2013) *New Mobilities in Europe: Polish migration to Ireland post-2004*. Manchester: Manchester University Press.

Kruk, M. (2020) 'Dlaczego studenci z zagranicy wybierają Lublin? Opinie młodzieży z krajów Partnerstwa Wschodniego o studiach w Lublinie', *Studia Migracyjne – Przegląd Polonijny*, 1(175): 143–60.

Krzaklewska, E. (2019) 'Youth, mobility and generations – the meanings and impact of migration and mobility experiences on transitions to adulthood,' *Studia Migracyjne – Przegląd Polonijny*, 1(171): 41–59.

Kubiciel-Lodzińska, S. and Ruszczak, B. (2016) 'The determinants of student migration to Poland based on the Opolskie Voivodeship study', *International Migration*, 54(5): 163–74.

Kulcsár, L. and Brădățan, C. (2014) 'The greying periphery: ageing and community development in rural Romania and Bulgaria', *Europe-Asia Studies,* 66(5): 794–810.

Kurniewicz, A., Swianiewicz, P. and Łukomska, J. (2023) 'Wpływ statusu stolicy wojewódzkiej na rozwój miast – przypadek reform w latach 1975 i 1999 w Polsce', *Studia Regionalne i Lokalne*, (91): 23–42.

Kurzajczyk, M. (2021) 'Ukraińcy w Kaliszu. W 1921 roku zaczęła się tworzyć kaliska wspólnota ukraińska', *Kalisz Nasze Miasto*, 17 May. Available at: https://kalisz.naszemiasto.pl/ukraincy-w-kaliszu-w-1921-roku-zaczela-sie-tworzyc-kaliska/ar/c7-8259048 (Accessed 3 July 2023).

Kuschminder, K. (2022) 'Reintegration strategies', in R. King and K. Kuschminder (eds), *Handbook of Return Migration*. London: Elgar, pp. 200–11.

Kwaśny, J. (2020) *Sytuacja byłych miast wojewódzkich 20 lat po reformie powiatowej*. Kraków: Uniwersytet Ekonomiczny w Krakowie and MSAP.

Kyliushyk, I. and Jastrzębowska, A. (2023) 'Aid attitudes in short- and long-term perspectives among Ukrainian migrants and Poles during the Russian war in 2022', *Frontiers of Sociology*, 8, 'Migration and Society': 1–8.

Łachowski, W. and Łęczek, A. (2020) 'Tereny zielone w dużych miastach Polski. Analiza z wykorzystaniem Sentinel 2', *Urban Development Issues*, 68(1): 77–90.

Łakomski, M. (2010) *Płock na emigracji*. Płock: ViaArtCity.

Leiber, S., Matuszczyk, K. and Rossow, V. (2019) 'Private labor market intermediaries in the europeanized live-in care market between Germany and Poland: a typology', *Zeitschrift für Sozialreform* 65(3): 365–92.

Lehmann, A. (2021) 'Największy wyrzut sumienia Kalisza. Historia rodziny Fibigerów zamknięta w fortepianach', *Gazeta Wyborcza Kalisz*, 27 October. Available at: https://kalisz.wyborcza.pl/kalisz/7,181359,27730625,historia-rodziny-fibigerow-zamknieta-w-fortepianach-o-jedynej.html (Accessed 28 October 2021).

Levchuk, P. (2021) 'Ukrainian language in Polish public space', *Cognitive Studies | Études cognitives* (21), Article 2476: 1–12.

Levitt P. (1998) 'Social remittances: migration driven local-level forms of cultural diffusion', *International Migration Review,* 32(4): 926–48.

Lewicka, M. (2011) 'Place attachment: how far have we come in the last 40 years?', *Journal of Environmental Psychology*, 31(3): 207–30.

Lewis, P. (1989) *Political Authority and Party Secretaries in Poland, 1975-1986*. Cambridge: Cambridge University Press.

Libanova, E. (2019) 'Labour migration from Ukraine: key features, drivers and impact', *Economics and Sociology*, 12(1): 313–28.

Lynnebakke, B. (2021) '"I felt like the mountains were coming for me." The role of place attachment and local lifestyle opportunities for labour migrants' staying aspirations in two Norwegian rural municipalities', *Migration Studies*, 9(3): 759–82.

Main, I. (2020) 'Proclaiming and practicing pro-immigration values in Poland', in E. Goździak, I. Main and B. Suter (eds) *Europe and the Refugee Response: a crisis of values?* London: Routledge, pp. 269–85.

Marszałkowski, M. (2018) 'Konferencja pn. "Imigracja - co o niej wiemy?"', 14 May. Available at: https://www.powiat.kalisz.pl/art,1381,konferencja-pn-imigracja-co-o-niej-wiemy (Accessed 25 November 2021).

Maksimovtsova, K. (2022) '"One nation – one language". The ambiguity of the state language policy and policy towards minorities in contemporary Latvia and Ukraine', *European Yearbook of Minority Issues*, 19(1): 239–67.

Massey, D., Arango, J., Hugo, G., Kouaouci, A., Pellegrino, A. and Taylor, J. (1993) 'Theories of international migration: a review and appraisal', *Population and Development Review*, 19(3): 431–66.

Massey, D. M. and Espinosa, K. (1997) 'What's driving Mexico-U.S. migration? A theoretical, empirical, and policy analysis', *The American Journal of Sociology*, 102(4): 939–99.

Matusz, P. and Pawłak, M. (2020) 'Multi-level governance of integration policy. Role of the cities. Comparison of Warsaw and Prague', *Przegląd Politologiczny*, 25(4): 23–41.

Mayblin, L., Valentine, G. and Winarska, A. (2016) 'Migration and diversity in a postsocialist context: creating integrative encounters in Poland,' *Environment and Planning A: Economy and Space*, 4(5): 960–78.

McAreavey, R. and Argent, N. (2018) 'Migrant integration in rural New Immigration Destinations: an institutional and triangular perspective', *Journal of Rural Studies*, 64: 267–75.

McCall, L. (2005) 'The complexity of intersectionality', *Signs: Journal of Women in Culture and Society*, 30(3): 1771–1800.

Miklas, A. (2021) 'Kaliszanie dla uchodźców na polsko - białoruskiej granicy', *Fakty Kaliskie*, 13 October. Available at: https://www.faktykaliskie.info/artykul/40279,kaliszanie-dla-uchodzc ow-na-polsko-bialoruskiej-granicy-zdjecia (Accessed 29 February 2024).

MN (2018) 'Ukraińcy marzą o zachodzie – w sadach zrobi się pusto?!', *Piła Nasze Miasto*, 14 December. Available at: https://pila.naszemiasto.pl/ukraincy-marza-o-zachodzie-w-sadach -zrobi-sie-pusto/ar/c10-4919212 (Accessed 4 July 2023).

MS (2021) 'Bezrobocie wzrosło. Tak na przestrzeni lat zmieniał się rynek pracy', *Fakty Kaliskie*, 16 August. Available at: https://www.faktykaliskie.info/artykul/39452,bezrobocie-wzroslo-tak-na-przestrzeni-lat-zmienial-sie-rynek-pracy (Accessed 17 August 2021).

Morawska, E. (2001) 'Structuring migration: the case of Polish income-seeking travelers to the West', *Theory and Society*, 30(1): 47–80.

Mulholland, J. and Ryan, L. (2022) 'Advancing the embedding framework: using longitudinal methods to revisit French highly skilled migrants in the context of Brexit', *Journal of Ethnic and Migration Studies*, 49(3): 601–17.

Musiyezdov, O. (2019) 'Ukrainian emigration in Poland: from "earners" to highly qualified specialists', *Ukrainskyy sotsiologichnyy zhurnal*, 21: 37–49.

Niskiewicz, A. (2017) *Niemieckie Towarzystwo Społeczno-Kulturalne w Pile 1992-2017*. Piła: NTSK.

Nowicka, M. (2019) '"I don't mean to sound racist but ..." Transforming racism in transnational Europe', *Ethnic and Racial Studies*, 41(5): 824–41.

Nowosielski, M., Głowala, A., Grażul-Luft, A., Zdanowicz-Kucharczyk, K., Zgorzelska, A., Slowik, J., Šafránková, D. and Zachová, M. (2021) *Edukacja elementarna uczniów z doświadczeniem migracji w Polsce i Czechach. Doświadczenia – Wnioski – Rekomendacje – Zasoby*. Płock: Wydawnictwo naukowe Mazowieckiej Uczelni Publicznej w Płocku.

Ociepa-Kicińska, E. and Gorzałczyńska-Koczkodaj, M. (2022) 'Forms of aid provided to refugees of the 2022 Russia–Ukraine war: the case of Poland', *International Journal of Environmental Research and Public Health*, 19(12), 7085–8001.

OECD (2020) *OECD Regions and Cities at a Glance: country note Poland*. Paris: OECD Publishing.

Okólski, M. (2001) 'Incomplete migration: a new form of mobility in Central and Eastern Europe. The case of Polish and Ukrainian migrants', in C. Wallace and D. Stola (eds), *Patterns of Migration in Central Europe*. London: Palgrave Macmillan, pp. 105–28.

Okólski, M. (2012) 'Transition from emigration to immigration. Is it the destiny of modern European countries?', in M. Okólski (ed.), *European Immigrations: trends, structures and policy implications*. Amsterdam: Amsterdam University Press, pp. 7–22.

Okólski, M. (2021) 'The migration transition in Poland', *Central and Eastern European Migration Review*, 10(2): 51–69.

Okólski, M. and Salt, J. (2014) 'Polish emigration to the UK after 2004: why did so many come?' *Central and Eastern European Migration Review*, 3(2): 11–38.

Omyła-Rudzka, M. (2022) 'Jak Polacy chcieliby mieszkać?'. Warsaw: CBOS.

Omyła-Rudzka, M. (2023) 'Stosunek do innych narodów rok po wybuchu wojny na Ukrainie'. Warsaw: CBOS.

Pacewicz, P. (2023) 'Gdzie jest milion uchodźców z Ukrainy? W danych SG widać też lęk przed rocznicą 24 lutego', *Oko.press*, 28 February. Available at: https://oko.press/ilu-jest-uchodzcow-z-ukrainy (Accessed 23 February 2024).

Parreñas, R. (2008) *The Force of Domesticity: Filipina migrants and globalization*. New York: New York University Press.

Parutis, V. (2014) '"Economic Migrants" or "Middling Transnationals"? East European migrants' experiences of work in the UK', *International Migration*, 52(1): 36–55.

Pędziwiatr, K., Brzozowski, J. and Nahorniuk, O. (2022) 'Refugees from Ukraine in Kraków'. Kraków: Cracow University of Economics and Multiculturalism and Migration Observatory (MMO).

Pełczyński, G. and Pomieciński, A. (2021) *Mały słownik mniejszości narodowych w Polsce*. Toruń: Oficyjna Wydawnicza Kucharski; Wrocław: Uniwersytet Wrocławski; and Poznań: Uniwersytet im. Adama Mickiewicza w Poznaniu.

Phillips, D. and Robinson, D. (2015) 'Reflections on migration, community, and place', *Population, Space and Place*, 21, 409–20.

Pieczyńska-Chamczyk, M. (2022) 'Już na drugi dzień po wybuchu wojny założyły grupę pomocową. "Pilanie Ukrainie" - tu się dzieją cuda'.' *Piła Nasze Miasto*, 12 April. Available at: https://pila.naszemiasto.pl/juz-na-drugi-dzien-po-wybuchu-wojny-zalozyly-grupe-pomocowa/ar/c1-8769693 (Accessed 27 October 2023).

Piore, M. (1979) *Birds of Passage: migrant labor and industrial societies*. Cambridge: Cambridge University Press.

Platts-Fowler, D. and Robinson, D. (2015) 'A place for integration: refugee experiences in two English cities', *Population, Space and Place*, 21: 476–91.

Prawdzic, I. (2021) 'Dwujęzyczność polsko-niemiecka w powiecie pilskim, czarnkowsko-trzcianeckim i złotowskim: zarządzanie językiem w trzech pokoleniach na podstawie reprezentatywnych biografii językowych', *Acta Baltico-Slavica*, 45(2550): 1–17.

Przygodzki, S. (no date) *Szlakiem wielokulturowego Kalisza*. Kalisz: Miasto Kalisz.

Pszczółkowska, D. (2024) *How Migrants Choose Their Destinations: factors influencing post-EU accession choices and decisions to remain*. London: Routledge.

Robinson, D. (2010) 'The neighbourhood effects of new immigration', *Environment and Planning A*, 42, 2451–66.

Rokitowska-Malcher, J. (2021) *Czynniki ekonomiczne i pozaekonomiczne poakcesyjnych remigracji Polaków ze szczególnym uwzględnieniem województwa dolnośląskiego*. Wrocław: Wydawnictwa Uniwersytetu Ekonomicznego we Wrocławiu.

Roszkowska, M. (2018) 'Do ciężkiej pracy w Polsce? Sprowadzimy niewolników z Nepalu', *Gazeta Wyborcza*, 1 October. Available at: https://wyborcza.pl/duzyformat/7,127290,23973472,do-ciezkiej-pracy-w-polsce-sprowadzimy-niewolnikow-z-nepalu.html (Accessed 1 June 2023)

Runge, A. (2012) 'Metodologiczne problemy badania miast średnich w Polsce', *Prace Geograficzne*, 129: 83–101.

Ryan L. (2010) 'Becoming Polish in London: negotiating ethnicity through migration', *Social Identities*, 16(3): 359–76.

Ryan, L. (2016) 'Looking for weak ties: using a mixed methods approach to capture elusive connections', *The Sociological Review*, 64(4): 951–69.

Ryan, L. (2023) *Social Networks and Migration: relocations, relationships and resources*. Bristol: Bristol University Press.

Ryan, L., Sales, R., Tilki, M. and Siara, B. (2008) 'Social networks, social support and social capital: the experiences of recent Polish migrants in London', *Sociology*, 42(4): 672–90.

Rzepnikowska, A. (2019) *Convivial Cultures in Multicultural Cities: Polish migrant women in Manchester and Barcelona*. London: Routledge.

Scannell, L. and Gifford, R. (2010) 'Defining place attachment: a tripartite organizing framework', *Journal of Environmental Psychology*, 30(1): 1–10.

Scovil, J. (2023) 'Polacy wobec wojny na Ukrainie i ukraińskich uchodźców'. Warsaw: CBOS.

Sheller, M. and Urry, J. (2006) 'The new mobilities paradigm', *Environment and Planning A: Economy and Space*, 38(2): 207–26.

Skalnicka-Kirpsza, P. (2021) 'Wyborcza.pl od dziś gra także w Kaliszu. Dosłownie! Zapraszamy na spotkanie i koncert', *Gazeta Wyborcza*, 27 October. Available at: https://kalisz.wyborcza.pl/kalisz/7,181359,27731269,wyborcza-pl-od-dzis-gra-takze-w-kaliszu-i-to-doslownie.html (Accessed 28 October 2021)

Słabig, A. (2013) 'Pozostać czy wyemigrować? Autochtoni i Ukraińcy w województwie pilskim w latach 1975–1989 w dokumentach służby bezpieczeństwa', *Zapiski Historyczne*, 78(2): 59–97.

Śleszyński, P. (2018) *Polska średnich miast. Założenia i koncepcja deglomeracji w Polsce*. Warsaw: Klub Jagielloński.

Ślęzak, E. and Bielewska, A. (2022) 'Cities' migration policies in a country with a deficit of migration policy: the case of Poland', *International Migration*, 60(3): 173–87.

Smith, J. (2017) 'Introduction: putting place back in place attachment research', in J. Smith, *Explorations in Place Attachment*. London: Routledge, pp.1–16.

Sobolak, J. (2022) 'Obywatele Sri Lanki na polskich budowach? Branża próbuje wypełnić wakaty', *Gazeta Wyborcza*, 12 July. Available at: https://wyborcza.biz/biznes/7,147758,28661095,obywatele-sri-lanki-na-polskich-budowach-branza-probuje-wypelnic.html?disableRedirects=true (Accessed 1 June 2023)

Solari, C. (2017) *On the Shoulders of Grandmothers: gender, migration, and post-Soviet nation-state building*. New York and London: Routledge.

Sorge, A. (2021) 'Anxiety, ambivalence, and the violence of expectations: migrant reception and resettlement in Sicily', *Anthropological Forum*, 31(3): 256–74.

Spetany, M. (2021) 'Bezrobocie wzrosło. Tak na przestrzeni lat zmieniał się rynek pracy', *Fakty kaliskie*, 16 August. Available at: https://www.faktykaliskie.info/artykul/39452,bezrobocie-wzroslo-tak-na-przestrzeni-lat-zmienial-sie-rynek-pracy (Accessed 20 October 2023).

Springer, F. (2016) *Miasto Archipelag. Polska mniejszych miast*. Kraków: Karakter.

Sribniak, I. (2019) 'Kalisz – centrum życia społeczno-politycznego ukraińskich kombatantów w Polsce (w pierwszej połowie lat 20.): na podstawie nowo odkrytych materiałów z polskich i ukraińskich archiwów', in I. Matiasz (ed.), *Ukraina i Polska: drogi relacji międzypaństwowych*. Kyiv: Instytut Polski, pp. 106–24.

Stevenson, P. (2006) '"National" languages in transnational contexts: language, migration and citizenship in Europe', in C. Mar-Molinero et al. (eds), *Language Ideologies, Policies and Practices*. Basingstoke: Palgrave Macmillan, pp. 147–61.

Syska, M. (2019) 'Polska średnich miast' Available at: https://www.youtube.com/watch?v=WYkJ016htqI, (Accessed 23 March 2024).

Szymaniak, M. (2021) *Zapaść. Reportaże z mniejszych miast* (Wołowiec: Czarne).

Szaban, D. and Michalak, P. (2020) 'When Ukrainian migrant meets a Polish official. Implementing migration policy in the opinions of temporary economic migrants from Ukraine in Poland in a neo-institutional perspective', *Przegląd Narodowościowy – Review of Nationalities*, 10: 181–95.

Szczech-Pietkiewicz, E. (2017) 'Competitiveness of cities and their regions in Poland – changes in the light of the growth pole concept' in G. Pascariu and M. Duarte (eds) *Core-Periphery Patterns across the European Union: Case studies and lessons from Eastern and Southern Europe*. Bingley: Emerald Publishing, pp. 233–47.

Szewczyk, A. (2015) '"European generation of migration": change and agency in the post-2004 Polish graduates' migratory experience', *Geoforum*, 60: 153–62.

Szmytkowska, M. (2017) *Kreacje współczesnego miasta. Uwarunkowania i trajektorie rozwojowe polskich miast średnich*. Gdańsk: Wydawnictwo Uniwersytetu Gdańskiego.

Szukalski, P. (2020) 'Małżeństwa polsko-ukraińskie zawierane w Polsce: przyczynek do badania integracji imigrantów ukraińskich z ostatnich lat', *Polityka Społeczna*, 8: 28–36.

Szkwarek, W. (2023a) '"Nikomu nie zabronię się bać". Inwestycja Orlenu dzieli lokalną społeczność', *Money.pl*, 24 May. Available at: https://www.money.pl/gospodarka/nikomu-nie-zabronie-sie-bac-inwestycja-orlenu-dzieli-lokalna-spolecznosc-6899414802283424a.html. (Accessed 12 October 2023)

Szkwarek, W. (2023b) 'Miasteczko pracownicze w Płocku gotowe. Tak wygląda', *Money.pl*,17 June. Available at: https://www.money.pl/gospodarka/miasteczko-pracownicze-w-plocku-otwarte-zamieszka-tam-6-tys-obcokrajowcow-6909988835482176a.html (Accessed 12 October 2023).

Szymańska-Matusiewicz, G. (2017) 'Remaking the state or creating civil society? Vietnamese migrant associations in Poland', *Journal of Vietnamese Studies*, 12(1): 42–72.

Tabaka, A. and Błachowicz, M. (2010) *Nowy Kaliszanin*. Kalisz: Miejska Biblioteka Publiczna.

Trąbka, A. (2019) 'From functional bonds to place identity: place attachment of Polish migrants living in London and Oslo', *Journal of Environmental Psychology,* 62: 67–73.

Trąbka, A., Klimavičiūtė, L., Czeranowska, O., Jonavičienė, D., Grabowska, I. and Wermińska-Wiśnicka, I. (2022) 'Your heart is where your roots are? Place attachment and belonging among Polish and Lithuanian returnees', *Comparative Migration Studies*, 10(1): 1–16.

Trevena, P. (2013) 'Why do highly educated migrants go for low-skilled jobs? A case study of Polish graduates working in London', in B. Glorius, I. Grabowska-Lusińska and A. Kuvik (eds), *Mobility in Transition: Migration Patterns after EU Enlargement*. Amsterdam: Amsterdam University Press, pp. 169–90.

Trevena, P., McGhee, D. and Heath, S. (2013) 'Location, location? A critical examination of patterns and determinants of internal mobility among post-accession Polish migrants in the UK', *Population, Space and Place,* 19(6): 671–87.

UdSC (Urząd do Spraw Cudzoziemców) (2021) *Obywatele Ukrainy w Polsce – raport*, 14 December. Available at: https://www.gov.pl/web/udsc/obywatele-ukrainy-w-polsce--raport (Accessed 6 March 2023).

UdSC (2022) 'Ochrona międzynarodowa w 2021 r.', 12 January. Available at: https://www.gov.pl/web/udsc/ochrona-miedzynarodowa-w-2021-r (Accessed 22 October 2023).

UdSC (2023) *Raport na temat obywateli Ukrainy* (wg stanu na dzień 1 styczeń 2023 r.) https://www.gov.pl/web/udsc/sytuacja-dotyczaca-ukrainy (Accessed 6 March 2023).

UNHCR (2022) *Lives on Hold: profiles and intentions of refugees from Ukraine*. UNHCR Regional Bureau for Europe.

Urbańska, S. (2009) 'Transnarodowość jako perspektywa ujęcia macierzyństwa w warunkach migracji', in K. Slany (ed.), *Migracje kobiet: Perspektywa wielowymiarowa*. Kraków: Uniwersytet Jagielloński.

USwP (Urząd Statystyczny w Poznaniu) (2020) 'Miasto Kalisz' (series Statystyczny Vademecum Samorządowca). Pdf no longer accessible online.

USwP (Urząd Statystyczny w Poznaniu) (2022) 'Cudzoziemcy na wielkopolskim rynku pracy w 2021 r.' Available at: https://poznan.stat.gov.pl/opracowania-biezace/opracowania-sygnalne/praca-wynagrodzenie/cudzoziemcy-na-wielkopolskim-rynku-pracy-w-2021-r-,10,4.html (Accessed 29 October 2023).

USwW (Urząd Statystyczny w Warszawie) (2020) 'Miasto Płock' (series Statystyczny Vademecum Samorządowca). Pdf no longer accessible online.

Van Mol, C., Snel, E., Hemmerechts, K. and Timmerman, C. (2018) 'Migration aspirations and migration cultures: a case study of Ukrainian migration towards the European Union', *Population, Space and Place,* 24(5): 1–11.

Wałachowski, K. and Król, S. (2019) *Uciekające metropolie: ranking 100 polskich miast*. Warsaw: Klub Jagielloński.

Walczak, A. (2021a) 'Ten konflikt ciągnie się od zaborów. Cebularze i bażanty, czyli sąsiedzkie niesnaski kalisko-ostrowskie', *Gazeta Wyborcza Kalisz*, 27 October. Available at: https://kalisz.wyborcza.pl/kalisz/7,181359,27727368,ten-konflikt-ciagnie-sie-od-zaborow-cebularze-i-bazanty-czyli.html (Accessed 30 October 2021).

Walczak, A. (2021b) 'Jest Kalisz najstarszym miastem w Polsce czy nie? Historycy spierają się o "Calisię" Ptolemeusza', *Gazeta Wyborcza Kalisz,* 29 October. Available at: https://kalisz.wyborcza.pl/kalisz/7,181359,27703986,najstarsze-miasto-w-polsce-oczywiscie-ze-kalisz.html (Accessed 30 October 2021).

Walczak, B. (2014) *Dziecko, rodzina i szkoła, wobec migracji rodzicielskich: 10 lat po akcesji do Uniii Europejskiej*. Warsaw: Pedagogium.

Walczak, K. and Andrysiak, E. (2006) *Mniejszości narodowe i religijne w dziejach Kalisza i Ziemi Kaliskiej*. Kalisz: Kaliski Towarzystwo Przyjaciół Nauki.

Wallinder, Y. (2019) 'Imagined independence among highly skilled Swedish labour migrants', *Sociologisk Forskning*, 56(1): 27–51.

Wallis, A. (1965, republished 2011) 'Hierarchia miast', *Studia Socjologiczne*, 1(200): 81–92.

Warzywoda-Kruszyńska, W. and Jankowski, B. (2013) *Ciągłość i zmiana w łódzkich enklawach biedy*. Łódź: Wydawnictwo Uniwersytetu Łódzkiego.

Wessendorf, S. (2007) '"Roots migrants": transnationalism and "return" among second-generation Italians in Switzerland', *Journal of Ethnic and Migration Studies*, 33(7): 1083–1102.

Wessendorf, S. (2015) '"All the people speak bad English": coping with language differences in a super-diverse context'. Birmingham Institute for Research into Superdiversity, IRiS Working Paper No. 9/2015.

White, A (2011) 'The mobility of Polish families in the west of England: translocalism and attitudes to return', *Studia Migracyjne – Przegląd Polonijny*, 1: 11–32.

White, A. (2014a) 'Double return migration: failed returns to Poland leading to settlement abroad and new transnational strategies', *International Migration*, 52(6): 72–84.
White A. (2014b) 'Polish return and double return migration', *Europe-Asia Studies*, 66(10): 25–49.
White, A. (2016a) 'Informal practices, unemployment, and migration in small-town Poland', *East European Politics and Societies* 30(2): 404–22.
White, A. (2016b) 'Polish circular migration and marginality: a livelihood strategy approach', *Studia Migracyjne – Przegląd Polonijny*, 1(159): 151–64.
White, A. (2016c) 'Social remittances and migration (sub)-cultures in contemporary Poland', *Central and Eastern European Migration Review*, 5(2): 63–80.
White, A. (2017, 2nd edition) *Polish Families and Migration Since EU Accession*. Bristol: Policy Press.
White, A. (2018a) 'Culture and Identity', in A. White, I. Grabowska, P. Kaczmarczyk and K. Slany, *The Impact of Migration on Poland: EU mobility and social change*. London: UCL Press, pp. 160–85.
White, A. (2018b) 'Lifestyles, livelihoods, networks and trust', in A. White, I. Grabowska, P. Kaczmarczyk and K. Slany, *The Impact of Migration on Poland: EU mobility and social change*. London: UCL Press, pp. 131–59.
White, A. (2018c) 'Polish society abroad', in A. White, I. Grabowska, P. Kaczmarczyk and K. Slany, *The Impact of Migration on Poland: EU mobility and social change*. London: UCL Press, pp. 186–212.
White, A. (2022a) 'Mobility, transnational and integration continuums as components of the migrant experience: an intersectional Polish-Ukrainian case study', *Central and Eastern European Migration Review*, 11(2): 17–32.
White, A. (2022b) 'Post-socialist mobility cultures', *Polish Sociological Review*, 220(4): 443–56.
White, A. (2024a) 'Ściągnąć (Poland)', in A. Ledeneva (ed.) *The Global Encyclopaedia of Informality: a hitchhiker's guide to informal problem-solving in human life, Volume 3*. London: UCL Press, pp. 403–6.
White, A. (2024b) 'Social remittances: the influence of fellow migrants', in N. Shah (ed.) *Social Remittances and Social Change: Focus on Asia and Middle East*. Lahore: Lahore School of Economics Graduate Institute of Development Studies, pp. 61–82.
White, A. and Grabowska, I. (2019) 'Social remittances and social change in Central and Eastern Europe', *Central and Eastern European Migration Review*, 8(1): 33–50.
White, A., Grabowska, I., Kaczmarczyk, P., and Slany, K. (2018) 'The impact of migration to and from Poland since EU accession', in A. White, I. Grabowska, P. Kaczmarczyk and K. Slany, *The Impact of Migration on Poland: EU mobility and social change*. London: UCL Press, pp. 10–41.
Wilson, A. (2022) *The Ukrainians: the story of how a people became a nation (new edition)*. New Haven: Yale University Press.
Winogrodzka, D. and Grabowska, I. (2022) '(Dis)ordered social sequences of mobile young adults: spatial, social and return mobilities, *Journal of Youth Studies*, 25(2): 242–58.
Wojnarowska, A. (2017) 'Quality of public space of town centre – testing the new method of assessment on the group of medium-sized towns of the Łódź region', *Space-Society-Economy*, 19: 43–63.
Woźniak, M. (no date) *Poznaj Kalisz, najstarsze miasto w Polsce*. Ostrzeszów: Oficyna Wydawnicza Kulawiak.
Woźniak, M. (2006) 'Eksterminacja ludności żydowskiej miasta Kalisza w okresie II Wojny Światowej', in K. Walczak and E. Andrysiak (eds) *Mniejszości narodowe i religijne w dziejach Kalisza i Ziemi Kaliskiej*. Kalisz: Kaliski Towarzystwo Przyjaciół Nauki, pp. 37–42.
Zaborowski, Ł. (2019) *Deglomeracja czy degradacja? Potencjał rozwoju średnich miast w Polsce*. Warsaw: Klub Jagielloński.
Zarobitchany.org (2020) 'Ukrainskie zarobitchane postepenno osedajut v Pol'she'. Available at: https://zarobitchany.org/news/ukrainskie-zarobitcsane-postepenno-osedauat-v-polshe 23.8.20 (Accessed 28 October 2020).
Zelinsky, W. (1971) 'The hypothesis of the mobility transition', *The Geographical Review*, 61(2): 219–49.
Zespół szkół ekonomicznych w Kaliszu 'Aktualności rok 2016/17'. Available at: https://www.zse.kalisz.pl/rok-szkolny-20162017.html?page=33 (Accessed 3 July 2023).
Zielińska, M. and Szaban, D. (2021) '(Nie) planowane (nie) powroty Ukraińców pracujących w Polsce w drugiej dekadzie XXI wieku. Czynniki warunkujące przeobrażenia migracji czasowych w osiadłe', *Acta Universitatis Lodziensis. Folia Sociologica* (76): 39–58.

Żuber, P. (ed.) (2012) *Koncepcja przestrzennego zagospodarowania kraju 2030*. Warsaw: Ministry of Regional Development. Available at: https://eregion.wzp.pl/sites/default/files/kpzk.pdf (Accessed 27 October 2023).

ZUS (Zakład Ubezpieczeń Społecznych) (2022) *Cudzoziemcy w polskim systemie ubezpieczeń społecznych – XII 2021*. Warsaw: ZUS.

Index

agencies, recruitment, 21n3, 23, 35, 51, 79–80, 109, 113, 124, 165–6, 169–73, 185, 187n1, 193, 197, 204, 214, 219, 242, 256, 266, 273, 290

agency
'easy', experimental, opportunistic, 13, 15, 38–9, 67, 69, 71, 74–9, 92–3, 97, 107, 117, 133–5, 149, 151, 158–9, 162, 168, 206, 259–60, 297
and livelihood strategies, 97, 191, 201
see also forced migration

agricultural work, 86, 90, 119, 124, 144, 169, 194, 197

'anchoring', 6, 38, 81, 103, 108, 143, 186, 189, 192, 205, 209, 215, 229, 262, 300

Armenia, Armenians, 116, 271, 285, 289

asylum
see refugees

attitudes towards migrants and migration, 9, 11, 15, 17–20, 84, 100, 113–31, 144, 219, 228, Chapter 11, 284–91

Australians, 276–7, 282, 284–5

Austria, 11, 78, 81, 85

Bangladeshis, 7, 271–5

beauticians, 90, 139, 179, 194–5, 208, 224, 235, 261, 299

Belarus, Belarusians, 6–7, 27, 29, 35, 40, 112, 236, 268–72, 274, 277, 282–4, 287, 290

Belgium, 76, 84, 105, 230, 253–4

Berlin, 33, 77, 81, 125

bi-national marriages, 5, 59, 61–2, 117, 143, 250, 267–8, 276–7, 279, 283

birthrates
see population decline/growth

Brexit, Brexit referendum, 12, 95, 100

bribery and corruption in Ukraine, 137, 149–50, 153–4, 161, 191, 241

bridging ties, 233, 241–3

brokers, labour
see agencies

builders
see construction workers

Bulgaria, Bulgarians, 74, 85, 116, 183, 254

businesses, small
failure as migration motive, 76, 134, 136, 149, 153, 156, 272, 281
setting up after migration/return, 89, 99, 106–7, 147–8, 178, 266, 271, 275, 281, 292

see also online working (including transnational)

Bydgoszcz, 55, 57, 135, 145, 152, 155, 165–6, 209

cafés
see food outlets

carers, migrant-worker, 66, 77–8, 85, 124, 129, 144

caring responsibilities towards family in sending country, 138–9, 150, 152, 158, 166, 168, 173–5, 183, 253

carpenters, 136, 151, 153

Chernihiv, 55, 160

children
Polish, 14–15, 68, 73, 75–6, 82, 92, 98, 100–1, 104, 106, 110, 128, 172, 224, 253, 257–8, 262
Ukrainian, 5–6, 121, 128, 136, 138, 146–51, 158, 160, 162, 167–8, 173–81, 183, 186, 198, 203, 205, 207–8, 216, 218–20, 225, 228, 232, 234, 236, 240–1, 253
other nationalities, 119, 267, 277–9, 285
see also caring responsibilities

children-friendly locations, 56–8, 60–1, 223, 298

Chinese migrants, 7, 115, 266, 290

churches
see religion

cities, Polish
rankings, 47–8
size and its significance, 45–8, 51–62, 151
see also metropolises, regional capitals

class, social, 8–9, 39, 65–6, 68, 74, 92, 97, 219–20, 227, 261, 272, 295–6, 299

co-ethnic networks
see networks, migrant/co-ethnic

colleges, adult education (*szkoły policealne*), 27, 151, 194, 206, 218, 288, 292

communities, 3, 7, 14–15, 20, 83, 118, 140, 212–4, 265–7, 271, 273, 281, 292

conditions, working, 51, 91, 169–70, 185, 191, 195–7, 202–3, 209, 255, 298
see also exploitation

construction workers, 29–30, 72, 77, 85, 99–100, 106, 114, 117, 119–20, 124, 146, 150, 152–3, 156, 194, 198, 214, 239, 261

contact
hypothesis, 83, 110, 113, 233–4, 245

INDEX   319

inter-ethnic, 21, 119, 141, Chapter 11, 275, 292, 300
conviviality and socialising, inter-ethnic, 83–5, 195, 234–41, 288
cooks, 91, 197, 208, 251, 280
corruption
    see bribery
cosmopolitanism
    see diversity
countries of emigration/immigration
    see migration transition
Covid-19 pandemic, 5, 23, 40, 56, 78, 98, 100, 136–7, 139, 144, 146, 152, 157, 178, 181, 190, 192, 196, 203, 205, 209, 256, 272, 275
crisis, humanitarian/'migration' (2015), 19, 266
Cubans, 119
culture of migration
    see migration cultures
cumulative causation, 14, 172
Czechia, Czechs, 12, 85, 141, 143–4, 155, 168, 180, 232n1, 261, 267

Darwich, Eskan, 266
deskilling (working without using formal qualifications and/or professional expertise)
    Poles abroad, 89–91
    migrants in Poland, 163, 283, 197–201
    Ukrainians in Ukraine, 135, 163, 299
    see also reskilling
debt (personal), 74–6, 92, 134, 153
diasporas
    see communities
disability, 75, 138, 151–2, 162
distance (studying/work)
    see online studying/online working
diversification of
    Polish migrant populations, 68, 75
    Ukrainian migration populations, 133, 135, 153, 197, 265, 299
diversity, ethnic, and attitudes towards diversity, 6, 8–9, 12, 17, 45, 85, 94n5, 110–11, 115, 126, 130, 252, 271, 284, 300–1
    see also Islamophobia, xenophobia
Dnipro (city), 55, 144, 160, 206
doctors
    see health and healthcare
double return migration, 73
drivers, 75, 89, 105, 119–20, 150, 153, 179, 181, 195–6, 209, 223, 227

educational migration
    see student migrants
elastic geography ('near/far', 'big/small'), 52–9, 282–3
empathy towards migrants, 18–20, 110, 114, 257–9
English language
    Lingua franca outside English-speaking countries, 119, 128, 157, 272, 274–5, 278, 280–3, 288
    skills of Polish migrants, 69, 75, 85, 88–90, 98–9, 105, 150, 255, 278, 288

teaching, 280, 283, 293n5
entrepreneurs
    see businesses, small
ethnic hierarchies, 7, 86, 111–12, 120, 123, 289, 292
EU accession (of Poland) and connected migration phenomena, 8, 12–13, 15, 58, 65–101, 10
EU long-term resident status, 138, 141, 143, 191
EU migrants in Poland, 6–7, 281
EU 'wave' and 'swell' (Poles moving westwards within EU after 2004)
    see EU accession; 'wave' self-identity
exploitation, 6–7, 84, 109, 113, 115, 120, 124, 171, 183, 209, 246, 272, 292

Facebook, 7, 27, 33–4, 36, 79, 97, 159–60, 217, 223, 239–40, 242, 272–3, 279–80
factories, factory jobs, 9, 14, 17, 20, 23, 27, 29, 31, 33, 36, 48, 75, 77, 86, 90–1, 96, 104, 107, 114–15, 117, 121, 124, 126, 128, 137, 139, 144, 147, 150, 153, 155–6, 159, 160–61, 169–70, 174, 176, 178–80, 190, 194–8, 200-205, 209, 218, 223–4, 227, 236–40, 246, 253–7, 260–1, 267, 271–3, 275, 288–9, 291
family decision-making and livelihood strategies, 37, 61, 100, 103–4, 108, 142, 149–50, 166, 172–82, 201, 299
family reunification, 2, 5, 13, 16, 21n9, 65, 75, 120, 138, 152–3, 156–7, 161, 166–7, 172–82, 186, 191, 216, 269, 273, 302
Filipinos, 289
food outlets, 51, 72, 76, 90, 117, 136, 148, 150, 158, 167, 183, 195, 239, 265, 267, 270–2, 273, 275, 277, 285, 289, 292, 293n8
Friends' reunification abroad, 182–3

Gdańsk-Gdynia-Sopot, 7, 45
geographical diffusion of migrants
    see migration transition
geographical imaginaries
    see elastic geography
Georgians, 35, 289
gendering
    of labour markets in KPP, 50, 67, 95, 104, 106–8, 190, 282
    of migration and migrants' experiences abroad, 6, 19, 37, 39–40, 74, 96–7, 121, 129, 138, 143–4, 147–154, 157, 162–3, 169, 172–4, 179, 190, 195, 200, 203, 210, 228–9, 232, 235, 237, 256–7, 261–2, 276, 299
generation born in 1980s Poland, 72
    see EU accession; 'wave' self-identity
Germans, Germany/Prussia, 6, 11, 19, 24, 26, 30–3, 66, 70, 72, 74, 76–80, 84–5, 92, 104, 120–1, 123–4, 127, 129, 139, 155, 157, 168–9, 180, 183, 191, 194, 206, 228, 230–1, 235, 243, 252–61, 283–4
Global Economic Crisis (2008), 12, 78, 84, 86, 100
governments, Polish
    civic platform, 2007–15, 4

320   POLISH CITIES OF MIGRATION

law and justice, 2005–7 and 2015–23, 3–4, 8, 30
graduate-entry jobs
 in Poland, 23, 67, 72, 89, 96, 98, 104
 in Ukraine, 121, 153
grandparents in Ukraine, 156, 158, 174, 186, 198

hairdressers, 146, 160, 197, 208, 224, 239, 249, 257, 261, 299
health and healthcare, 57, 60, 95, 100, 128, 144, 152, 182, 207, 210n6, 225, 279, 291, 300
holidays, foreign, 81–2, 223, 227, 232n, 235, 269
home, 21n2, 52, 55, 61, 83, 88, 93n4, 95, 102, 111, 138–9, 141, 143, 186, 210–11, 214, 216, 222, 224–7, 234–5, 238–9, 245, 259, 275, 282, 298
 homemaking roles, 150–1
 see also place attachment
homesickness, 119, 225, 257
hostels, migrant, and houses in multiple occupancy, 17, 35–6, 92, 137–8, 141, 167, 170–1, 173, 177, 179, 197, 205, 217–18, 220, 222, 224–5, 234–5, 239–40, 275, 289, 292
hotspots, migration, 14, 17, 96, 261
household decision-making
 see family decision-making
housing, 47, 290
 buying/building, 1, 3, 48, 74, 78, 99, 148, 158, 178, 226, 229, 241, 259, 281
 renting and rents, 25, 44, 62, 75, 92, 134, 146, 151, 170, 205, 215, 226, 242, 272, 274
 selling (in Ukraine), 141, 226
 see also home; hostels

'immigrants light', 266, 275
Indians, 6, 30, 116, 119, 123, 243
industrialisation, industry
 see factories
informal work, 205, 242
inflation, 79, 136, 204, 272, 274
inspection visits, 178–9, 272
integration
 conceptual frameworks/definitions, 11, 37–8, 68
 experiences of interviewees, 80–92, 143, 178, Chapter 9, 239, 245, 255, Chapter 12
 policies in Polish cities, 7–8, 11, 35, 43
 see also return migration (re-integration)
intentional unpredictability, 69, 73, 78, 97, 138
internal migration, 8, 10, 21n2, 23–4, 26, 30, 37, 51, 53–4, 56, 99, 101, 105, 133–4, 151, 182–3, 217, 228, 244, 248, 270, 272, 281–2, 291, 297
inter-ethnic relations between non-Poles, 288–91
intersectionality, 3, 37, 39, 96–7, 134, 162, 190, 299
Ireland, Irish people, 2, 5, 9, 15, 18, 26, 69–73, 78, 82–5, 88–9, 93n4, 99–100, 102–3, 118, 120–1, 126–7, 167, 230, 258, 288

Islam and Islamophobia, 30, 85, 110, 112, 123, 130, 255, 275, 285, 290–1
Israel, 144, 147, 169
Italy, Italians, 4, 6, 18, 74, 80, 117–18, 157, 158, 169, 185, 228, 230, 267, 276–8
Ivano-Frankivsk, 155–7, 160, 215

Jews, 29, 31–2, 111
jobs
 manual/white-collar, 40, 50, 75, 86, 89–90, 104–7, 113, 144, 151, 153, 197, 272
 security and contracts, 190, 196–7, 202, 257
 see also mobility, occupational/social; deskilling; reskilling

Kalisz (except joint mentions with Płock and Piła), 24–29, 30–32, 46, 48, 50, 55, 58–60, 62, 67, 104, 116, 118–19, 121, 124, 126–7, 152, 157, 160, 177, 190, 193–5, 202, 209, 214–16, 218, 223, 226–8, 241, 243–4, 248, 261, 266–7, 281, 288–9
Kamianets-Podilskyi, 157, 160
Kazakhs, 268–70, 292
Kherson, 160
Kraków, 6–7, 43, 117
Kryvyi Rih, 60, 160
labour brokers
 see agencies
labour markets
 in KPP, 104–7, 195
 dual/segmented, 104, 121–2, 125, 194
 see also gendering of labour markets
language
 learning and competence, 27, 33, 36, 69, 80, 84, 88–9, 95, 98, 105, 119, 122, 141–2, 148, 150, 168, 178, 190–1, 194, 201–2, 206–7, 210, 235, 239, 256, 259, 269, 272, 274–5,
 ideologies and strategies, 246, 255, 277–8, 280–3, 288–9, 292
 see also linguistic landscape; Russian language; teachers; Ukrainian language
leisure activities of migrants, 60, 71–2, 76, 81–2, 195, 232, 270, 274
life stage, 39, 61, 69, 81, 95–6, 100, 145–8, 162, 166, 213, 232, 234, 268
lifestyle, 1, 6, 44, 61, 65, 67, 84, 93, 95, 107–8, 145–8, 163, 213, 267, 274, 277, 281
linguistic landscape and soundscape, 116, 118, 125–6
Lithuania, Lithuanians, 5, 86, 91, 155, 195
livelihood strategies, 9, 14, 17, 37, 44, 52, 65–6, 71, 74–9, 92–3, 97, 99, 103–4, 107–8, 122–3 Chapter 7, 198, 201, 232, 256, 262, Chapter 12
Łódź, 14, 21n7, 48, 52
London, 12, 54, 72, 74, 77, 83, 85, 87, 98, 117, 195, 198
Lviv and Lviv region, 55–6, 146, 155–8, 180, 215, 251

manual work
 see jobs

INDEX 321

Mariupol, 56, 160, 162, 184, 228, 230, 237
Mazowieckie region (Mazowsze), 24, 28–9, 50, 74
metropolises (Polish cities of over 500,000), 7–10, 43–7, 66
migration
    attitudes and opinions concerning, Chapters 6 and 11
    circular/repeated, 5, 20, 66, 74, 77–9, 107, 109, 133, 138, 143, 146, 162, 181, 202, 206, 226, 232, 246, 255–6, 261, 276, 297
    cultures, 11, 13–17, 19–20, 37, 69, 71, 76, 79, 87, 91–3, 96, 103, 109–10, 162, Chapter 8, 262, 287, 296
    cycle/process, 11
    incomplete (solo-parent), 15, 74–5, 78, 146
    motives
        see motives to migrate
    successive generations', 68
    transit/onward, 4, 10, 229–31
    transition (general comments), 3–13
minority minorities, 3, 7, 21, Chapter 12
mobility, 'mobility turn', 2–3, 13, 15, 39, 65, 67, 96, 133, 139, 162, 182, 281, 297
mobility cultures
    see migration cultures
mobility, occupational/social, 90–1, 135, 147, 150, 154, 168, 194–202, 208–9, 212, 228, 280
    see also deskilling; reskilling
mobility transition (Zelinsky), 10
mortgages, 66, 74, 134, 216, 226–7
motives to migrate/settle/return
    minority minorities, Chapter 12
    Polish migration abroad, 69–80
    Polish return to Poland, 97–101
    Ukrainian migration from Ukraine, Chapter 7
    Ukrainian migration to Poland, 167–9
    Ukrainian settlement in smaller cities, 44, 51–58, 96, Chapter 10
    see also family reunification; lifestyle; student migrants
Muslims
    see Islam and Islamophobia

neighbours, 83–4, 119, 126, 226, 235, 240–1, 251, 286
neighbourhoods, 83, 213, 215, 227, 241
Netherlands, 50, 60, 72, 76–7, 79, 84, 86, 92, 125, 252, 257, 259–60
networks, migrant/co-ethnic
    Polish, 77, 79, 86–8
    Ukrainian, Chapter 8, 214–21
NGOs and online support groups, 8, 23, 29, 34–5, 43
    see also Facebook
Normalny (Polish, Russian and Ukrainian adjective meaning 'proper', 'appropriate')
    behaviour, livelihood and living standards, 14, 17, 19–20, 93, 107, 110, 123, 135–6, 150, 184, 204, 220, 225, 243, 244–5, 257, 260, 262, 289, 298
    definition and discussion, 136

Norway, Norwegians, 72, 80, 93n4, 113, 123, 260
nurses, 135, 147, 154, 158
    see also health and healthcare

online studying, 206, 225, 269, 280
online working (including transnational), 178, 201
onward migration (to a third country)
    see transit migration
Orlen, company/oil refinery, 29–30, 59–61, 71, 104, 129, 279, 282, 293n5
Ostrów Wielkopolski, 25, 31, 104, 146

parents
    see children
persuasion to migrate/return, 15, 73, 76–7, 90, 98, 100, 138, 166–7, 177, 179–80, 182–3, 235, 277, 291
place attachment, ambivalence and alienation (as processes), 44–5, 52–3, 62, 211–12
    Poles abroad, 80–83, 86, 88, 93
    Ukrainians in Poland, 172, 178, 190, 196, 209, Chapter 10, 239
    other nationalities in Poland, 275, 279, 281, 296

Piła (except joint mentions with Płock and Kalisz), 7, 23–9, 32–6, 48–9, 53–60, 62, 67, 72, 74, 77, 81, 102–4, 107, 114, 116–17, 126, 128–9, 138, 144, 151, 169, 175, 177, 191, 195, 205, 214–16, 218, 223, 226, 240, 244, 249–50, 252, 256, 267, 289–90
Płock (except joint mentions with Piła and Kalisz), 23–30, 34–5, 47–50, 57, 59–61, 66–7, 73, 76, 78, 98, 101, 104–5, 114, 116–20, 127, 129–30, 141, 153, 157, 161, 169, 173, 177, 203, 205, 221–2, 224, 238–40, 244–5, 267, 279, 281–3, 288–9
Poles speaking Ukrainian
    see Ukrainian language use in KPP by Poles
Polish card (Karta Polaka) and Polish ethnic affinity, 140–3, 178, 268
Polish migration viewed by Ukrainians, 252–61
pollution, 27, 29, 60–2, 134, 160–2, 279, 291
Poltava, 158–9
population decline/growth, 2, 24–6, 28–30, 45–6, 49
post-accession migration
    see EU accession
Poznań, 27, 55–6, 58, 67, 71, 99, 101, 116, 147, 151, 182, 192, 228, 244, 270, 282

refugees, 4–6, 11, 17–20, 23, 26, 29, 40, 85, 111–13, 115, 119, 128–30, 161–2, 167, 169, 192, 200, 240, 271
regional capitals, pre- and post-1999, 48–50
religion and religious institutions, 32–3, 85, 168, 217–18, 223, 275
remote (studying/working)
    see online studying; online working
remoteness and poor transport links, 27, 46, 283
renting and rents
    see housing

residence/work permits, employer 'invitations' and visas (Polish), 5–6, 21n3, 51, 137–40, 156, 168, 170, 189–94, 197, 220, 266, 268, 271, 273, 283, 293n3, 301
reskilling, 89–90, 197–8
'experience path', 105
restaurants
see food outlets
return migration
motives, 96–101
planning, strategies, 72, 96–7
re-acculturation, 101–4
re-integration, 104–7
sustainability, duration, 96, 101–2
Romanians, 74, 110, 116, 120
Russia, Russians, 5, 17, 34–5, 85–6, 112, 144, 155, 180, 218, 279
Russian language use in KPP
Poles, 119, 128, 205, 246, 262
Ukrainians, 36, 155, 218

salaries
see wages
Scotland, 74, 87
seasonal migrants, 4, 21n3, 79, 107, 129, 144, 174, 245
secondary employment
see informal work
shops as migrant workplaces, 74, 90, 117–19, 125, 144, 215
skilled work
see jobs
Slovaks, 85
'small groups' of migrants, 3, 7, 267
social capital
see networks
social media, 7, 115, 128, 170, 182, 192, 214, 217, 239–40, 255
see also Facebook, YouTube
social remittances, 9, 16, 83–6, 102, 168–9, 207–8, 298
social ties and mutual relations
Poles with foreigners except Ukrainians, 284–7
Ukrainians with other non-Poles, 288–91
Ukrainians with Poles, 114–31, Chapter 11
student migrants, 5–8, 69, 77, 90–1, 115, 140, 178–9, 239, 266–7, 268–70
Sumy, 160
Sweden, Swedes, 53, 84, 107, 127, 272
'swell' (Poles going abroad after the 2004–8 'wave')
see EU accession
Switzerland, Swiss, 81, 85, 88

teachers, 35, 66, 72, 75, 90, 108, 148, 152, 154, 176, 195, 200, 202, 206, 207–8, 219, 230, 238, 243, 251, 261, 267–8, 278–81, 287, 293n5
Ternopil, 155, 157–8, 219
tolerance
see diversity
Turks, 114, 119, 125, 271, 274

Ukrainian exiles in Kalisz, 1920s–30s, 32
Ukrainian language use in KPP
by Poles, 119, 237, 240
by Ukrainians, 218–19
(un)employment
see labour markets
United Kingdom
migrants from Poland, 6, 9, 12, 15, 36, 69, 71–4, 83–4, 87–91, 98, 110, 120, 122, 254–7, 274, 278, 288
Ukrainian (would-be) migrants, 167–8, 228
UK attitudes towards CEE migrants, 12, 83, 100, 111
Uruguay, 278–8, 280–1

Venezuelans, 202, 271–3, 275, 288–9
Vietnamese minority and migrants, 6–7, 26, 115, 118, 266, 288, 290
visas
see residence permits
visibility of migrants to receiving society, 3, 7, 114–20, 265, 279–80, 286

wages
in Poland, 28–9, 47, 59, 75–8, 95, 102, 104–8, 117, 122, 124–5, 127–9, 171, 185, 196–8, 201–2, 204, 226, 251–4, 261, 272–5, 281
in Ukraine, 134–6, 149–50, 152–3, 251, 254, 261
Wales, 82, 89
Warsaw, 6, 8, 14, 23, 26–7, 30, 32, 43, 46, 50, 53, 57, 66–7, 101, 105, 116–17, 144, 165, 205, 214–15, 228, 243–4, 248, 253, 266, 269, 272, 274, 282–3, 290, 299
'wave' self-identity
Polish migrants, 2004–8, 72–3, 76–7, 88
Ukrainian migrants, 2014–22, 159, 213–14, 231, 265
other nationalities, 273–4
welders, 40, 142, 153–4, 203–4, 209, 228, 237, 276
white-collar work
see jobs
work ethic, Ukrainian self-stereotyping, 198–9
working hours
see wages
Wrocław, 7, 14, 21n8, 26, 50, 58, 66, 101, 117, 147, 244, 267, 272, 295

YouTube, 46, 182, 186

xenophobia, 9, 19
see also diversity; Islamophobia

Zaporizhzhia, 159–61